VISUAL QUICKSTART GUIDE

MAYA 6

FOR WINDOWS AND MACINTOSH

Danny Riddell and Adrian Dimond

Peachpit Press

Visual QuickStart Guide
Maya 6 for Windows and Macintosh
Danny Riddell and Adrian Dimond

Peachpit Press

1249 Eighth Street
Berkeley, CA 94710
510/524-2178
800/283-9444
510/524-2221 (fax)
Find us on the World Wide Web at: http://www.peachpit.com
To report errors, please send a note to errata@peachpit.com
Peachpit Press is a division of Pearson Education

Editors: Rebecca Gulick and Whitney Walker
Technical Editor: Greg Berridge
Production Coordinators: Myrna Vladic and Pat Christenson
Compositors: Rick Gordon, Emerald Valley Graphics, Deborah Roberti, Espresso Graphics
Indexer: FireCrystal Communications
Cover Design: The Visual Group
Cover Production: George Mattingly/GMD

ISBN 0-321-24746-9

9 8 7 6 5 4 3 2 1

Printed and bound in the United States of America

Dedication

To my incredible wife, Yee-Ju, and family for inspiring me, believing in me, and challenging me. Without their love, dedication, and support, this book would not have been possible.

—Danny Riddell

To Violet, for putting up with my loud typing.

—Adrian Dimond

Acknowledgements

Danny would like to thank Andrew Britt, for his writing and knowledgeable technical review of the first edition; Rebecca Gulick, for her direction and encouragement throughout the book project; Marjorie Baer, for her constant encouragement and leadership; and Eric Anderson for his technical contributions to the second edition. Many thanks to Adrian Dimond for his invaluable insights and for making this revision possible.

Adrian would like to thank Rebecca Gulick, for bringing him on board; Greg Berridge, for his thorough technical review of the third edition; Whitney Walker, for putting things the right way; Myrna Vladic and her production team, for making everything look good; and finally, Danny Riddell, for laying such wonderful groundwork for this book in the first two editions. Also, special thanks to all the artists who submitted their spectacular work for the gallery, and to Alias, for making it all possible.

TABLE OF CONTENTS

INTRODUCTION

Figure i.1 This voracious prehistoric lizard is just one of the myriad creatures you can bring to life in Maya.

Welcome to *Maya 6 for Windows & Macintosh: Visual QuickStart Guide*.

Alias Maya is the high-end 3D program that has brought to life many of the three-dimensional people, animals, plants, cars, and machines you see in film, videos, and games. Whether you want to create pod races, realistic anatomy, or scenes with an artistic flair, Maya can help you achieve the desired look and feel. Maya's only restriction is your imagination; if you can think it up, you can create it in Maya, with precise control over the final imagery (**Figure i.1**).

Maya is an extremely powerful character animation application. By offering tools for both cartoon and photorealistic character animators, Maya has become the preferred 3D character animation program.

This book introduces you to Maya's interface and features. You'll soon realize, though, that Maya has enough depth to keep you learning for years. What makes Maya spectacular is that the average user can learn enough to build incredible images relatively quickly. Maya offers ease of use for beginners and extreme depth for advanced users, propelling it to the top of the 3D software genre.

Who Is This Book For?

If you want to learn basic 3D concepts, or if you are familiar with other 3D software and want to learn Maya, this book is for you. You should be familiar with computers and other graphics software packages, but you don't need prior 3D knowledge (though it will make Maya easier to learn). This book will guide you through the expansive Maya interface and show you how to animate and render your 3D projects. If you work through this book from cover to cover, you'll end up with a solid Maya foundation—familiarity with the user interface and the capability to model, texture, and animate 3D content.

Once you've completed this book and mastered the Maya basics, you'll be ready to explore Maya's more advanced features. Good resources for tutorials can be found at *www.learningmaya.com, www.highend3d.com,* and *www.cgtalk.com.*

After exploring Maya modeling, rendering, and animation, you may find that you're better at one or the other. As you work through this book, think about which area interests you most. Using Maya could develop into a hobby or even a career in creating 3D content for movies, product ads, and interactive entertainment!

What You Will Need

For starters, of course, you'll need a license for Maya or the Maya PLE (the free Personal Learning Edition) for Windows or Macintosh installed on your computer. For advanced features like Fluids, you will need Maya Unlimited. See Maya's documentation for instructions on installing the program.

In terms of hardware, Maya's incredible power comes at a price. Maya is the most resource-intensive software I know of, so I recommend beefing up your machine with as much RAM and processor power as you can manage—you'll definitely notice the difference.

Another very important aspect is what kind of display card you use with Maya. You can visit the Alias Web site (*www.alias.com*) and go to the support section for Maya to find the most current list of qualified display cards. For Windows, Nvidia Quadro 4 XGL and Quadro FX cards are highly recommended. ATI FireGL cards are also supported, as well as a few 3Dlabs cards. See the Alias Web site for specific models and driver versions. For Mac, ATI Radeon 9800 Pro Special Edition is recommended. Always check the card manufacturer's Web site for driver updates, since out-of-date drivers are often shipped with cards.

Also, be aware that Maya requires a three-button mouse, since the middle mouse button is used as a Virtual Slider feature for many functions. Where possible, we've offered alternatives for anyone who only has a two-button mouse, but any serious Maya user will want to purchase a three-button mouse.

Check out the Maya documentation for minimum system requirements or visit the Alias Web site.

Figure i.2 This is the Maya 6 interface as it appears in Windows.

Figure i.3 Here's a look at the interface of Maya 6 for Mac OS X.

Maya Versions and Flavors

This book covers Maya 6 for Windows and Mac OS X (**Figures i.2** and **i.3**). With Maya 6, there's very little difference between the two versions—at least in the features covered here. However, whenever there is a difference in functionality, I'll point it out.

One difference between the Maya interface in the Windows and Mac versions is that the Mac version lets you tear off Hotbox menus.

Let's take a closer look at the different flavors of Maya for Windows:

◆ **Maya Complete** comes with a full set of modeling tools for working with NURBS, polygons, and subdivision surfaces. It also includes advanced character animation tools, dynamics (the use of physics to simulate real-world forces), and effects. Maya complete is everything you need to get started doing production work for games, video, and film.

◆ **Maya Unlimited** includes all of Maya Complete's tools and features, plus Maya Cloth, Maya Fur, Advanced Modeling Tools, Fluid Dynamics and Maya Live for Matchmoving.

Because this book is for beginning to intermediate users, it covers only those features and tools found in Maya Complete. However, it also covers Fluid Dynamics, which is part of Maya Unlimited, even though it's not available in Maya Complete.

What's new in Maya 6?

Maya 6 contains hundreds of new features and improvements, many of which were the direct result of customer requests.

Notable improvements include a revamped Trax editor, Mental Ray 3.3, new animation abilities, modeling tools, project organization features, workflow enhancements, improved integration with support applications like Adobe Photoshop, and much more.

Maya 6 enhances the user's ability to work in real time with a new feature called High Quality rendering, which works in the shaded views. High Quality rendering takes advantage of the latest display card hardware for accelerating OpenGL and provides higher quality real time feedback of what your scene will look like with textures, shadows, and lighting.

Maya 6 also now has automatic LOD (Level of Detail) for dense polygonal objects. This means that objects with lots of faces will be drawn with fewer faces so that they are more interactive. These and many other enhancements are covered in this book. For a full list of all the new improvements in Maya 6, go to *www.alias.com/eng/products-services/maya/ file/maya6_features_in_detail_whitepaper.pdf*.

Additional Resources

There are hundreds of Maya- and 3D-related resources on the Web. One of my favorites is *www.highend3d.com*. Highend3D offers tutorials, forums, and listservs to which many talented 3D artists contribute daily. Some other good 3D tutorial and informational sites include CGtalk (*www.cgtalk.com*), 3D Café (*www.3dcafe.com*), 3D Ark (*www.3dark.com*), and Animation World Network, or AWN (*www.awn.com*).

✔ Tip

■ Chapter 16, "Cameras and Rendering," and Chapter 17, "MEL and Expressions Primer," cover scripting. Because the column in this book is narrower than the common text editor screen, sometimes lines of code printed in the steps have to be broken where they do not otherwise break in your editor. A small gray arrow indicates when this kind of break occurs. For example:

```
print "This is going to be a longer
→ line of code.";
```

You should continue to use one line in your scripts, or else you'll encounter errors when executing.

Versions and Flavors/Additional Resources

MAYA BASICS

Maya's layered user interface is very easy to use, yet it lets you access the application's great depth of functionality. This chapter introduces you to that interface and shows you how to set preferences, start a project, and access online help. First, though, it's a good idea to know something about the way Maya works.

About Maya

Maya is a node-based program. A *node* is a visual representation of an element, such as a surface, texture, or animation curve. Every element in Maya is represented by a node or several connected nodes (**Figure 1.1**). The nodes themselves are made up of many *attributes*, which are the information that defines the node, such as an object's position or size. You access nodes in the Outliner and Hypergraph (**Figure 1.2**) windows. The advantage of this node-based architecture is that it gives you precise control over which nodes get connected to or disconnected from other nodes—which in turn determines the behavior and look of the object. Maya lets you view all of a scene's connections from within the Hypergraph (**Figure 1.3**). The arrows and lines represent the connections. (The Hypergraph is covered in more detail later in this chapter.)

Figure 1.1 Nodes can be viewed in the Hypergraph or the Outliner. A new node is created for each object.

Figure 1.2 A Maya scene file can consist of a limited number of nodes and connections, or it can have thousands of nodes in more complex scene files.

Figure 1.3 Node connections can be seen in the Hypergraph, with arrows showing the connections between the nodes and the directions of those connections.

ABOUT MAYA

Figure 1.4 Flat, 2D graphics work with the *x* and *y* axes but lack a depth axis that enables images to become three-dimensional.

Figure 1.5 Adding another axis allows objects to become three-dimensional. These 3D models can now become accurately represented.

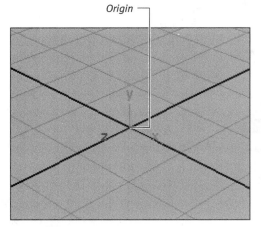

Figure 1.6 The center point of the Maya scene is called the *origin*. All directional values start at 0 from the origin.

Maya's coordinate system

Traditional animation and graphics applications, like Adobe Photoshop, work with two axes, usually *x* and *y* (**Figure 1.4**). An *x* and *y* coordinate system provides height and width but lacks the depth to make objects appear three-dimensional. Maya adds a third axis, *z*, which gives objects depth (**Figure 1.5**). The addition of the third axis lets you create proportionally accurate models and animations.

Within the XYZ coordinate system are two kinds of coordinates, *world* and *local*. World coordinates start at the center of the scene in location 0, 0, 0, called the *origin* (**Figure 1.6**). Local coordinates are those around the area of the object.

Objects themselves have what's called *UV coordinate space*. A surface has a U direction and a V direction. In the simple example of a plane, the U direction goes from left to right, and the V direction goes from top to bottom (**Figure 1.7**). It's like latitude and longitude on a world map. Just as you can find a position on earth by its latitude and longitude, you can determine a position on a surface by its U and V coordinates. This becomes especially important when positioning textures on a surface.

Figure 1.7 Each surface is described with a U direction and a V direction. You can place curves on surfaces using U and V coordinates.

Maya's Interface

The Maya interface can appear daunting at first glance, but it's actually very organized and easy to get around once you're familiar with it (**Figure 1.8**). Along the top of the Maya interface is the main menu bar, which contains all the major Maya commands. Because Maya contains more menus than can fit in a window, you can't view all of them simultaneously in the menu bar. For this reason, Maya's menus are grouped into menu sets, arranged by tasks, which can be accessed from the menu at the far left of the status line.

The status line, located directly beneath the main menu bar, holds many important selection functions. Below the status line is the Shelf, which holds often-used tools.

Along the left side of the interface is the toolbar, which holds Maya's manipulation tools. You use these tools to select, rotate, move, and scale objects or pieces of objects, called *components*.

The typical Maya layout shows four views: Front, Side, Top, and Perspective. The areas containing these views are called *panes*. The default layout has four panes. At the bottom of the interface are the *Range Slider* and *Time Slider*, which allow you to control your position in time for animation. At the right-hand side of the interface is the *Channel Box*, which holds shortcuts to object attributes. Below the Channel Box are the *Display Editor* and *Render Layer Editor*.

Figure 1.8 This is the Maya interface as it appears by default. Many of the elements seen here can be hidden or customized to suit the task at hand.

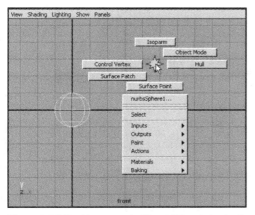

Figure 1.9 A Marking menu holds additional shortcuts for turning different components on and off.

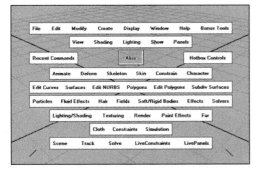

Figure 1.10 The Hotbox is a convenient way to access the program's menus and commands. It can be modified to suit a user's workflow in the Hotbox Controls menu.

Figure 1.11 You can interactively change values by first selecting the attribute's name in the Channel Box, moving the mouse over a view pane, and then dragging the pointer back and forth in the view using the middle mouse button to alter the attribute numbers.

In addition to the main menu bar, there are menus that can be accessed from within individual panes and through *Marking menus* (**Figure 1.9**). Marking menus represent a convenient way to quickly access tools or commands. They appear when you right-click an object or when you click in one of the five Hotbox regions (see "About the Hotbox," later in this chapter). Maya is full of menus, and it can take a significant amount of time to truly master them.

One of Maya's best features is the Hotbox (**Figure 1.10**). It holds all of Maya's menu sets and appears directly above the mouse pointer when you hold down the (Spacebar) (and then disappears again when you release the key). The Hotbox can be a great time-saver because you can access it from wherever your mouse is—without going up to the main menu bar and selecting a command.

To change an object's position, rotation, or scale (collectively known as *transforms*), you can type values in the Channel Box (**Figure 1.11**) or use Maya's *manipulators*, which allow you to change an object's value by clicking and dragging an interactive handle (**Figure 1.12**).

Figure 1.12 This cone is surrounded by a Rotate manipulator. By clicking and dragging the circles, you can make the cone rotate.

Using the Shelf

The Shelf is where you can store often-used tools and commands. You can use multiple Shelf sets to organize your favorite and most frequently used tools. Maya provides an extensive set of preset shelves (**Figure 1.13**). It is convenient to categorize items into individual Shelf sets. For instance, you could create one Shelf for all the modeling tools you frequently use and another Shelf for all your favorite rendering tools. You might even have a third Shelf that just holds your 10 or 15 most frequently used tools and commands.

In the Shelf you can add or delete items or choose from any of the preset Shelf commands. Although the Shelf is useful, it also takes up a lot of screen space. You can show and hide the Shelf when you need more screen space. To hide the Shelf, simply choose Display > UI Elements > Shelf (**Figure 1.14**). You can also hide the Shelf by clicking on the dimpled strip to the left of it.

Figure 1.14 Maya's many windows can make screen space scarce. To save screen space, you can hide many interface elements by deselecting them in the Display › UI Elements submenu.

MAYA'S INTERFACE

Figure 1.13 The Shelf holds tools and commands. You can customize it, or create additional Shelves, to contain frequently used commands and tools to suit the current task. All of the default shelf sets are shown (from top): General, Curves, Surfaces, Polygons, Subdivs, Deformation, Animation, Dynamics, Rendering, and Paint Effects.

Figure 1.15 The Help Line shows important information about commands and translations. Here, at the bottom of the image, it is showing the rotation of a sphere in degrees.

The items you add to a Shelf retain their most recent settings—which means you can add the same tool to the Shelf twice but with different settings. For example, you could add two Create > Primitive > Sphere icons to the Shelf but adjust one's option to be a full 360 degrees and the other to less than 360 (for example, 240). You could then just click each of these icons to produce the sphere with the amount of degrees you want without having to go back into the options.

To add an object to the Shelf:

◆ Select the menu item you want to add to the Shelf while pressing [Ctrl]/[Control] and [Shift] at the same time.
The object is added to the Shelf.

To remove an object from the Shelf:

◆ Using the middle mouse button, drag the icon from the Shelf to the trash.
The object is removed from the Shelf.

About the Help Line

The Help Line provides information on object transformations and hints as to what your next step should be. When you move the mouse pointer over a menu item, text appears in the Help Line describing the steps needed to complete the command. If you rotate an object, the Help Line will reflect the change numerically (**Figure 1.15**).

The Numeric Input field to the right of the status line is where you can type precise values for the transformations. This can be useful when you need to have exact positioning for objects such as architectural buildings and product designs. Maya gives you the option to build things by eye or by entering exact position and size figures. When these changes are made, the new values appear in the Help Line.

About the Channel Box

The Channel Box, which lists a selected object's *keyable* attributes, is located on the right side of the Maya interface (**Figure 1.16**). Keyable attributes are object properties that can be animated. You can change an attribute's value quickly in the Channel Box without having to open another full window (thus saving screen space). You can enter values in any attribute's field, or you can click on the attribute's name and interactively change its value by using the middle mouse button—to drag in any view pane.

✔ Tip

■ If you hold down Ctrl/⌘ while dragging to scale an object the two unselected axes will scale together.

Ten default attributes in the Channel Box display when an object is selected (**Figure 1.17**): Translate X, Translate Y, Translate Z, Rotate X, Rotate Y, Rotate Z, Scale X, Scale Y, Scale Z (known collectively as *transforms*), and Visibility. The values for these attributes can be typed in one at a time, in small sets, or all at once. More attributes can be added to the Channel Box list by using the Channel Control.

Below the transforms are the Shapes and Inputs nodes (**Figure 1.18**). The Shapes section lists the node name of every object that is defined by a node, and these node names collectively define the geometry. Take a close look, for example, at how the Shapes section lists pSphereShape every time you create a sphere. If more than one shape makes up an object, the nodes for those shapes will be listed under the shapes section. The Inputs section usually holds attributes that affect the construction history of the selected object. (See "About construction history," later in this chapter.)

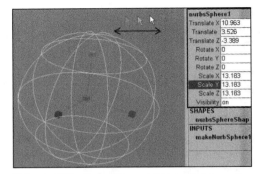

Figure 1.16 The Channel Box, at right, holds information about an object, including its position (Translate), scale and rotation.

Figure 1.17 The Channel Box includes ten default attribute listings for an object; however, you can also add or change attributes.

Figure 1.18 Inputs node attributes can be adjusted to change a surface's attributes after it is created.

Figure 1.19 Once multiple attributes in the Channel Box are selected, they can be changed simultaneously.

Figure 1.20 The Attribute Editor contains all of the information about a selected object (or objects).

Figure 1.21 Each of the five Hotbox regions—North, South, East, West, and Center—holds a different Marking menu. The center region is defined by the Alias symbol.

If more than one object is selected, the Channel Box displays the last object selected; however, any value change to an attribute will affect all selected objects. You can click and drag across multiple values in the Channel Box to select them (**Figure 1.19**). With multiple attributes selected, you can change all the values at once, as opposed to making the same change to each attribute one at a time. As your scenes become larger with more objects, lights and shaders, being able to adjust many attributes quickly will become essential.

✔ Tip

- MEL (Maya Embedded Language) is a scripting language that is very handy for manipulating a list of selected objects. This is something we will cover in Chapter 17, "MEL and Expressions Primer."

About the Attribute Editor

The Attribute Editor is similar to the Channel Box in that it allows you to access attributes that can be changed. However, the Attribute Editor provides a much more detailed representation of the attributes (**Figure 1.20**). In addition to the attributes in the Channel Box, the Attribute Editor contains attributes that are not keyable (that is, they cannot be animated).

About the Hotbox

The Hotbox is a collection of menu sets you can access from anywhere your pointer is located, simply by holding down the (Spacebar). The Hotbox is divided into five regions: North, South, East, West, and Center (**Figure 1.21**). Each of these regions has an associated Marking menu.

continues on next page

The default Marking menu for the North region holds shortcuts to different interface layouts (for example, a Single Perspective window) (**Figure 1.22**). The South Marking menu changes the contents of the selected pane (**Figure 1.23**)—for example, from a Perspective view to an Outliner (see "About the Outliner," later in this chapter). The West Marking menu holds preset selection masks (**Figure 1.24**), which filter the object types that can be selected. The East Marking menu hides or displays specific user-interface elements (**Figure 1.25**)—for example, allowing you to hide the Shelf to create more screen space. The Center Marking menu offers shortcuts for switching camera views (for example, from a Front view to a Perspective view) (**Figure 1.26**).

In addition to providing access to all of the Marking menus, the Hotbox also provides access to all of Maya's menu sets. The top row of menus in the Hotbox includes the most commonly used commands (such as those for saving and opening scene files). The second row of menus includes those that you'll find at the top of each panel. In the third row are the Recent Commands and Hotbox Controls menus.

Figure 1.22 In the North region Marking menu, you can select from different interface layouts.

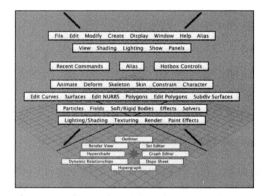

Figure 1.23 The South region Marking menu allows you to change contents of panes.

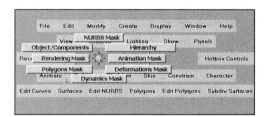

Figure 1.24 You can change object and component selection modes with the Hotbox's West region Marking menu.

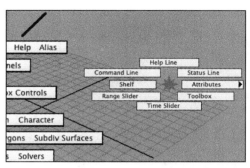

Figure 1.25 You can toggle interface elements on and off with the East region Marking menu to make more room for modeling and animation.

Figure 1.26 You can change views using the Hotbox's Center Marking menu.

Figure 1.27 This is the Hotbox with all of the menus visible.

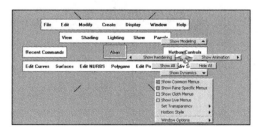

Figure 1.28 You can view one or all of the menu sets inside the Hotbox.

The Hotbox Controls allow you to hide or show rows of menus in the Hotbox. You can choose to show only the middle row of menus, or you can choose to make other, specific, menu sets visible. You can even display all of the rows of menus simultaneously (**Figure 1.27**).

To show all menu sets in the Hotbox:

1. Hold down the (Spacebar).

   The Hotbox will appear for as long as you hold down the (Spacebar).

2. Click Hotbox Controls.

   A Marking menu appears over that button (**Figure 1.28**).

3. While still holding down the (Spacebar) and the mouse button, select Show All. Release the mouse button but continue to hold down the (Spacebar).

   All of the menus appear (see Figure 1.27). If you have trouble finding a menu, this is a good way to make it easier.

About the Hypergraph

The Hypergraph window shows how all the nodes in your Maya scene are organized and connected. These connections are very important to the quality of the final animation and rendering. Character setup and movement rely on proper node connections in order for character body parts to move naturally as one entity. This organization and connection of individual nodes is called a *hierarchy* (**Figure 1.29**). A scene's hierarchy is shown in the Hypergraph as well as in the Outliner and can be adjusted and deleted within these windows or from inside a pane.

Each Maya object type has an associated icon (**Figure 1.30**). Without these icons, each node would look exactly the same. As you get more familiar with Maya, you will begin to recognize each object type's icon. For example, a CV (Control Vertice) Curve tool's icon is , and a Spot Light's icon is . In the Hypergraph, you can view nodes by object type (**Figure 1.31**), or you can view all object types at once (**Figure 1.32**). In the Hypergraph, non-animated nodes appear rectangular; animated nodes appear slanted (**Figure 1.33**).

To show the Hypergraph

◆ From the Window menu, choose Hypergraph.

Figure 1.29 Any number of nodes connected together creates a hierarchy. The order of the hierarchy is shown in the Hypergraph and Outliner.

Figure 1.30 A small icon on each node reveals that node's object type. For example, a surface node has a small, blue icon that resembles a simple surface.

Figure 1.31 You can have the Hypergraph display just one type of node to make it easier to find and select specific objects. For modeling, for example, you might only want to see curves and surfaces. However, for animating, you might choose to see just joints and IK handles. Joints and IK handles are used to select and move portions of a character to simulate motion.

Figure 1.32 The default setting for the Hypergraph is Show All. This view helps illustrate how geometry is connected to a joint, and other hierarchy information.

Figure 1.33 Animated nodes appear slanted, making it easy to isolate unwanted animation on an object.

Figure 1.34 The input and output connections of an object reveals additional dependencies of the object. Some of these dependencies may be shading groups, lights, or textures.

About dependencies

Each node in the Hypergraph has connected *dependencies*, which display additional nodes connected to the selected object. Say you were selecting a newly created sphere and showing its input and output connections in the Hypergraph (**Figure 1.34**). The sphere's Shape node, the default Shader node, and the connected makeNurbs Construction History node would all become visible. Arrows between the nodes show the directions of the connections. One way you can view a node's dependencies is to click the Show Input and Output Connections icon. When you've finished viewing these connections, you can click the Scene Hierarchy icon to set the Hypergraph back to showing the scene hierarchy.

continues on next page

Connected nodes can be collapsed to shrink the number of simultaneously displayed nodes and then expanded again when needed. A red arrow appears on a collapsed node hierarchy (**Figure 1.35**). To collapse a hierarchy, double-click the topmost node. Double-clicking the top node of a collapsed hierarchy expands the hierarchy one node at a time (**Figure 1.36**). To expand the entire hierarchy, click the topmost node using the right mouse button and select Expand All from the pop-up menu (**Figure 1.37**).

The Hypergraph is one of the most heavily used windows in Maya. The ability to connect, disconnect, and move nodes around is essential to keeping your scene organized and functional.

Figure 1.35 You can collapse a hierarchy to make more room in the Hypergraph. A collapsed hierarchy is indicated by a red arrow under the top node.

Figure 1.36 A collapsed hierarchy can be expanded one node at a time, which is often useful for temporarily showing a node and then collapsing it again.

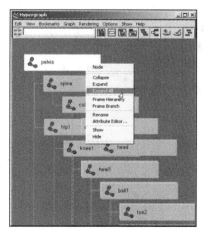

Figure 1.37 When you want to see the whole hierarchy again, you can right-click the top node and select Expand All.

Figure 1.38 The Outliner appears in a slim window, which makes it easy to select and move objects.

Figure 1.39 In the Outliner, as in the Hypergraph, the user can control which objects are viewed.

Figure 1.40 The four default camera views appear in the Outliner.

Figure 1.41 To see which objects are connected to other objects, click the arrows to expand the hierarchy. Each object in the Outliner has its own icon to indicate its object type.

About the Outliner

The Outliner is similar to the Hypergraph, but it displays the hierarchy in a small, vertical window (**Figure 1.38**), which makes it easier to find and select objects. The Outliner's menus contain functions for filtering out specific object types, thereby reducing the number of nodes displayed at one time (**Figure 1.39**). You can use the Outliner to change an object's position in the hierarchy as well as to quickly select objects deep down in the hierarchy.

When the Outliner is opened and before any new objects are created, you will see colored listings of the top, front, side, and perspective camera nodes in addition to the defaultLightSet and defaultObjectSet icons (**Figure 1.40**). As each new object is created, a new node becomes visible. Once connections are made and a hierarchy has been established, a plus sign appears next to the top object in the hierarchy; you click this to expand the list of objects within the hierarchy (**Figure 1.41**).

Its small size makes the Outliner a convenient tool for selecting objects. However, although the Outliner occupies much less screen space than the Hypergraph, it doesn't give the user as much flexibility in node placement.

MAYA'S INTERFACE

About construction history

As you build surfaces in Maya, the software maintains connections to the original curves or surfaces used to create them. This connection is referred to as *construction history*. The construction history remembers the steps you used to create an object and allows you to change the final object's shape by altering the original curve or surface geometry. This is very useful when you want to tweak a surface without having to rebuild it. An example might be drawing a curve that defines the shape of the outside of a vase (**Figure 1.42**) and revolving it to complete the vase shape (**Figure 1.43**). Once the vase is created, the construction history remembers the curve's position and ties it to the shape of the final surface. When you want to change the shape of the vase, you can select part of the original curve and move it; the final surface will follow the changes of the curve (**Figure 1.44**).

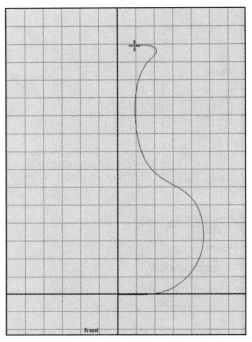

Figure 1.42 Curves can be used to outline a shape that can later be revolved to create a surface.

Figure 1.44 The entire curve or just individual points on it can be selected and moved to alter the surface shape. The surface is attached to the curve through history and must follow the curve's edits.

Figure 1.43 One curve can be revolved and then edited to affect the final surface shape after it's created through the object's history.

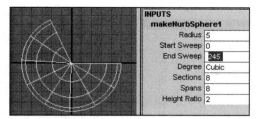

Figure 1.45 An object's primitive surface can be altered via its Inputs node, which contains multiple editable attributes specific to each object type.

Most of the *NURBS* (nonuniform rational B-splines) and polygon primitives have construction histories attached to their surfaces. The History nodes for the primitives appear in the Channel Box under the Inputs heading. These Inputs nodes are useful for altering common object attributes after the original object creation. An example of this is adjusting the End Sweep of a primitive sphere to take a slice out of the shape (**Figure 1.45**).

To turn the construction history on or off:

◆ Click the Construction History On/Off icon in the Status bar. ⊠ is on and ⊠ is off.

✔ Tip

■ Once you've turned off the construction history, no objects that you create will include one. To include a construction history, you must rebuild the object.

To delete an object's construction history:

1. From the Create menu select NURBS Primitive > Sphere to create a sphere or select an object.

2. From the Edit menu select Delete by Type > History.

Workflow

As your Maya skills develop, you'll be able to doodle and experiment in 3D and create work using just your imagination without much planning, but for large projects, an efficient, well-planned workflow is essential. The more thought that goes into what will be created before a single pixel is manipulated onscreen, the fewer problems you'll have later on.

Obviously you cannot render without first having modeled and textured your objects. How do you know what to model unless you have a sketch of the character or you have collected some reference material? Good actors can improvise, but will your CG characters improvise on their own without a script?

Once you've completed your project's pre-production tasks—tasks such as writing the script, creating storyboards to illustrate the action, and sketching to develop the characters and environments—you can begin working in the 3D world.

Modeling is usually the first major phase in your project workflow after pre-production. You can also begin to block out the camera moves and animation using low-res geometry or primitives as placeholders. Before you can begin animating a character you need to create its skeleton. Once the hi-res models have been completed, it's time for texturing and shading. Then the geometry or skin will be stuck to the character's skeleton. Lighting is another step that can take place as the major elements start to come together.

Rendering and compositing occur near the end of your workflow. You can conduct rendering tests throughout the course of the project so that problems are solved and the scene looks just the way you want it to before the final rendering.

Workflow may seem like common sense until your client or the director asks you to change the camera move the night before the project is due. Having to change the camera move in most cases would mean re-rendering everything for a shot, which is usually not something that you can do in a hurry. That's why it's important to block out your scenes using stand-in models and low-res geometry so that you can lock in the camera moves before rendering.

Of course, there will be many times when you will have to go back into an earlier part of your workflow to make revisions. Compositing can often allow you to revise any number of elements in a 3D scene without re-rendering the entire image. For example, if a character's shirt was textured as polka dots but needs to be changed to plaid, you can render just the shirt and apply it over the previously rendered image. (For more information on rendering see Chapter 16, "Cameras and Rendering.") You can revise texture maps and shaders fairly easily at any point in the process using this method. If you edit a texture map in a program like Adobe Photoshop and save it over the original, the next time you open Maya the revised texture will be loaded as well. For more instruction on texturing see Chapter 15, "Shaders and Material."

Figure 1.46 Keeping all the different files organized is essential for a steady workflow. You can either use Maya's preset folder set or create your own folders.

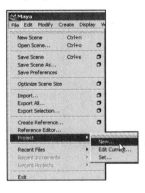

Figure 1.47 Creating a new project places a main project folder on your hard drive with multiple folders to organize images, renders, textures, and scene files.

Figure 1.48 Browse to a folder where you want to consistently place new project files.

Beginning a Project

Because of Maya's complexity and the numerous files that may be produced for each project, you need to create a folder set that has multiple folders for specific types of files. You can use Maya's premade folder set, called a *project*, to quickly organize all the files you create (**Figure 1.46**).

Once you create a new project, you can tell Maya where you want your files to go by setting that project as the working project. When a project is set, Maya knows which folders to put your renders in and which folders to put your scene files in.

The Maya working file, called a *scene file*, should be saved in the Scenes folder. The best way to create a successful file structure is to first create a new project, set the project, create a new scene, and save the scene in the Scenes folder. The following section describes that process step by step.

To create a new project:

1. From the File menu, select Project > New (**Figure 1.47**).

2. Enter a name for the project in the Name field at the top of the dialog box that appears.

3. Click Browse (next to the Location field) and select a folder in which to create the project folders (**Figure 1.48**).

4. Click Use Defaults to use preset folder names.

continues on next page

5. Click Accept.

A project folder is created at the specified location; it has multiple subfolders created with the default folder names (**Figure 1.49**).

For Maya to know which folder set you want to store your files in, you must set a project to be associated with your current working files. The final rendered files will go into the set project, so be careful to set the correct project before rendering. (Rendering is the process of turning your wireframe 3D scene into a final 2D image. For more on this topic, see Chapter 15.)

To set a project:

1. Create a project by following the steps in the previous section.

2. From the File menu, select Project > Set (**Figure 1.50**).

3. Browse to and select the folder for the project you want to use.

4. Click OK to set the project.

A Maya working file is called a *scene file;* it can be saved, opened, and imported into other scene files.

To create a new scene:

◆ From the File menu, select New Scene (**Figure 1.51**).

A blank Maya scene is created.

Figure 1.49 Using the default names for the folders helps maintain consistency among projects.

Figure 1.50 Once a project and its folders have been created, you can set the project as Current and Maya will place saved files into the correct folders—scene files into the Scenes folder, for instance.

Figure 1.51 Scene files can be used to create separate models or scenes to be imported or opened at a later date. The scene file stores information about textures, models, animation, particles, and all the user settings.

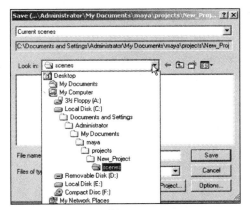

Figure 1.52 If a project has been set, the Save As command will automatically open the scene folder for the set projects, into which you can save the file.

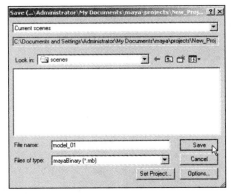

Figure 1.53 It's good practice to name your files in a numbered sequence since projects often use multiple scene files.

Figure 1.54 You can set the Default Scene by clicking the option box next to New Scene in the File menu.

To save a scene:

1. From the File menu, select Save Scene.

   The Save dialog box appears the first time a file is saved.

2. Click the pop-up menu next to "Look in" to select a folder in which to save the file (**Figure 1.52**).

   If you have set the project correctly, the pop-up menu should already show the Scenes Folder inside the project folder you set.

3. Enter a name for the file in the "File name" field, and click Save (**Figure 1.53**). The scene is now saved in the Scenes folder.

In many cases when you create a new scene you'll want it to have customized settings by default. This could be anything from your favorite preferences to a 3-point lighting rig or a particular sphere. Maya makes it easy to set a default scene file.

To set the default scene:

1. Customize and save a scene file that you want to use as your default.

2. In the File menu, click the box next to New Scene (**Figure 1.54**).

   The New Scene Options dialog box opens.

continues on next page

3. Click the Enable Default Scene check box (**Figure 1.55**).

This enables the Default Scene parameter field below the check box.

4. Click the folder icon next to the Default Scene parameter field to open a file browser.

5. Navigate to your scene folder and select the customized scene you want to use as your default scene (**Figure 1.56**), and click Open.

6. Click Apply to save this preference.

A Warning dialog box appears to prevent you from losing any work that is currently open.

7. Click Save (**Figure 1.57**) to save the scene you currently have open.

Maya creates a new scene with the default you just picked, replacing the scene you currently have open. Now every time you select New Scene, your customized scene will open

Figure 1.55 Enable the use of the Default Scene by clicking the check box.

Figure 1.56 Select the scene file that you would like to be your default scene.

Figure 1.57 Using a default scene will save you time from re-entering commonly used settings.

Figure 1.58 Referencing a file into multiple scenes allows the original scene file to be edited; the reference files will inherit the changes.

Figure 1.59 Changes made to a referenced file are automatically included in each scene in which the referenced file is used.

Importing, Exporting, and Referencing

There are two ways to bring files and geometry into a Maya scene: importing and referencing. When you import a file into Maya, you are permanently merging the file into the current scene. This is recommended if you're working with just one file that is not very large.

Often, you'll want to use the same model in multiple scenes (**Figure 1.58**). You can use referencing to bring the same file into multiple scenes simultaneously. Referencing gives you a chance to edit the original file and have those revisions updated in all the scene files that use the reference. For instance, you can create a character in one file and then reference it into different files for each camera shot. If you later want to make changes to the character, you can open the original character file and make the changes, then save the file. The updates are automatically made to all files that reference the character (**Figure 1.59**).

Referencing can be particularly helpful when more than one person is working on the same project. In such cases, you can have the modeler create a low-resolution character for the animator to reference into a scene. This way, the modeler can continue making additions to the character while the animator is creating its motion. As the model is updated, the animator can see the changes as he or she works. The other advantage is that the low-resolution model will draw faster onscreen

continues on next page

because there isn't as much geometry for the CPU to process (**Figure 1.60**).

Using references is a powerful way to manage your large projects. Larger scenes can be segmented by storing the individual parts in separate files, so the new scenes that you do save will be smaller. This saves you time (saving large scene files to the hard drive can be time consuming) and disk space.

✔ Tips

- When editing referenced files the names of nodes and objects become extremely important. If the names change then the scene that refers to them will no longer be-able to find those objects.

- Maya can assign a locator when you import a reference. For large scenes this allows you to unload a referenced object by right-clicking the reference's name in any of the views and choosing Unload Related Reference. You will still see the cross hairs of the locator and the references name, but since the geometry is no longer loaded, your scene's display will be much faster while you focus on another part of the scene (**Figure 1.61**).

Figure 1.60 From left to right we have smoothed deformable geometry, a polycage, and then a stand-in created from primitive cubes.

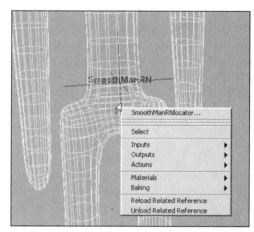

Figure 1.61 Unloading references will greatly improve real-time performance while animating.

Figure 1.62 To export everything in the scene, use the Export All command.

In addition to importing and referencing, you can also export objects out of a scene. There are two export options: Export All and Export Selection. The Export All command exports everything in the current scene to a new file. The Export Selection command exports currently selected objects. Export also exports cameras, but when you import the scene only the cameras with unique names will be included. The cameras with default names like Front, Top, Side, or Persp will be ignored when you import.

To export an entire scene:

1. From the File menu, select Export All (**Figure 1.62**).
   The Export window opens.

2. Navigate to the folder in which you want to place the exported file.

3. Click Export.
   All the file components are exported.

To export selected objects:

1. Select the objects you want to export (**Figure 1.63**).

Figure 1.63 This creature is being selected in the Outliner so that it can be exported separately from the rest of the scene.

2. From the File menu, select Export Selection (**Figure 1.64**).
   The Export window opens.

3. Navigate to the folder where you want to place the exported file.

4. Click Export.
   The selected objects are exported.

Figure 1.64 To export only the items that are selected in a scene, use the Export Selection command.

IMPORTING, EXPORTING, AND REFERENCING

To import a file:

1. From the File menu, select Import (**Figure 1.65**).

The Import dialog box opens.

2. Navigate to the folder where the file you want to import is located.

3. Click the file you wish to import, and then click Import (**Figure 1.66**).

The file is imported into the scene.

To reference a file:

1. From the File menu, select Create Reference (**Figure 1.67**).

The Reference dialog box opens.

2. Navigate to the folder where the file you want to reference is located.

3. Click the file you want to reference, and then click Reference (**Figure 1.68**).

The file is referenced into the scene.

✔ Tip

■ Do not group referenced objects to non-referenced objects. If you translate the group node in-between loading and unloading the references, Maya may loose track of where the reference is supposed to be.

Figure 1.65 Importing a file into another scene combines the imported file with the open file.

Figure 1.66 A creature scene file is being imported into the currently open scene.

Figure 1.68 Browse to the file you want to reference and click Reference, or double-click the file name to use it as the reference file.

Figure 1.67 Select File > Create Reference to bring a file into an existing scene.

Figure 1.69 By setting preferences, you get the interface configuration you want each time you start the software.

Figure 1.70 In Preferences, Undo is selected to change the number of undos allowed.

Figure 1.71 In most cases, you want your Undo Queue to be set to Infinite.

Setting Maya Preferences

Maya has multiple preferences that can be altered to suit your working style as well as your favorite color scheme. In this section, we'll look at just a few of the most essential preference settings. If you want to learn more about preferences, you can refer to the Maya help files.

You can set the number of "undos" that are allowed, determining the number of times you can back out of previous commands.

To change the number of undos:

1. From the Window menu, select Settings/Preferences > Preferences (**Figure 1.69**).
   The Preferences dialog box opens.

2. Click Undo under Categories to view the Undo preferences (**Figure 1.70**).
   The Preferences dialog box opens.

3. The default number of undos is 10. Change the Queue setting to Infinite (**Figure 1.71**).
   Setting the Queue to Infinite allows you to back out of every command you've executed—up to the last saved version.

4. Click Save to lock in the changes.
   You now have an unlimited number of undos.

✔ Tip

- Each saved undo takes up memory, which means your machine may run slowly if you have too many stored undos. If this is the case then set your undo level to 50 or less instead of infinite.

The manipulator settings control the look and size of the manipulators. Larger manipulators can often be easier to grab and move.

To change the size of a Maya manipulator:

1. From the Create menu, select NURBS Primitive > Sphere.

   A sphere is created at the origin.

2. Select the Move tool by pressing [w] or clicking the Move icon in the toolbox ![icon].

3. From the Window menu, select Settings/ Preferences > Preferences.

   The Preferences dialog box opens.

4. Select Manipulators in the Categories list (**Figure 1.72**).

   The Manipulator Display Preferences are displayed to the right.

5. Move the Preferences dialog box so you can view the sphere. Click the sphere to make sure it's selected (**Figure 1.73**).

6. In the Manipulator Display Preferences move the Global Scale slider slowly to the left and right. Adjust it until the spacing of the manipulator is to your liking (**Figure 1.74**).

   Watch the manipulator on the sphere while adjusting the slider. The overall scale of the manipulator is changed (**Figure 1.75**).

Figure 1.72 Under Manipulators in the Preferences dialog box, you can change the size of the manipulators.

Figure 1.73 With Preferences still open, click the sphere to select it.

Figure 1.74 Global Scale changes the overall size of the manipulators. Here, they have been made smaller.

Figure 1.75 Moving the slider to the right scales the manipulator larger; moving the slider to the left shrinks the manipulator.

Figure 1.76 The Handle Size setting adjusts the bold part of the manipulators—the arrows, in the case of the Move tool.

Figure 1.77 The handle icons for the manipulator get smaller when you move the slider left and larger when you move the slider right.

Figure 1.78 You can reset the options to defaults by selecting Edit > Restore Default Settings inside the Preferences window.

7. Adjust the Handle Size slider back and forth to a position of your liking (**Figure 1.76**).

The handle icons for the manipulator get smaller when you move the slider left and larger when you move the slider right (**Figure 1.77**).

✔ Tip

■ You can change the size of manipulators on the fly by using the ⊞ and ⊟ keys.

To set preferences back to the default set:

◆ In the Preferences dialog box select Edit > Restore Default Settings (**Figure 1.78**). The default settings are restored.

✔ Tip

■ Remember to change your undos back to Unlimited after you restore the default settings.

To alter your Maya color scheme:

1. From the Window menu, select Settings/Preferences > Colors (**Figure 1.79**).

   The Colors dialog box opens.

2. Click the 3D Views arrow ▼ **3D Views** to view the Background color slider (**Figure 1.80**).

3. Click the color swatch next to Background to open the Color Chooser.

4. In the Wheel, click the color you would like for your Maya background (**Figure 1.81**).

5. Click Accept to lock in the color.

   Your Maya background becomes the color chosen.

✔ Tip

- You can follow the same steps to change any part of the interface color scheme.

- Pressing Ctrl b will toggle the background color in your camera views between several shades of gray.

Figure 1.79 You can change the colors of many interface items using the Colors preference settings.

Figure 1.80 In the Colors dialog box, click the color swatch next to Background to open the Color Chooser.

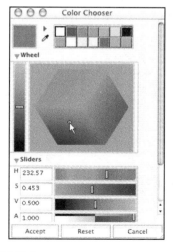

Figure 1.81 Click in the Wheel to pick a color for the background.

SETTING MAYA PREFERENCES

Figure 1.82 Hotkeys can be set to add keyboard shortcuts to nearly any command.

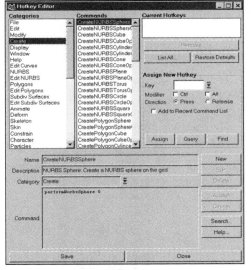

Figure 1.83 In the Hotkey Editor, select the name of the menu and the menu item in the Categories and Commands lists, respectively, to add a shortcut.

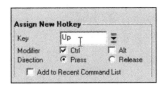

Figure 1.84 In the Assign New Hotkey portion of the Hotkey Editor, choose the key and modifier you want to use as a hotkey for the selected command.

Keyboard Shortcuts

Any function in Maya can have an associated keyboard shortcut, or *hotkey*. Hotkeys can be huge time-savers, because you can use them rather than go to the menu bar to select a function or command. Maya has many default hotkeys, which we recommend keeping until you become more adept with the interface. Later, you may find that you want to set up hotkeys for particular commands that you use regularly. The following describes how to create a new hotkey or view the currently set hotkeys.

To create a new hotkey:

1. From the Window menu, select Settings/ Preferences > Hotkeys (**Figure 1.82**). The Hotkey Editor opens.

2. In Categories, click the category name for the command you want to set (**Figure 1.83**).

   The category name is the same as the name of the menu the command is under.

3. Under Commands select the command name you want to create a hotkey for.

   If the command already had a hotkey assigned to it, you would see which key it was in the upper-right corner of the window.

4. In the Hotkey Editor under Assign New Hotkey, choose a Key and a Modifier for the command (**Figure 1.84**).

   You should remove any current hotkey currently assigned to the command before assigning a new hotkey.

5. Click Assign and close the Hotkey Editor.

✔ Tip

- Maya creates a folder in your user directory to store preferences so you can take your preferences with you to multiple computers.

Maya Help

Maya's manual comes preloaded in the help files. You can search these files by topic or browse through them page by page. The help files are a good resource when you want additional information about a specific topic.

Maya offers an integrated Web browser that's a great way to view the help files instead of having to toggle from one program from another. Because it is integrated into Maya it allows the Web pages to execute MEL commands that can control what happens in Maya (**Figure 1.85**).

You can load the Web browser into your pane by selecting Panels > Panel > Web Browser (**Figure 1.86**).

Figure 1.85 The new integrated Web browser gives you convenient access to help docs and tutorials.

Figure 1.86 You can assign the Web browser to a panel in your viewport through the panel menu.

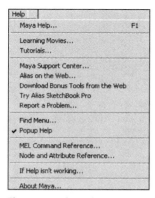

Figure 1.87 The Help menu provides ways to search and browse for information on specific topics.

Under the Help menu in the upper right-hand corner of the Maya interface are links to the tutorials, search functions, an index of topics and definitions, and a Find menu feature in case you forget where a menu item is located (**Figure 1.87**).

The Tutorials and Learning Movies include tutorials and references that are easy to navigate, many of which offer step-by-step instructions for common Maya tasks.

The Contents and Search function allows you to type in a topic on which you would like more information and shows you a list of links categorized by the percentage of relevance to the topic you chose (**Figure 1.88**).

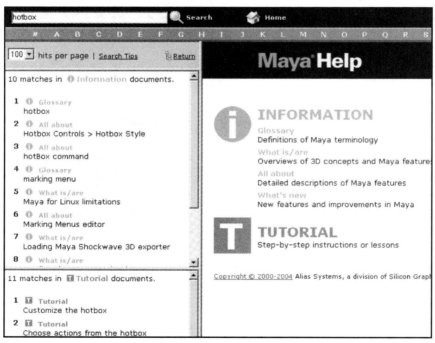

Figure 1.88 The Contents and Search window in the Help menu shows multiple listings for additional information on a specified topic.

MAYA HELP

The Find a Menu Item feature allows you to type in the name of a topic or function and get the item's menu and path (**Figure 1.89**). This can be particularly useful when you know what a function is called but can't remember on what menu it resides.

Maya's Index is similar to an index in the back of a book. You pick the topic you want from an alphabetical listing, and Maya gives you a definition as well as relevant information on the topic (**Figure 1.90**).

Figure 1.89 The Find a Menu Item feature is a quick way to find every menu in which any given command is located.

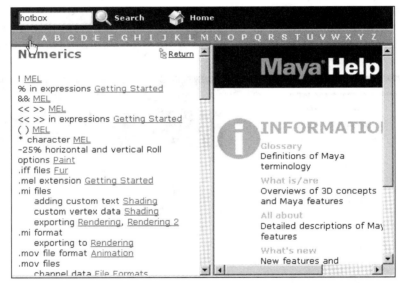

Figure 1.90 The Index contains command definitions and tutorials for all the Maya help files.

MAYA HELP

NAVIGATING AND CHANGING THE INTERFACE

Figure 2.1 The Maya interface can be changed to suit each user.

Figure 2.2 The Hotbox is a set of menus that appear where your mouse is when you hold down the
Spacebar.

Maya's interface is fully customizable (**Figure 2.1**), which means you can alter its layout to suit your current project and workflow. For example, you can hide each menu and window until you're viewing only one pane—a panel or window in which to work—while the rest of the interface is hidden. However, even when menus are hidden, you can still access them via the Hotbox (**Figure 2.2**).

You can also hide and show specific object types in a pane using the Show menu. Once you're viewing the object types you want in the pane, you can *dolly*, *track*, and *tumble* around the objects (movie-industry terms for specific camera movements) to get a better, more three-dimensional view.

Maya provides many ways to accomplish the same task—another way it helps speed users' workflow. It includes hotkeys (keyboard shortcuts) for commonly used commands, and you can add hotkeys for just about any command you want.

In the pages that follow, I'll describe the ways you can change the interface and navigate the scene.

Dollying, Tracking, and Tumbling

Dollying, tracking, and tumbling allow you to change your view of a scene, controlling how far or near its objects appear. Since you're always looking through a camera, dollying, tracking, and tumbling provide ways to move that camera around the scene. These are some of the most important tools in Maya because you need to see objects from every direction and dimension. The point of view from which you're viewing your scene becomes important to the alignment and placement of objects.

Tracking a view moves that view up, down, or sideways. You might track a view to get a look at an object that's currently out of view.

To track a view:

1. Move the mouse over any pane.

2. Hold down [Alt] ([⌘] on a Macintosh) and use the middle mouse button to drag the scene in the desired direction (**Figure 2.3**).

Dollying a view visually enlarges or shrinks the view, bringing objects closer (zooming in) or moving them farther away (zooming out).

To dolly a view:

1. Move the mouse over any pane.

2. Hold down [Alt]/[⌘] plus the right mouse button, dragging left to shrink the view and right to enlarge the view (**Figure 2.4**).

Tumbling a view visually rotates it around the center of interest—useful for getting the full 3D effect of the objects and scene. For example, you could tumble around an object to get a view of its front, back, and sides from any angle.

Figure 2.3 Tracking drags the scene up, down, or sideways.

Figure 2.4 Dollying is used to zoom in and out of specific areas of the scene; dollying right (bottom) enlarges the view.

To tumble the view:

1. Move the mouse over the Perspective view.

2. Hold down Alt /⌘ and use the left mouse button to drag and rotate the scene in the direction desired (**Figure 2.5**).

✔ Tips

■ You can also use the scroll wheel on your mouse to dolly without holding down any other mouse buttons. Scrolling up enlarges the view, scrolling down shrinks it.

■ You can marquee-zoom in by pressing Ctrl /Control and Alt /⌘ while dragging a marquee from upper left to lower right with the left mouse button. You can zoom out by dragging lower right to upper left. The smaller the square, the larger the zoom.

■ You can hold Shift while tumbling to constrain the tumble along a specific axis.

Figure 2.5 This is the Maya interface with four panes visible. Tumbling (which only works in the Perspective view) rotates the view around an object or scene.

DOLLYING, TRACKING, AND TUMBLING

Changing the Layout

Maya has two windows that are easily confused because their names are so similar, *pane* and *panel*. A pane is conceptually the same as a window pane. If you look inside a window with panes, you might see something different in each pane. The same is true here. A pane can hold a Front, Top, Side, or Perspective view, or a panel.

A panel is a type of Maya window that helps with different Maya functions. For example, the Hypergraph and Outliner are panels that show all of the nodes in a scene, and the Graph Editor is a panel used to edit animation curves. Many of these panels can be opened in their own windows (**Figure 2.6**) or within a specific pane (**Figure 2.7**). One advantage to opening a panel inside a pane is the ability to then tap the Spacebar to minimize (**Figure 2.8**) or maximize (**Figure 2.9**) the pane. You can temporarily access the pane and then shrink it back down, gaining access to the other panes as well.

Figure 2.6 The Outliner is open in its own window.

Figure 2.7 The Outliner is in one pane and can be enlarged and shrunk for convenience.

Figure 2.8 Minimizing a pane allows you to view multiple panes at once.

Figure 2.9 Maximizing a pane enlarges the view over any other panes, giving you more workspace within that pane.

Maya's programmers understood that different users would want to work with Maya and its interface layout differently. With this in mind, they've provided many ways to change Maya's interface and layout. (When I talk about the *layout*, I'm referring to the number of panes the user is viewing and the specific panels and views that are placed within those panes, **Figure 2.10**).

Figure 2.10 Layouts can be sized, saved, and changed to accommodate the user's current needs. The top image is a four-pane layout; the bottom image is a two-pane (side-by-side) layout.

To switch from Maya's single view to its four-view layout, place your cursor over any one of the views and press the (Spacebar). The Front, Side, and Top views are orthographic, meaning they present a 2D view of the surfaces (**Figure 2.11**). This allows you to view the surfaces straight on from the selected view angle. Viewing the surfaces in this manner can be important for proper placement and alignment of objects. The three orthographic views combine to provide an accurate portrayal of the objects' placement relative to the rest of the scene. Users new to 3D often forget to check their objects in multiple views, which can cause placement problems for other objects. While the objects may look perfectly placed from the Front view, they could be completely off in the Side or Top view. The Perspective view gives you a full three-dimensional view of your scene (**Figure 2.12**). The combination of all of these views makes it possible for you to access your scene from virtually any angle.

Figure 2.12 The Perspective view is the only view that allows you to tumble around the scene, giving you the full 3D effect.

Figure 2.11 Orthographic views are the same as the views you would use when drafting with a pencil. You have three views that are from a straight-on camera, making editing and placement easier.

Figure 2.13 Any pane can be changed into a Perspective view by selecting Perspective > persp.

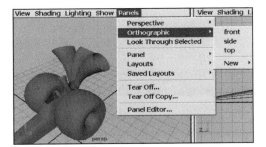

Figure 2.14 Any pane can be changed to any orthographic view (for example, Front or Top) by selecting the Orthographic menu.

Maya allows you to change the layout of the panes, save a new layout, or change just one panel. In this chapter, we'll show you how to perform each of these layout changes.

To change a pane into a Perspective view:

◆ From the Panels menu inside the pane you want to change, select Perspective > persp (**Figure 2.13**).

To change a pane into an orthographic view:

◆ From the Panels menu inside the pane you want to change, select Orthographic > front, side, or top (**Figure 2.14**).

Panes don't always have to be view panes like Front or Perspective; they can also be panels that provide access to other areas and windows within Maya. These panels are often animation windows, like the Graph Editor (see Chapter 1, "Maya Basics") (**Figure 2.15**), or node representations of your scene, like the Hypergraph (see Chapter 1) (**Figure 2.16**) or even a Web browser. As you learn more about Maya, you will learn what each of these panels does to help your workflow.

To change a pane into a nonview panel:

◆ From the Panels menu inside any pane, select Panel and choose the panel name you want—Outliner, for example—to change the pane into its respective view (**Figure 2.17**).

Figure 2.15 The Graph Editor holds all of the animation curves that can be edited. This panel can be embedded in a pane or opened in a window.

Figure 2.16 The Hypergraph holds visual representations of all the objects in the scene and can be embedded in a pane or opened in a window.

Figure 2.17 Many different panels can be embedded inside a pane.

Figure 2.18 Preset layouts give you quick access to the number of panes visible and the panel sets that will go in them.

Figure 2.19 The layout icon shortcuts can be altered after being chosen by holding down the arrows at the bottom of the tool box. You could change a preset pane into a Perspective view with the arrows. The number of arrows varies with the layout selected.

To change the pane layout:

◆ From the Panels menu inside any pane, select Layouts and choose the preset layout name you want—Two Panes Side by Side, for example (**Figure 2.18**).

If you select Two Panes Side by Side, you will have only two panels to work with, and they will be laid out adjacent to one another.

or

◆ Select the icon of the layout you want from the toolbar on the left side of Maya's interface (**Figure 2.19**).

To save a layout:

1. Set up the layout you would like to save and use later.

2. From the Window menu, select Save Current Layout.

3. Enter a name for the layout and click OK.

To change your current layout to a saved layout:

◆ From the Panels menu inside any pane, select Saved Layouts and choose the name of the saved layout you would like to use.

To edit a layout:

1. From the Panels menu inside any pane, select Saved Layouts > Edit Layouts.

2. Under the Layouts tab select the name of the layout you would like to edit (**Figure 2.20**).

3. Under the Edit Layouts tab, change the Configuration pop-up menu to the new configuration you would like to use (**Figure 2.21**).

4. Pull any of the center dividers for the numbered blocks to adjust the blocks' size relative to the size of the other blocks (**Figure 2.22**).

5. Click the Close button to close the window. You can now access the new layout from the Panels > Saved Layouts menu.

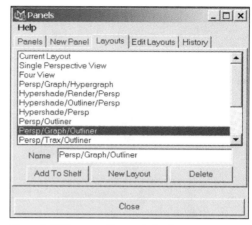

Figure 2.20 You can edit an existing layout or create a new layout under the Layouts tab.

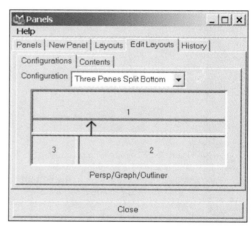

Figure 2.22 It can be helpful to resize the panes at this point to make the size of each one comparable to its use. For instance, you might want to make the Perspective pane larger so that you always have more working area in that view.

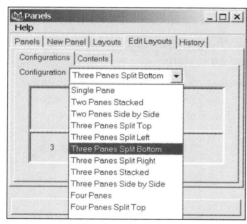

Figure 2.21 You can change the number of panes the layout uses by selecting Edit Layouts tab › Configurations tab › Configuration menu.

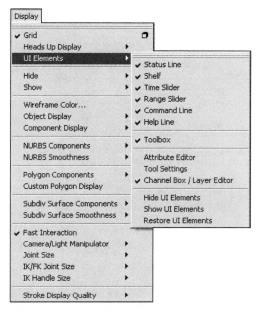

Figure 2.23 Each interface element or related section can be turned on and off to save screen space when the element is not needed.

Figure 2.24 A quick way to gain more working space is to use the Hide UI Elements command.

To hide or show a UI element:

◆ From the Display menu, select UI Elements, and choose the UI elements you would like to hide or show (**Figure 2.23**).

Each UI element name toggles between hidden and shown. If it is hidden, selecting it will show it, and vice versa.

To hide all UI elements:

◆ From the Display menu, select UI Elements > Hide UI Elements.

All elements become hidden except the main and pane menu bars and your current pane layout (**Figure 2.24**).

To show all UI elements:

◆ From the Display menu, select UI Elements > Restore UI Elements (**Figure 2.25**).

All UI elements are shown.

Figure 2.25 You can quickly show all interface elements when needed by using the Restore UI Elements command.

CHANGING THE LAYOUT

To hide or show the main and pane menu bars:

◆ Hold down the ⎡Spacebar⎤ anywhere in a pane, and select Hotbox Controls > Window Options > Show Main Menubar (Windows only) or Show Pane Menubars (**Figure 2.26**).

Show Main Menubar and Show Pane Menubars are toggled on and off. If they're on, selecting them will turn them off, and vice versa.

Using the Show menu

The Show menu comes in handy when you want to isolate a particular type of object (and hide other types), such as curves or lights. It offers a convenient way to display only the object types you want, or to edit and hide all other object types. When animating, for example, you might want to show only the character's surface in one pane and only its bones in another (**Figure 2.27**).

The Show menu allows you to turn all types of objects on and off at once. It also lets you turn objects on and off individually. You may want to turn off all objects first, then turn back on just the object type you want to isolate (**Figure 2.28**).

The Show menu only visually hides or shows object types; it does not delete the objects. Object types turned off in the Show menu will still appear in the final render.

Figure 2.26 The main menu bar and the pane menus must be turned on and off individually.

Figure 2.27 You can open two of the same panes, in this case Perspective views, and show different object types in each pane, making it easier to select and visualize objects.

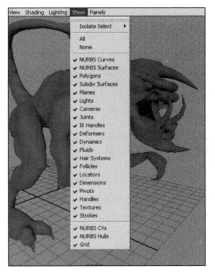

Figure 2.28 Turning all objects off or on in the Show menu helps you to quickly turn on only the relevant object types in the pane.

Figure 2.29 The Show menu hides and shows all objects of the chosen type. If you choose Lights, all lights in the view will be hidden.

Figure 2.30 There's no way to see or select an object type in a pane while it's hidden through the Show menu. In the right pane, Lights have been turned off in the Show menu.

To hide object types with the Show menu:

◆ From the Show menu inside any pane, select the object type you want to hide (**Figure 2.29**).

The object type selected is hidden from view (**Figure 2.30**).

To show hidden object types with the Show menu:

◆ From the Show menu inside any pane, select the object type you want to show in the pane (**Figure 2.29**).

The object type selected becomes visible in the view pane.

You can temporarily enlarge a pane to get a better view of its contents.

To focus a pane to full screen:

1. Move the mouse over the pane you would like to make larger (**Figure 2.31**).

2. Tap the ⬚Spacebar⬚ once.

The pane expands to full view (covering any other panes) (**Figure 2.32**).

Figure 2.31 The border of the pane turns blue to indicate that it's selected.

Figure 2.32 Tapping the ⬚Spacebar⬚ zooms the pane; however, *holding down* the ⬚Spacebar⬚ opens the Hotbox. Be careful to use the ⬚Spacebar⬚ correctly.

CHANGING THE LAYOUT

✔ Tip

■ Tap the [Spacebar] again to reset the pane's size (uncovering any additional panes).

■ Press [Ctrl]/[Control] [Spacebar] to hide most of Maya's interface so that the pane uses the maximum screen space.

To frame a selected item in a view:

1. Click the item you want the camera to zoom in on.

2. Press [f].

The view zooms to the object (**Figure 2.33**).

✔ Tips

■ You can make all of the view panes frame the selected item at the same time by pressing [Shift] [f].

■ You can toggle between the previous view and the next view by using the square bracket keys ([[] and []]).

To frame all objects in a view:

◆ Press [a].

The view frames all of the objects in the scene (**Figure 2.34**).

✔ Tip

■ You can make all of the view panes frame all of the objects at the same time by pressing [Shift] [a].

Maya has four main menu sets: Animation, Modeling, Dynamics, and Rendering. Each of these sets holds menus specific to its topic as well as the common menus File, Edit, Modify, Create, Display, Window, and Help. The common menus are always accessible from the main menu—regardless of which menu set you're currently using.

Figure 2.33 Press [f] to zoom in closer to a selected object.

Figure 2.34 When [a] is pressed, the camera moves from the view on top to the view on the bottom. Now all of the objects in the scene are framed within the view.

Figure 2.35 Each menu set holds menus specific to the type of process you're working on. If you're in the modeling stage of a project, you can use the Modeling menu set to access modeling-related menus.

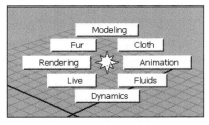

Figure 2.36 You can use Marking menus to change your menu sets when you've hidden the status line or you just want to speed your workflow.

To change the menu set:

Do any of the following:

◆ On the left side of the status bar, use the pop-up menu to select the appropriate menu set (**Figure 2.35**).

◆ In any view pane, hold down the ⓗ key and the left mouse button to select a menu set from the Marking menu (**Figure 2.36**). (Most objects have a menu specific to their object type called a Marking menu.)

◆ Press �F2 for the Animation menu set, �F3 for the Modeling menu set, �F4 for the Dynamic menu set, and �F5 for the Rendering menu set.

To show and hide the Hotbox:

1. Show the Hotbox by holding down the Spacebar (**Figure 2.37**).

2. Hide the Hotbox by releasing the Spacebar.

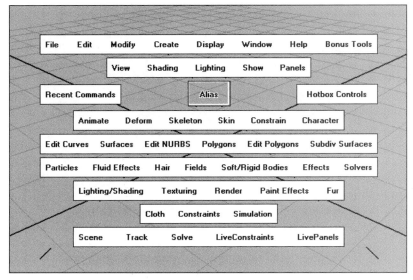

Figure 2.37 You can quickly open and close the Hotbox by holding down the Spacebar.

To show and hide specific menu sets in the Hotbox:

1. Show the Hotbox by holding down the [Spacebar] in any pane.

2. Hold down the left mouse button over the Hotbox Controls to show the Hotbox Controls Marking menu (**Figure 2.38**).

3. Move the mouse over the menu set name you want to show—Show Animation, in this example.

   This opens an additional Marking menu.

4. Select Show/Hide (menu set name) (**Figure 2.39**).

   The menu set is shown if it was hidden, and vice versa.

To show all menu sets in the Hotbox:

1. Show the Hotbox by holding down the [Spacebar] in any pane.

2. Hold down the left mouse button over the Hotbox controls to show the Hotbox Controls Marking menu.

3. Select Show All to show all the menu sets in the Hotbox (**Figure 2.40**).

To hide all menu sets in the Hotbox:

1. Show the Hotbox by holding down the [Spacebar] in any pane.

2. Hold down the left mouse button over the Hotbox Controls to show the Hotbox Controls Marking menu.

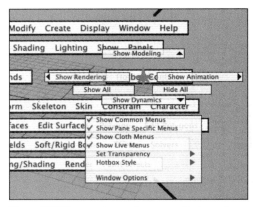

Figure 2.38 You can change the menus that are shown in the Hotbox by using the Marking menu in the Hotbox Controls.

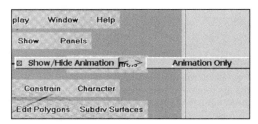

Figure 2.39 You can hide and show individual menus to control the size and accessibility of the Hotbox.

Figure 2.40 One advantage of using the Hotbox is that you can turn on all of the menu sets at once, or you can activate just one or two.

CHANGING THE LAYOUT

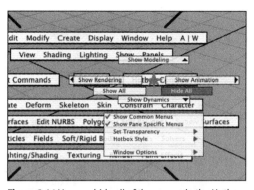

Figure 2.41 You can hide all of the menus in the Hotbox.

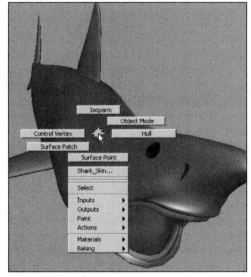

Figure 2.42 Each object has an associated menu set, called a Marking menu, which you can access by Right–clicking the object.

3. Select Hide All to hide all the menu sets in the Hotbox (**Figure 2.41**).

Hiding all of the menus in the Hotbox leaves only the Recent Commands and the Hotbox Controls menus available for selection. Along with these two menus, all of the Hotbox's Marking menus are still accessible.

Most objects have a menu specific to their object type called a Marking menu. The Marking menu holds shortcuts to the selected object's most commonly used commands. If you're in the habit of using Marking menus, you'll save yourself a lot of time.

To show an object's Marking menu:

1. Move your pointer directly over an object.

2. Click the object using the right mouse button to show its Marking menu (**Figure 2.42**).

✔ Tip

■ Once you're familiar with the location of specific commands in the Marking menus, you can quickly drag in the direction of the command you want to select without waiting for the menu item names to appear.

To show and hide the grid:

◆ From the Display menu, select Grid to toggle the grid on and off.

✔ Tip

■ You can adjust the size, closeness, and colors of the grid lines in the Grid options.

CHANGING THE LAYOUT

The Channel Box provides an easy way to adjust many of a selected object's attributes. Located on the right side of the interface in the default layout (**Figure 2.43**), the Channel Box can also be retrieved after being hidden, or toggled on and off using the steps outlined below.

To show or hide the Channel Box:

◆ Click the "Show or hide the Channel Box/Layer Editor" icon 🔲 on the right side of the status line. (The status line sits directly below the main menu bar.)

or

◆ From the Display menu select UI Elements > Channel Box/Layer Editor (**Figure 2.44**).

The Channel Box appears on the right side of the Maya interface.

Figure 2.43 The Channel Box can be hidden to save screen space or shown to give the user easy access to keyable object attributes.

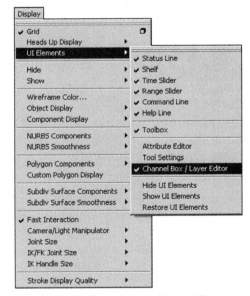

Figure 2.44 The Channel Box and Layer Editor can be shown together to make better use of available screen space.

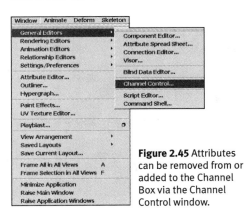

Figure 2.45 Attributes can be removed from or added to the Channel Box via the Channel Control window.

By default, the Channel Box holds the keyable attributes of the selected object. You can add attributes to the Channel Box list by following the steps outlined below.

To add preset attributes to the Channel Box:

1. Create or select an object to which you want to add an attribute.

2. From the Window menu, select General Editors > Channel Control (**Figure 2.45**). The Channel Control window opens.

3. Under the Keyable tab select the attribute name in the Non Keyable area of the Channel Control window (**Figure 2.46**).

4. Click the Move button 〈〈 Move .

5. The attribute is added to the Keyable list of attributes (**Figure 2.47**).

6. Click the Close button to close the Channel Control window.

   The new attribute is shown in the Channel Box (**Figure 2.48**).

Figure 2.46 The Non Keyable area of the Channel Control window holds attributes that can be added to the Channel Box.

Figure 2.47 You can move additional attributes to the Keyable area to add them to the Channel Box.

Figure 2.48 The Channel Box displays the newly added attribute, ready for use.

The Attribute Editor contains additional attributes not available in the Channel Box. The Channel Box is a great shortcut for accessing many of an object's attributes; however, it's too small to hold all of them. The Attribute Editor remains empty until an object is selected.

To show or hide the Attribute Editor:

Do any of the following:

◆ Click the "Show or hide the Attribute Editor" icon 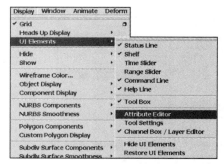 on the right side of the status line.

Make a selection to view its attributes.

◆ From the Display menu, select UI Elements > Attribute Editor (**Figure 2.49**).

The Attribute Editor appears on the right side of the Maya interface.

◆ Press (Ctrl) / (Control) (a).

The Attribute Editor opens (**Figure 2.50**).

◆ From the Window menu, select Attribute Editor (**Figure 2.51**).

The Attribute Editor opens on the right side of the interface.

✔ Tip

■ The field below the Attribute Editor conveniently allows you to store notes about the node and save them with the scene file.

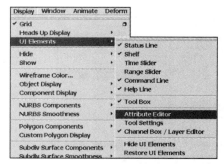

Figure 2.49 The Attribute Editor can be opened from the Display › UI Elements menu.

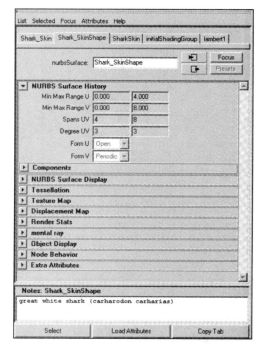

Figure 2.50 When opened in a new window, the Attribute Editor can be moved around and minimized (to get it out of the way).

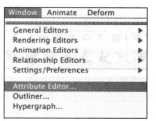

Figure 2.51 The Attribute Editor can be opened in a new window.

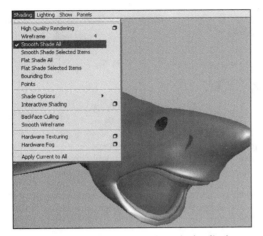

Figure 2.52 The Shading menu controls the display mode for each individual pane.

About Display Options and Smoothness

By using Maya's display options, you can change the way objects are viewed within the pane. You can view your scene in wireframe, smooth-shaded, flat-shaded, bounding-box, or points mode, and you can change your display options to match your current needs. Bounding-box and points mode, for example, can be used to speed interaction when tumbling around a complex scene. Wireframe mode is handy for selecting components (because you can see the components through the object), and smooth and flat shading can provide a more complete surface view (which makes it easier to model a surface). Each of the display options is useful for specific situations, so switching between them can improve workflow.

Included among the display options are hardware texturing and lighting options, which provide quick feedback when adding texture or lighting to a scene. Most of these settings have associated keyboard shortcuts.

You can display NURBS and Subdiv objects in one of three smoothness levels: rough, medium, or fine. (However, the display smoothness levels do not apply to polygonal objects.) Objects are displayed rough by default, but you can change the setting using the shortcuts described below. Choosing a setting of rough can ease component selection because fewer surface lines are shown. A fine setting comes closest to matching the final surface—which means this is the setting to use when you need to focus on fine details.

To change the display options from the Shading menu:

◆ From the Shading menu in any pane, select one of the following shading options: Wireframe, Smooth Shade, Flat Shade, Bounding Box, or Points (**Figure 2.52**).

ABOUT DISPLAY OPTIONS AND SMOOTHNESS

Shading and smoothness shortcuts

1️⃣ = Rough smoothness (**Figure 2.53**)

2️⃣ = Medium smoothness (Figure 2.53)

3️⃣ = Fine smoothness (Figure 2.53)

4️⃣ = Wireframe mode (**Figure 2.54**)

5️⃣ = Shaded mode (**Figure 2.55**)

6️⃣ = Hardware Texturing (**Figure 2.56**)

7️⃣ = Hardware Lighting (**Figure 2.57**)

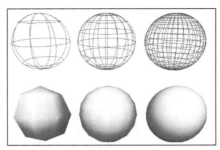

Figure 2.53 Rough smoothness (left) shows the object in low resolution. Medium smoothness (middle) shows the object with some additional resolution but not enough to obstruct the view of the object. Fine smoothness (right) provides the closest representation of the surface's shape.

Figure 2.54 Wireframe mode allows you to see through objects and view their geometry on the front and back of the surface.

Figure 2.55 Shaded mode presents the surface in gray by default to show its final skin.

Figure 2.56 Hardware Texturing shows the surface textures within the pane.

Figure 2.57 Hardware Lighting shows the scene's lighting scenario interactively within the pane by generalizing the effects that the lights would have on the scene—somewhat of a very rough version of the final render. The Hardware Lighting option can save large amounts of rendering time because you can see the results as soon as you change a light's position.

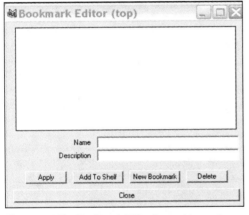

Figure 2.58 The View menu is used to alter, save, and restore camera viewpoints.

Figure 2.59 The Bookmark Editor is used to create user-defined camera angles.

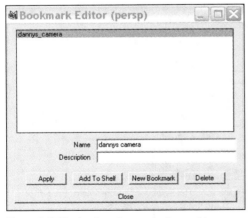

Figure 2.60 The bookmark name is changed to dannys_camera.

Using the View menu

The View menu lets you control what the camera is focused on inside a view pane (**Figure 2.58**). You can bookmark your current pane's viewpoint to later return to that camera angle. This option is most useful on the Persp view to return to a pre-defined or user-defined viewpoint.

To bookmark the current pane viewpoint:

1. From the View menu inside any pane, select the Bookmarks > Edit Bookmarks menu item.

   The Bookmark Editor window opens (**Figure 2.59**).

2. Click the New Bookmark button.

3. In the Name field, type a new name for your bookmark (**Figure 2.60**).

4. Click Apply, and then Close to complete the bookmark.

To access a bookmarked pane viewpoint:

◆ From the View menu inside any pane, select the Bookmarks > (bookmark name) menu item (**Figure 2.61**).

The view returns to the bookmarked viewpoint.

The View menu is also used to select the camera you are currently looking through, as well as to frame selected objects into view.

To select the camera you are currently looking through:

◆ From the View menu inside any pane, click the Select Camera menu item (**Figure 2.62**).

The Camera you are looking through becomes selected, and the Attribute Editor for the camera opens on the right side of the interface (**Figure 2.63**).

Figure 2.61 The saved view named dannys_camera is accessed by selecting View › Bookmarks › dannys_camera.

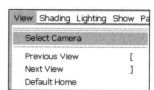

Figure 2.62
The View › Select Camera menu item is found at the top of any view pane.

Figure 2.63 The selected camera's Attribute Editor holds all of the camera settings.

CREATING PRIMITIVES AND TEXT

3

As pre-made geometry sets that simplify the creation of more complex shapes, primitives are the building blocks of 3D modeling. To understand this, just take a look at the objects around you: Everything in nature, no matter how complex, can be broken down into a few primitive shapes—something you can do right now with the objects in front of you. Is the object you're looking at built around many cylinders like a metal chair, or is it a squashed cube like a door or a wall? Many objects combine a number of different primitives. Take, for example, the bicycle: Its wheels combine a cylinder (for each spoke) and a slim torus (which defines the tires' shape). Likewise, you can use a number of primitives to create a detailed face from a simple sphere, or employ just a few well-placed cubes to construct a building.

Because they can be manipulated in a variety of ways, primitives have become an important part of Maya and other 3D programs. NURBS primitives can speed workflow because the curves have already been drawn and, in many cases, have been replaced with surface geometry. You can stretch, cut, scale, translate, trim, and rebuild them, making them essential to your workflow and great time-savers as well.

Maya includes three primary types of primitives: *NURBS, polygons,* and *subdivs.* To help you understand which type is appropriate for the task at hand, this chapter takes a close look at NURBS (**Figure 3.1**), Polygons (**Figure 3.2**) and Subdivs (**Figure 3.3**), explaining the strengths and weaknesses of each.

Figure 3.1 The NURBS primitives (top to bottom): sphere, cube, cylinder, cone, plane, torus, circle, and square.

Figure 3.2 The polygon primitives (top to bottom): sphere, cube, cylinder, cone, plane, and torus.

Figure 3.3 The subdiv primitives (top to bottom): sphere, cube, cylinder, cone, plane, and torus.

Weighted control points

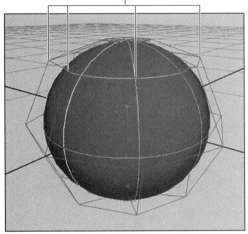

Figure 3.4 NURBS surfaces are changed using weighted control points.

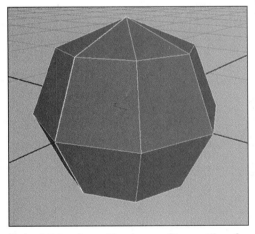

Figure 3.5 A surface with a degree of 1, or setting of linear.

About NURBS

NURBS curves, surfaces, and primitives are an important part of Maya modeling. You can use NURBS objects to produce long, smooth surfaces (such as car hoods) or sharp, angular surfaces (such as stop signs). NURBS objects make it possible for you to adjust the look of a surface by manipulating just a few weighted control points (**Figure 3.4**).

Each of the NURBS curves and surfaces has an associated degree that controls the smoothness of the NURBS object. A surface degree of 1, or a setting of *linear*, will produce a straight connection between each control point, creating a very angular surface (**Figure 3.5**). As you raise the degree of the NURBS object, you create a smoother curve and surface (**Figure 3.6**). The higher the degree of the curve, the more points are needed to define it. For more about NURBS degrees, see Chapter 7, "NURBS Curves and surfaces."

continues on next page

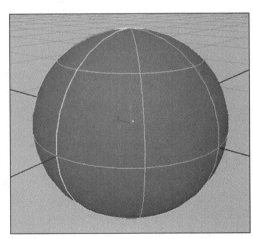

Figure 3.6 A surface with a higher degree will appear smoother.

NURBS, or *nonuniform rational B-spline*, describes objects whose shapes are defined by mathematical equations. Luckily for us, Maya takes care of most of the math behind the scenes. *B-spline* refers to the underlying curve that defines all NURBS objects. When creating a NURBS object, you use multiple curves to produce a wire representation of the surface's appearance. After using curves to lay down the shape of the surface, you add a skin atop the curves to create the final surface: This process of creating a surface that extends from one curve to the next is called *lofting* (**Figure 3.7**).

You can break down NURBS objects into separate components that work together to define the shape of the NURBS object. Components include (among others) *CVs* (control vertices), *edit points*, and *hulls*—each of which can be manipulated to sculpt the surface or define the curves' shapes. (You can manipulate components together or separately to change the shape of an object.) For more information on NURBS components, see Chapter 7.

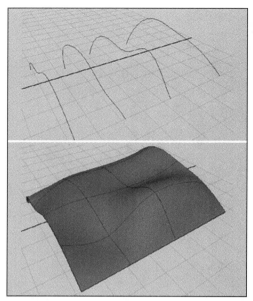

Figure 3.7 The top object has curves only; the bottom object has curves plus a skin.

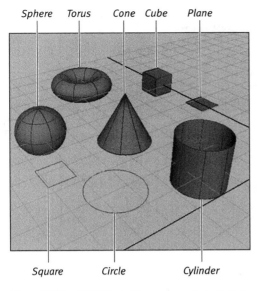

Sphere Torus Cone Cube Plane

Square Circle Cylinder

Figure 3.8 The NURBS primitives are used as starting points for more complex models.

Figure 3.9 A primitive's attributes can be changed in its Options dialog box.

Figure 3.10 The construction history allows you to change an existing surface's attributes.

About NURBS Primitives

NURBS primitives represent a collection of frequently used, predefined curves and surfaces. Maya includes eight NURBS primitives: *sphere, cube, cylinder, cone, plane, torus, circle,* and *square* (**Figure 3.8**).

These predefined primitive surfaces are not only time-savers for creating simple objects; you can also use them as a starting point for more detailed shapes. The circle and square primitives are NURBS curves without surfaces attached to them; the other six NURBS primitives are predefined surfaces ready to be placed in the Maya scene or further manipulated.

Each primitive includes a number of attributes that you can set for an object. You can change each primitive's attributes in its Options dialog box *before* you create an object (**Figure 3.9**). In addition, most primitives include a construction history that's attached to their surfaces: This is where you can adjust and fine-tune the surface's properties *after* it's been created (**Figure 3.10**). The construction-history attributes appear in the Channel Box under each primitive's makeNurb heading, but only if construction history was enabled when the primitive was created. In this chapter, we'll show you how to create NURBS primitives and change some of their attributes (both before and after the object has been created). For more information on construction history, see Chapter 1, "Maya Basics."

Creating NURBS primitives

NURBS primitives are found in the Create > NURBS Primitives submenu (**Figure 3.11**). You create a primitive by selecting the primitive's name from the submenu. You can also create a NURBS primitive through the Hotbox, as described below. And by simply clicking their icons in the Surfaces Shelf, you can quickly create any of the primitive NURBS surfaces (**Figure 3.12**).

When you create a primitive surface or curve, Maya will place the object's center point at the origin of the scene (at 0, 0, 0 coordinates). This centers most objects over the *Y*-axis line (so that half of the object is above the axis, and half is below) (**Figure 3.13**). The exception is the cone, whose center point is at its base. You can create NURBS primitives by following the steps that follow.

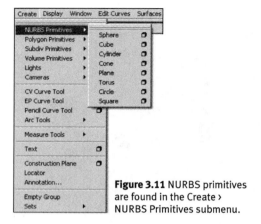

Figure 3.11 NURBS primitives are found in the Create › NURBS Primitives submenu.

Figure 3.12 You can quickly create NURBS primitives by clicking their icons in the Surfaces Shelf.

Figure 3.13 Maya places the center point of the primitive at the origin of the scene.

ABOUT NURBS PRIMITIVES

Figure 3.14 Select the name of the primitive you want to create from the NURBS Primitives submenu.

Figure 3.15 The NURBS primitive appears at the origin of the Maya scene (the Sphere is shown).

Figure 3.16 You can use the Hotbox to select the NURBS Primitives submenu (here Cube is selected).

To create a NURBS primitive using the main menu:

1. From the Create menu, select the NURBS Primitives submenu.

2. Select the name of the primitive you want to create—in this case, the sphere (**Figure 3.14**).

   The NURBS primitive appears at the origin of the Maya scene (**Figure 3.15**).

The Hotbox is a great time-saver because you can create objects and primitives without accessing the main menu. You can display the Hotbox from anywhere within the Maya window, providing even faster access to Maya's menus.

To create a NURBS primitive using the Hotbox:

1. Hold down (Spacebar) anywhere in the scene to show the Hotbox.

2. From the Create menu in the Hotbox, select the NURBS Primitives submenu.

3. Select the name of the primitive you want to create—in this case, the cube (**Figure 3.16**).

   The NURBS primitive is created at the origin of the Maya scene (**Figure 3.17**).

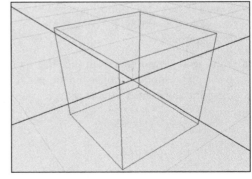

Figure 3.17 The NURBS primitive is created at the origin of the Maya scene (the cube is shown).

ABOUT NURBS PRIMITIVES

Maya's Surfaces Shelf contains shortcut icons for all of the primitive NURBS surfaces (**Figure 3.18**). By selecting these primitives from the Shelf, you can save yourself the two or three steps required to select the same primitive from the Create menu.

To create a NURBS primitive using the Shelf:

◆ From the Surfaces Shelf, select the NURBS primitive icon for the object you would like to create (for example, a sphere or cone).

The primitive is created at the origin of the Maya scene (**Figure 3.19**).

✔ Tips

■ If the Shelf is not already open, open it by going to the Display menu and selecting UI Elements > Shelf (**Figure 3.20**).

■ To add primitives or other objects to the Shelf, hold down [Shift] and [Ctrl]/[Control] while selecting the menu item in the main menu. This stores the command you selected from the menu in the Shelf with its currently selected options. Thus, if you were to change the object's attributes in the Options dialog box before adding it to the Shelf, you could have one sphere in the Shelf with an end-sweep angle of 20 and another with an end-sweep angle of 360—another way to speed your workflow for commonly used settings.

■ You can remove items from the Shelf by pressing the middle mouse button while dragging the items to the trash.

Figure 3.18 The default Shelf in Maya holds shortcut icons for the Sphere and Cone NURBS primitives.

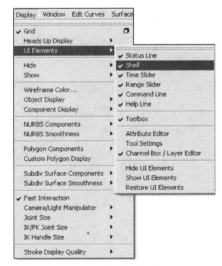

Figure 3.19 Select the primitive NURBS icon in Surfaces Shelf; here the Cone has been chosen.

Figure 3.20 To view the Shelf, select UI Elements > Shelf.

Figure 3.21 The radius attribute, which is common to the objects shown above, makes the object larger.

Figure 3.22 Select the box next to the name of the primitive for which you want to set the radius.

Figure 3.23 Adjust the Radius slider to half the diameter that you desire for the primitive.

Changing Attributes of NURBS Primitives

Each NURBS primitive has an associated set of attributes. Some attributes are common to all NURBS primitives, and others are specific to just one or two. By changing these attributes, you can alter a surface's appearance.

You change all NURBS primitive attributes in the same way. In this section, we'll show you how to change the radius attribute of a NURBS primitive. You can follow the same steps to change other object attributes. The following section defines many of the NURBS primitives' attributes.

The radius attribute is common to the NURBS primitive sphere, cone, cylinder, torus, and circle (**Figure 3.21**).

To set the radius of a NURBS primitive sphere, cone, cylinder, torus, or circle from the Create menu:

1. From the Create menu, select the NURBS Primitives submenu.

2. Select the box next to the name of the primitive for which you want to set the radius—in this case, the cylinder (**Figure 3.22**).

3. In the selected primitive's Options dialog box, adjust the Radius slider to half the desired diameter of the primitive (**Figure 3.23**).

✔ Tip

■ You can type in a value larger than the slider's highest value.

To change the radius of a NURBS primitive for an existing object:

1. Select a primitive NURBS sphere, cone, cylinder, torus, or circle.

2. Click the makeNurb title under the Inputs heading in the Channel Box to show the selected primitive's changeable attributes (**Figure 3.24**).

3. Click once in the Radius field to select it (**Figure 3.25**).

4. Change the number to the size you want the radius to be.

5. Press ⌈Enter⌋ to complete the radius change (**Figure 3.26**).

✔ Tips

- You can also click the attribute's name (in our example, Radius) in the Channel Box, and then click and drag the middle mouse button left or right in the View window to interactively change the object's radius.

- If the construction history is turned off, the makeNurb node will not be available in the Channel Box.

- The makeNurb history will not be available on a duplicated object unless you go into the Edit > Duplicate options and check Duplicate Upstream Graph.

Figure 3.24 Select the makeNurb title under the INPUTS heading in the Channel Box (the cylinder is shown).

Figure 3.25 Click the Radius field once to select it (Cylinder settings are shown).

Figure 3.26 Before (left) and after (right) the radius change (the cylinder is shown).

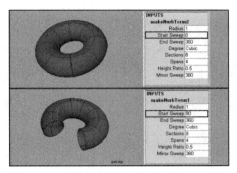

Figure 3.27 Adjusting the start sweep causes the beginning and end of the surface to be separated (the torus is shown). The picture on top shows the torus before the start sweep has been adjusted. The picture on the bottom shows the torus after the start sweep has been adjusted.

Figure 3.28 Adjusting the Minor Sweep attribute unfolds the surface along the U direction (the torus is shown). The picture on top represents the torus before minor sweep has been adjusted; the picture on the bottom shows the result of the adjustment.

Figure 3.29 If the Degree attribute is set to Cubic (default), the surface will be curved (top). If the Degree attribute is set to Linear, the surface will be planar and faceted (bottom).

NURBS primitive attributes

The following are some important NURBS primitive attributes, with their definitions. You set these in the Channel Box or in the object's Options dialog box.

- ◆ **Radius**—The radius of an object is half of its diameter. Adjusting the radius scales the object proportionally on all three axes.

- ◆ **Start Sweep**—Adjusting the start sweep causes the surface to separate from its end in a clockwise direction. The result is a slice of the surface, or a surface of less than 360 degrees (**Figure 3.27**).

- ◆ **End Sweep**—Adjusting the end sweep has a similar effect to adjusting the start sweep; however, instead of working clockwise from the end point, it works counterclockwise from the starting point to open the surface. The result is a slice of the surface, or a surface of less than 360 degrees.

- ◆ **Minor Sweep**—Adjusting the Minor Sweep attribute, which is specific to the torus primitive, unfolds the surface along the U direction, creating (for a torus) a slice of the surface similar to a spool (rather than a full doughnut shape) (**Figure 3.28**).

- ◆ **Degree**—A NURBS primitive can be linear or cubic. If the Degree attribute is set to Linear, the surface is planar and faceted. If the Degree attribute is set to Cubic (default), the surface is more curved and smooth (**Figure 3.29**).

continues on next page

- **Sections**—Adjusting the Sections attribute adds more detail to the surface in the U direction, which makes it easier to edit its shape (**Figure 3.30**).

- **Spans**—Adjusting the Spans attribute adds detail to the surface in the V direction, which makes it easier to edit its shape (**Figure 3.31**).

- **Height Ratio**—This is the ratio of the height in relation to the depth. If the height ratio is set to 2, the height will be twice the size of the depth.

- **Length Ratio**—This is the ratio of the length in relation to the depth. If the length ratio is set to 2, the length will be twice the size of the depth.

- **Patches U and Patches V**—Patches U and V are specific to the plane and cube primitives. Adjusting these attributes will increase the surface geometry in the U or V direction (**Figure 3.32**).

Figure 3.30 Adjusting the Sections attribute adds more detail to the surface in the U direction.

Figure 3.31 Adjusting the Spans attribute adds isoparms in the V direction.

Figure 3.32 Adjusting Patches U and Patches V attributes increases the surface geometry in the U or V direction.

Figure 3.33 A low-polygon model renders fast and can be developed quickly (this one is by Andrew Britt).

Figure 3.34 Faces, edges, and vertices make up the polygon components.

About Polygons

Polygon meshes facilitate extremely flexible modeling because they can be used to produce high-quality, smooth surfaces as well as low-resolution, fast-rendering surfaces. Games can use only a small amount of polygons per surface (called *low-poly* models) in order for game engines to render them on the fly. Thus, polygons are the surface type of choice for game and Internet developers. A proficient modeler can create a good-looking, fast-loading model by using just a few well-placed polygons (**Figure 3.33**).

Polygons have many components, which you use to manipulate the final look of the surface. The components themselves are made up of *faces, edges,* and *vertices* (**Figure 3.34**)—all of which combine to help define the shape of the polygonal object. Each of these components can be manipulated individually, giving the creator precise control of polygon construction.

continues on next page

You can create polygons, or *polys* for short, one at a time, slowly adding to the surface's resolution. Or you can start with a very simple poly object (for example, a poly primitive; see the next section), and use the Smooth command to add more individual polys, increasing the surface's resolution and smoothness (**Figure 3.35**). To learn more about the Smooth command, see Chapter 8 "Polygons."

Subdivisions are an important part of a polygonal mesh. The number of subdivisions in the poly surface determines how smooth the final surface will render (**Figure 3.36**). Decreasing the number of subdivisions results in fewer faces, making the surface appear much more angular. You can set the number of poly subdivisions before or after you create an object. You can also subdivide individual polygons, giving you precise control over the final number of polygons. (Note that use of the word subdivision in reference to subdividing polygons is not the same as subdiv surfaces, discussed later in this chapter.)

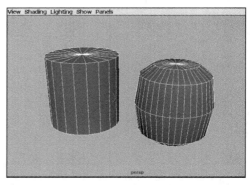

Figure 3.35 You can start with a simple poly object, like a poly primitive (left), and use the Smooth command to add more individual polys (right).

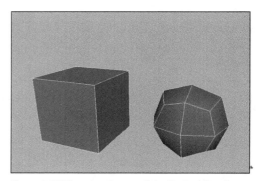

Figure 3.36 The smoothness of the final surface is determined by the number of subdivisions in the poly surface. The default surface is on the left; subdivisions have been added on the right.

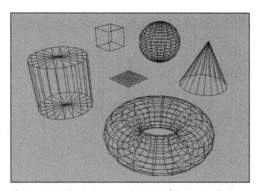

Figure 3.37 The polygon primitives (clockwise from left): cylinder, cube, sphere, cone, torus, and plane (center).

Figure 3.38 Polygon primitives can be extruded, split, subdivided, merged, beveled, and separated (among other things). Here, a beveled primitive cube is shown.

About Polygon Primitives

Polygon primitives, like NURBS primitives, represent a collection of frequently used predefined surfaces. These predefined primitive surfaces can save you time in creating objects and give you a head start on creating more detailed shapes.

Maya includes six polygon primitives: sphere, cube, cylinder, cone, plane, and torus (**Figure 3.37**). You can use polygon primitives to speed workflow because each face that describes the surface has already been drawn for you.

Once you've created polygon primitives, you can (among other things) extrude, split, subdivide, merge, bevel, and separate them. This allows for fast modeling of objects and precise control over the number of faces used for the surface—which means you can control the amount of render time needed to produce the final image (**Figure 3.38**).

Creating polygon primitives

Polygon primitives are found in the Create menu within the Polygon Primitives submenu. You can access polygon primitives via the Hotbox, as described below. By clicking their icons in the Polygons Shelf, you can quickly create any of the poly primitives.

When you create a poly primitive, Maya places the center point of the object at the origin of the scene (just as it does when you create a NURBS primitive).

You can create poly primitives by following the steps outlined below.

To create a polygon primitive using the main menu:

1. From the Create menu, select the Polygon Primitives submenu.

2. Select the name of the primitive you want to create (the torus is shown here) (**Figure 3.39**).

   A polygon primitive is created at the origin (0, 0, 0) of the Maya scene (**Figure 3.40**).

The Hotbox is a great time-saver because it allows you to select objects and primitives without returning to the main menu.

To create a polygon primitive using the Hotbox:

1. Hold down (Spacebar) anywhere in the scene to display the Hotbox.

2. From the Create menu in the Hotbox, select the Polygon Primitives submenu (**Figure 3.41**).

Figure 3.39 You can create a polygon primitive by choosing Create > Polygon Primitives. Here Torus primitive is selected.

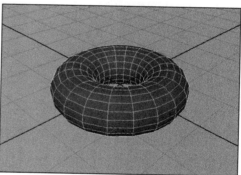

Figure 3.40 A polygon primitive appears at the origin of the Maya scene; the torus is shown.

Figure 3.41 You can access the Polygon Primitives submenu via the Hotbox.

Figure 3.42 Select the name of the primitive you want to create.

Figure 3.43 A polygon primitive appears at the origin of the Maya scene.

Figure 3.44 Shortcut icons for the polygon primitives in the Polygons Shelf.

Figure 3.45 The primitive appears at the origin of the Maya scene (the cube is shown).

3. Select the name of the primitive you want to create (the cone is shown here) (**Figure 3.42**).

A polygon primitive is created at the origin of the Maya scene (**Figure 3.43**).

The default Shelf in Maya holds shortcut icons for the cube and cylinder polygon primitives (**Figure 3.44**). Selecting these primitives from the Shelf can save the two or three steps you would take to select the primitive from the Create menu.

To create a polygon primitive using the Shelf:

◆ From the Polygons Shelf, select the icon of the polygon primitive you would like to create—for example, the cube or cylinder.

The primitive is created at the origin of the Maya scene (**Figure 3.45**).

✔ Tips

■ If the Shelf is not already open, open it by going to the Display menu and selecting UI Elements > Shelf.

■ To add primitives or other objects to the Shelf, hold down s and Ctrl/Control while selecting the primitive in the Create menu.

Changing a Polygon Primitive's Attributes

Like NURBS primitives, each poly primitive has a number of attributes that you can set for the object before or after it's created. You can change each primitive's default attributes in the Options dialog box before you create an object (**Figure 3.46**). Most of these primitives have a construction history attached to their surface, which means you can fine-tune surface properties after the surface has been created (**Figure 3.47**). The construction-history attributes appear under each primitive's poly heading in the Channel Box.

You change all of the polygon primitives' attributes in the same way. In the text that follows we'll show you how to change the Subdivisions Height attribute of a polygon primitive. You can follow the same steps to change other object attributes. The next section defines many of the poly primitives' other attributes.

The Subdivisions Height attribute (common to all of the polygon primitives) determines the number of times the surface's height is divided. By raising the number, you add polygons to describe the surface along the height of the object (**Figure 3.48**). If you lower the number, you will use fewer polygons to describe the surface along the height of the object (**Figure 3.49**).

Figure 3.46 Each poly primitive has many attributes that can be set for the object before or after it is created.

Figure 3.47 You can fine-tune polygon primitives after the surface has been created by adjusting their poly attributes.

Figure 3.48 If you raise the Subdivisions Height attribute, you are adding polygons to describe the surface along the height of the object.

Figure 3.49 Additional polygons are added to the surface along its height.

Figure 3.50 Select the box next to the name of the primitive for which you want to set Subdivisions Height.

Figure 3.51 Adjust the Subdivisions Along Height slider to the amount of divisions you want along the height of the surface.

To set the Subdivisions Height attribute of a polygon primitive from the Create menu:

1. From the Create menu, select the Polygon Primitives submenu.

2. Select the box next to the name of the primitive for which you want to set Subdivisions Height (the cylinder is shown here) (**Figure 3.50**)

3. In the Options dialog box, adjust the Subdivisions Along Height slider to the number of divisions you want along the height of the surface (**Figure 3.51**).

4. Click Create to create a new primitive with the new Subdivisions Height settings.

✔ Tip

■ You can type in a value that's higher than what the slider will allow.

CHANGING A POLYGON PRIMITIVE'S ATTRIBUTES

To change the Subdivisions Height attribute of a polygon primitive after the object has been created:

1. Select a polygon primitive.

2. Select the poly(object) title under the Inputs heading in the Channel Box (**Figure 3.52**).

3. Click the Subdivisions Height field to select the number there (**Figure 3.53**).

4. Change the number to reflect the number of times you want to divide the height.

5. Press (Enter) to complete the change (**Figure 3.54**).

✔ Tip

- You can also click the attribute's name (Subdivisions Height in our example) in the Channel Box, and then click and drag the middle mouse button left or right in the view window to interactively change the Subdivisions Height value.

Figure 3.52 Select the poly(object) title in the Channel Box (the title of a cone is shown).

Figure 3.53 Click the Subdivisions Height field to select its contents (the number for the cone is shown).

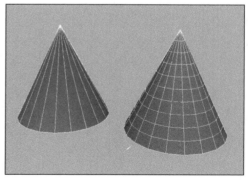

Figure 3.54 Press (Enter) to complete the change. The cone with default settings is on the left; the cone with the altered Subdivisions Height setting is on the right.

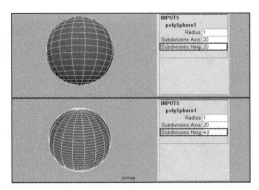

Figure 3.55 Adjusting the Subdivisions Height attribute adds or subtracts polygons to or from the height (a sphere is shown).

Figure 3.56 Adjusting the Subdivisions Axis attribute adds or subtracts polygons to the object along the center axis.

Figure 3.57 Adjusting the Subdivisions Cap attribute adds or subtracts polygons to or from the object's cap, radiating out from the center.

Polygon primitive attributes

The following are some of the most important polygon primitive attributes.

◆ **Subdivisions Height, Width**—These attributes adjust the number of times the height or width of the surface is divided. Adjusting these attributes adds or subtracts faces in the direction of the axis (**Figure 3.55**).

◆ **Subdivisions Depth**—This attribute adjusts the number of times the depth of the surface is divided. Adjusting this attribute adds or subtracts faces along the depth of the object.

◆ **Subdivisions Axis**—This attribute adjusts the number of times the surface is divided along the center axis. Adjusting this attribute adds or subtracts faces to the object in the same way you would add slices to a pizza (**Figure 3.56**).

◆ **Subdivisions Cap**—Two poly primitives have caps, the cone and the cylinder. Caps are pieces of geometry used to cover a surface's round hole(s). The cylinder has a cap on the top and bottom of its surface; the cone only has a cap on the bottom of its surface. The Subdivisions Cap attribute adjusts the number of times the surface's cap is divided. Adjusting this attribute adds or subtracts faces to or from the object's cap—like a water droplet sending concentric circles out from the center (**Figure 3.57**).

continues on next page

◆ **Radius**—An object's radius is half its diameter. Adjusting the Radius attribute scales the object proportionally on multiple axes.

◆ **Section Radius**—This attribute is only used by the torus polygon primitive. Adjusting the section radius fattens or slims the torus' doughnut-like shape (**Figure 3.58**).

◆ **Width, Height, and Depth**—These attributes adjust the object's width, height, or depth.

◆ **Twist**—This attribute is used only by the torus polygon primitive. Adjusting the twist moves the faces around the center axis inside the tube shape from 0 to 360 degrees (**Figure 3.59**).

Figure 3.58 Adjusting the section radius fattens or slims the Torus' shape.

Figure 3.59 Putting a twist on a torus.

CHANGING A POLYGON PRIMITIVE'S ATTRIBUTES

Figure 3.60 A subdiv model is one mesh that defines a complex surface. The model on the left shows a single subdiv surface, whereas the model on the right is a NURBS patch model containing over a hundred individual surfaces.

About Subdiv Surfaces

Subdivision surfaces, or *subdivs*, have been around since 1978. But only recently has computer hardware become fast enough to make working with subdivs manageable. More programs have adapted to using subdiv surfaces in their modeling workflow and more professional studios are using them in their production pipelines for feature films and broadcast work. Video games, however, are still dominated by polygons.

Subdivs combine the best of both NURBS and polygons. A subdiv surface is like a polygon model in that it can define complex surfaces with only one mesh (**Figure 3.60**), whereas NURBS models may require many surfaces to create a complex "patch model." Like a NURBS model, a subdiv can easily be increased in detail at any point in time to more precisely draw curvature, whereas polygon models are generally un-wieldy after adding more detail.

Working with subdivs is, however, very reliant on the polygon modeling toolset in Maya. So becoming familiar with polygons paves the way for a better understanding of subdivs.

continues on next page

Subdivs, like NURBS and polys, have components like points/vertices, lines/edges, and faces that can be directly manipulated to shape your model (**Figure 3.61**).

Subdivs in Maya are based on levels of detail. The top level known as the Level 0 mesh and has the coarsest level of detail. Below that are more levels of increasing detail. You can also use the Level 0 mesh as a sort of stand-in geometry for binding and animating. Subdivs are very versatile in this way. You can display more or less detail of the selected subdiv model you're working on by pressing ①, ②, or ③ on your keyboard (**Figure 3.62**).

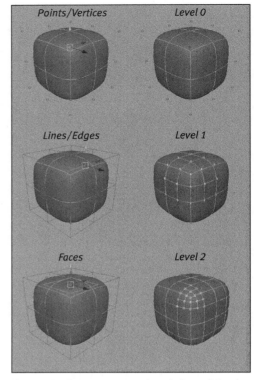

Figure 3.61 The components of a Subdiv model and the levels of detail from coarse to refined.

Figure 3.62 You can display increasing levels of detail in a Subdiv primitive by pressing ①, ②, or ③ on the keyboard.

Figure 3.63 The six subdiv primitives: cube, sphere, cylinder, plane, cone, and torus.

About Subdiv Primitives

Subdiv primitives come in the same six basic shapes as the polygon primitives (**Figure 3.63**) with one major difference—there are no attributes to adjust.

Like the other primitives you have read about, you can use these six basic shapes to start modeling from and add detail using the modeling tools. As we will discuss in more detail in Chapter 9, "Subdiv Surfaces," you can also convert the other primitives into subdiv surfaces and use the polygonal modeling tools to indirectly manipulate a subdiv model.

Creating Subdiv Primitives

Subdiv primitives are found in the Create menu within the Subdiv Primitives submenu. You can access subdiv primitives via the Hotbox, as described below. By clicking their icons in the Subdiv Shelf, you can quickly create any of the six subdiv primitives.

When you create a subdiv primitive, Maya places the center point of the object at the origin of the scene (just as it does when you create a NURBS or Polygonal primitive).

You can create subdiv primitives by following the steps outlined below.

To create a subdiv primitive using the main menu:

◆ From the Create menu, select the Subdiv Primitives submenu and select the primitive you want to create (**Figure 3.64**).

A subdiv primitive is created at the origin (0, 0, 0) of the Maya scene (**Figure 3.65**).

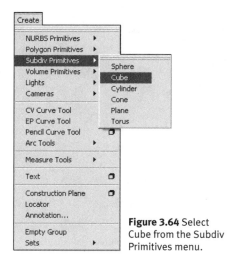

Figure 3.64 Select Cube from the Subdiv Primitives menu.

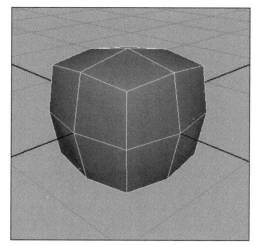

Figure 3.65 A primitive Subdiv Cube appears at center of the Maya scene.

CREATING SUBDIV PRIMITIVES

Figure 3.66 Selecting Cylinder from the Subdiv Primitives menu using the Hotbox.

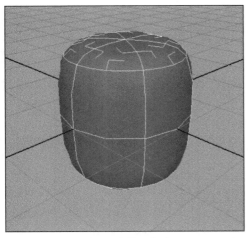

Figure 3.67 A primitive subdiv cylinder appears at the world origin.

Figure 3.68 Shortcut icons for the subdiv primitives in the Polygons Shelf.

To create a subdiv primitive using the Hotbox:

1. Press the (Spacebar) while the cursor is anywhere in the scene to display the Hotbox.

2. From the Create menu in the Hotbox, select the Subdiv Primitives submenu and select the name of the primitive you want to create (**Figure 3.66**).

   A subdiv primitive is created at the "world origin," the virtual space in which you place objects, of the Maya scene (**Figure 3.67**).

The default Shelf in Maya holds shortcut icons for the Cube and Cylinder subdiv primitives (**Figure 3.68**). Selecting these primitives from the Shelf can save the two or three steps you would take to select the primitive from the Create menu.

To create a subdiv primitive using the Shelf:

◆ From the Subdivs Shelf, select the icon of the subdiv primitive you would like to create—for example, the Cube or Cylinder.

   The primitive is created at the world origin of the Maya scene (**Figure 3.69**).

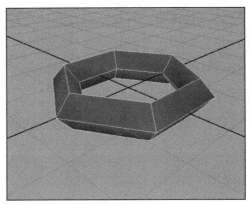

Figure 3.69 A primitive subdiv torus is created at the world origin.

About Text

You can create three types of text in Maya: *curves, trims,* and *polys* (**Figure 3.70**). You can find all of these text types in the Create > Text Options dialog box. Each text type has its place, and the type you use will depend on the application.

All of the text types in Maya create flat text objects made of curves, trimmed surfaces (see Chapter 7), or polygons. Although text starts out flat, there are many ways to make it three-dimensional. Once the two-dimensional text is created, you can do anything to it that you would do to any other curve or surface. For instance, if you create text made of curves, you can loft—a function that creates a surface over two or more curves—between a copy and an original (**Figure 3.71**). You can also take text made of polygons and extrude it to make it three-dimensional. See Chapter 7 for more on lofting.

The Curves text-type option creates versatile text with curves but no attached surfaces. This means you can make the front face of the text planar to create a surface over it, or you can leave it open and loft between two copies of the text to make it three-dimensional while leaving a hole for the front face, as in Figure 3.71.

Notice that the text is created in separate, selectable pieces. For instance, the letter *D* would have a curve for the outside part of the letter and another curve for its center.

To create curve-based text:

1. From the Create menu, select the box next to Text (**Figure 3.72**).

2. In the Options dialog box, click the Text field, and type in new text.

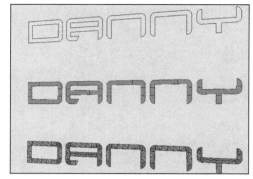

Figure 3.70 Maya includes three types of text (from top): curves, trims, and polys.

Figure 3.71 Once the 2D text is created, you can do anything to it that you would do to any other curve or surface. This is an example of a loft.

Figure 3.72 Go to the Create menu and select the box next to Text.

ABOUT TEXT

Figure 3.73 Click the arrow next to the Font field, and select the font for the text.

Figure 3.74 Make sure the Curves button is selected for Type.

Figure 3.75 Text is placed in the Maya scene with the bottom-left corner of it at the origin.

Figure 3.76 Trim text type can save you some steps if you're looking for text with surface geometry on its front face.

Figure 3.77 You can manipulate the curve's components to change an individual letter's shape.

3. Click the arrow next to the Font field and select the font for the text. Then click Create (**Figure 3.73**).

4. Make sure Curves is selected for the Type option (**Figure 3.74**).

5. Click Create to complete the text.

Text appears in the Maya scene with the bottom-left corner of the text at the origin (**Figure 3.75**).

Another text-type setting is Trim. Using this text type is the same as selecting the curves and making them planar (see Chapter 7). This text type can save you some steps if you're looking for text with surface geometry on its front face (**Figure 3.76**).

With trimmed text, you have surfaces attached to curves through history, allowing you to manipulate the curves to change an individual letter's shape (**Figure 3.77**).

To create trimmed text:

1. From the Create menu, select the box next to Text.

2. In the Options dialog box, click the Text field, and type in your new text (**Figure 3.78**).

3. Click the arrow next to the Font field, and select the font for the text. Click OK.

4. Make sure Trim is selected for the Type option (**Figure 3.79**).

5. Click Create to complete the text.

   Text appears in the Maya scene with the bottom-left corner of the text at the origin, as in Figure 3.75.

The third text type setting is Poly. It's best to use this text type if you want to work the text into other polygon surfaces. This text type includes numerous options for controlling the number of polygons used on the text, as well as other helpful text attributes.

The Poly text type also uses surfaces attached to curves through history, allowing you to manipulate the curves to change an individual letter's shape.

To create poly-based text:

1. From the Create menu, select the box next to Text.

2. In the Options dialog box, click the Text field, and type in new text.

3. Click the arrow next to the Font field, and select the font for the text.

4. Make sure Poly is selected for Type; use the default options for best results (**Figure 3.80**).

5. Click Create to complete the text.

   Text appears in the Maya scene with its bottom-left corner at the origin (**Figure 3.81**).

Figure 3.78 Click the Text field, and type in new text.

Figure 3.79 Make sure the Trim button is selected for Type.

Figure 3.80 Make sure the Poly button is selected for Type.

Figure 3.81 Text appears in the Maya scene with its bottom-left corner at the origin.

Figure 3.82 The default name for the seventh NURBS sphere created in the scene would be nurbsSphere7.

Figure 3.83 Select the object's default name at the top of the Channel Box.

Figure 3.84 Replace the default name with the new name.

Naming Objects

Each time you create an object, Maya gives it a default name. This name is a description of the actual object, followed by the number of times that object type has been used. For example, nurbsSphere7 would be the default name for the seventh NURBS sphere created in the scene (**Figure 3.82**). To make an object easy to find later, you will want to change its default name to something more descriptive. For example, if you created a sphere that you intended to use as a head, you could change its name to *head*. This keeps things organized and clear as you to add objects to your scene.

To change an object's name:

1. Create an object, or select an existing one by clicking it.

2. Select the object's default name at the top of the Channel Box (**Figure 3.83**).

3. Replace the default name by typing in a new name—for example, dannysSphere (**Figure 3.84**).

4. Press (Enter) to complete the name change.

continues on next page

✔ Tip

■ You can also change an object's name via the Attribute Editor's Transform panel (the first tab) (**Figure 3.85**). Once the object is selected, you can access the Attribute Editor with ⌃Ctrl/⌃Control Alt.

Every time you create a primitive or other object in Maya, a node is created to represent the object. You can view this node and any of its connections in the Hypergraph. You can also change the name of the object in the Hypergraph. For more information on the Hypergraph, see Chapter 1.

To change an object's name in the Hypergraph:

1. Create an object, or select an existing one.

2. From any view, select Panels > Panel > Hypergraph to change the current view into a Hypergraph (**Figure 3.86**).

   This menu is at the top of each view's panel.

3. Press f to zoom in on the selected object's node.

4. Hold down ⌃Ctrl/⌃Control and double-click the node's object name (**Figure 3.87**).

5. Replace the default name with the new name—for example, dannysSphere.

6. Press Enter to complete the name change.

Figure 3.85 You can also change the object's name in the Attribute Editor's Transform panel (the first tab).

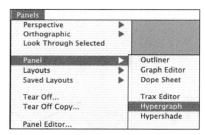

Figure 3.86 From any view, select Panels › Panel › Hypergraph to change the current view into a Hypergraph.

Figure 3.87 Hold down ⌃Ctrl/⌃Control, and double-click the node's object name to change it.

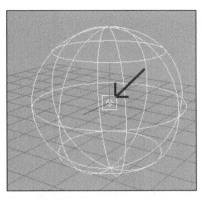

Figure 3.88 The pivot point manipulator can be moved to adjust the rotation axis.

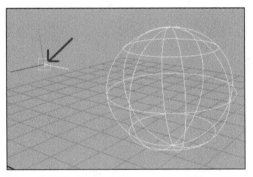

Figure 3.89 The pivot point is moved to a new position.

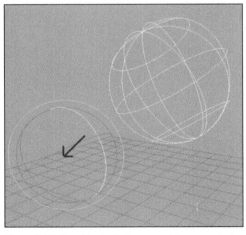

Figure 3.90 The object rotates around the new pivot point position.

About Pivot Points

Each object in Maya has a pivot point. When you rotate an object, it rotates around its pivot point, and when you scale an object, it scales to and from the pivot point. By default, the object's pivot point is at the center of the object, but Maya lets you move the pivot point according to your needs. That can be very useful when you want to create certain kinds of animations and movements. For example, if you want to have the camera rotate around a sphere while keeping the sphere in the center of the camera's view, you can move the camera's pivot point to the center of the sphere. When you then rotate the camera, the sphere stays in the center of the camera's view. If the camera's pivot point were in the default position at the center of the camera, it would spin in place instead of rotating around the object.

To change an object's pivot point position:

1. Select the object whose pivot point you would like to move.

2. Click (Insert)/(Home) to go into pivot point mode.

   The pivot point manipulator is now visible (**Figure 3.88**).

3. Click one of the pivot point manipulator handles and move the pivot point to a new position (**Figure 3.89**).

   The new position will be the new rotation point for the object.

4. Click (Insert)/(Home) to disable pivot point mode.

5. Rotate the object to view the pivot point changes (**Figure 3.90**).

continues on next page

ABOUT PIVOT POINTS

✔ Tip

■ For a real-world example of using a pivot point, see the task "To create a simple staircase" in Chapter 5, "Transforming Objects and Components."

To position the pivot point in the center of an object:

1. Select the object whose pivot point you would like to center (**Figure 3.91**).

2. From the Modify menu select Center Pivot.

   The selected object's pivot point is now at the center of the object (**Figure 3.92**).

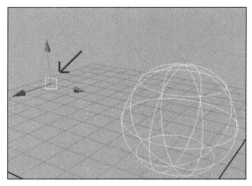

Figure 3.91 The selected object's pivot point is currently next to the object.

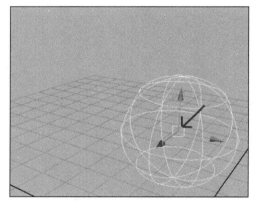

Figure 3.92 The selected object's pivot point is now at the center of the object.

SELECTION MODES, HIDING, AND TEMPLATING

4

A Maya scene can include hundreds of joints, thousands of polygons, and *hundreds of thousands* of points—all of which can amount to a major headache when you're trying to locate just one small point in the middle of huge amounts of geometry (**Figure 4.1**). Not to worry: Maya provides a number of tools that you can use to hide, template, layer, and select objects, eliminating much of the frustration of organizing and selecting objects.

Figure 4.1 A model can have hundreds of selectable points. Luckily, Maya provides helpers for selecting specific ones: Here, the component Pick mask is used to select one of this creature's many points.

For new users, however, selecting a specific object type or piece of an object (known as a *component)* can be tricky. For instance, a curve may be positioned in front of the surface you are trying to select, making it difficult to select it without using the Pick Mask. The object might be a curve, light, surface, or any of an array of other object types, each of which can be turned off using the Pick mask (**Figure 4.2**). You use the Pick mask controls to mask certain object types (so that only the object types you wish to select are displayed). For example, if you're only interested in selecting curves, you can turn off the ability to select other object types (**Figure 4.3**). Once you do this, when you try to click anything *except* a curve, nothing will happen. When you click a curve, however, it will become selected. We'll devote much of this chapter to this useful tool and the selection process.

Sometimes you'll find that certain objects inhibit your view of other objects. This is where hiding, templating, and layering come in to play. You can use these functions to separate objects so that they no longer hinder your view, making it easier to select the objects that you *are* interested in.

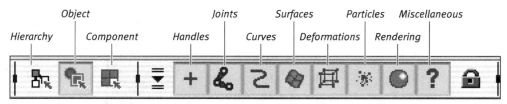

Figure 4.2 The controls in the Pick mask determine which objects can be selected at any given time.

Figure 4.3 Individual object types, such as curves, can be selected in the Pick mask to limit a selection to that type of object.

Object

Hierarchy   Component

Figure 4.4 Hierarchy, object, and component Pick mask buttons control whether an object or an object component can be selected.

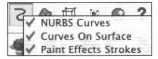

Figure 4.5 Each Pick mask has additional masking selections that you can view by clicking its icon with the right mouse button.

Figure 4.6 Using a marquee can be an easy way to select multiple objects.

Selecting Objects and Using the Pick Mask

Most commands in Maya require that you select an object, or object component, in order for the command to be executed. To do so, you will need to use the Pick mask. Sometimes referred to as the Selection mask, this tool is used to select an object or component by type (not just by where you click).

The Pick mask has three modes: *Hierarchy*, *Object*, and *Component* (**Figure 4.4**). Each of these modes also has multiple subsets to help you mask off everything but the specific object or component you're interested in. Under each of these subsets you can mask off even more objects to further limit your selection. To view additional subsets, right-click the mode's icon (**Figure 4.5**). You can toggle between Object mode (which allows you to select entire objects) and Component mode (which allows you to select pieces of an object) by pressing F8 .

This chapter describes the function of each Pick mask mode.

To select an object:

1. Choose the Select by Object Type icon.

2. Move the mouse over an object.

3. Click the object to select it.

or

Drag a marquee that overlaps part of the object you want to select (**Figure 4.6**).

4. Release the mouse button to select the object(s).

To add objects to a selection:

◆ While holding down (Shift), click each object you want to add to the current selection.

   or

◆ While holding down (Shift), draw a marquee that overlaps part of each object you want to add to the selection.

✔ Tip

■ If you drag a marquee around part of an object that's already been selected, you will deselect the object.

To subtract objects from a selection:

◆ While holding (Shift), click each object you want to subtract from the current selection. The objects are subtracted.

   or

◆ While holding down (Shift), drag the mouse to draw a marquee that overlaps part of each selected object you want to subtract.

   or

◆ While holding down (Ctrl)/(Control), drag the mouse to draw a marquee that overlaps part of the objects you want to subtract. This will only remove objects that you have selected, whereas using (Shift) will add unselected objects if your marquee overlaps them.

To invert the selection:

1. Select an object (**Figure 4.7**).

2. From the Edit menu, select Invert Selection (**Figure 4.8**).

   Deselected objects become selected; selected objects become deselected (**Figure 4.9**).

Figure 4.7 Click an object or drag a marquee to make a selection.

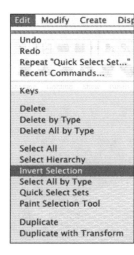

Figure 4.8 From the Edit menu, select Invert Selection.

Figure 4.9 When Invert Selection is used, deselected objects become selected, and selected objects become deselected.

Figure 4.10 Click in the background of a pane to deselect all objects, or [Shift]-click a selected object to deselect it.

Figure 4.11 Select Outliner from the Window menu, and click the name of the object you want to select.

Figure 4.12 Click the node of the object you want to select.

To deselect all objects:

◆ Click once in open space to deselect all objects, or [Shift]-click a selected object to deselect it (**Figure 4.10**).

To select an object using the Outliner:

1. From the Window menu, select Outliner.

2. Click the name of the object you want to select (**Figure 4.11**).

   The object becomes selected.

To select an object using the Hypergraph:

1. From the Window menu, select Hypergraph.

2. Click the node of the object you want to select (**Figure 4.12**).

   The object becomes selected.

Selecting objects using Hierarchy mode

Hierarchy mode is used to select objects within a hierarchy. You can select the top node in a hierarchy; a descendent, called a *leaf* (**Figure 4.13**); or a templated object. There are three major masks in Hierarchy mode, all of which are defined in **Table 4.1**. In the following examples we will first group two spheres to create a hierarchy, then show how to select objects within that hierarchy. For more information on hierarchies, see Chapter 6, "Grouping, Parenting, and Aligning."

To select the top object in a hierarchy:

1. Create two spheres.

2. Drag a marquee around the spheres to select both (**Figure 4.14**).

3. From the Edit menu, select Group.
   The two objects are grouped together.

4. From the Window menu, select Outliner (**Figure 4.15**).
   The Outliner window opens.

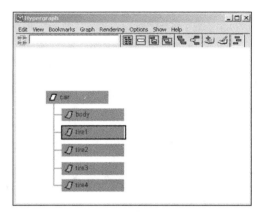

Figure 4.13 A *leaf* is a node lower down in a hierarchy, such as tire4 in this figure.

Figure 4.14 A marquee selects all objects it touches; you don't need to box in the entire object.

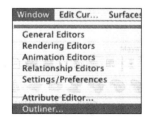

Figure 4.15 The Outliner lists all the nodes in the scene.

Table 4.1

Hierarchy Mode Selection Masks		
ICON	NAME	FUNCTION
	Root	Selects the top node in a hierarchy.
	Leaf	Selects a descendant object.
	Template	Selects a templated object. You must select a templated object before untemplating it.

Figure 4.16 Clicking the plus sign expands the view of all of the object names in the hierarchy.

Figure 4.17 The group node at the top of the hierarchy becomes selected no matter which object in the hierarchy you originally selected.

Figure 4.18 The selected node becomes gray, and the top node in the hierarchy becomes green.

5. Click the plus (+) sign to the left of the group name in the Outliner to show the entire hierarchy (**Figure 4.16**).

6. Set the Pick mask to Select by Hierarchy mode by clicking its icon in the Status Line.

7. Set the submask to Select by Hierarchy: Root by clicking its icon in the Status Line.

8. Click one of the objects.

   The group node at the top of the hierarchy becomes selected, in turn selecting both of the spheres beneath it (**Figure 4.17**).

To select an object within a hierarchy:

1. Follow Steps 1 through 6 of the preceding task.

2. Set the submask to Select by Hierarchy: Leaf by clicking its icon .

3. Click one of the objects.

   The object clicked, not the group node, becomes selected (**Figure 4.18**). In the outliner, the selected node is shown in gray.

✔ Tip

- You can move up and down the hierarchy to the group node by pressing the up ↑ and down ↓ arrows.

Selecting objects using Object Type mode

Selecting by Object Type mode (usually just called *Object mode*) selects entire objects. There are eight masks for Object mode, all of which are described in **Table 4.2**.

This mask is extremely useful when you want to select an object of a specific type that has other object types overlapping it—preventing the object from being selected. Take, for example, a character that has already been set up for animation—with joints, Inverse Kinematics, also known as *IK*, handles, selection handles, and geometry sitting directly on top of each other. It can be difficult to select the joints behind the geometry. To get around this problem, you can use the Object Pick mask to turn off all object types *except* for joints (**Figure 4.19**). Now the only selectable objects are the joints themselves, making them much easier to select.

Table 4.2

Object Mode Selection Masks		
ICON	**NAME**	**FUNCTION**
+	Handles	Selects selection handles and IK handles.
	Joints	Selects skeleton joints.
	Curves	Selects NURBS curves, curves on surfaces, and paint effects strokes.
	Surfaces	Selects NURBS, polys, and sub-division surfaces as well as planes.
	Deformations	Selects lattices, clusters, non-linears, and sculpt objects.
	Dynamics	Selects particles, emitters, fields, springs, rigid bodies, and constraints.
	Rendering	Selects lights, cameras, and textures.
?	Miscellaneous	Selects IK end effectors, locators, and dimensions.

Figure 4.19 When only the Joints Pick mask is selected, joints are the only object type that can be selected.

Figure 4.20 Zoom the camera up to an object by pressing (f); press and hold (Shift) (f) to zoom the object in all the views.

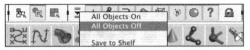

Figure 4.21 Select All Objects Off in the Pick mask to set the mask to select nothing.

✔ Tip

■ You can follow the same steps to mask any object type.

To select surfaces only with the Object Pick mask:

1. From the Create menu, select NURBS primitive > Sphere.

2. From the Create menu, select Lights > Spotlight.

3. Press (f) to bring the objects closer to the camera view (**Figure 4.20**).

4. Set the Pick mask to Select by Object Type by clicking the icon ▣.

5. Click the arrow to the right of the Object Pick Mask icon ▤, and select All Objects Off from the pop-up menu (**Figure 4.21**). All object types are turned off in the Pick mask.

6. Set the submask to Select by Object Type: Surfaces by clicking its icon ▨.

7. Drag a marquee around the two objects. Because it is a surface, the sphere becomes selected. However, since the spotlight is *not* a surface, it isn't selected (**Figure 4.22**).

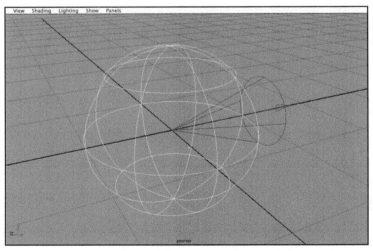

Figure 4.22 Only the sphere, which is a surface, is selected (even though the marquee overlaps the spotlight).

Selecting parts of objects using Component mode

Every Maya object is made up of components, which define the final shape of a curve or surface. A curve, for example, is made up of hulls, CVs, and edit points (**Figure 4.23**). The positions of each of these components determine the look of the curve. Each object's components can be selected and edited individually using Component mode and Maya's manipulation tools. (For more information on curve and surface components, see Chapter 7, "NURBS Curves and Surfaces.")

There are eight major masks in Component mode, all of which are defined in **Table 4.3**.

Figure 4.23 There are three main selectable components of a curve: hulls, CVs, and edit points.

Table 4.3

Component Mode Selection Masks

Icon	Name	Function
■	Points	Selects NURBS CVs, poly vertices, subdiv vertices, lattice points, and particles.
●	Parameter Points	Selects NURBS edit points, curve points, surface points, and subdiv UVs.
✎	Lines	Selects NURBS isoparms and trim edges, poly and subdiv edges, and springs.
◆	Faces	Selects NURBS patches, and poly and subdiv faces.
✐	Hulls	Selects NURBS hulls.
◉	Pivots	Selects rotate, scale, and joint pivots.
+	Handles	Selects selection handles.
?	Local Rotation	Selects local rotation axes and image planes.

Figure 4.24 Click the four CVs to create the curve.

Figure 4.25 Click one or more curve CVs to select them.

Figure 4.26 CVs can be moved to re-form the curve.

To select and move a curve's CVs:

1. Draw a curve using the CV Curve tool ![icon], or open a file that uses curves (**Figure 4.24**). See Chapter 7 for more on creating curves.

2. Click the Select by Component icon ![icon] in the Pick mask.

3. Click the Set the Component Type icon ![icon] arrow and select All Components Off from the menu.

4. Click the Points Submask icon ![icon].

5. Select the curve to show its points.

6. Click one or more curve CVs to select them (**Figure 4.25**).

7. Click the Move icon ![icon] in the toolbar. The Move tool manipulator appears.

8. Click and drag the Move tool manipulator to move the CVs and manipulate the curve (**Figure 4.26**).

Pick mask shortcuts

The Pick mask has preset shortcuts for specific settings.

`F8`—Toggles between Object and Component modes.

`F9`—Sets the Pick mask to select vertices (**Figure 4.27**).

`F10`—Sets the Pick mask to select edges (**Figure 4.28**).

`F11`—Sets the Pick mask to select faces (**Figure 4.29**).

`F12`—Sets the Pick mask to select UVs (**Figure 4.30**).

Often, you will want to select the same group of points or the same objects again and again; however, making the selection more than once can be tedious and unnecessary. You can save time by saving and naming the selection for later use—a function called a Quick Select Set. You can use a Quick Select Set again and again to reselect the same objects and components.

Figure 4.27 Press `9` to have the Pick mask change to select vertices (without selecting other common components).

Figure 4.28 Press `0` to have the Pick mask change to select edges (without selecting other common components).

Figure 4.29 Press `-` to have the Pick mask change to select faces (without selecting other common components).

Figure 4.30 Press `=` to have the Pick mask change to select UVs (without selecting other common components).

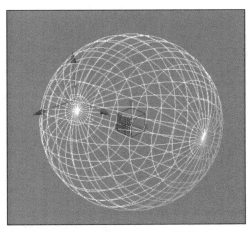

Figure 4.31 Select the points you would like to use for a saved selection.

Figure 4.32 Select Quick Select Set to lock in your selection for future use.

Figure 4.33 Give your selection set a descriptive name to make later use easier.

To create a Quick Select Set:

1. In Component mode select multiple points (**Figure 4.31**), or in Object mode select multiple objects.

2. From the Create menu, select Sets > Quick Select Set (**Figure 4.32**).

   The Create Quick Select Set dialog box opens.

3. Enter a name in the "Enter Quick Select Set name" field (**Figure 4.33**).

4. Click OK.

   The named selection is now available from the Edit > Quick Select Sets > [set name] menu (**Figure 4.34**).

Figure 4.34 After creating a Quick Select Set, you can remake the selection by choosing Edit > Quick Select Sets > [set name].

105

To hide a selected object:

1. Select an object to hide (**Figure 4.35**).

2. From the Display menu, choose Hide > Hide Selection (**Figure 4.36**), or press Ctrl / Control h .

   The selected object becomes hidden from view (**Figure 4.37**).

To show all hidden objects:

◆ From the Display menu, choose Show > All (**Figure 4.38**).

   All hidden objects become visible.

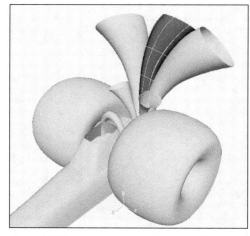

Figure 4.35 Select one or more objects to hide.

Figure 4.36 Hide the selection by choosing Display > Hide > Hide Selection.

Figure 4.38 Choose Show > All to show all objects that have been hidden.

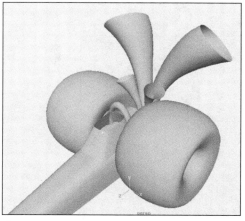

Figure 4.37 The selection becomes totally hidden from view. You can show all objects at once or show the last object hidden.

Figure 4.39 Choose Show > Show Last Hidden to have the last object hidden appear.

Figure 4.40 Any selected object can be templated. A templated object appears gray until it has been selected.

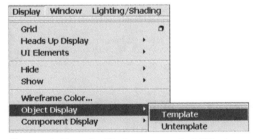

Figure 4.41 From the Display menu, select Object Display > Template.

To show the last hidden object:

◆ From the Display menu choose Show > Show Last Hidden (**Figure 4.39**), or press [Ctrl] / [Control] [Shift] [h].

The last object hidden becomes visible.

Templating an object allows you to see how it's placed without it getting in the way of other selections. When you template an object, it turns gray and becomes selectable only via the Select Template Pick mask.

To template an object:

1. Select the objects you want to template (**Figure 4.40**).

2. From the Display menu, select Object Display > Template (**Figure 4.41**).

3. The object becomes grayed out (**Figure 4.42**) and is only selectable with the Hierarchy: Select Template Selection mask.

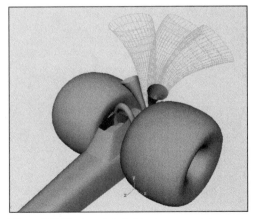

Figure 4.42 The templated objects are gray when not selected and pink when selected with the Template Selection mask.

SELECTING OBJECTS AND USING THE PICK MASK

107

To untemplate an object:

1. Set the Pick mask to Hierarchy mode and click the Template icon 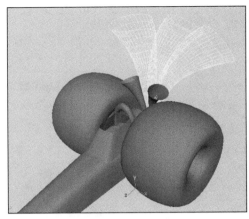 to select templates.

2. Select the templated objects you want to untemplate (**Figure 4.43**).

   The selected templated objects become light pink.

3. From the Display menu, select Object Display > Untemplate (**Figure 4.44**).

   The objects become untemplated.

Figure 4.43 To select a templated object you must set the Hierarchy Pick mask to Select Template.

Figure 4.44 To untemplate an object, select Object Display > Untemplate.

SELECTING OBJECTS AND USING THE PICK MASK

Figure 4.45 You can create additional layers in the Layers menu.

Figure 4.46 The Edit Layer dialog box holds the Name, Display Type, and Color options.

Figure 4.47 Select a descriptive name for the layer.

Figure 4.48 Select a color swatch for the objects on the layer. The wireframes of any objects on the layer will become the color of the selected swatch.

About Layers

Layers are used to separate objects so they can be viewed and edited separately. Each layer can have an associated color, which makes objects on that layer easily recognizable. A layer can be hidden, shown, templated, or referenced. Objects can be moved from layer to layer as needed, and new layers can be created at any time.

To create, rename, and color-code a layer:

1. Open the Channel Box, and click the Layer Editor icon.

2. From the Layers menu, in the Layer Editor select Create Layer (**Figure 4.45**), or click the Create Layer icon.
   A new layer is created, called layer1.

3. Double-click layer1 to open the Edit Layer dialog box (**Figure 4.46**).

4. Type a descriptive name for the layer in the Name field (**Figure 4.47**).

5. Choose Normal.
   The Display Type pop-up menu lets you choose to have the objects on the layer viewed as normal (or standard), as a template, or as a reference.

6. Select a color swatch (**Figure 4.48**).
   The wireframe of each object on the layer will display in the selected color.

7. Click Save.

continues on next page

ABOUT LAYERS

✔ Tips

- By default, new objects created reside on the default layer, not the newly created layer. To place each new object on the current layer, choose Use Current Layer from the Layer Options menu (**Figure 4.49**).

- You can make each new layer the current layer by choosing Make New Layers Current from the Layer Options menu.

- You can delete a layer by clicking on the layer with the right mouse button and selecting Delete from the menu.

- You can choose the order in which the layers are listed by selecting Layers>Sort Layers Alphabetically or Sort Layers Chronologically.

To move an object to a different layer:

1. Select the objects you want to move (**Figure 4.50**).

2. Right-click the layer to which you want to move the objects. Then choose Add Selected Objects from the menu (**Figure 4.51**).

To delete a layer:

1. In the Layer Editor, select the layer(s) you want to delete.

2. Select Layer > Delete Selected Layer(s). The layer is removed from the Layer Editor.

✔ Tips

- If a layer containing objects is deleted, those objects are assigned to the default layer.

- To delete unused layers, select Layer > Delete Unused Layers.

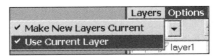

Figure 4.49 To have each new object be placed on the current layer, choose Use Current Layer from the Layer Options menu.

Figure 4.50 Select the objects you want to move to a new layer.

Figure 4.51 Choose Add Selected Objects to move objects to a different layer.

To toggle a layer's visibility:

◆ In the Layer Editor, click the square furthest left of the layer name.

If the layer is currently visible, it will become invisible; if the layer is invisible, it will become visible.

To add an annotation to an object:

1. Select the object you would like to annotate.

2. From the Create menu. select Annotation. The Annotate Node dialog box appears.

3. Type your annotation in the Enter Annotation field, then press OK.

An annotation appears with a line pointing to the annotated object.

ABOUT LAYERS

TRANSFORMING OBJECTS AND COMPONENTS

- Arrow selection
- Lasso selection
- Move
- Rotate
- Scale
- Soft Modification
- Show Manipulator
- Last tool used

Figure 5.1 Maya's manipulation tools.

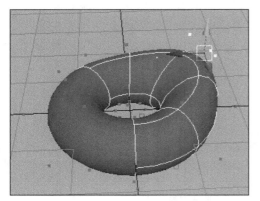

Figure 5.2 The Move tool's translation manipulator is used to move objects and components around the scene.

Maya gives you many ways to move, rotate, and scale objects around a scene, and many shortcuts for completing these common tasks. To move an object (referred to as translating an object), you can type in the coordinates in the Channel Box or use one of the many manipulation tools (**Figure 5.1**) to drag the object freely around the scene or constrain it to an axis.

Using the same tools you would employ to manipulate objects in the scene, you can also manipulate *parts* of an object, known as *components*. Each object type has its own components that can be translated (**Figure 5.2**), rotated, and/or scaled to change their look and position, in turn changing the appearance of the object.

Maya's developers have done a great job of making the program easy to learn while still providing plenty of depth: Most tools include advanced features that you can explore as your knowledge base grows. The Duplication options provide a good example of this. Once you get used to using them, you can employ a number of advanced options like duplicating an object multiple times by setting the number of copies, or indicating exactly where you want to place the duplicated object in the scene.

Moving, Rotating, and Scaling Objects

Maya provides multiple tools for moving, rotating, and scaling objects and components. Each of these tools has axes that you can grab and move to transform an object. These axes, called *manipulators* (**Figure 5.3**), are used to translate (move), rotate, or scale the object. Manipulators make it easy to constrain objects along a particular axis: You simply click and drag the colored line for the axis along which you want to constrain the object. The colors remain consistent for each tool. RGB colors coincide with the *X-Y-Z* axes (**Figure 5.4**): The manipulator's *X* axis is red; the *Y* axis is green; and the *Z* axis is blue. If you forget an axis' color, simply check the View axis in the lower left-hand corner of each pane (**Figure 5.5**). The axis selected on the manipulator is always yellow.

Move tool

Rotate tool

Scale tool

Figure 5.3 The Move, Rotate, and Scale manipulators.

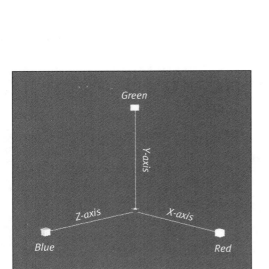

Figure 5.4 RGB colors match the *X-Y-Z* axes.

Figure 5.5 Check the View axis in the lower-left corner of each pane to remind yourself which color is associated with each axis.

Figure 5.6 You can freely translate an object by selecting the center of the Move tool's manipulators, scaling proportionally with the center of the Scale tool's manipulator, or clicking and dragging anywhere in the sphere of the Rotate tool to rotate freely.

Figure 5.7 The manipulation tools and their shortcut keys.

In addition to constraining an object along an axis, you can freely manipulate the object by clicking and dragging the square in the middle of the Move and Scale tool manipulators, or by clicking and dragging anywhere inside of the Rotate manipulator (**Figure 5.6**).

Each of the tools in the toolbar, with the exception of the Lasso tool and the Soft Modification tool, has an associated shortcut—all of which are easy to remember because they coincide with the [q][w][e][r][t][y] keys on the keyboard. You can just press a tool's key to turn on its manipulator.

The [q][w][e][r][t][y] keys and the manipulators they turn on are as follows (**Figure 5.7**):

[q] Arrow selection tool

[w] Move tool

[e] Rotate tool

[r] Scale tool

[t] Show Manipulator

[y] Last tool used

✔ Tip

- Be aware that these keys will not work if the Caps Lock key is on. In Maya, capitals represent different hotkeys with different functions mapped to them. For example, the Move, Rotate, and Scale tools' associated keyboard shortcuts are [w], [e], and [r], respectively. However, when those same keyboard letters are capitalized, they're used as follows: [W] keyframes translation; [E] keyframes rotation; and [R] keyframes scaling.

To translate an object or component using the Move tool:

1. Select an object or component by clicking it.

2. Press [w] or click the Move tool icon [📱] in the toolbar.

   The Move manipulator will now be visible on the object or component (**Figure 5.8**).

3. Click and drag the manipulator's arrow in the direction you want the object to move (**Figure 5.9**).

   This translates the object along the selected axis.

   or

   Hold down [Shift], and then with the middle mouse button, click and drag in the direction you want the object to move (**Figure 5.10**).

   This selects the appropriate manipulator axis and translates the object in that direction. This is particularly useful if you've just created an object at the origin but moved the camera away from the grid. You can pull the object into your camera view if you know the direction of the origin.

Figure 5.8 The Move manipulator is used to move the object around the scene.

Original position   *New position*

Axis manipulator

Figure 5.9 Click and drag the axis to which you want the object constrained so that you can maintain precise control over the surface's position. This is particularly useful in the Perspective view.

Figure 5.10 By dragging left and right with the middle mouse button, you can change values interactively. Here, a translation value is changed; therefore, the object is moved.

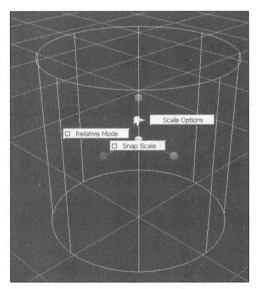

Figure 5.11 The Scale tool's Marking menu includes shortcuts for scaling proportionally as well as along an axis.

✔ Tips

■ You can also hold down ⓧ to activate grid snap. In addition, if you drag with the middle mouse button anywhere on the grid, the object will snap to that location.

■ You can use the ⊞ and ⊟ keys to enlarge or shrink the manipulators.

■ From anywhere in a view pane you can hold down the keyboard shortcut for the Move (ⓦ), Rotate (ⓔ), or Scale (ⓡ) tool and click to bring up that tool's Marking menu (**Figure 5.11**). Maya's Transform Marking menus include shortcuts to many of the tools' options.

MOVING, ROTATING, AND SCALING OBJECTS

117

To scale an object or component:

1. Click an object or component to select it.

2. Press ⌐r⌐ or click the Scale tool icon in the toolbar.

   The Scale manipulator should now be visible on the object or component (**Figure 5.12**).

3. Click the small square of the axis on which you want to scale the object or component, and drag in the direction you want the object to scale (**Figure 5.13**).

   or

   While pressing ⌐Shift⌐, click and drag with the middle mouse button anywhere in the pane in the direction in which you want the object to scale (**Figure 5.14**).

   This selects the appropriate manipulator axis and scales the object in that direction.

Figure 5.12 You use the Scale tool's manipulator to scale an object proportionally or along a single axis.

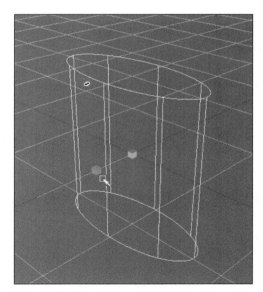

Figure 5.13 Click and drag a Scale tool's axis to scale it along a particular axis.

Figure 5.14 This cylinder is being scaled along the *X* axis by clicking and dragging with the middle mouse button.

Figure 5.15 The Rotate manipulator is used to rotate the surface on one or more axes.

Figure 5.16 Click and drag the axis circle to which you want the object constrained. A gray pie slice shows you how many degrees you have rotated the object.

To rotate an object or component:

1. Select an object or component by clicking it.

2. Press [e] or click the Rotate tool icon ![icon] in the toolbar.

   The Rotate manipulator is now visible on the object or component (**Figure 5.15**).

3. Click the circle of the axis you want to rotate the object or component around, and drag in the direction you want the object to rotate (**Figure 5.16**).

✔ Tips

- You can click anywhere within the Rotate manipulator sphere, and click and drag to rotate the object without being constrained to any axis.

- Once the axis you want to use is yellow on the manipulator, you can click and drag anywhere in the pane with the middle mouse button to rotate the object around that axis without touching the axis or the object.

- The light-blue outer ring rotates the object or component around an axis that always faces the camera view (**Figure 5.17**).

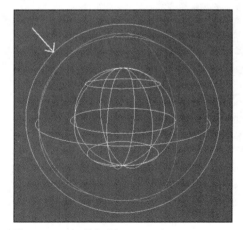

Figure 5.17 The light-blue outer ring rotates the object or component.

To translate, rotate, or scale an object or component using the Channel Box:

1. Click an object or component to select it.

2. In the Channel Box, click once in the field next to the attribute you want to change (**Figure 5.18**).

3. Type a new value in the selected field.

   The object reflects the value change (**Figures 5.19** and **5.20**).

   or

   Click to select the Attribute's name, and then move the mouse over a view pane. Hold down the middle mouse button and drag left or right to interactively change the value of the selected attribute (**Figure 5.21**).

Figure 5.18 Click the field name of the attribute you want to change (in this case, Translate X).

Figure 5.19 The position of the cone with Translate X set to *0*.

Figure 5.20 Changing the Translate X value to *3* moves the cone three units in the positive *x* direction.

Figure 5.21 You can use the middle mouse button to interactively change values anywhere in a pane.

MOVING, ROTATING, AND SCALING OBJECTS

Figure 5.22 The additional manipulator on the Show Manipulator tool controls additional Revolve attributes, saving you from going to the Channel Box. In this example, the revolve was changed to less than 360 degrees by moving the manipulator at the center of the object.

Figure 5.23 Two manipulators appear, giving you more precise control over what objects the spotlight is pinpointing and the direction in which the light is aimed.

Using the Show Manipulator tool

The Show Manipulator tool ▨ lets you access the Input node of an object (known as its *construction history*) to alter a surface or curve. This tool is most useful for surfaces that originated from curves because the manipulator provides shortcuts to altering the Input node attributes (**Figure 5.22**). (For more information, see Chapter 7.)

Another great use of the Show Manipulator tool is to direct a spotlight or camera. When used on a spotlight, the light will have two manipulators instead of one—one to move the light, and one for the light to point at, which makes adjusting lighting easier.

The Show Manipulator tool most commonly appears with two manipulators. In the case of a spotlight, one manipulator translates the camera, while the second indicates where the spotlight will be aimed. Follow the steps below to create a spotlight and aim it using the Show Manipulator tool.

To aim a spotlight using the Show Manipulator tool:

1. From the Create menu, select Lights > Spotlight.

2. Click the Show Manipulator icon ▨ in the toolbar.

   The spotlight now has one manipulator at its base and another in front of the light (**Figure 5.23**).

continues on next page

3. Select the manipulator at the base of the spotlight (**Figure 5.24**).

4. Move the manipulator up the *Y* axis.

   The spotlight moves with the manipulator but continues to point at the second manipulator (**Figure 5.25**).

5. Select the manipulator in front of the spotlight.

6. Move the manipulator along the *Z* axis.

   The spotlight remains in place but continues to point at the manipulator (**Figure 5.26**).

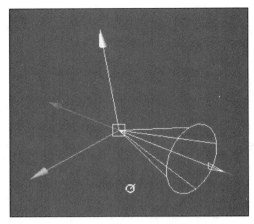

Figure 5.24 Select the manipulator attached to the spotlight to translate the light.

Figure 5.25 You can move the manipulators separately or together (which you would do when you want to maintain the same relationship between the manipulators).

Move light with this manipulator

Change light direction with this manipulator

Figure 5.26 To place a light directly on an object, you can group one of the show manipulators to it: The spotlight will then always shine on that object.

Changes which history
node is currently viewed

Adjusts cone
angle

Figure 5.27 Most objects will display a blue ring from which you can access that object's input nodes.

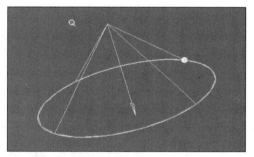

Figure 5.28 The cone angle controls the width of the light beam.

7. Click twice on the light blue ring.

The manipulators change into a ring around the cone of light. Each time you click the ring, it takes you through the cone's History nodes (**Figure 5.27**).

8. Click and drag on the square atop the circle that surrounds the cone.

The cone angle will change interactively as you drag the mouse (**Figure 5.28**).

To use the Lasso Selection tool to select a set of components:

1. Create a primitive NURBS sphere.

2. Press F8 .

3. Click the Lasso selection icon in the toolbar.

4. Drag in a circle around the CVs you would like to select (**Figure 5.29**).

5. Release the mouse.

The CVs within the circle become selected (**Figure 5.30**).

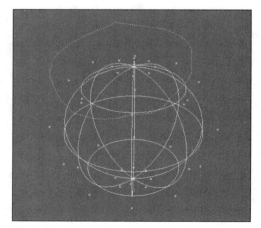

Figure 5.29 The Lasso Selection tool will close itself after the mouse is released.

Figure 5.30 The top CVs become selected because they were within the selection circle.

Duplication Options

Maya provides duplication shortcuts for modeling objects with repetitive geometry—for example, a staircase. To model a staircase, you could use one elongated cube and one duplicate action to produce the whole staircase in a minimum number of steps (**Figure 5.31**).

You can use the Duplicate tool for simple object duplications as well as for more complex duplications, including rotations, translations, and scales of an object. What's more, the Duplicate option includes additional valuable tools for mirroring and creating instances of objects.

You can duplicate objects either with or without their Inputs, History nodes (**Figure 5.32**). (See Chapter 1, "Maya Basics," for more information on construction history.) It's important to note, however, that history duplication is set to *off* by default.

Mirroring and instancing objects

In addition to translating objects, you can use the Duplication options to create a mirror image of an object (that is, a reversed copy of the original). Body parts make good candidates for mirroring because many (eyes, ears, arms, and legs) include near-identical versions on the other side of the body (**Figure 5.33**). If you mirror one of these objects—say an ear—you can create a second object in the perfect mirrored position with just a click of your mouse.

Figure 5.31 This staircase was made with two objects and one duplication.

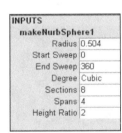

Figure 5.32 The sphere's Inputs node holds its editable history attributes.

Figure 5.33 By mirroring an arm, you can save time in modeling a second arm.

Figure 5.34 Instances of objects will mimic the edits of the first object interactively.

Figure 5.35 From the Edit menu select the box next to Duplicate to open the Duplicate Options dialog box.

In addition to duplicating and mirroring objects, you can create *instances* of objects—duplicates that retain a connection to the shape of the original (**Figure 5.34**). The beauty of this is that you can then edit the original and have each of the instanced objects follow those edits interactively. For example, if you were creating a building with multiple identical pillars, you could create one pillar and then create a number of *instances* of it to get those additional pillars. If you later decide to change the look of the pillars, all you have to do is edit one, and the rest will be updated automatically.

To duplicate an object:

1. Click an object to select it.

2. From the Edit menu, select the box next to Duplicate (**Figure 5.35**).

   This opens the Duplicate Options dialog box.

3. Enter the amount of duplicates desired in the Number of Copies field (**Figure 5.36**).

4. Click Duplicate.

   The specified number of copies are duplicated and placed on top of each other.

Figure 5.36 Enter the number of duplicates you desire in the Number of Copies field.

To duplicate an object with rotation:

1. Select an object.

2. From the Edit menu, select the box next to Duplicate.

   This opens the Duplicate Options dialog box.

3. Select a rotation amount for each additional copy, and type that amount in the Rotate field of the axis you want to rotate around (**Figure 5.37**). The fields are, left to right. X axis, Y axis, and Z axis.

   If you've used a sphere, you'll only notice a rotation in wireframe mode.

4. Click the Duplicate button to duplicate the object.

✔ Tips

- You can use the same technique to translate or scale a copy.

- You can reset the duplication options to their original state by selecting Edit > Reset Settings inside the Options window.

Now that you have a general idea of how to duplicate an object, let's put the options into action and create a simple staircase. We'll use the same technique we employed to create a simple copy with rotation, but now we'll use the Translate, Rotate, and Scale options together.

The key to successfully creating a duplicate with translation is placing the pivot point in the correct position for the objects to rotate around (**Figure 5.38**).

DUPLICATION OPTIONS

Figure 5.37 Enter the amount of rotation desired in the first field of the Rotate attribute. The first field is the rotate X field.

Pivot point

Figure 5.38 The pivot point's placement determines the placement of a duplicated surface.

Figure 5.39 Type *0.5* in the Translate Y field to move the cube's bottom so that it sits on the grid.

Figure 5.40 Type *6* in the Scale X field to scale the *X* axis of the object by six units.

Figure 5.41 The pivot point determines the point in space that the staircase will rotate around.

To create a simple staircase:

1. From the Create menu, select Poly Primitive > Cube.

   A cube is created at the origin.

2. Type *0.5* in the Translate Y field in the Channel Box and press [Enter] (**Figure 5.39**).

   This moves the cube up so that its base sits on the grid.

3. Type *6* in the Scale X field in the Channel Box and press [Enter] (**Figure 5.40**).

   This widens the cube.

4. Press [w] or click the Move tool icon in the toolbar.

5. Press [Insert]/[Home] on the keyboard to go into pivot-point edit mode.

6. Move the pivot point to the far-left edge of the cube, using the *X*-axis manipulator (**Figure 5.41**).

7. Press [Insert]/[Home] again to turn off pivot-point edit mode.

8. From the Edit menu, select the box next to Duplicate to open the Duplicate Options window.

   continues on next page

DUPLICATION OPTIONS

9. Set the Duplicate options as follows (**Figure 5.42**):

   ▲ **Translate: 0, 1, 0**—This moves each new duplicate up the Y axis one unit. Our cube is one unit high, so each copy will sit on top of the previous one.

   ▲ **Rotate: 0, 15, 0**—This rotates each duplicate 15 degrees more than the previous one around the Y axis.

   ▲ **Scale: .95, .95, .95**—This scales each duplicate proportionately to 95 percent the size of the last. The staircase will get smaller as it goes higher.

10. Enter *20* in the Number of Copies field. This will create 20 new steps.

11. Select Duplicate.

    The specified number of copies are made and placed on top of each other after being rotated and scaled (**Figure 5.43**).

✔ Tips

■ It's a good idea to check your options before duplicating. The previous settings will be retained unless you reset them. To return the options to their default settings, with the Duplicate Options window open, select Edit > Reset Settings.

■ Move the pivot point farther down the X axis before duplicating to make room for a pole in the center (**Figure 5.44**).

Figure 5.42 Set the Duplicate options as shown to properly duplicate the cube.

Figure 5.43 A staircase can be built with the click of a button if the proper Duplicate options have been set.

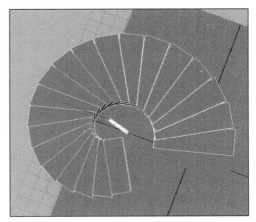

Figure 5.44 Move the pivot point farther from the original object to vary the center of the staircase.

Figure 5.45 You can create half a face and then mirror it to complete the rest of the face.

Figure 5.46 By combining instancing and mirroring, you can update both sides of the face with a single movement.

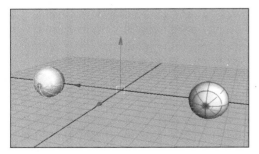

Figure 5.47 Body parts are ideal for mirroring because they have identical counterparts. The pivot point's placement in the scene determines how far apart the mirrored objects end up.

Mirroring an object produces a precise reverse copy of the object. This technique is great for creating one side of a face and then mirroring the face across an axis to complete it (**Figure 5.45**). The pivot point is used as the mirror axis, which means that the farther the pivot point is from the object, the farther the mirrored copy will be from the original. Often, this command is used in conjunction with instancing so that the user can continue to manipulate the original side of the face and have *both* sides of the face reflect those changes (**Figure 5.46**). (We'll take a closer look at instancing after the following task.)

You can also use instancing to place objects an equal distance away from an axis line, creating a mirrored copy perfectly placed (**Figure 5.47**).

In the following example, we'll mirror a sphere across an axis, as if to create two eyes.

To mirror an object:

1. From the Create menu, select NURBS Primitives > Sphere, or select an object to mirror.

2. Type *-2* in the Translate X field in the Channel Box (**Figure 5.48**).

   This moves the object two units down the negative *X* axis.

3. Press ⬜w or click the Move tool icon in the toolbar.

4. Press ⬜Insert/⬜Home on the keyboard to go into pivot-point edit mode.

5. Holding down ⬜x, move the pivot point to the origin (**Figure 5.49**).

   ⬜x snaps to the grid, which ensures that the pivot point is precisely at the origin.

6. Press ⬜Insert/⬜Home to get out of pivot-point edit mode.

7. From the Edit menu, select the box beside Duplicate.

   This opens the Duplicate Options window.

8. Select Edit > Reset Settings in the Duplicate Options window to reset the settings, then set the Scale X field to *–1*.

9. Select Duplicate.

   A mirrored copy is duplicated an equal distance from the pivot point (**Figure 5.50**).

Figure 5.48 Type *-2* in the Translate X field of the Channel Box to move the object two units in the negative *X* direction.

Figure 5.49 Move the pivot point to the origin to send the copy an equal distance away from the origin.

Figure 5.50 A mirrored copy is duplicated an equal distance from the pivot point.

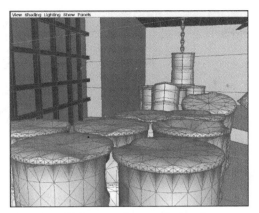

Figure 5.51 Oil drums are instanced to cut down on the amount of edits that need to be made. The objects are rotated to hide their similar attributes.

Figure 5.52 Set the Translate X field (the field on the left) to *2*.

Figure 5.53 Selecting Copy simply duplicates the object; however, selecting Instance results in an additional connection to the original object.

Instancing is a great way to save time, both in modeling and in rendering. An instanced object will follow the edits of the original, making instancing ideal for any object that will have identical copies anywhere else in the scene (**Figure 5.51**). You can still scale, rotate, and move the objects independently once they've been instanced.

To make an instance of an object:

1. Select an object by clicking it.

2. From the Edit menu, select the box next to Duplicate.

    This opens the Duplicate Options window.

3. Set the Translate X field to *2* and the rest of the Translate and Rotate fields to *0* (**Figure 5.52**).

    We add a translate here so the copy does not sit directly on top of the original.

4. For Geometry Type, select Instance (**Figure 5.53**).

5. Select Duplicate.

    The duplicate is now an instance, or virtual copy, of the original.

6. With one of the objects selected, press ⌐F8⌐ to go into component-selection mode.

continues on next page

7. Marquee-select across the top third of the object to select one of its components (**Figure 5.54**).

8. Press $\boxed{w}$, and translate the components in any direction.

Note that the other object follows the translation of the selected surface (**Figure 5.55**).

✔ Tip

■ Once you've created an instance of an object, you can't modify its components independently.

Figure 5.54 Marquee-select across the top third of the object to select CVs to manipulate.

Figure 5.55 The other object follows the translation of the selected surface but in the opposite direction, like an object in a mirror.

Figure 5.56 A primitive sphere's Inputs node holds the editable history of the sphere.

Figure 5.57 Check the Duplicate Input Connections check box in the Duplicate Options window to copy the input connections to the new object.

Figure 5.58 The Number of Copies slider determines how many copies of the object will be produced.

Often, you'll want the construction history to remain attached to an object when you create a copy of it. You can do this by selecting the Duplicate Input Connections check box in the Duplicate Options window. The objects will then share the same Input node, and both the original and the duplicates will be changed by it.

To duplicate an object with its input connections:

1. Select an object that has input connections attached to it—a primitive sphere, for example (**Figure 5.56**).

2. From the Edit menu, select the box next to Duplicate.

    This opens the Duplicate Options window.

3. Check the box next to Duplicate Input Connections (**Figure 5.57**).

    This connects the duplicated object to the Input node of the original. This way, if you alter the Input node of one, the duplicates will be affected as well.

4. Type the number of duplicates you want to produce in the Number of Copies field (**Figure 5.58**).

continues on next page

5. Click Duplicate.

A copy of the object is made, and its connections are attached to it (**Figure 5.59**). The new object sits directly on top of the original.

6. Select the Move tool, and move the duplicated object away from the original.

7. In the Channel Box select the End Sweep attribute name, and drag the middle mouse button in the View pane to confirm the connections.

The End Sweep is changed on both objects interactively.

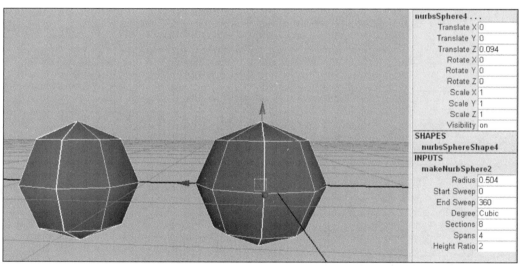

Figure 5.59 When you retain the Inputs node on duplicated objects, you can continue to make individual changes to the surfaces.

DUPLICATION OPTIONS

Undo	Ctrl+z
Redo	Z
Repeat "Duplicate with Transform"	g
Recent Commands...	
Keys	▸
Delete	
Delete by Type	▸
Delete All by Type	▸
Select All	
Select Hierarchy	
Invert Selection	
Select All by Type	▸
Quick Select Sets	▸
Paint Selection Tool	❑
Duplicate	Ctrl+d ❑
Duplicate with Transform	D
Group	Ctrl+g ❑
Ungroup	❑
Level of Detail	▸
Parent	p ❑
Unparent	P ❑

Figure 5.60 The Edit › Duplicate with Transform menu.

The standard Duplication tool can be cumbersome for simple duplications since there are so many options to adjust, or reset, for even a simple duplication. The Duplicate with Translation tool, on the other hand, comes in handy when all you want to do is make a copy and move it down an axis, or if you only want to produce one or two copies.

To duplicate an object with simple translation:

1. Create a primitive sphere.

2. From the Edit menu, select Duplicate with Transform (**Figure 5.60**).

3. Move the duplicated sphere a few units in the *z* direction (**Figure 5.61**).

4. From the Edit menu, select Duplicate with Transform.

   A new Sphere is created the same distance from the second sphere as that one was from the original (**Figure 5.62**).

5. Press (Shift)(d).

   Another duplicate is made, an equal distance from the last (**Figure 5.63**).

Figure 5.61 Move the sphere the distance you would like your future duplications to copy.

Figure 5.62 Duplicate the object again.

Figure 5.63 Each new copy moves down the axis the same amount as the original copy.

Soft Modifying Objects

The Soft Modification tool adds the ability to push and pull surfaces like they were clay (**Figure 5.64**).

You can use this tool for modeling as well as animation because its parameters are keyframeable, as long as the construction history has been enabled (see Chapter 1 for more about construction history). The Soft Modification tool's uses range from putting warts on a nose to creating sloping hills to animating bulging muscles on a superhero's arm (**Figure 5.65**).

Essentially, the Soft Modification tool works by tapering the effect of moving points on surfaces so that they blend in. That's especially useful when you're working with dense surfaces: Without the Soft Modification tool, it would be far too time consuming to individually move the large number of components required to make smooth changes.

As with the other translation tools, you can activate the Soft Modification tool and then select the area of the object you want to soft modify. Or, if you select an object first and then choose the Soft Modification tool, the effect will automatically be applied to the center of the object. The effect can be moved at any time, unless you delete the construction history.

Soft Modification tool

Figure 5.64 Choose the Soft Modification tool from the toolbox.

Figure 5.65 Warts, hills, and muscles are just a few examples of what softMods can do.

Figure 5.66 In the Channel Box, increase the subdivision width and height to create a dense polygon plane.

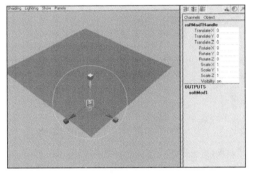

Figure 5.67 Add a softMod to a surface.

Figure 5.68 Drag the *Y* axis of the softMod manipulator.

To soft modify an object:

1. Create a primitive polygonal plane and give it Subdivision Height and Width of *100* and scale it to about 20 times its original size (**Figure 5.66**).

   For more on creating polygonal primitives, see Chapter 3, "Creating Primitives and Text."

2. Click the Soft Modification tool 🗗 in the toolbar.

3. Click the part of the object where you want to create the softMod.

   A softMod node is added to the surface and its manipulator becomes active (**Figure 5.67**).

4. Select the *Y* translate axis of the manipulator and drag it up (**Figure 5.68**).

5. Click the Cycling Index to display the Falloff manipulator (**Figure 5.69**).

   continues on next page

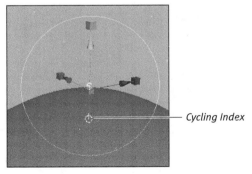

Cycling Index

Figure 5.69 The Cycling Index is a circle with a line through it under the softMod manipulator. Click the Cycling Index to toggle on the Falloff manipulator.

SOFT MODIFYING OBJECTS

6. Click and drag the red circle surrounding the Falloff manipulator to increase or decrease the drop-off area (**Figure 5.70**).

7. Press ⓦ and use the Move tool to click and drag the S icon on the Falloff manipulator (**Figure 5.71**)

8. Press (Ctrl)/(Control) ⓐ to open the Attribute Editor for the softMod (**Figure 5.72**).

Figure 5.70 Click and drag the red circle around the Falloff manipulator to adjust the drop-off area.

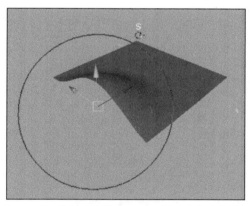

Figure 5.71 Using the Move tool, click and drag the Falloff manipulator.

Figure 5.72 Edit the falloff curve in the softMod Attribute Editor.

Figure 5.73 Click the graph in the Falloff Curve section...

Figure 5.74 ...to create edit points.

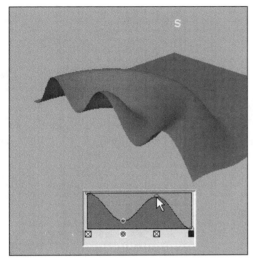

Figure 5.75 The softMod has a smooth, wavelike shape.

9. In the Falloff Curve section of the Attribute Editor (**Figure 5.73**), click the ramp to create a new edit point (**Figure 5.74**).

10. Click and drag the edit point into the desired position.

    or

    Click the box with an x in it to delete the edit point (**Figure 5.75**).

11. Add two edit points and position them as they are in Figure 5.75.

    You can see the results of editing the falloff curve on the surface of the softMod you created.

✔ Tips

- Before clicking the Soft Modification tool in the toolbar, be sure that you don't have any objects selected on your screen. If you do, a softMod node will be added to any selected objects when you choose the tool.

- If you deselect the Falloff manipulator, you can click the S icon floating above the surface and then press ⟨t⟩ to reactivate it (see **Figure 5.75**).

- Soft modification can work on selected components, as well as the entire object.

SOFT MODIFYING OBJECTS

GROUPING, PARENTING, AND ALIGNING

6

Grouping, parenting, and *aligning* provide ways of organizing and controlling an object's relationship to other objects. If you wanted to move a number of objects around a scene simultaneously, you might want to consider *grouping* those objects so you could move them as a single unit—one selection vs. multiple selections.

You can think of parenting as a distant cousin to grouping. The difference between the two functions boils down to this: Parented surfaces (**Figure 6.1**) have a relationship in which one follows the other (**Figure 6.2**), while objects in a group can act both independently and as a single, grouped entity. We'll be exploring the differences between parenting and grouping throughout this chapter.

Aligning objects, surfaces, and curves can be tricky if you're trying to do it by sight alone. Luckily, Maya offers a few tools to help, including the Align and Snap Together tools.

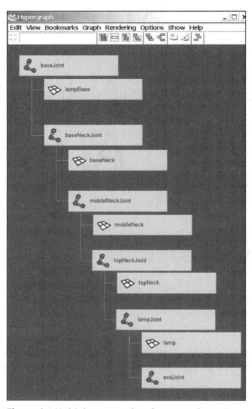

Figure 6.1 Multiple parented surfaces are shown in the Hypergraph.

Figure 6.2 When a parent joint is moved, all of the children move along with it.

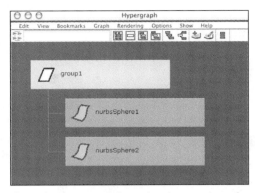

Figure 6.3 The top node is used to change values of the entire group without changing the current values of the individual objects.

Figure 6.4 Rotating the group node rotates all of the surfaces in the group at the same time around one pivot point.

Figure 6.5 The sphere on the left is parented to the sphere on the right. This means that the sphere on the left moves when the sphere on the right is moved.

Grouping vs. Parenting

Grouping two or more objects connects those objects with an additional node, called Group(*n*) (**Figure 6.3**), which you use when you want to perform an action to both, such as moving them at the same time. (The *(n)* in Group(n) represents the number of the group node.) Even though the objects are grouped, you can still select one and move or perform an action on it without affecting the other objects in the group. Alternatively, you can select the Group node and have your actions affect the grouped objects as if they were only one object (**Figure 6.4**).

Parented objects react a bit differently than objects that are grouped. Parented objects have a child-parent relationship. In real life, when a child is holding a parent's hand, the child must follow the parent wherever he or she goes (at least in theory). The same is true in 3D—an object that is parented to another object has to follow the other object around (**Figure 6.5**). When you parent one object to another, no extra node is created. Maya knows which object you want to be the parent and which you want to be the child by the order in which you select them.

To group two or more objects together:

1. Marquee-select two or more surfaces with the Arrow tool (**Figure 6.6**), or Shift-click to select multiple objects.

2. From the Edit menu, select Group (**Figure 6.7**).

   The objects are grouped together with an additional node.

3. From the Window menu, select Hypergraph.

   The Hypergraph opens in a new window.

4. Press f to zoom the Hypergraph to the selection.

   There is now one more node than the number of objects. This additional node is the group node, named group# (**Figure 6.8**).

✔ Tip

■ You can select the Group node and set the Pick mask to hierarchy mode to move the grouped objects together, or you can select a surface's node and set the Pick mask to object mode to move that surface separately from the group.

Figure 6.6 You can drag a marquee to select multiple surfaces. The marquee only needs to touch a part of the surface.

Figure 6.7 Select Edit > Group to group objects together.

Figure 6.8 The top node is created at the same time the group is created. You use it to control the nodes beneath it.

Figure 6.9 The Group node's default name is group#, with # representing the number of groups created so far.

Figure 6.10 Select Edit > Ungroup to pull objects out of the group.

To ungroup an object:

1. Select the Group node in the Hypergraph (**Figure 6.9**).

2. From the Edit menu, select Ungroup (**Figure 6.10**).

The geometry is no longer grouped, and the Group node is deleted.

Once objects are grouped together, they can be translated, rotated, or scaled as if they were a single object. One of the reasons Maya creates an extra group node is to give you an additional pivot point to use as the center point that the objects rotate or scale around. When an object is grouped, the pivot point of the Group node is placed at the origin. The pivot point can then be moved anywhere in the scene to determine its rotation and scale center point.

To translate, rotate, or scale a group:

1. Select the Group node in the Hypergraph, or click one of the grouped objects with the Pick mask set to hierarchy mode 🔳 to select the Group node.

2. Select the Rotate, Scale, or Move tool in the toolbar, or use their respective hotkeys.

3. Press [Insert]/[Home] to go into pivot-point edit mode.

4. Move the pivot point to the position you want the group to rotate around or scale from (**Figure 6.11**).

You can ignore this step if you're just translating the object.

5. Press [Insert]/[Home] to get out of pivot-point edit mode.

continues on next page

Figure 6.11 The Group node's pivot point is used as the center point for the entire group.

GROUPING VS. PARENTING

6. Translate, rotate, or scale the group by selecting a manipulator's (**Figure 6.12**) axis and dragging left or right in the pane with the middle mouse button to change the axes' value.

✔ Tip

■ You can move the pivot point to the center of a selected Group node by selecting Modify > Center Pivot (**Figure 6.13**).

To move one object within a group:

1. Select the object you want to move with the Pick mask set to object-type mode ![icon].

2. Select the Move tool icon from the toolbox, or press [w].

3. Translate the object by selecting any axis of the Move tool's manipulator, and then dragging left or right in the pane with the middle mouse button to change its value.

The selected object moves, but the rest of the group does not (**Figure 6.14**).

✔ Tips

■ You can follow these same steps to rotate or scale an object within a group without affecting the rest of the group.

■ Once you've selected a member of a group, press [↑] to move up the hierarchy and select the Group node.

Figure 6.12 You translate, rotate, or scale a group the same way you do an individual object.

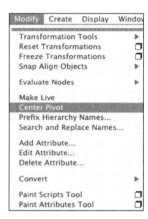

Figure 6.13 The Modify › Center Pivot command is useful for quickly centering the pivot of a group.

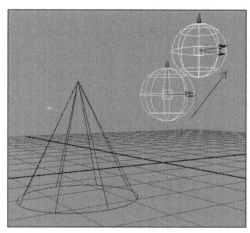

Figure 6.14 Grouped objects can still be edited individually by selecting just that object and not the group node.

GROUPING VS. PARENTING

Figure 6.15 The fingers are children of the palm, and the palm is a child of the lower arm. When the lower arm is rotated, all the joints and surfaces below the parent joint follow.

Figure 6.16 An entire hierarchy is formed by parenting one bone to another until they're all connected.

A solid parenting example is a biped skeleton. For our example, we'll use an arm. Your arm starts at your shoulder blade and continues down, connecting your shoulder to your upper arm to your lower arm to your wrist to your palm to your fingers. A relationship is created that forces the fingers to follow the rest of the arm. This relationship is called a parent-child relationship. In this case, the parent is the upper arm and its child is the lower arm. The lower arm is the parent of the wrist, which itself is the parent of the palm. Whenever the upper arm is moved, all the children beneath it move, creating the whole arm movement (**Figure 6.15**).

The overall relationship of the parts of the skeleton is called a *hierarchy* (**Figure 6.16**). A hierarchy determines which objects control other objects. The order of the hierarchy is important to both selecting and translating.

When parenting two objects together, the order in which you select the objects is very important. The second object you select becomes a parent of the first object selected. Once it's parented, the child will follow the parent's translations.

GROUPING VS. PARENTING

147

To parent two objects together:

1. Select the object you want to become the child by clicking it.

2. Select the object you want to become the parent by [Shift]-clicking it (**Figure 6.17**).

3. From the Edit menu, select Parent, or press [p].

   The second selected object becomes a parent of the first object (**Figure 6.18**).

✔ Tips

■ Because no additional node is added when objects are parented, the pivot point of the parent is used as the center point for controlling the entire hierarchy.

■ If more than two objects are selected, all selected objects become children of the last object selected.

■ You can parent one object to another by using the middle mouse button to drag the child onto the parent in the Hypergraph and Outliner.

To unparent objects:

1. Select each of the children you want to unparent by clicking the first child and then [Shift]-clicking additional children in the Hypergraph or with the Pick mask set to object mode.

2. From the Edit menu, select Unparent to unparent the object, or press [Shift] [p] (**Figure 6.19**).

   This pulls the object out of the hierarchy, so that it now acts separately from the parented hierarchy.

✔ Tip

■ You can also use the middle mouse button to drag the object out of the hierarchy in the Hypergraph and the Outliner, disconnecting the selected object from the rest of the hierarchy.

Figure 6.17 [Shift]-click additional objects to add them to the selection.

Figure 6.18 The cube is the parent of the cylinder—shown in the Hypergraph by a connecting line.

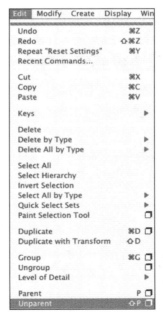

Figure 6.19 Select Edit › Unparent to separate two or more parented surfaces.

Figure 6.20 You can align one point on one surface to one point on another surface. Here one point on each surface has been selected and the point-to-point command has been run, so that now the two select points are on top of each other (inside the square).

About Aligning and Snapping Objects

In the real world, objects touch each other to form other objects. A room, for example, is formed by multiple adjoining walls. You can use Maya's alignment tools to line up objects and components (**Figure 6.20**), saving the additional steps it would take to align objects by eye and eliminating the uncertainty over whether the objects actually touch each other.

Maya's alignment options include the Snap Align and Snap Together tools. The Snap Align tool is especially easy to control because it's completely icon-based (**Figure 6.21**)—which means there's no Options window to fuss with. This is a great tool for aligning one object to another, giving you multiple alignment choices (for example, aligning one object to another's center, top, or bottom just by clicking the respective icon). The Snap Together tool takes alignment even further by allowing you to move and rotate an object while aligning it (**Figure 6.22**).

Figure 6.21 Graphical elements are used as quick alignment tools.

Figure 6.22 Arrows appear when the alignment tool is invoked to show how the alignment command will affect the surfaces when [Enter] is pressed, completing the command.

Snaps are alignment shortcuts used to quickly align objects or components to gridlines, curves, points, or view planes—for example, moving a selected object to a specific gridline (**Figure 6.23**). You can also use Snaps to make sure curve components and surfaces actually overlap other curves or surfaces. This is important in Maya because many commands require that curves and/or surfaces actually touch in order for the command to work properly. The best way to confirm that a selected point is touching the desired curve is to select the point and use curve snap to move the point to the curve. Snapping can also help bring selected, out-of-view surfaces into view by snapping the selected object to a gridline or curve that is within view.

The four snaps

Let's take a look at the four snaps (**Figure 6.24**) available in Maya:

◆ **Snap to Grids** ▦ ((x̄))—Snaps a CV, pivot point, or polygonal vertex to a grid corner. If you turn on this option before you draw a curve, the CVs will snap to the grid corners (**Figure 6.23**).

◆ **Snap to Curves** ▨ ((c̄))—Snaps a CV, pivot point, or polygonal vertex to a curve or curve on a surface (**Figure 6.25**).

◆ **Snap to Points** ▧ ((v̄))—Snaps a CV, pivot point, or polygonal vertex to another point (**Figure 6.26**).

◆ **Snap to View Planes** ▨—Snaps a CV, pivot point, or polygonal vertex to a view plane (**Figure 6.27**).

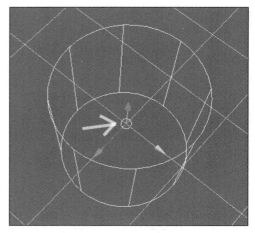

Figure 6.23 Snaps help surfaces jump into alignment with gridlines, curves, and points.

Figure 6.24 The four Snaps, from left to right: Grid, Curve, Points, and View Planes.

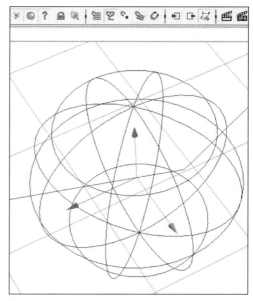

Figure 6.25 Snap to Curves moves the surface into alignment with the curve.

Figure 6.26 The two curve's endpoints are snapped together using Snap to Points.

Figure 6.27 Use Snap to View Plane to snap the surface along the plane axis.

To snap an object to the grid:

1. Select an object.

2. Select the Move tool.

3. Hold down ⌧ and drag with the middle mouse button along the grid you would like the object to snap to (**Figure 6.28**).

   or

   Click 🏢 in the status bar and drag with the middle mouse button along the grid you would like the object to snap to.

   The pivot point of the object snaps to the grid corner where you clicked with the middle mouse button.

4. Release the mouse to finalize the snapping position.

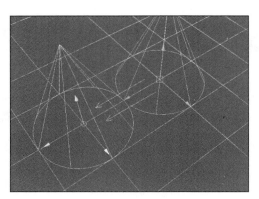

Figure 6.28 The center point of the surface is used to snap from gridline to gridline.

ABOUT ALIGNING AND SNAPPING OBJECTS

To snap an object to a curve:

1. Select an object.

2. Select the Move tool.

3. Hold down c and drag with the middle mouse button on the curve where you would like the object to snap to (**Figure 6.29**).

   or

   Click 🐍 in the status bar and drag with the middle mouse button on the curve where you would like the object to snap to.

   The pivot point of the object jumps to the curve where you clicked with the middle mouse button.

4. Release the mouse to finalize the snapping position.

To snap an object to a view plane:

1. Select an object.

2. Select the Move tool.

3. Click 🐍 in the status bar and drag with the middle mouse button on the view plane where you would like the object to snap to.

   The pivot point of the object snaps to the view plane where you clicked with the middle mouse button (**Figure 6.30**).

Figure 6.29 The surface's center point will slide across the curve until you release the mouse button.

Figure 6.30 The pivot point of the object snaps to the view plane where you clicked with your middle mouse button.

Figure 6.31 Separate two primitive planes so that you can easily view the snapping results.

Figure 6.32 Select the point you would like to snap into alignment with another point.

Figure 6.33 Any selected point can be snapped to any edit point or CV.

To snap a point on one surface to a point on another surface:

1. Create two NURBS planes (**Figure 6.31**).

2. Select both planes and press F8 .
   The selection mode switches into CV components.

3. Select a corner CV on one of the planes (**Figure 6.32**).

4. Select the Move tool.

5. Hold down Clear and click and drag with the middle mouse button on a second plane near the CV where you would like the object to snap to.
   The pivot point of the selected CV snaps to the CV on the second plane that's closest to where you clicked with your middle mouse button (**Figure 6.33**).

✔ Tips

- Although you can use the left mouse button when snapping, using the middle mouse button prevents unwanted objects from accidentally being selected.

- Although we showed snapping points on a curve in this example, the same technique can be used to snap a point on one object to a point on another object. You can snap any point to any other point on a surface or a curve, on the same object or a different object.

The Snap Align tools

The Snap Align tools are a set of alignment aids for placing multiple objects. Alignment is very important in the world of 3D modeling because an object can appear to be aligned in the Perspective view but be completely off in the orthographic views (**Figure 6.34**). This happens because the camera angles of orthographic views are straight on from the side, top, and right; whereas the Perspective view can be viewed at any angle, often giving you an inaccurate perception of the scene.

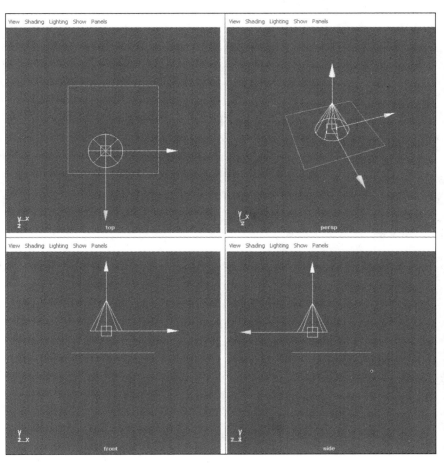

Figure 6.34
The cone seems to be centered on the plane in the Perspective view, but in the orthographic views, you can see that it's actually very much out of alignment.

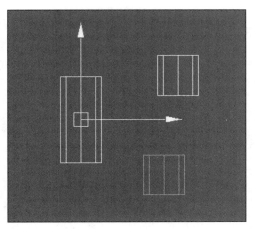

Figure 6.35 The cylinders are different sizes to better illustrate the change after alignment.

Figure 6.36 Min aligns the surfaces with the minimum *Y* value of the two.

Figure 6.37 The bases of the two surfaces are now placed on the same grid line.

The Snap Alignment tools include the Point-to-Point Snaps, Snap Align Objects, Snap Align Tool, and the Snap Together Tool—all of which are essential to a streamlined work-flow. Many of the alignment tools are similar; you'll soon determine which one best fits your workflow.

To align two or more objects using the Align Objects tool:

1. Create two primitive cylinders (making one taller along the *Y* axis) with some space between them (**Figure 6.35**).

2. Select the cylinders.

3. From the Modify menu select the box beside Snap Align Objects > Align Objects. The Align Objects Options dialog box opens.

4. Select Min ▮ for the Align Mode, and check Align in World Y (unchecking World X and Z) (**Figure 6.36**).

   Setting the World to Y forces the movement to happen along the *Y* axis.

5. Click Apply.

   One cylinder moves up the *Y* axis, and one cylinder moves down the *Y* axis until the base of each object is aligned (**Figure 6.37**).

continues on next page

6. With the Align Objects Options dialog box still open, select Mid ![icon] for the Align Mode, and check Align in World Y (unchecking World X and Z).

7. Click Align.

One cylinder moves up the *Y* axis, and one cylinder moves down the *Y* axis until the center of each object is aligned (**Figure 6.38**).

To evenly distribute multiple objects along an axis using the Align Objects tool:

1. Create a primitive cylinder.

2. Duplicate the cylinder four times.

3. Move one of the cylinders up the *Y* axis 10 grid units (**Figure 6.39**).

4. Select all of the cylinders.

5. From the Modify menu select the box beside Snap Align Objects > Align Objects. The Align Objects Options window opens.

6. Select Dist ![icon] as the Align Mode, and check Align in World Y (unchecking World X and Z) (**Figure 6.40**).

Setting the World to Y forces the objects to be distributed along the *Y* axis.

7. Click Apply.

Each of the cylinders moves up the *Y* axis until they're all evenly spaced between the two cylinders farthest from the others (**Figure 6.41**).

Figure 6.40 The Dist option can be used to evenly distribute the selected objects along the selected axes.

Figure 6.38 The two surfaces are aligned to their centers.

Figure 6.39 Only the placement of the two surfaces farthest away from each other matters now because the rest of the objects will be distributed evenly between them.

Figure 6.41 The cylinders are perfectly spaced along the *Y* axis.

Figure 6.42 The order of selection becomes important because the objects are aligned to the last selected object.

To align two or more objects using the Align tool:

1. Create five primitive cylinders and randomly space them away from each other (**Figure 6.42**).

2. Select one cylinder by clicking it, then [Shift]-select each of the others one at a time until all are selected.

3. From the Modify menu, select the box beside Snap Align Objects > Align Tool.

   A gray box appears around the selected cylinders. On the edges of the box are icon manipulators used to align the objects (**Figure 6.43**).

4. Click 🖳 on the surrounding box (**Figure 6.44**).

   The cylinders fall into alignment with the selected icon.

5. Press [z] to undo the alignment, then click on another icon to see its alignment type.

6. Repeat the last step until you feel comfortable with each of the alignment icons functions.

✔ Tip

■ Objects are aligned to the last selected object (blue).

Figure 6.44 Note that each icon actually illustrates the side, or center, on which the alignment will occur.

Figure 6.43 A gray bounding box is for visualization purposes only: You need to click the icons for the Align function to work.

ABOUT ALIGNING AND SNAPPING OBJECTS

To use the Point-to-Point Snap Align tool:

1. Create one primitive cylinder and one primitive cone.

2. Select the objects and press [F8].

3. Select one CV from the cylinder, then [Shift]-select a CV from the cone (**Figure 6.45**).

4. From the Modify menu, select the box beside Snap Align Objects > Point to Point.

The entire object associated with the first selected point moves into alignment with the second object. The two selected points are now stacked on top of one another (**Figure 6.46**).

✔ Tip

■ If you only want the points to move into alignment, not the entire object, use Point Snap (explained earlier in this chapter) instead of the Point-to-Point Snap Align Tool.

Figure 6.45 You can select any edit point or CV to be aligned with any edit point or CV on another surface.

Figure 6.46 The two selected points now appear as one but are actually sitting on top of each other.

Figure 6.47 The selected set of points will be aligned to the other selected points as closely as possible without changing the shape of the surface.

Figure 6.48 The Snap Align Objects drop-down menu holds many of the alignment commands.

Figure 6.49 The cylinder's placement shifts into alignment with the selected points on the cone's surface.

To use the 2 and 3 Point-to-Point Snap Align tools:

1. Create one primitive cylinder and one primitive cone.

2. Select the objects and press F8 .

3. Select two CVs from the cylinder, then Shift -select two CVs from the cone (**Figure 6.47**).

   or

   Select three CVs from the cylinder, then Shift -select three CVs from the cone.

4. If you selected two CVs on each object, from the Modify menu, select the box beside Snap Align Objects > 2 Points to 2 Points. If you selected three points on each object, select the box beside Snap Align Objects > 3 Points to 3 Points (**Figure 6.48**).

   The entire object with the first selected points moves into alignment with the second object's selected points. The points may not stack on top of one another if the spacing between points is different on each of the objects (**Figure 6.49**).

NURBS CURVES AND SURFACES

Figure 7.1 You can edit a revolved surface using the original NURBS curve you used to create it.

You can use NURBS curves to create nearly any object—a medieval knight, a detailed car, an alien, or just about any other object you can imagine. Because they can be highly organic, characterized by sinuous, rounded shapes, NURBS surfaces are great for creating trees, faces, and streamlined vehicles.

For anyone who has used other software programs with Bézier curves (for example, Adobe Illustrator), NURBS curve creation should come quite naturally. Although NURBS curves are different than Bézier curves, you create and edit them similarly. Bézier and NURBS curves represent curved lines whose shape you can edit by translating points along the curve (the placement of the original points was specified at the curve's creation). You can use NURBS curves to create a framework for a final surface, outline the profile of surfaces that you plan to later *revolve* to create the final surface, and fine-tune a surface (**Figure 7.1**).

About NURBS Objects

NURBS object creation is a Maya strong-point because of the precise control it affords the user over the final surface. There are two types of NURBS objects: *curves* and *surfaces*.

NURBS curves have three main components: *CVs (control vertices)*, *edit points*, and *hulls* (**Figure 7.2**). You use these components to create and edit curves in different ways. As you grow familiar with creating NURBS curves, you'll likely come to prefer one component to the others, making it your primary editing method.

In addition to CVs, edit points, and hulls, NURBS surfaces have the following more advanced components: *surface normals*, *patch centers*, and *surface origins* (**Figure 7.3**). You can edit any NURBS surface that was created from a curve (for example, a revolved surface) by editing components of the original curve or by editing the surface's components directly. When a surface is created from one or more curves, it remains linked to that curve through a history connection. Thus, when you modify a curve, you're also editing the surface.

Figure 7.2 NURBS components are used to easily and quickly change the look of the curve or surface.

Figure 7.3 NURBS surface components are used to manipulate the look and feel of the surface.

Figure 7.4 Surface edit points can be shown by themselves to make selection and editing easier. You can select each component by clicking its icon, in this case a small *x*.

Each NURBS component (edit points, CVs, and so on) can be displayed and edited both individually (**Figure 7.4**; edit points are shown) and with other components (**Figure 7.5**; edit points and hulls are shown). NURBS curves are an important part of NURBS modeling because they help you create and edit surfaces. This chapter will provide the foundation you need to control the look of NURBS curves and surfaces.

Figure 7.5 Maya allows you to show or hide as many components as you want to view at any given time. This helps you narrow down your selection while still getting a good idea of what the object's other components look like.

Creating NURBS Curves

By learning how to create and edit curves, you'll gain a better understanding of how to take full advantage of Maya's modeling tools. Multiple edit points give you precise control over the shape and placement of NURBS curves.

Curves are often used to create a wire representation of a surface. Once you've done this, you can place a skin over the curves to create the final surface (**Figure 7.6**). You can create this final surface using a number of Maya commands, including *lofting, extruding,* and *revolving*—all of which we'll examine in depth in this chapter.

Anatomy of a curve

Each NURBS curve has an associated direction, derived from the order in which the CVs were created. A curve's direction is important in determining the look of the final surface. If you don't pay attention to the direction in which a curve is created, you will often get undesirable results when you go to create the final surface. Curves that are oriented in opposite directions can twist and fold the final surface.

The direction of a curve is determined by the first and second CVs created for the curve. The first CV, or *start point*, is represented by a small square. The second CV is represented by the letter *U*. The start point followed by the *U* shows the user the direction in which the curve is headed; this determines the *U* direction of any surface created from the curve (**Figure 7.7**).

Because NURBS curves are used mainly as modeling aids, they don't appear when the scene is rendered.

Figure 7.6 Curves used to create a framework for the surface (top), and the same curves with a surface laid over them (bottom).

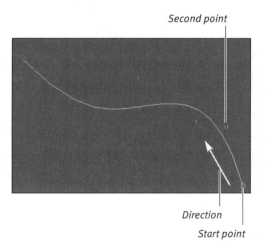

Second point

Direction

Start point

Figure 7.7 The *U* direction of a curve is determined by the first and second CVs created.

Edit point *Curve point* *Direction*

Hull *Span* *Start point*

Figure 7.8 This image shows NURBS curve components.

Each curve has the following components (**Figure 7.8**):

◆ **Control vertices**—CVs are points placed slightly away from the curve and are the components most often used to edit a curve's shape.

◆ **Edit points (knots)**—Edit points, placed directly on the curve and indicated by a small *x*, represent another way of editing a curve's shape.

◆ **Hulls**—Hulls are straight lines connecting each CV. Showing the hulls can help clarify which row of CVs each CV is connected to. By clicking a hull, you select the entire row of CVs along the hull.

◆ **Spans**—A span is the area between two edit points. Each time an edit point is added, a span is added as well. You can't edit spans directly (like edit points); instead, they represent the results of your edits. You use spans to create and rebuild curves and surfaces. The more spans you add when rebuilding a surface, the more edit points you're adding— which means the more spans you have, the more detailed, and heavy, your surface becomes.

◆ **Curve point**—A curve point is an arbitrary point on a curve—often used as a point to detach a curve from or to align it with. A curve point can be located anywhere along a curve.

◆ **Start point**—The start of a curve is the first CV created for the curve, represented by a small square.

◆ **Curve direction**—The direction of a curve is determined by the first and second CVs created for the curve.

Creating curves of various degrees

Every curve has a certain degree; the higher the degree, the smoother the curve. A curve can have a degree of 1, 2, 3, 5, or 7. A curve with a degree of 1 is a linear curve and only requires two points to define it (**Figure 7.9**). Linear curves and surfaces are characterized by straight lines and sharp corners. A curve degree of 3 will produce a smooth curve without using an excessive number of CVs to describe it (**Figure 7.10**). A curve with a degree of 3 is the most common and versatile curve because it only requires four points and is smooth enough to create a high-quality surface. Because of the accuracy needed for manufacturing, car designers often use degrees higher than 5. For animation, however, a degree of 3 is usually high enough.

Each curve requires CVs that total one more than its degree to create it. For example, a curve with a degree of 3 requires four CVs (**Figure 7.10**), and a 7-degree curve requires eight CVs, thereby creating a heavier surface (**Figure 7.11**). It is for this reason that a degree of 3 or 5 is usually most ideal.

Figure 7.9 A curve degree of 1 creates a linear curve and a linear surface (if a surface is created from the curve).

Figure 7.10 A curve degree of 3 produces a smooth curve without using an excessive number of CVs.

Figure 7.11 This is a 7-degree curve, which means it requires eight CVs.

Figure 7.12 This surface was created with one revolved curve.

Creating profile curves

You can create many objects by drawing an outline curve in the shape of the object's profile. This profile curve can then be revolved to complete the final surface (**Figure 7.12**). In addition, you can alter the profile curve to tweak the object's shape after the final surface has been created. You can do this because the profile curve and final surface are connected through the object's construction history (**Figure 7.13**).

If you're drawing a profile curve for a vase, glass, pot, or any other object that has thickness to it, you should draw the profile of the inside as well as of the outside (**Figure 7.14**). If you don't draw both profiles, your object will be paper-thin: Since most real objects have some depth or dimension, you need to re-create that thickness in Maya to keep your objects looking realistic. The thickness of the glass is defined by the way you draw the profile curve.

Figure 7.13 By tweaking a point of the curve—which is how this revolved surface was created—you can interactively sculpt the object.

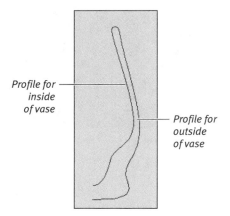

Profile for inside of vase

Profile for outside of vase

Figure 7.14 When drawing a profile curve, make sure you add the inside of the surface to add thickness to the final object.

Typically, you create a curve in one of three ways: with the CV Curve tool, the EP Curve tool, or the Pencil Curve tool.

To create a curve with the CV Curve tool:

1. From the Create menu, select CV Curve Tool.

2. In the Top view, click in several places.
   A CV will appear with each mouse click, and a curve will appear on the fourth click (**Figure 7.15**).

3. Press [Enter] to complete the creation of the curve.
   The curve becomes highlighted to indicate that it's selected.

To create a curve with the EP Curve tool:

1. From the Create menu, select EP Curve Tool.

2. In the Top view, click in several places.
   A curve is created once the second edit point is placed, and it continues to take shape with each subsequent point (**Figure 7.16**).

3. Press [Enter] to finish creating the curve.

To create a curve with the Pencil Curve tool:

1. From the Create menu, select Pencil Curve Tool.

2. Click and drag in the Top view to draw a line.
   The curve is completed once you release the mouse. The Pencil Curve tool tends to be a less efficient way of creating a curve because you end up with more points than you need to describe the shape (**Figure 7.17**).

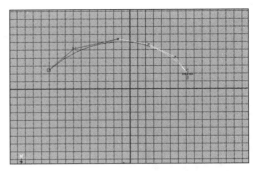

Figure 7.15 This curve was created by placing points using the CV Curve tool.

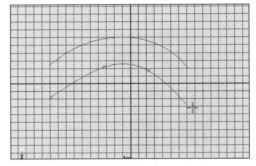

Figure 7.16 This curve was created using the EP Curve tool.

Figure 7.17 The bottom curve was created using the Pencil Curve tool.

Figure 7.18 Curve direction can cause unwanted surface problems. It is best to keep all curves of the same surface facing in the same direction.

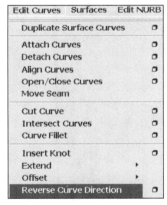

Figure 7.19 Select Edit Curves > Reverse Curve Direction to change the direction of a curve.

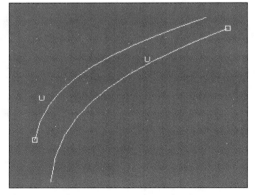

Figure 7.20 The curve on top shows the direction before it was reversed; the curve beneath it shows the direction after the curve has been reversed.

As stated earlier, each curve has a direction, called the *U* direction. Sometimes you'll want to reverse a curve's direction because you are getting undesirable surfaces from the curves (**Figure 7.18**).

To reverse a curve's direction:

1. Select a curve in object mode.

2. From the Edit Curves menu, select Reverse Curve Direction (**Figure 7.19**).

3. Press F8 to view the new curve direction in component mode (**Figure 7.20**).

Circular 2D fillets

A *fillet* is a concave junction where two curves or surfaces meet. You can create 2D fillets to combine multiple curves with an arc between them. Sometimes it's easier to create two curves and fillet them together in order to create a corner than it is to draw out one curve with the corner in it. An example might be when you need to create a corner out of two perpendicular curves (**Figure 7.21**).

To create a circular 2D fillet:

1. Create two curves to fillet between (**Figure 7.22**).

2. Right-click the first curve and select Curve Point from the Marking menu (**Figure 7.23**).

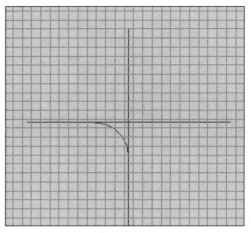

Figure 7.21 A 2D fillet serves as a good tool for adding smooth corners to a set of curves.

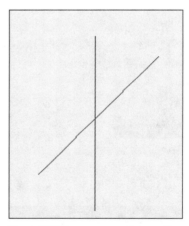

Figure 7.22 Two curves are intersecting.

Figure 7.23 A Marking menu appears when you click the curve with your right mouse button. This is a convenient way to choose which component type you'd like to be able to select.

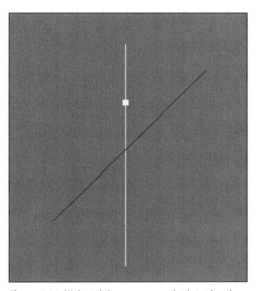

Figure 7.24 Click and drag a curve point into the place where you would like the arc to begin.

3. Click the first curve, and drag the point to where you want the fillet to arc (**Figure 7.24**).

4. Right-click the second curve and select Curve Point from the Marking menu.

5. (Shift)-click the second curve and drag the point to where you want the fillet to arc (**Figure 7.25**).

6. From the Edit Curves menu, select Curve Fillet.

   An arc is created between the two curve points (**Figure 7.26**).

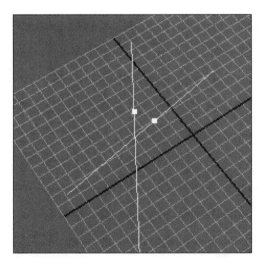

Figure 7.25 The two curve points determine the start and end points of the arc.

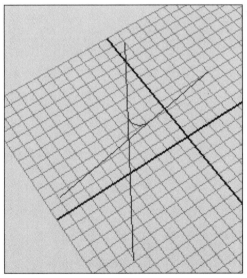

Figure 7.26 An arc is created between the two curve points selected on each curve.

Opening and closing curves

A curve that does not start and end on the same point is called an open curve (**Figure 7.27**). Many Maya commands will not function correctly on open curves, so the curves must be closed. A closed curve has the same start and end point, making it continuous (**Figure 7.28**).

To open or close a curve:

◆ From the Edit Curves menu, select Open/Close Curves (**Figure 7.29**).

An open curve will become closed, and a closed curve will become open.

Figure 7.27 An incomplete circle is called an open curve.

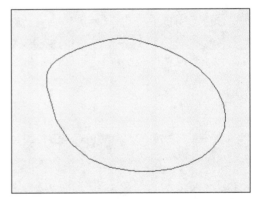

Figure 7.28 A closed curve has the same start and end point.

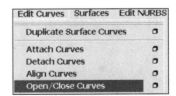

Figure 7.29 The Open/Close Curves command opens a closed curve and closes an open curve.

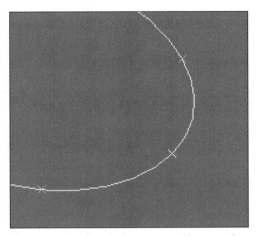

Figure 7.30 An edit point is represented by an *x*; when selected, it can be used as a curve's breaking point.

Figure 7.31 Two curves are created out of the detachment at the edit point.

To detach a curve:

1. Select a curve with the Pick mask set to Component: Parm Points mode.

2. Select the edit point *x* where you would like to detach the curve (**Figure 7.30**).

3. From the Edit Curves menu, select Detach Curves.

   The curve is now broken into two curves (**Figure 7.31**).

✔ Tip

■ If Keep Originals is selected in the Detach Curves Options dialog box, you will have three curves after detaching—the original curve and two detached curves. Deselect Keep Originals before you detach to automatically delete the original curve (see the "Keep Originals" sidebar later in this chapter).

Locking the length of a curve

Curves are like rubber bands in that you can pull and stretch them apart. That is, you can edit CVs to be any distance from one another that you want. However, for the practical purposes of animation, you'd be better off making your curve behave like a piece of string that stays the same length while you bend it. You can do that by locking the length of the curve so that the CVs remain the same distance from one another when you animate the curve.

To lock the length of a curve:

1. Select a curve and choose Edit Curves > Modify Curves > Lock Length (**Figure 7.32**).

2. Press F8 to switch to component mode and select the Points component type ▣.

3. Select the first CV in the curve, press W and move it around.

   The curve will now follow the CV you selected like a piece of string (**Figure 7.33**).

✔ Tip

■ Select a curve and choose Edit Curves > Modify Curves > Unlock Length.

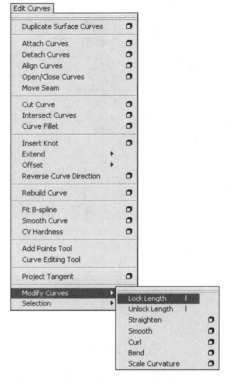

Figure 7.32 Select Edit Curves > Modify Curves > Lock Length.

Figure 7.33 With Lock Length enabled, drag a CV to animate the curve like a piece of string.

Figure 7.34 Select Edit Curves > Modify Curves > Straighten.

Figure 7.35 Set the options for Straighten.

To straighten a curve:

1. With a curve selected, choose Edit Curves > Modify Curves and click the option box next to Straighten (**Figure 7.34**).

   The Straighten Curves Options dialog box opens.

2. Uncheck the Preserve Length check box.

3. Adjust the Straightness slider to *1* (or simply type *1* in the text box) (**Figure 7.35**).

4. Click Apply.

   The wavy Curve becomes a straight line (**Figure 7.36**).

Figure 7.36 The top Curve is wavy before being straightened. The bottom curve is the result.

To smooth a curve:

1. With a curve selected, choose Edit Curves > Modify Curves and click the option box next to Smooth (**Figure 7.37**).

   The Smooth Curves Options dialog box opens.

2. Set the Smooth Factor to *10* (**Figure 7.38**).

3. Click Apply.

   The jagged curve becomes smoother (**Figure 7.39**).

Figure 7.37 Select Smooth from the Edit Curves > Modify Curves menu.

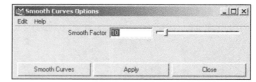

Figure 7.38 Set the Smooth Factor to *10*.

Figure 7.39 The top curve is jagged before applying the Smooth function. The bottom curve is the result.

Figure 7.40 Select the option for Edit Curves › Rebuild Curve.

Figure 7.41 Set the Number of Spans to *25*.

Figure 7.42 Select Edit Curves › Modify Curves › Curl.

Figure 7.43 Set the options for Curl Curves.

To curl a curve:

1. With a curve selected, choose Edit Curves and click the option box next to Rebuild Curves (**Figure 7.40**).

   The Rebuild Curves Options dialog box opens.

2. Set the Number of Spans to *25* (**Figure 7.41**).

3. Click Rebuild.

   The effect of curl will be more apparent if your curve has many CVs in it.

4. Choose Edit Curves > Modify Curves and click the option box next to Curl (**Figure 7.42**).

   The Curl Curves Options dialog box opens.

5. Set the Curl Amount to *2* and the Curl Frequency to *1* (**Figure 7.43**).

6. Click Apply. The curve becomes a spiral (**Figure 7.44**).

Figure 7.44 The top curve is straight before being curled. The bottom curve is the result.

To bend a curve:

1. With a curve selected, choose Edit Curves > Modify Curves and click the option box next to Bend (**Figure 7.45**). The Bend Curves Options dialog box opens.

2. Set the Bend Amount to *.15* (**Figure 7.46**).

3. Click Apply. The curve becomes more like a circle (**Figure 7.47**).

Figure 7.45 Select Edit Curves > Modify Curves > Bend.

Figure 7.46 Set the options for Bend Curves.

Figure 7.47 The top curve is straight before being bent. The bottom curve is the result.

Figure 7.48 Select from the Edit Curves > Modify Curves > Scale Curvature.

Figure 7.49 Set the options for Scale Curvature.

To scale curvature:

1. With a curve selected, choose Edit Curves > Modify Curves and click the option box next to Scale Curvature (**Figure 7.48**).

   The Scale Curvature Options dialog box opens.

2. Set the Scale Factor to *.5* and the Max Curvature to *1* (**Figure 7.49**).

3. Click Apply. The curve expands (**Figure 7.50**).

✔ Tip

- You can also apply the Straighten, Smooth, Curl, Bend, and Scale Curvature effects to selected CVs instead of to the entire curve.

Figure 7.50 The top curve is tighter before applying Scale Curvature. The bottom curve is the result.

Creating Surfaces from Curves

There are several commands in Maya that you can use to turn curves into surfaces. They include Revolve, Loft, Planar, Extrude, Birail, and Boundary.

To revolve a curve to make a vase:

1. In the Front view, draw a curve for the shape of the vase's profile (**Figure 7.51**).

2. Select the curve in object mode.

3. In the Surfaces menu select the box next to Revolve (**Figure 7.52**).
   The Revolve Options window opens.

4. Select the axis you want the object to revolve around (**Figure 7.53**). We'll use the *Y* axis for our illustration.

5. Click Revolve to create the surface of the vase.
   If you get unexpected results, you may have the object revolving around the wrong axis.

6. Press ③ to increase the smoothness to see the full surface (**Figure 7.54**).

✔ Tips

- You can adjust Start Sweep Angle and End Sweep Angle in Revolve Options to create a revolved surface that is not a complete 360 degrees.

- To interactively change the shape of a revolved surface by changing the angle of the axis revolution, you can use the Show Manipulator tool.

Figure 7.51 A profile curve illustrates the outline of the object used for revolving.

Figure 7.52 From the Surfaces menu select the box next to Revolve to open the Revolve Options window.

Figure 7.53 The revolve axis is very important to the look of the final surface. You want to choose the axis that goes through the middle of the final surface.

Figure 7.54 Increasing surface smoothness helps clarify where the actual revolved surface lies.

CREATING SURFACES FROM CURVES

Figure 7.55 When creating curves to loft across, you must consider each curve describing the contour of the final surface.

Figure 7.56 A lofted surface maintains a connection to the original curves, so that you can edit them in the future using the original curves.

One of the best ways to create a surface from multiple curves is by using the Loft command. The Loft command creates a surface that extends from one selected curve to the next until each curve is covered with a surface. Each of the isoparms on the final surface is derived from the edit point placement on each curve. As a general rule, you want to have the same amount of edit points on each curve.

To loft across multiple curves:

1. Create two or more curves with which to create a surface (**Figure 7.55**).

2. (Shift)-select each curve in the order in which you would like the surface to loft across them.

   The order in which you select curves is important. The surface will start at the first selected curve and cover each additional curve in the order you select them.

3. With all the curves selected, choose Surfaces > Loft to create a surface over the curves (**Figure 7.56**).

✔ Tip

■ A new surface displays in rough mode and will look as if it is not fully touching the curves that were used to create it. Select the surface and press ③ to view the surface in smooth display mode.

CREATING SURFACES FROM CURVES

The Extrude command creates a surface by sweeping one curve (the profile) along another curve (the path). The Extrude command is often used to add depth to text and create long, tubelike objects such as power cords.

To extrude a curve:

1. Create a profile curve that is the shape you'd like the final extruded surface to be. For example, if you want to extrude a tube, you could create a circle (**Figure 7.57**).

2. Starting from the already created curve, create a CV curve the length of the final surface you want to create (**Figure 7.58**).
   This is referred to as the *path curve*.

3. Select the circle, then [Shift]-select the path curve.

4. From the Surfaces menu, select Extrude to sweep the profile curve along the path curve.
   A new extruded surface is created (**Figure 7.59**).

✔ Tip

- By default, the new surface starts at the angle of the profile curve and mimics its angles. With this default setting, the extruded surface only follows the path curve if the profile curve is perpendicular to the path curve. To ignore the angle of the profile curve and have the curve follow the path curve, select At Path in the Extrude Options window.

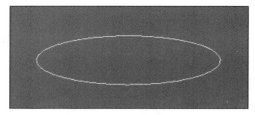

Figure 7.57 Any curve shape can be used for an extrude—for example, if you're looking for a tubelike shape, you could use a closed curve.

Figure 7.58 The second curve you create for an extrude is used for the path and length of the extruded surface.

Figure 7.59 A surface is created from the extrude that follows the angle of the profile curve.

Figure 7.60 The Make Planar command works well for any closed, flat curve out of which you would like to make a flat surface.

Figure 7.61 This closed curve will determine the outline of the surface. Use grid snap to be sure that all of the points of the curve lie on the same plane.

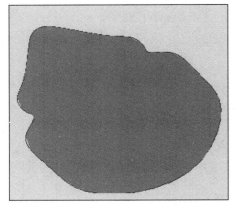

Figure 7.62 A flat surface is created, with the curve used as the border of the surface.

The Make Planar command is used to make a flat surface out of a curve. An example of its use would be to create the flat top of a guitar (that is, the part with the hole in it) (**Figure 7.60**). You could create the outline of the guitar's body with a curve, and then use the Make Planar command to complete the flat surface.

To make a curve planar:

1. Create a closed curve with all the CVs on the same axis (**Figure 7.61**).

2. From the Surfaces menu select Planar. A planar surface is created from the curve (**Figure 7.62**).

✔ Tips

- The curve must be closed or self-intersecting for the Planar command to work.

- All CVs must lie on the same axis for the command to work. To ensure that this is the case, you can grid-snap each CV to a grid plane.

The Birail tool is similar to Extrude, except that instead of having one path curve and one profile curve, it has two path curves (rails) and any number of profile curves. The hull of a boat provides a good example: Two path curves can determine the hull's outline, and profile curves can determine its depth and shape (**Figure 7.63**).

To create a birail surface:

1. Draw two curves to use for the rails of the surface (**Figure 7.64**).

2. Draw a new curve that extends from the first curve to the second curve using curve snap (hold down [c] and click and drag on the rail curve) for the first and last points (**Figure 7.65**).

   The curves must touch each other for the operation to work. Curve snap helps ensure that the profile curve touches both rails.

3. From the Surfaces menu select Birail > Birail 1 Tool (**Figure 7.66**).

   Use Birail 2 Tool if you have two profile curves. Use Birail 3+ if you are using three or more profile curves.

4. Click the profile curves, and then click the rail curves (**Figure 7.67**).

   The birail surface is created.

Figure 7.63 The hull of a boat can be created from a few profile curves and two rail curves.

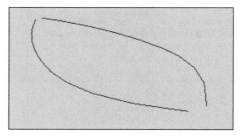

Figure 7.64 You always use two curves for the rails.

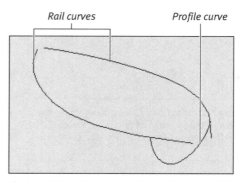

Figure 7.65 For the command to function correctly, your must curve-snap the ends of each profile curve to the rails.

Figure 7.66 From the Surfaces menu select Birail > Birail 1 Tool.

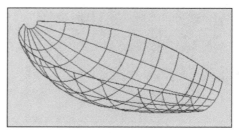

Figure 7.67 A surface is created from the three curves using the Birail tool.

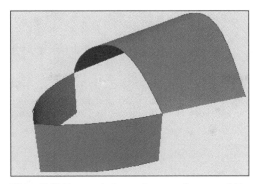

Figure 7.68 The gap between these surfaces would be a good candidate for filling via the Boundary command.

Figure 7.69 With boundary surfaces, as with birail surfaces, it is essential to curve-snap each end point.

Figure 7.70 You can select curves or isoparms on which to use the Boundary command.

The Boundary command requires three or four curves that intersect or meet at each other's ends. One use for a boundary surface would be when you have three surfaces connecting at a corner and you want to use three of the edges to complete a rounded corner between the surfaces (**Figure 7.68**).

To create a boundary surface:

1. Draw three or four curves with intersecting ends (**Figure 7.69**).

   You can make sure the ends intersect by curve-snapping the first and last CVs to the other curves.

2. Select all the curves that complete the boundary (**Figure 7.70**).

3. From the Surfaces menu, select Boundary.

   The boundary surface is created (**Figure 7.71**).

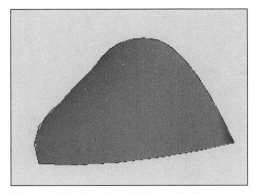

Figure 7.71 A surface is created across the three curves.

To create beveled text:

1. From the Create menu, select the box next to Text.

   The Text Curves Options dialog box opens.

2. In the Text field, type the text you want.

3. Select a font for the text.

4. Select Curves for Type.

5. Click Create (**Figure 7.72**).

6. From the Surfaces menu, select Bevel (**Figure 7.73**).

   The text bevel can be edited with the Inputs node afterward or in the Text Curves Options dialog box before creation.

   The text now appears with a bevel (**Figure 7.74**).

✔ Tip

- You can adjust the width and depth of the extrude in the bevel's Inputs node (accessible from the Channel Box).

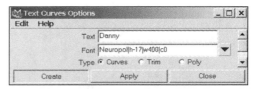

Figure 7.72 In the Text Curves Options dialog box set the Text, Font, and Type options, and then click Create.

Figure 7.73 From the Surfaces menu select Bevel.

Figure 7.74 The curves that outlined the letters have been turned into beveled surfaces.

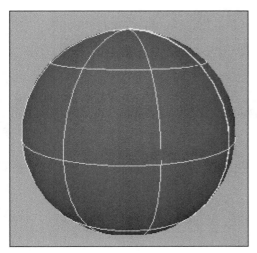

Figure 7.75 The sphere has been selected to make it live so that a curve can be drawn on it. Any surface can be made live.

Figure 7.76 When the surface is live, the wireframe turns green.

To draw a curve directly on a surface, you must make the surface live. Once a surface is live, a curve can be created and edited directly on the surface itself.

To make a surface live:

1. Select a surface (**Figure 7.75**).

2. From the Modify menu, select Make Live or click 🔁 .

   The surface wireframe turns green to indicate that it is a live surface (**Figure 7.76**).

✔ Tip

■ To deactivate a surface that's live, select Make Not Live from the Modify menu.

To draw a curve on a live surface:

1. Make the surface live.

2. From the Create menu, select CV Curve Tool (**Figure 7.77**).

3. Click points on the surface where you want to create the curve (**Figure 7.78**).

4. Press ⌐Enter⌐ to complete the curve.
   A curve is created on the surface.

5. From the Modify menu, select Make Not Live to bring the surface back into normal mode (**Figure 7.79**).

✔ Tip

■ You can move the curve along the surface in the U or V direction using the Move tool.

When you project a curve, it creates a new curve on the selected surface. Imagine projecting the image of a curve at an object from a slide projector. The shape of the object may warp the image of the curve. Likewise, when you project a curve in Maya, the resulting curve projected on an object's surface is warped to some degree.

Figure 7.77 From the Create menu, select CV Curve Tool.

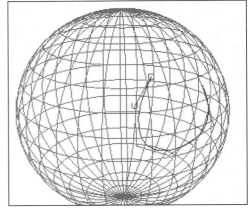

Figure 7.78 It's helpful to tumble your view around the surface to get a straight look at where you want to place each CV.

Figure 7.79 From the Modify menu select Make Not Live to return to normal mode.

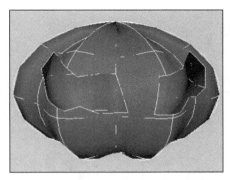

Figure 7.80 Curves on surfaces work well when you want to later trim out part of a surface, as with this pumpkin.

Figure 7.81 This circle will be projected onto the surface of the sphere.

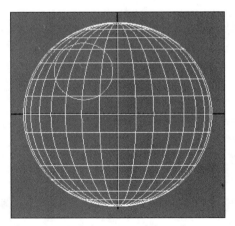

Figure 7.82 Both the curve and the surface must be selected for the projection to work.

Figure 7.83 The active view becomes the angle from which the curve is projected.

A pumpkin's eyes provide a good example of this: You can draw the shape of the eyes you want to cut out of a pumpkin in the Front view, and project these curves onto the pumpkin shape so that you can later trim them out of the surface (**Figure 7.80**). The trim function is often used after projecting a curve onto a surface to cut out the curve shape.

To project a curve onto a surface:

1. Create a surface for the curve to be projected onto—a primitive sphere, for example.

2. In the Front view, create a curve to project onto the surface; in this example, we'll use a primitive circle (**Figure 7.81**).

3. Select the curve to be projected, and the surface (**Figure 7.82**).

4. With the Front view active, select Edit NURBS > Project Curve on Surface (**Figure 7.83**).

   The curve becomes projected on both sides of the sphere's surface (**Figure 7.84**).

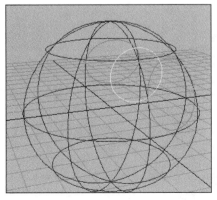

Figure 7.84 The curve is projected on both sides of the object.

189

To trim out a hole in a surface:

1. Follow the steps outlined in the previous task, "To project a curve onto a surface."

2. From the Edit NURBS menu, select Trim Tool.

3. Click the sphere.

   The object becomes transparent and the lines turn white to indicate that you're in the Trim tool (**Figure 7.85**).

4. Click in an area you want to keep—*not* the area in which you want a hole.

   A yellow diamond indicates the area you want to retain (**Figure 7.86**).

5. Click [Enter] to trim the surface.

   Because the curve was projected on both sides of the sphere, there are now two holes in the surface (**Figure 7.87**).

✔ Tip

■ You can click on each area you want to retain. In our sphere example, you can click on the main surface of the sphere and inside the area of one of the circles to create only one hole in the surface.

Figure 7.85 The object becomes transparent and each area that has an option to trim is filled with a grid.

Figure 7.86 The small, yellow diamond indicates that the region will be kept intact.

Figure 7.87 The surface now includes two holes where the original curve originally appeared on the surface.

Keep Originals

Many of the curve and surface manipulation and rebuild commands have a Keep Originals option. When you rebuild a curve using a command such as Detach, the Keep Originals option lets you retain the original curve in addition to creating the new curve(s) as a result of the specific rebuild command.

Be aware that you may not notice that the original curve or surface is still present because the new curves or surfaces will sit directly on top of the original.

POLYGONS

View Shading Lighting Show Panels
Verts:
Edges:
Faces:
UVs:

Figure 8.1 This polygon model was designed to have the least number of faces possible. The textures make up for the lack of detail. Modeled and textured by Toby Marvin.

Polygons provide a fun, easy way to model a surface. A polygon is a surface made up of smaller, flat surfaces with three or more sides. These smaller surfaces are called faces. Working with polygons has more of a rigid construction feel, and working with NURBS has a more pliable, sculptural feel.

Games make extensive use of polygons because the complexity of a game must be limited if it is to offer fast interaction with real-time rendering. If your character has a low poly (short for polygon) count—that is, a low number of faces—it will render and interact quickly. A character in a game is usually limited to a certain number of polygons so that the game can run in real time (**Figure 8.1**).

You can, however, use polygons to make smooth, highly detailed, even organic surfaces (**Figure 8.2**). Some surfaces may be easier to build in polygons than in NURBS surfaces. For example, you can create a character's body from a single seamless polygon surface—something you can't achieve without using many NURBS surfaces.

Figure 8.2 Polygons can be used to make both smooth shapes, such as a banana, and hard edges like the ones on this shoe. Shoe and trouser leg modeled by Adrian Niu.

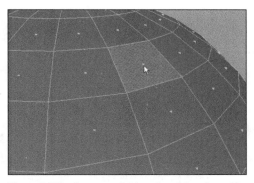

Figure 8.3 The faces are displayed on this sphere. The highlighted face was selected by clicking the dot in the center of the face.

Figure 8.4 The selected edge is shared by the faces on either side of it. Any change to the position or size of this edge will affect all of the faces it touches.

Figure 8.5 The selected vertex is at the corner of four faces.

About Modeling Polygons

The most common way to create a complex polygon model is to start with a primitive poly cube. By transforming this simple object and manipulating its existing components, you can get the basic shape for your model. From there, you can build on the object by adding more complexity to the surface.

Polygons include four types of components, which are important for both modeling and texturing: faces, edges, vertices, and UV.

◆ A **face** is one of the many smaller surfaces that make up the polygon object as a whole. You can choose it by selecting the point in the center of each face (**Figure 8.3**).

◆ An **edge** is one border of a polygonal face (**Figure 8.4**).

◆ A **vertex** is at the corner of a face. Vertices become yellow when selected (**Figure 8.5**). If a vertex is moved, it will change the shape of the four faces that include it.

◆ **UVs** are used for creating texture, not for modeling; they become green when selected (see Chapter 14, "Using Lights").

Two of the most commonly used polygon tools are the Extrude Face tool and the Split Polygon tool. Many other tools are used to manipulate a poly surface, including Extrude Edge and Subdivide.

✔ Tip

■ Once a face, vertex, or edge is selected, you can move, rotate, or scale the component. For the fastest workflow, use the Marking menu.

To select and transform polygon components:

1. Create any polygon primitive (see Chapter 3, "Creating Primitives and Text").

2. Right-click a polygon surface to open the Marking menu.

3. From the Marking menu, select Vertex (**Figure 8.6**).

4. Select some vertices.

   You can marquee-select by clicking and dragging (**Figure 8.7**).

5. Press ⓦ or click the Move tool icon 🔧 in the toolbar.

6. Move the vertices (**Figure 8.8**).

✔ Tips

■ If you are in wireframe mode, you must click a component of the surface, such as an edge, for the Marking menu to show up. If you are in shaded mode, you can click anywhere on the surface.

■ You can use the method described here to select and transform any of the polygon components, except for UVs. You can select UVs in a 3D view, but you can only move them in the UV Texture Editor. For more information on UV textures, see Chapter 15, "Shaders, Materials, and Mapping."

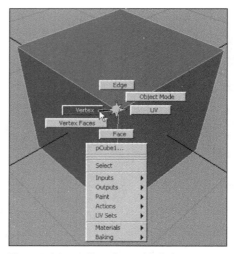

Figure 8.6 Generally, only one kind of component is displayed at a time. This Marking menu, accessible with the right mouse button, provides a convenient way to switch among the different component displays.

Figure 8.7 Three vertices are selected simultaneously using marquee-select.

Figure 8.8 The selected vertices are moved using the Move tool. The shape of every face that shares these vertices is changed.

Figure 8.9 In the top image, the faces of a torus have been selected in the Side view. (It's often helpful to switch views to get a better angle on your selection.) In the bottom image, you see the torus after the selected faces have been deleted.

When using polygons, you often work with a large number of components. Maya has several tools to help you select components and to prevent you from selecting components by mistake. These include Backface Culling, which prevents you from picking points on the far side of the object by hiding them, and tools that allow you to grow, shrink, and convert your existing selections.

To use Backface Culling:

1. From the Create menu, select Polygon Primitives > Torus.

2. Right-click a polygon surface to open the Marking menu and select Face.

3. In the Side view, marquee-select the top half of the torus and then delete the faces (**Figure 8.9**).

4. From the Display menu, select the box next to Custom Polygon Display.

   The Custom Polygon Display Options dialog box opens (**Figure 8.10**).

continues on next page

Figure 8.10 In the Custom Polygon Display Options dialog box, you can choose whether to have the display options affect all polygon objects or just the selected one(s)—for Objects Affected, choose Selected or All.

5. From the Backface Culling menu, select On and click Apply.

The portions of the torus on the far side of the camera view disappear. They cannot be selected (**Figure 8.11**).

6. From the Backface Culling menu, select Keep Wire. Click Apply.

You can see the wireframe of the back side, but you cannot select components from that part of the surface (**Figure 8.12**).

7. From the Backface Culling menu, select Keep Hard Edges. Click Apply.

You can see the hard edges of the back side only—that is, the edges along the sides of holes in the surface (**Figure 8.13**).

8. From the Backface Culling menu, select Off. Click Apply.

The Custom Polygon Display Options are reset to their default values. Now you can select the back sides of polygon surfaces again.

Figure 8.11 When Backface Culling is turned on, the components on the far side of the object disappear so you can't select them. This feature works for all kinds of polygon components.

Figure 8.12 Backface Culling is set to Keep Wire. This setting allows you to see the shape of the object while preventing you from selecting unwanted components on its back side.

Figure 8.13 Keep Hard Edges lets you see the object's basic shape, but only the edges that border a hole in the object.

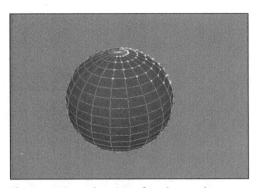

Figure 8.14 Several vertices of a polygon sphere are selected. With Backface Culling off, points on the back of the sphere are selected as well.

Selected vertices

Figure 8.15 Surgically picking poly vertices one by one can be difficult. One way to save time is to use Edit Polygons › Selection › Grow Selection Region. This selects the points surrounding the ones that are currently selected, making the selected area larger.

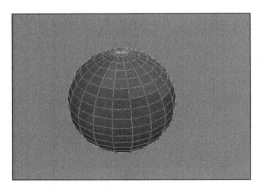

Figure 8.16 The faces that were surrounded by selected vertices are now selected, and the points are deselected.

To grow, shrink, and convert a selection:

1. From the Create menu, select Polygon Primitives > Sphere.

2. Right-click a polygon surface and select Vertex from the Marking menu.

3. Select several vertices (**Figure 8.14**).

4. From the Edit Polygons menu, choose Selection > Grow Selection Region.

   The vertices surrounding the existing selection are also selected. Repeat this step to increase the size of the selected area (**Figure 8.15**).

5. From the Edit Polygons menu, choose Selection > Shrink Selection Region.

   The region of selected vertices becomes smaller. Repeat this step to further shrink the region.

6. From the Edit Polygons menu, choose Selection > Convert Selection to Faces.

   The vertices are deselected, and the faces they surrounded are selected (**Figure 8.16**).

✔ Tips

■ A selection of any kind of polygon component can similarly be converted to edges, vertices, or UVs.

■ Some polygon-modeling tools, such as Extrude Face, work only on faces. If you've already selected the region as vertices, Convert Selection saves you the time of meticulously selecting the faces one by one in order to run this tool on the faces.

ABOUT MODELING POLYGONS

You can start a model by creating a single face using the Create Polygon tool.

To create a polygonal house using the Create Polygon tool:

1. Select Panels > Orthographic > front to switch to the front orthographic view (**Figure 8.17**).

   The orthographic view makes it easier to draw a planar face (where all the vertices of the surface fall onto one plane).

2. From the Polygons menu, choose the Create Polygon tool.

   The cursor changes to a crosshairs icon, indicating you are ready to create a polygon.

3. In the Front view, click where you want to create the first vertex in the face.

   A light green square represents the current vertex.

4. Click and hold to create the next vertex, then drag to see the connection to the previous vertex (**Figure 8.18**).

Figure 8.17
Switch to the front orthographic view.

Figure 8.18 Place the second vertex in a face using the Create Face tool.

Tris and Quads

For most of your modeling you will want your final polygonal mesh to have three-sided faces (tris) or four-sided faces (quads). Faces can also be planar or non-planar, meaning that the vertices making up the face fall into the same plane.

For example, if a playing card is a four-sided polygonal face, it is planar. If you bend it from one corner to the other corner so that it is shaped like a taco, it becomes non-planar.

Tris are always planar. Quads can be non-planar, as in the example above, but are appealing for many reasons and can easily be converted to tris.

However, when you create n-sided faces with more than four sides, the results can be unpredictable, especially if the face is non-planar or if it is being deformed. For that reason, it's best to avoid n-sided faces.

Figure 8.19 Place the third vertex to form a right angle.

Figure 8.20 Place the fourth vertex to form a square.

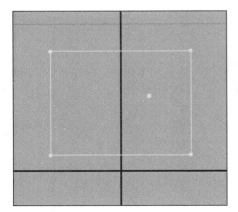

Figure 8.21 Click inside the first face created to begin creating a window.

5. Release the mouse button to finish the creation of the second vertex.

Once you've created the second vertex, click and drag to see the connection between two vertices.

6. Repeat steps 4 and 5 to create the third vertex (**Figure 8.19**).

7. Create the fourth vertex and press Enter (**Figure 8.20**).

This simple polygonal face is the first step in creating any number of models. Now let's add some "windows" to your polygonal house.

To make windows for the house:

1. Follow the previous set of steps to create a four-sided polygonal face.

2. Hold Ctrl/Control and click inside the face to create a single vertex (**Figure 8.21**).

3. Create at least three more vertices to create a square hole inside the face (**Figure 8.22**).

4. Repeat steps 2 and 3 to create another hole and press Enter.

Figure 8.22 Place the fourth vertex in a window using the Create Face tool.

ABOUT MODELING POLYGONS

When you build a polygonal model one face at a time, you need to connect those faces together by merging two vertices or edges into one. However, the polygon tools only work on components in the same mesh, so you will have to first combine the separate faces into one mesh.

Figure 8.23 Select two separate polygon meshes.

To merge vertices:

1. Select the surfaces (**Figure 8.23**) and choose Polygons > Combine. The surfaces are highlighted in one color, indicating that they are one mesh.

2. Press [F8] to switch to component mode.

3. Choose Points ▪ and select a vertex from each face (**Figure 8.24**).

    The selected vertices become yellow.

4. From the Edit Polygons menu, select the box next to Merge Vertices.

    The Merge Vertex Options dialog box opens (**Figure 8.25**).

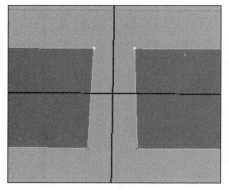

Figure 8.24 Select two vertices to merge using the Merge Vertices Tool.

5. In the Merge Vertex Options dialog box, adjust the Distance slider so that it spans the space between the selected vertices (in this case, a value of *1*).

6. Click Apply.

    The two vertices merge (**Figure 8.26**).

Figure 8.25 Set the Distance to *1* in the Merge Vertex Options dialog box.

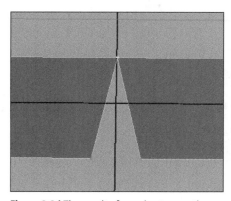

Figure 8.26 The result of merging two vertices.

Figure 8.27 The cursor changes to an arrowhead when you select the Merge Edge tool.

Figure 8.28 The potential target edges have arrows assigned to them.

Figure 8.29 The result of merging edges.

To merge edges:

1. Select the surfaces and choose Polygons > Combine.

   The surfaces are highlighted in one color, indicating that they are one mesh.

2. From the Edit Polygons menu, choose Merge Edges tool.

   The cursor changes to an arrowhead (**Figure 8.27**).

3. Click an edge of one of the faces.

   The selected edge turns tan, while violet arrow shapes appear on all of the edges that are available for merging (**Figure 8.28**).

4. Click one of the available edges and press [Enter].

   The two edges merge (**Figure 8.29**).

When you are editing a mesh, you may need to delete a face. You can simply select and delete most component types of a polygonal mesh, but if you delete a face, it usually leaves a hole. However, the Collapse tool removes the selected faces or edges and then draws the surrounding vertices into a point, without leaving a hole.

To collapse the faces of a cube:

1. From the Create menu, select Polygon Primitives > Cube.

2. Right-click the cube to open a Marking menu and select Face.

3. Click a face on the cube to highlight it (**Figure 8.30**).

4. Select Edit Polygons > Collapse.

   The selected face is removed and the remaining vertices are drawn into a single point (**Figure 8.31**).

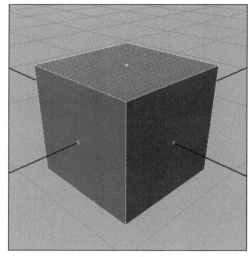

Figure 8.30 Select a face to collapse.

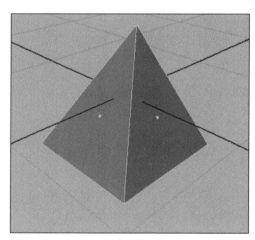

Figure 8.31 The result of collapsing the face.

Figure 8.32 Place a face to use as a hole cutout.

Figure 8.33 Select the face using the Make Hole tool.

Figure 8.34 Select the face from which to cut the hole.

Figure 8.35 The result of making the hole.

When you need to cut a hole out of another polygon, you can use a face to do so in an almost cookie cutter manner, as long as the faces involved belong to the same mesh.

To cut a hole in a cube:

1. From the Create menu, select Polygon Primitives > Cube.

2. From the Create menu, select Polygon Primitives > Plane.

3. Press ⓦ or click the Move tool icon 🔧 in the toolbar.

4. Using the Move tool, place the plane above the cube (**Figure 8.32**).

5. Select the cube and the plane and choose Polygons > Combine to combine them into a single mesh.

6. From the Edit Polygons menu, select the Make Hole tool.

   The cursor changes to an arrowhead and the mesh switches to face component mode.

7. Click the square in the middle plane to select its face as the shape for the hole (**Figure 8.33**).

   The face becomes highlighted tan.

8. Click the square in the middle of the top of the cube to select its top face as the face from which to cut the hole (**Figure 8.34**).

9. Press (Enter) to finish making the hole (**Figure 8.35**).

ABOUT MODELING POLYGONS

Extrude Face is a great way to begin constructing your surface. It allows you to pull additional geometry from the surface. You simply select a face or faces, extrude them, and then manipulate the new faces.

To extrude faces of a cube:

1. From the Create menu, select Polygon Primitives > Cube.

2. Right-click the cube and select Face from the Marking menu.

3. Marquee-select all of the faces (**Figure 8.36**).

4. From the Edit Polygons menu, select Extrude Face.

   A manipulator appears that you can use to move, rotate, and scale the new faces (**Figure 8.37**). Even though the manipulator shows up on only one face, it affects all of the faces that were just extruded. It transforms them locally, which means that they move relative to their surface normal, which is a line perpendicular to the center of each individual face.

5. Move one face out from the center of the cube with the Translate manipulator.

   All newly extruded faces move out from the center as well (**Figure 8.38**). This procedure is very helpful for creating symmetrical objects.

✔ Tips

■ When you first extrude a face, points appear on the center of each edge of the face you chose (see Figure 8.37). These points remain flat until you move or scale the selected face. Beware any time you see these points along an edge: They can cause problems later in the final rendering because you actually have two surfaces sitting directly on top of each other. To avoid this, make sure that you scale or move a face after every extrusion.

Figure 8.36 When you use marquee-select around the entire object, even the faces on the far side of the object are selected.

Figure 8.37 This manipulator appears when Edit Polygons › Extrude Face is selected.

Figure 8.38 When one face is moved outward, all of the faces move outward. When you scale with the Extrude Face tool, all of the selected faces are scaled simultaneously, relative to their centers.

ABOUT MODELING POLYGONS

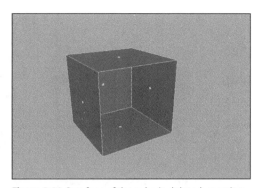

Figure 8.39 One face of the cube is deleted, creating an opening.

Figure 8.40 The edges on the left and right sides of the opening are selected.

- After extruding a face, you will often want to scale it proportionally. Simply click any of the scale manipulators, and a proportional scale manipulator will appear in the center. To rotate along a single axis, click the outside rotate manipulator, and three rotate manipulators (one for each axis) will appear.

- When you extrude more than one face at a time, Maya will extrude those faces separately. To extrude them as one piece, choose Polygons > Tool Options > Keep Faces Together.

To extrude edges:

1. From the Create menu, select Polygon Primitives > Cube.

2. Right-click the cube and select Face from the Marking menu.

3. Select a face on the side of the cube and press Delete.

   The face disappears, and you see the inside of the cube (**Figure 8.39**). (You can also delete an edge or vertex, but this does not make an opening, just a larger face defined by the edges left behind. To try this, pick some vertices and select Delete Vertex from the Edit Polygons menu.)

4. Right-click the cube and select Edge from the Marking menu.

5. Select the left edge and press Shift to select the right edge of the hole you created (**Figure 8.40**).

continues on next page

ABOUT MODELING POLYGONS

6. From the Edit Polygons menu, select Extrude Edge.

7. Move the edge out and away from the cube.

Two new faces have been created, and the cube should now look like an open box (**Figure 8.41**).

✔ Tip

■ An edge should not be shared by more than two faces. This means that you should extrude only edges that are adjacent to an opening in the polygon. Although you can do otherwise, I don't recommend it (**Figure 8.42**).

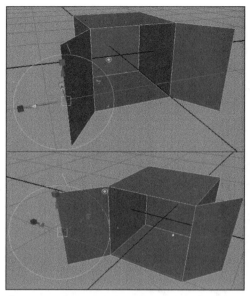

Figure 8.41 The edges have been extruded, which creates new faces. When one edge is moved, the other edge moves in the same direction for one axis but in the opposite direction for the other axis (depending on which side of the cube is removed). This figure shows two possible results.

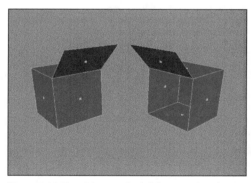

Figure 8.42 The object on the left has an edge that is shared by three faces; the object on the right does not because it has an opening in the front. It's not good construction to have an edge shared by more than two faces. One problem is that the polygon object cannot be converted to subdivision surfaces.

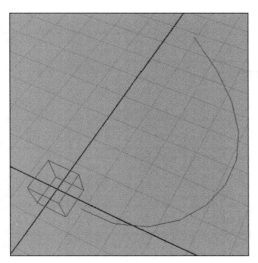

Figure 8.43 The CV curve is used as an extrusion path for the new surfaces.

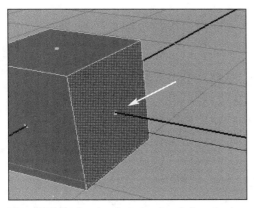

Figure 8.44 The face is selected and ready for extrusion.

Figure 8.45 The Use Selected Curve for Extrusion option is on to ensure that the extruded surfaces follow the path defined by the curve.

The Extrude Face and Extrude Edge tools allow you to extrude a selected face or edge along a predefined curve. Setting the number of divisions in the Extrude Face, or Extrude Edge options controls the number of additional polygons added for the extrusion. The higher the Divisions value, the more surface detail and curvature will be added to the final surface.

To extrude edges and faces along a path curve:

1. From the Create menu, select Polygon Primitives > Cube.

2. From the Create menu, select CV Curve Tool.

3. Create a curve that starts near the face or edge you want to extrude and stops where you want the extrusion to end (**Figure 8.43**).

4. Right-click the cube and select Face or Edge from the Marking menu.

5. Select the face or edge you want to extrude along a path (**Figure 8.44**).

6. Press [Shift] to select the curve to extrude along.

7. From the Edit Polygons menu, select the box beside Extrude Face if you have a face selected, or Extrude Edge if you have an edge selected.

   The Extrude Face or Extrude Edge Options dialog box opens.

8. Make sure that under the Other Values arrow, the Use Selected Curve for Extrusion option is on (**Figure 8.45**).

continues on next page

9. Click Apply.

The selected surface component is extruded. By default, only one division is set in the options, so the new surface goes straight from the start point on the surface to the end of the curve (**Figure 8.46**).

10. With the options dialog box still open, use the middle mouse button to click the program's title bar and then press [z] to undo the extrusion and keep the component and curve selected.

11. In the options dialog box under the Other Values arrow, change Divisions to *10* (**Figure 8.47**).

12. Click Extrude Face or Extrude Edge.

The selected face or edge is now extruded along the path curve (**Figure 8.48**).

✔ Tips

■ Changing the twist setting rotates extruded polygons as they travel along the curve.

■ Changing the Taper/Taper Curve setting scales extruded polygons as they travel along the curve (**Figure 8.49**).

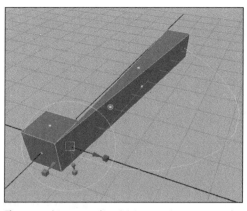

Figure 8.46 Because the Divisions option is set to *1* by default, the resulting surface is a straight extrusion.

Figure 8.47 Upping the Divisions setting to *10* gives the final extruded surface enough extra geometry to appear as though it is following along the curve.

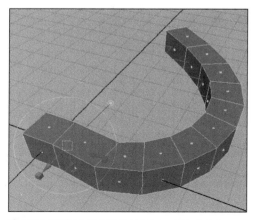

Figure 8.48 The selected face is now extruded along the path curve.

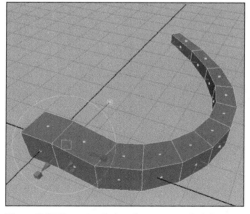

Figure 8.49 The extruded surfaces are scaled down as they get farther from the original face.

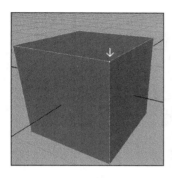

Figure 8.50
The corner vertex is selected in preparation for the extrusion.

Figure 8.51 The Extrude Length setting determines how far the selected vertex will be moved away from the surface.

Figure 8.52 A pyramid-like shape is created when the vertex is extruded.

Figure 8.53 Divisions is set to *2*, creating additional surface geometry on the extrusion.

The Extrude Vertex tool is a great addition to the Maya polygon toolset. The Extrude Vertex tool creates additional polygons around the selected vertex in a pyramid-like shape, moving the vertex away from the surface at a user-defined length.

To extrude faces from a vertex:

1. From the Create menu, select Polygon Primitives > Cube.

2. Right-click the cube and select Vertex from the Marking menu.

3. Select the vertex you want to extrude (**Figure 8.50**).

4. From the Edit Polygons menu, select the box next to Extrude Vertex.
   The Extrude Vertex options opens.

5. Set Extrude Length to *2* (**Figure 8.51**).
   The Extrude Length setting determines how far the selected vertex will be moved away from the surface.

6. Click Extrude Vertex.
   The vertex is extruded, and additional faces are created to produce a pyramid-like shape (**Figure 8.52**).

✔ Tips

■ Changing the Extrude Width setting adjusts the percentage of supporting edges used to create the extrusion, making the pyramid-like shape wider.

■ Changing the Divisions setting to a higher number divides the extruded surface into additional polygons (**Figure 8.53**).

ABOUT MODELING POLYGONS

The Split Polygon tool is used extensively in polygon modeling and has been improved in recent versions of Maya. It allows you to split one face into two or more faces along an edge that you create. You can split multiple faces simultaneously to save time.

Because of the way perspective distorts the view of an object, it can be difficult to select the center of an edge. To help you split a face in the right place, the Split Polygon tool snaps to the center of an edge, or to a user-defined point along an edge.

In general, it's best to limit yourself to three- and four-sided faces, known as triangles and quads, respectively. Quads and triangles respond more predictably to other polygon modeling tools. If a face has five or more sides, you should split it into multiple faces with fewer sides each.

To split a face:

1. From the Create menu, select Polygon Primitives > Cube.

2. From the Edit Polygons menu, select the box next to Split Polygon Tool.

   The Tool Settings dialog box opens with Split Polygon Tool options.

3. Turn on Snap to Magnets and Snap to Edge and adjust the Magnet Tolerance slider to about the middle of the range (**Figure 8.54**).

4. Click and drag along a top edge to the center.

   The point should snap to the center of the edge (**Figure 8.55**).

5. Release the mouse button.

6. Click and drag along the edge on the opposite side of the top of the cube to the center of that edge (**Figure 8.56**).

   With Snap to Edge set to on, only points along an edge can be selected.

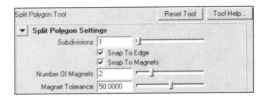

Figure 8.54 The options for the Split Polygon tool make it easy to split a polygon in halves, thirds, quarters, and so on.

Figure 8.55 Using the Split Polygon tool, you can place a point at the center of an edge.

Figure 8.56 The new edge is defined by the two points placed by the Split Polygon tool. Pressing (Enter) now completes the command. However, you could continue splitting (and go all the way around the cube) by clicking a point on one edge at a time.

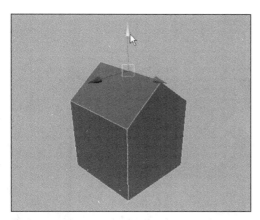

Figure 8.57 The new edge is moved up, creating a simple house shape. Note that the front of the house has five edges. More than four edges is generally considered bad construction.

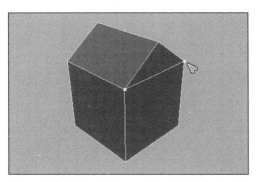

Figure 8.58 A new edge is created, splitting the front face into two separate faces.

7. Press Enter.

   The face is now split in half.

8. Right-click the cube and select Edge from the Marking menu.

9. Select the new edge you created and move it up so that the object looks like a simple house (**Figure 8.57**).

10. From the Edit Polygons menu, select Split Polygon Tool.

11. Click and drag up the left side of the cube until the point snaps to the corner. Repeat for the right side (**Figure 8.58**).

12. Press Enter.

    Now the five-sided face, which formed the front of the house, is split into a three-sided face and a four-sided face.

✔ Tips

- Make sure that your split always creates an edge. If you click one edge and press Enter without successfully clicking another edge of the same face, you will put a vertex on that edge—another example of bad construction. To avoid this problem, just make sure to undo the action if the Split Polygon tool does not create a new edge.

- Snapping can make it difficult to create a split where you want. To turn off snapping, under the Split Polygon Tool options in the Tool Settings dialog box, uncheck Snap to Edge.

- You are not limited to snapping to the middle of an edge—you can snap to more than one point of an edge. If you want to split a polygon into thirds, snap to a point one-third of the way along an edge. You can enter 2 for Number of Magnets in the Split Polygon Tool options in the Tool Settings dialog box. This creates two points, evenly spaced along the edge, that the tool will snap to (Snap to Magnets must also be selected).

ABOUT MODELING POLYGONS

Splitting multiple polygons using the Split Polygon tool can be a tedious process, but the Cut Face tool can cut through a surface like a knife cutting through a block of cheese (**Figure 8.59**). To be more specific, the Cut Face tool adds edges to a poly (or an entire poly object) through a projected line that you position to your liking (**Figure 8.60**). The line is projected from the view angle of the camera, slicing through all of the selected intersecting polygons.

With the Cut Face delete option selected, one side of the cut object will be deleted. This option is useful if you later want to create an instance of the object or mirror the object to complete it (as you would the head of a character).

To slice a surface using the Cut Face tool:

1. Create a primitive polygon cube and select it.

2. From the Edit Polygons menu, select the box beside Cut Faces.

   The Polygon Cut Face Tool Options dialog box opens (**Figure 8.61**).

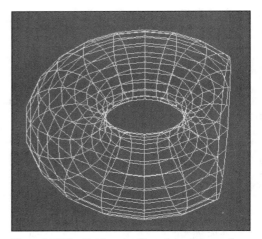

Figure 8.59 The Cut Face tool is an interactive surface-cutting tool that will either delete one side of the cut surface (shown here), or just slice the surface, leaving you with both sides.

Cutting line

Short line indicates side to be deleted

Figure 8.60 The Cut Face tool can be used to slice a piece of a surface by directing the cutting line into the exact position on the surface where you want the cut made. The short line defines which side of the cutting line will be deleted.

Figure 8.61 The Polygon Cut Face Tool Options dialog box provides many commands for cutting the surface in an exact, numeric position, or for interactively placing a cutting line. You can adjust the direction (or the plane) in which the cut is made.

Figure 8.62 You can move and rotate the cut line until it is perfectly aligned with your cut.

Figure 8.63 The cut line is projected from the selected camera angle to make a cut straight through the surface.

Figure 8.64 Deleting cut faces removes part of the original surface.

Figure 8.65 The surface on one side of the cutting line is deleted, leaving only a portion of the original surface.

3. Click Enter Cut Tool.

A line appears that is used as the cutting plane (**Figure 8.62**).

4. Click and drag the line to position the cutting plane on the surface.

5. Release the mouse to cut the surface (**Figure 8.63**).

The line is projected across the object, and cuts are made where it crosses a surface. Notice that no surfaces were deleted, just added.

6. In the Cut Face options, check the box beside Delete the Cut Faces (**Figure 8.64**).

7. Click Enter Cut Tool and Close.

The mouse icon becomes an arrow.

8. Click and drag the line across a surface to choose another cutting plane.

9. Release the mouse to cut the surface.

The surface on one side of the cutting line is deleted (**Figure 8.65**).

✔ Tips

- A short line, perpendicular to the cutting line, appears to show you which side of the line will be deleted (see Figure 8.60).

- Hold (Shift) to snap the cutting line horizontally, vertically, or at a 45-degree angle, to make a more precise cut.

- Both polygonal objects and their components can be cut. When you use the cut tools on selected faces in component mode, only those faces will be cut.

Poke Faces is another Maya tool for speeding up your polygon-modeling workflow. You can use it to subdivide a selected face, adding more detail to your model and more selection points.

The Poke Faces tool is similar to Subdivide in that it cuts the selected face into perfect triangles. However, the Poke Faces tool offers several workflow advantages, one of which is that once the surfaces have been divided, you're left with a manipulator to move the new polygons.

To poke the face of a polygon using the Poke Faces tool:

1. Create a primitive polygon cube.

2. Right-click the cube's surface and select Face from the Marking menu.

3. Select one or more faces to poke (**Figure 8.66**).

4. From the Edit Polygons menu, select Poke faces.

   Each selected face is split into four faces (**Figure 8.67**).

5. Select the manipulator and move it away from the surface.

   A pyramid-like shape appears as the manipulator is pulled away from the surface (**Figure 8.68**).

Selected face

Figure 8.66 The selected face is the face that will be split with the Poke command.

Figure 8.67 Each selected face is split into four faces, each one a perfect triangle.

Figure 8.68 The Poke tool creates a manipulator at the center point of the poked face, which is used to push the new geometry into, or pull it away from, the surface.

Figure 8.69 A wedged primitive cube.

Figure 8.70 The selected edge (top-right) defines the wedge's axis rotation point and determines the direction of the extrusion.

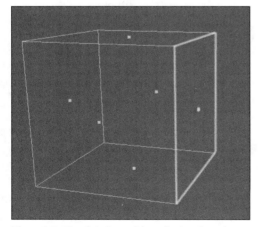

Figure 8.71 The right face of the cube is selected.

The Wedge Face tool is a variation of the Extrude Face tool. It creates angled wedges by extruding selected polygonal faces in an arc (**Figure 8.69**). This tool is a great time saver when you're creating poly surfaces that will need to be moved and rotated.

To create a wedge without using the new Wedge Face tool, you would have to extrude the faces of a surface one at a time and then rotate each into position to create the arc shape. You can perform the same task in just a few easy steps using the Wedge Face tool.

To wedge the face of a polygon:

1. Create a primitive polygon cube.

2. Right-click the surface and select Edge from the Marking menu.

3. Select a surface edge that you want the extruded surfaces to curve, or arc, around (**Figure 8.70**).

4. Right-click the surface and select Face from the Marking menu.

5. Press (Shift) to select a face of the same edge (**Figure 8.71**).

6. From the Edit Polygons menu, select Wedge Faces.

   The Polygon Wedge Face Options dialog box opens (**Figure 8.72**).

continues on next page

Figure 8.72 In the Polygon Wedge Face Options dialog box, you can set the wedge angle and the desired number of wedge divisions for the new surface.

215

7. Click Apply.

New geometry is created in an arc around the selected edge, ending 90 degrees from the original selected face (**Figure 8.73**).

8. Right-click the surface and select Edge from the Marking menu.

9. Select a surface edge of the face on the opposite side of the cube that you want the extruded surfaces to curve, or arc, around (**Figure 8.74**).

10. Right-click the surface and select Face from the Marking menu.

11. Press (Shift) to select a face of the same edge (**Figure 8.75**).

12. Change Wedge Angle to *120* and Wedge Divisions to *8*; then click Apply.

New geometry is created in an arc around the selected edge, ending 120 degrees from the original selected face and with eight divisions defining the arc (**Figure 8.76**).

Figure 8.73 New geometry is created in an arc around the selected edge, and additional polygons are created to make the wedge a smoother curve.

Figure 8.74 Surface edges become important to the Wedge command's rotation and extrusion. Select the edge you want the extrusion to wedge around.

Figure 8.75 Select the face to be arced.

Figure 8.76 You can control the arc amount by changing the Degree attribute.

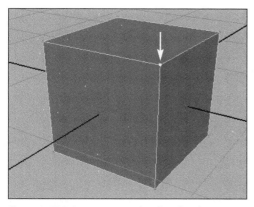

Figure 8.77 Select a vertex to be chamfered.

Edit Polygons	Subdiv Surfaces	
Texture	▶	
Subdivide		□
Split Polygon Tool		□
Extrude Face		□
Extrude Edge		□
Extrude Vertex		□
Chamfer Vertex		□
Bevel		□

Figure 8.78 Select Chamfer Vertex to chamfer the selected vertex.

The Chamfer Vertex tool removes a selected vertex and creates a chamfered corner; a three-sided polygon is created and the original vertex is removed.

To chamfer the corner of a polygon:

1. From the Create menu, select Polygon Primitives > Cube.

2. Right-click the cube and select Vertex from the Marking menu.

3. Select the vertex on the corner you want to chamfer (**Figure 8.77**).

4. From the Edit Polygons menu, select Chamfer Vertex (**Figure 8.78**).

   The corner of the polygon becomes chamfered, creating a three-sided triangle to replace the corner vertex (**Figure 8.79**).

✔ Tips

- When the Delete Faces option in the Chamfer Vertex options is on, Chamfer Vertex leaves a triangular hole for the chamfered corner, instead of creating a new face.

- Adjusting the Width option in the Chamfer Vertex options changes the distance down the edges that the chamfer runs, making the newly created triangle wider.

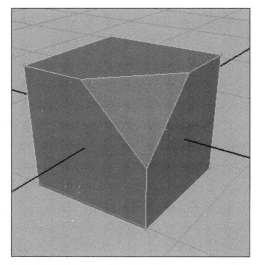

Figure 8.79 The completed chamfer.

The Bevel tool removes an edge and replaces it with an angled face. Since most real life objects do not have perfectly sharp edges, you'll probably use the Bevel tool a lot.

To bevel an edge:

1. From the Create menu, select Polygon Primitives > Cube.

2. Right-click the cube and select Edge from the Marking menu.

3. On the cube, select the edges you want to bevel (**Figure 8.80**).

4. From the Edit Polygons menu, select Bevel (**Figure 8.81**).

   The edges become beveled, creating angled faces (**Figure 8.82**).

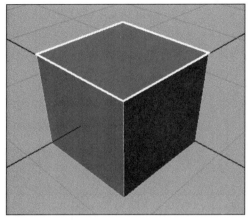

Figure 8.80 Select the edges to be beveled.

Figure 8.81 Select the Bevel command.

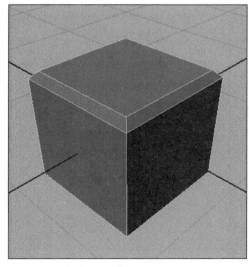

Figure 8.82 The beveled box.

Figure 8.83 Select the curves you want to bevel.

Figure 8.84 Select the Edit Polygons › Bevel command options.

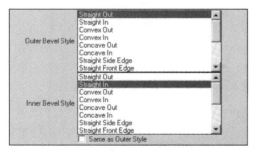

Figure 8.85 Select Straight In for the Inner Bevel Style.

You can also use the Bevel Plus tool to create objects with bevels. Bevel Plus uses curves to extrude objects and give them caps and beveled edges.

To create a beveled object with a hole:

1. Create two closed curves.

   For more information on creating NURBS primitives, see Chapter 3.

2. Select the outer curve first and the inner curve(s) next (**Figure 8.83**).

3. From the Surfaces menu, select the box next to Bevel Plus.

   The Bevel Plus Options dialog box opens (**Figure 8.84**).

4. In the Bevel tab, set the Bevel Width and Bevel Depth to *0.1* and the Extrude Distance to *0.25* .

5. From the Outer Bevel Style list, select Straight Out.

6. Uncheck the Same as Outer Style check box.

   The Inner Bevel Style list becomes active.

7. From the Inner Bevel Style list, select Straight In (**Figure 8.85**).

8. In the Output tab, select Polygons.

9. Click Apply to create the beveled object (**Figure 8.86**).

Figure 8.86 The beveled button.

The Sculpt Polygons tool allows you to manipulate polygon surfaces just as you would work with clay. Unlike the Soft Modification tool, Sculpt Polygons acts more like a brush that pushes and pulls the surface in strokes.

To sculpt polygons:

1. From the Create menu, select the box next to select Polygon Primitives > Plane.

   The Plane Options dialog box opens.

2. In the Plane Options dialog box, set the Subdivisons Along Width and Height to *50* and click Apply (**Figure 8.87**).

   A dense surface is created (**Figure 8.88**).

3. From the Edit Polygons menu, select the box next to the Sculpt Polygons tool.

   The Sculpt Surfaces/Polygons Tool dialog box opens in the Attribute Editor (**Figure 8.89**).

Figure 8.87 Set Subdivisions Along Width and Height to *50*.

Figure 8.88 Create a dense surface to sculpt.

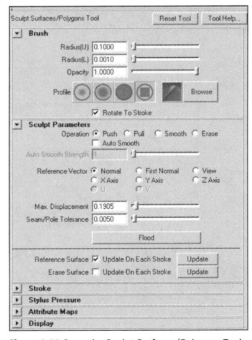

Figure 8.89 Open the Sculpt Surfaces/Polygons Tool Attribute Editor.

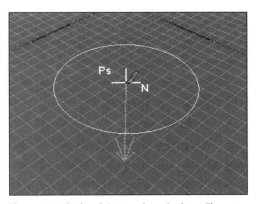

Figure 8.90 The brush icon and manipulator. The outer circle represents the size of the brush and the arrow represents the direction and amount of the effect.

Figure 8.91 Set Max. Displacement to *.4762* in the Sculpt Parameters section.

Figure 8.92 Select the second brush profile in the Brush Profiles section.

Figure 8.93 The sculpted surface.

4. Place the cursor over an active surface.

   The cursor turns to a paintbrush icon when the Sculpt Polygons tool is activated and the Sculpt Polygons brush appears when you move the cursor over a selected surface (**Figure 8.90**).

5. Hold down b and click and drag to the right to increase the size of the brush, or to the left to decrease its size.

6. In the Sculpt Parameters section of the Sculpt Surfaces/Polygons Tool dialog box, use the Max. Displacement slider to change the amount of the effect (**Figure 8.91**).

   The higher the amount, the more the surface will be displaced. It is usually best to set this value low so that it is easier to control the effect.

7. Check Pull to change the direction of the effect.

   Pull displaces the surface towards the brush, whereas Push displaces the surface away from the brush.

8. In the Brush section, choose one of the four Profile shapes to change the shape of the brush (**Figure 8.92**).

9. Drag the brush across the surface to see the effect (**Figure 8.93**).

ABOUT MODELING POLYGONS

When modeling, you often create symmetrical objects. Humans, for example, are bi-symmetrical in that one half looks like the other half, but flipped. The Mirror Geometry command will flip one half of an object so you have two symmetrical parts. That means you only have to model one half of a body, then use Mirror Geometry to make a whole person.

To mirror geometry:

1. Select the object to be mirrored (**Figure 8.94**).

2. From the Polygons menu, select the box next to Mirror Geometry.

   The Polygon Mirror Options dialog box opens (**Figure 8.95**).

3. Select a Mirror Direction of +X and click Apply.

   The model becomes two halves joined in the middle (**Figure 8.96**).

Figure 8.94
Select half
of an object.

Figure 8.95 Select +X as the Mirror Direction.

Figure 8.96 The symmetrical object.

Low-res

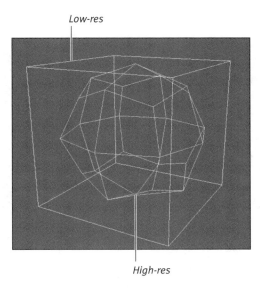

High-res

Figure 8.97 Smooth Proxy allows you to view a smooth version of your model while you work on a lower-res version. In this figure, the low-res version of the model looks like a primitive square; the high-res version looks similar to a sphere.

Low-res

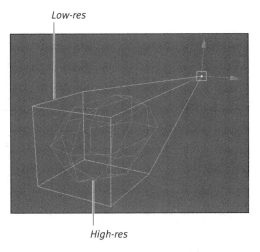

High-res

Figure 8.98 Adjusting the minimal points on the low-res surface adjusts many points on the high-res surface.

The Smooth Proxy tool is ideal for situations when you want to work on a low-res model but still want to see how the model will look when it's smoothed or converted to a subdiv surface. Using the Smooth Proxy tool, you can view a smooth version of your low-res model (just as if you had applied the Smooth command to it). The original low-res surface remains visible, allowing you to manipulate fewer points while still viewing the final smoothed shape.

When you run the Smooth Proxy command on a polygonal model, Maya creates a new layer that holds the higher-resolution proxy version—convenient for modeling because you can choose between viewing the low-res and smooth versions simultaneously or individually (by hiding one of the layers).

To facilitate surface modeling using the Smooth Proxy tool:

1. Select a polygonal object in object mode.

2. From the Polygons menu, select Smooth Proxy.

   Maya creates a new, smooth version of the model while also retaining the original. Each shape is added to its own layer; you can make one or the other layer invisible to simplify modeling (**Figure 8.97**).

3. Right-click the original object and select Vertex from the Marking menu.

4. Select and move one of the vertices.

   The high-res version of the model mirrors the manipulations of the low-res model (**Figure 8.98**).

✔ Tip

- In the Smooth Proxy options, you can set the smoothness of the high-res version of the model by changing the number of subdivisions.

The Subdivide tool splits a face into quads (four-sided faces) or triangles (three-sided faces). It provides a quick way of adding detail to your surface in the form of additional faces. These should not, however, be confused with subdivision surfaces. In this example, we'll combine the Subdivide and Extrude Face tools to create a door.

To subdivide a polygon face:

1. From the Create menu, select Polygon Primitives > Cube.

   It's common to start with a cube roughly scaled to the size of an object and then use the Edit Polygon tools to model the surface.

2. Scale the cube to the shape of a door (**Figure 8.99**).

3. Right-click the cube and select Face from the Marking menu.

4. Select the face on the front of the cube.

5. From the Edit Polygons menu, select Subdivide.

   The face splits into four faces (**Figure 8.100**).

6. From the Edit Polygons menu, select Extrude Face.

   The manipulator and new faces appear.

7. Scale the faces down a little using the Manipulator tool (**Figure 8.101**).

8. From the Edit Polygons menu, select Extrude Face again.

   The manipulator and new faces appear.

9. Scale the new faces down a little and move them in toward the middle of the object, which should now look like a door with four panels (**Figure 8.102**).

Figure 8.99 The cube is scaled to the shape of a door.

Figure 8.100 The face is subdivided into four smaller faces. To subdivide a face into more faces, select Edit Polygons > Subdivide > Options and adjust the Subdivision Levels setting.

Figure 8.101 The extruded faces are scaled down relative to their centers.

Figure 8.102 A completed four-panel door. Had the face on the opposite side of the door been selected before the Subdivide function, the exact same steps would have modeled the back side of the door simultaneously.

ABOUT MODELING POLYGONS

Figure 8.103 The Polygon Smooth Options dialog box.

Figure 8.104 The original door and the smoother door, side by side.

Polygons start out with sharp edges and corners. You can round them by using the Polygons > Smooth function, which subdivides surfaces into many smaller polygons to round out their corners and edges.

To smooth a polygon:

1. Select a polygon object, such as the door from the previous task.

2. From the Polygons menu, select Smooth.

   The Polygon Smooth Options dialog box opens (**Figure 8.103**). Higher subdivision levels in the Polygon Smooth Options dialog box create smoother objects with more faces. The Continuity setting determines how closely the new shape resembles the original (versus how rounded it is). A low Continuity setting makes the object appear more similar to the original shape; a high Continuity setting produces a very rounded shape.

3. Adjust the Subdivision Levels slider to set it to *3*.

4. Click Smooth.

   The object becomes smooth (**Figure 8.104**).

✔ Tips

- The basic structure of a polygon object should be complete before you apply the Smooth function. Smoothing produces a dense object with many faces, making it more difficult to work with.

- You can set Subdivision Levels in the Polygon Smooth Options dialog box as high as *4*; however, *3* is generally high enough (and any higher could give you a cumbersome surface due to an abundance of point information).

- You can change the level of smoothing after the function is complete by clicking polySmoothFace1, which should be at the top of the list of inputs in your Channel Box. You will then see a field labeled Divisions, which you can change from *0* (no smoothing) to *4* (very smooth) (**Figure 8.105**).

- You can smooth a portion of a polygon surface by selecting the faces of the part of the surface you want smoothed and then applying the Smooth operation (**Figure 8.106**).

Figure 8.105 The inputs in the Channel Box allow you to change the Smooth options after the function has been run. However, once additional tweaks are made to the surface, going back and changing the options in the polySmoothFace input field will produce undesirable results.

Figure 8.106 On the left, faces on the top and bottom of the object have been selected. On the right, you see the result of smoothing. The Smooth function works by selecting whole polygon objects or faces of the object; you cannot smooth by selecting vertices or edges.

Figure 8.107 A poly object with too many polygons.

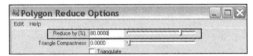

Figure 8.108 Set Reduce by (%) to the desired percentage of reduction; here, 80% is used.

Figure 8.109 The poly object now has 80% fewer polygons than before the reduction.

The Polygons > Reduce command reduces the number of faces in a selected mesh or subset of a mesh by a user-defined percentage. Keeping the polygon count as low as possible is very important in games and interactive media to keep rendering time to a minimum. The Reduce tool can help achieve this.

To reduce the number of faces in a polygonal mesh:

1. Select the polygon object or the set of faces you want to take polygons away from (**Figure 8.107**).

2. From the Polygons menu, select Reduce. The Polygon Reduce Options dialog box opens.

3. Set the Reduce by (%) field to the percentage of polygons by which you want to reduce the mesh—80%, for example (**Figure 8.108**).

4. Click Reduce.

   The polygonal mesh is reduced to 20% of the original number of polygons (**Figure 8.109**).

✔ Tip

■ If you want to keep a copy of the original, higher-res surface, select Keep Original in the Polygon Reduce Options dialog box.

Working with Vertex Normals

All surfaces have normals, but Polygons give you a great deal of control over them. Normals tell the renderer how to shade the surface. The direction and angle of a normal determines how hard or soft to render the edge between two faces.

To display vertex normals:

1. Select the polygon object.

2. From the Display menu, select the box next to Custom Polygon Display.

   The Custom Polygon Display Options dialog box opens (**Figure 8.110**).

3. In the Vertices section, check Normals and click Apply.

   The selected object displays the vertex normals with lines pointing from the vertices (**Figure 8.111**).

By controlling the angle of the vertex normal, you can make a low resolution surface look smoother than it actually is.

To soften vertex normals:

1. Create a polygon sphere by selecting Create > Polygon Primitives > Sphere.

2. Press ⑤ to switch to shaded mode.

3. From the Polygon menu, choose Edit > Normals and select the box next to Soften/Harden.

   The Polygon Soften/Harden Edge Options dialog box opens (**Figure 8.112**).

Figure 8.110 Use the Custom Polygon Display Options dialog box to display vertex normals.

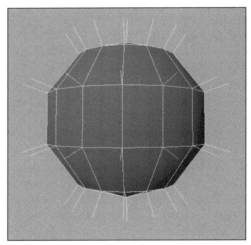

Figure 8.111 The selected object displays the vertex normals with lines pointing from the vertices.

Figure 8.112 Change the appearance of your object in the Polygon Soften/Harden Edge Options dialog box.

WORKING WITH VERTEX NORMALS

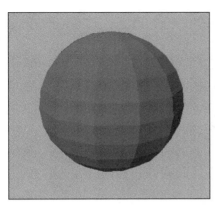

Figure 8.113 Click All Hard (0) to make the sphere look a little like the Death Star.

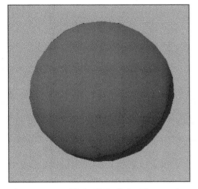

Figure 8.114 Click All Soft (180) to make the sphere look smooth again.

Figure 8.115 The Edit Vertex Normal tool manipulator appears on the selected vertex and is ready to be rotated.

4. Click All Hard (0) and then click Apply.

The sphere now has the appearance of a harder surface (**Figure 8.113**)

5. Click All Soft (180) and then click Apply.

The sphere now has the appearance of a smooth surface again (**Figure 8.114**).

The Vertex Normal Edit Tool lets you manually edit individual vertex normals, giving you precise control over the shading of a face.

To edit a vertex normal:

1. Select the polygon object.

2. Press ⑤ to switch to shaded mode.

3. Press F8 to switch to component mode and select Points ▣.

4. Select a single vertex to edit.

5. From the Edit Polygons menu, choose Normals > Vertex Normal Edit Tool.

The vertex normals are displayed on the selected object and the Vertex Normal Edit Tool manipulator appears (**Figure 8.115**).

6. Click one of the manipulator circles and drag it to rotate the vertex normal (**Figure 8.116**).

As you rotate the vertex, you will see the change in shading on the surface.

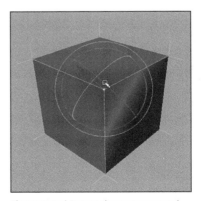

Figure 8.116 Rotate the vertex normal.

If you see diamond-shaped black areas on a mesh, that probably means that your vertex normals are locked or won't respond to attempts to soften them. To solve this, you need to unlock the vertex normal.

To unlock vertex normals:

1. Select the polygon object (**Figure 8.117**).

2. Press [5] to switch to shaded mode.

3. Press [F8] switch to component mode and select Points [■].

4. Select the locked vertex or vertices.

5. From the Edit Polygons menu, choose Normals and select the box next to Set Vertex Normal.

   The Set Vertex Normal Options dialog box opens (**Figure 8.118**).

6. Check Unlock Normals and click Apply.

   The normals return to a default orientation (**Figure 8.119**).

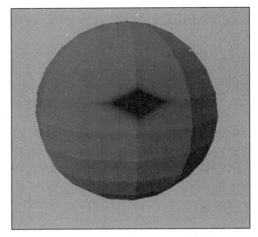

Figure 8.117 Locked normals appear as black diamond shapes on a surface.

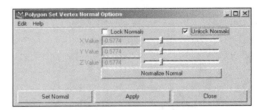

Figure 8.118 Check Unlock in the Polygon Set Vertex Normals Options dialog box.

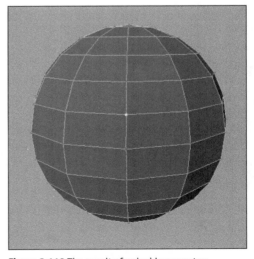

Figure 8.119 The result of unlocking a vertex.

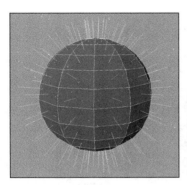

Figure 8.120
Face normals project from the center of each face in a polygon object.

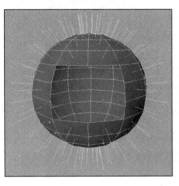

Figure 8.121
Select a double-sided object.

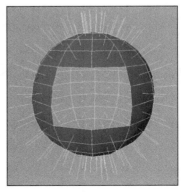

The face normal determines which side of the surface to render.

To display face normals:

1. Select the polygon object.

2. From the Display menu, select Polygon Components > Normals.

   The face normals are displayed as perpendicular lines pointing up from the center of each face (**Figure 8.120**).

By default, Maya creates double-sided polygons. If you create a single-sided polygon, the side of the face that has the normal will be displayed. If you look at the polygon from the other side, you see right through it. This is also referred to as Backface Culling.

To make a mesh single sided:

1. Press 5 to switch to shaded mode.

2. Select the polygon object (**Figure 8.121**).

3. Press Ctrl / Control a to open the Attribute Editor for the selected object.

4. In the Render Stats section, uncheck Doubled Sided (**Figure 8.122**).

   The object updates and only one side of the object's surface is visible (**Figure 8.123**).

Figure 8.122 Uncheck Double Sided in the polygon's Attribute Editor.

Figure 8.123
You can see through the back face of a single-sided surface.

WORKING WITH VERTEX NORMALS

Whether you are working with single- or double-sided polygons, it is important that normals on the same mesh all point in the same direction. However, normals on one surface might not face the same direction as those on another surface to which you are attaching. When this happens, many Maya functions will not behave as expected. To correct this, select the offending faces and reverse their face normal.

To reverse a face normal:

1. Select the polygon object.

2. Display the face normals for the object as described above.

   The face normals project from the centers of all the faces (**Figure 8.124**).

3. From the Edit Polygons menu, select Normals > Reverse.

   The face normals now project in the opposite direction (**Figure 8.125**).

✔ Tip

- You can set Maya to create single-sided polygonal surfaces by selecting Polygons > Tool Options > Create Meshes Single Sided.

- All of the above normal tools can be applied to an entire object or just to selected faces, and many of these tools will also work on selected vertices, faces, and edges.

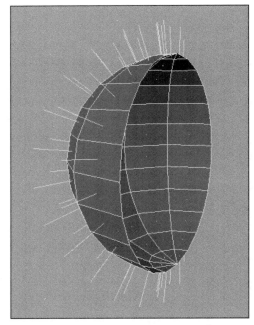

Figure 8.124 The face normals point outward...

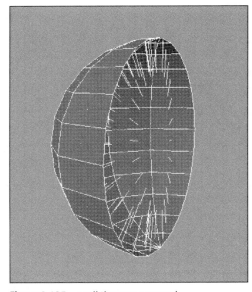

Figure 8.125 ... until they are reversed.

SUBDIV
SURFACES

Figure 9.1 This odd creature is called a Huffer. It was designed by Roy Miles and modeled by Andrew Britt using subdivision surfaces. Left, polygon mode; right, standard mode with vertices visible; top, standard mode with no components visible.

Figure 9.2 These are two copies of a subdivision cylinder. The one on the left is at display level-0, and the one on the right is at display level-1.

Subdivision surface modeling—also known as subdiv modeling or sub-Ds—combines NURBS and polygons and has two modeling modes: standard and polygon. In polygon mode, you can use all of the polygon tools on the surface. In standard mode, you work primarily with vertices, which act similarly to NURBS control vertices (CVs). But subdiv surfaces in standard mode also have edges and faces, similar to a polygon. Standard mode gives you the unique capability of moving between display levels—that is, different levels of detail. This allows you to move back and forth between low and high levels of detail on an object (**Figure 9.1**).

In polygon mode, you see the edges of a polygon shape surrounding a smooth surface, which is the subdiv surface. In this mode, all of the components are the same as in any other polygon.

Standard mode includes a different set of components, which can be manipulated at different display levels. Note that subdiv surfaces, like NURBS surfaces, have smoothness levels of rough, medium, and fine that can be activated by the 1, 2, and 3 keys, respectively (**Figure 9.2**). However, these should not be confused with display levels, which actually make the surface more complex.

Subdiv Surface Components

Subdiv surfaces have four types of components in standard mode: face, vertex, UV, and edge.

◆ A **face** generally appears offset from the subdiv surface. It can have three or more sides; however, the most efficient subdiv surfaces have four sides. The number in the center indicates the display level (**Figure 9.3**).

◆ A **vertex** generally appears offset from the surface. It is represented by the number of the display level it occupies. When moved, the vertex controls the area of surface nearest to it (**Figure 9.4**).

◆ **UVs** are points that turn green when selected (**Figure 9.5**). They are used for texturing, not modeling. See Chapter 15, "Shaders, Materials, and Mapping."

◆ An **edge** is one border of a face (**Figure 9.6**).

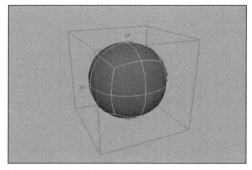

Figure 9.3 This subdiv surface sphere is at display level-0 and has its faces displayed.

Figure 9.4 A subdiv vertex, at display level-1, has been moved. The surface responds much as a NURBS surface responds to movement of a control vertex.

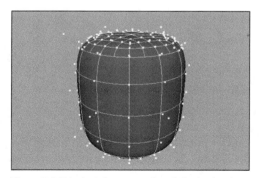

Figure 9.5 UVs don't have associated display levels. Thus, they show up as points, not numbers.

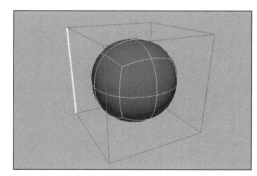

Figure 9.6 An edge of the sphere is selected in standard mode.

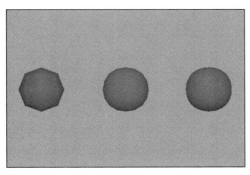

Figure 9.7 From left to right, Rough, Medium, and Fine Subdiv Smoothness settings.

Figure 9.8 To access the Marking menu for subdiv surfaces, right-click the sphere's surface. Much of what is needed to work with subdiv surfaces is right here.

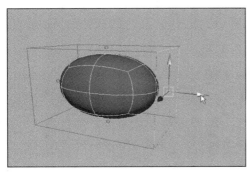

Figure 9.9 A face is moved, and the sphere is elongated.

To select a subdiv surface component:

1. From the Create menu, select Subdiv Primitives > Sphere.

2. Press ③ to select the Fine level of subdiv surface display smoothness (**Figure 9.7**).

   The surface should appear smoother in the view. Changing these settings does not affect the construction of the model, just its display.

3. Right-click the sphere and select Face from the Marking menu that appears (**Figure 9.8**).

   The faces should now appear surrounding the sphere.

4. Select and move the face (**Figure 9.9**).

Sculpting Subdiv Surfaces

Subdiv surfaces let you move back and forth between different levels of detail.

◆ **Display level**—Subdiv surface objects have different display levels—that is, different levels of refinement. This means that you can work with many points close together on the surface that affect only a small area, or with fewer points farther apart on a surface that affect a large area. You can move back and forth between these levels (**Figure 9.10**). Level-0 is your base mesh. It's the first level on which you will work since it's where all the polygonal components exist. These components can only be adjusted using the polygon tool set in polygon mode. When you start adding detail to your model, the subdivision edits (which have their own tools and workflows and are available in standard mode) go on subsequent levels—level-1, level-2, level-3, and so on.

◆ **Refine**—This function gives the selected area of the surface a higher level of detail. If the surface is at level-1, Refine will show the selected area with level-2 points.

◆ **Finer and Coarser**—These functions allow you to move quickly to a higher (Finer) or lower (Coarser) level of detail.

To change display levels on a subdiv surface:

1. From the Create menu, select Subdiv Primitives > Cylinder.

2. Press ③ on the keyboard to select the Fine level of subdiv surface smoothness.

3. Right-click the cylinder and select Vertex from the Marking menu.

4. Right-click the cylinder and select Display Level > 2 from the Marking menu (**Figure 9.11**).

   Many more points appear labeled as 2 (**Figure 9.12**).

Figure 9.10 A subdiv surface sphere is shown at display levels 0 (from top left), 1, 2, and 3. By default, the sphere has only levels 0 and 1. It needs to be refined to access higher levels.

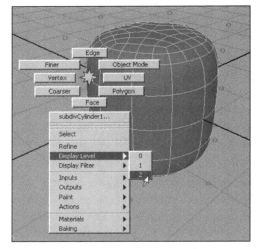

Figure 9.11 Display Level allows you to choose from any of the existing levels.

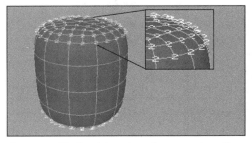

Figure 9.12 The level-2 vertices show up only on the default cylinder where detail is needed. If you need the 2s to be evenly distributed, go to display level-1 and refine.

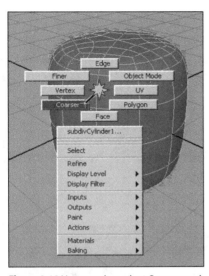

Figure 9.13 You can also select Coarser and Finer to change the display level.

Figure 9.14 The subdiv surface cylinder at display level-1.

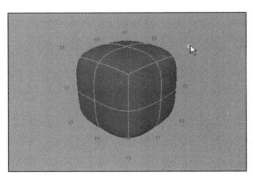

Figure 9.15 A vertex is selected to determine the area that will be refined.

5. Right-click the cylinder and select Coarser from the Marking menu (**Figure 9.13**).

The display level is reduced to 1 (**Figure 9.14**).

6. Right-click the cylinder and select Finer from the Marking menu.

The display level goes back up to 2.

To add detail to a subdiv surface:

1. From the Create menu, select Subdiv Primitives > Cube.

2. Press ③ to select the Fine level of subdiv surface smoothness.

3. Right-click the cube and select Vertex from the Marking menu.

4. Select a vertex (**Figure 9.15**).

5. Right-click the cube and select Refine from the Marking menu.

The zeros are replaced by ones in the area around the original point, and there are now more of them (**Figure 9.16**).

6. Right-click the cube and again select Refine from the Marking menu.

continues on next page

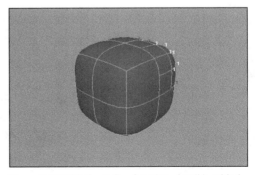

Figure 9.16 With the Refine function, detail is added only around the selected component.

7. Select and move a point (**Figure 9.17**).

8. Right-click the cube and select Display Level > 0 from the Marking menu.

9. Select and move a point (**Figure 9.18**).

The changes to the level-2 points remain while you work with level-0 points. You can move back and forth between the display levels.

✔ Tips

■ The Refine function also works with edges and faces.

■ You can refine up to a display level of 13. However, we don't recommend that you go above 3 because the speed of inter-activity decreases dramatically as the level increases.

■ You cannot delete a subdiv surface com-ponent. However, if you transform any component at a display level of 1 or higher and then try to delete it, the component will return to its original position.

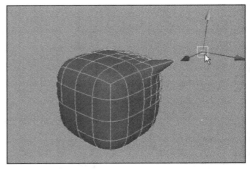

Figure 9.17 A point is selected and moved. This refined area allows tweaks to small portions of the surface.

Figure 9.18 You can tweak large portions of the surface by returning the display level to 0.

Figure 9.19 The sphere is scaled flatter to resemble a turtle shell.

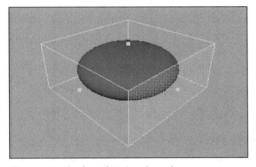

Figure 9.20 The front face is selected.

Working in Polygon Mode

Subdiv surfaces can speed the modeling process because you can choose between viewing the surface in high-res with many points or low-res with just a few points. If you know how to model polygons, you can model a subdiv surface as well because they use many of the same tools.

While standard mode is good for adding fine details, polygon mode is essential for creating the basic structure of the surface. One common tactic is to model a polygon to get the rough form and then convert it to subdiv surfaces. This approach is helpful because it lets you work quickly, and the polygon primitive cube has a simpler construction than the subdiv primitive cube.

It's good practice to finish all of the manipulation you plan to do in polygon mode before you begin refining the surface in standard mode. This is because you can lose changes made to the surface if you frequently switch between modes.

To model a turtle out of subdiv surfaces using polygon mode:

1. From the Create menu, select Subdiv Primitives > Sphere.

2. Press ③ to select the Fine level of subdivision surface smoothness.

3. Scale the sphere down the *Y* axis to make it flatter (**Figure 9.19**).

4. Right-click the sphere and select Polygon from the Marking menu.
   A rectangular polygon shell appears around the sphere.

5. Right-click the sphere and select Face from the Marking menu. Select the face on the front side of the polygon (**Figure 9.20**).

continues on next page

WORKING IN POLYGON MODE

6. From the Edit Polygons menu, select Extrude Face. Scale the face down (**Figure 9.21**).

7. From the Edit Polygons menu, select Extrude Face again. Move the face forward and up (**Figure 9.22**).

This will be the neck of the turtle.

8. From the Edit Polygons menu, select Extrude Face again. Proportionally scale the face up (**Figure 9.23**).

9. From the Edit Polygons menu, select Extrude Face again. Move the face forward (**Figure 9.24**).

This will be the head of the turtle.

Figure 9.21 The face is scaled down. To get the Proportional scale manipulator in the center, click any of the other scale manipulators.

Figure 9.22 The neck is formed by moving the face out and up.

Figure 9.23 The scale of this face determines the size of the back of the turtle's head.

Figure 9.24 Move this face forward to give the head some length.

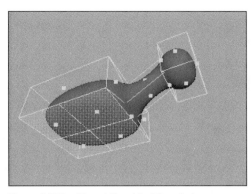

Figure 9.25 Looking at the object from below, you can see that the bottom has been subdivided.

Figure 9.26 The bases of the legs are scaled down simultaneously.

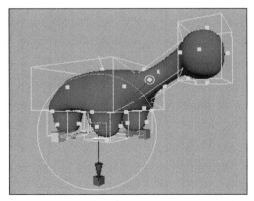

Figure 9.27 Move these faces down to determine the length of the legs. A simple turtle shape is completed.

10. Select the face on the bottom of the sphere.

11. From the Edit Polygons menu, select Subdivide (**Figure 9.25**).

12. From the Edit Polygons menu, select Extrude Face and proportionally scale the faces smaller (**Figure 9.26**).

13. From the Edit Polygons menu, select Extrude Face again and move the faces down (**Figure 9.27**).

You've created a turtle!

To model a subdiv telephone receiver, starting with a polygon:

1. From the Create menu, select Polygon Primitives > Cube.

2. Scale down the cube in the *Z* direction so that it is flatter. Scale it down in the *X* direction so that it is narrower (**Figure 9.28**).

3. Right-click the cube and select Face from the Marking menu.

4. Select the top face of the cube.

5. From the Edit Polygons menu, select Extrude Face and move the face up to double the height (**Figure 9.29**).

6. From the Edit Polygons menu, select Extrude Face again. Move the top face up so that you have three equal faces on the front of the object (**Figure 9.30**).

7. Select the top and bottom faces of the front of the object.

Figure 9.28 The polygon cube is scaled flatter and narrower.

Figure 9.29 The height of the object is doubled by extruding the top face.

Figure 9.30 The three faces on the front of the object should be about equal.

Figure 9.31 Move out the extruded faces to form the earpiece and mouthpiece of the telephone receiver.

Figure 9.32 The telephone receiver before conversion to subdiv surfaces. The mode has been switched from pick mask to object.

8. From the Edit Polygons menu, select Extrude Face and move the faces along the Z axis (**Figure 9.31**).

9. Press F8 to switch the pick mask mode to object mode (**Figure 9.32**). The object should be selected.

10. From the Modify menu, select Convert > Polygons to Subdiv (**Figure 9.33**). You've created a simple telephone receiver (**Figure 9.34**).

✔ Tips

■ You can turn subdiv surfaces back into polygons by choosing Modify > Convert > Subdiv to Polygons.

■ You can convert a NURBS surface to a subdiv surface by selecting Modify > Convert > NURBS to Subdiv. Whether you're converting from NURBS or polygons, you should always start with a simple surface. An already-dense surface converted to subdivs will prove very difficult to work with because of the number of points created by the conversion.

Figure 9.33 Select Modify > Convert > Polygons to Subdiv.

Figure 9.34 The subdiv telephone receiver's surfaces are smooth and rounded.

WORKING IN POLYGON MODE

Using the Crease Tools

Subdiv surfaces tend to be smooth all around. To get flatter areas and sharp edges, Maya has provided the Crease tools.

To add a partial crease:

1. Create the telephone receiver according to the instructions in the previous exercise.

   Be sure you are in standard mode. (From the Subdiv Surfaces menu, select Standard Mode.) The remaining steps will not work in polygon mode.

2. Right-click the surface and select Edge from the Marking menu.

3. Select the eight edges that form a cube around the top part of the telephone receiver (**Figure 9.35**).

4. From the Subdiv Surfaces menu, select Partial Crease Edge/Vertex (**Figure 9.36**).

5. Repeat steps 3 and 4 for the mouthpiece of the telephone receiver.

   The mouthpiece and earpiece of the receiver now have a flatter, more squared look (**Figure 9.37**).

Figure 9.35 With the camera lined up correctly, you can use marquee-selection to easily select several edges at once.

Figure 9.36 Note that in addition to creasing edges from this menu, you can uncrease them by selecting Uncrease Edge/Vertex.

Figure 9.37 This is the resulting telephone receiver after using partial crease on the top and mouthpiece.

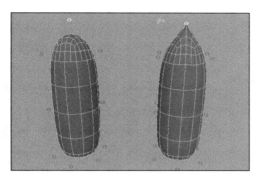

Figure 9.38 Left, the point has been moved up. Right, the surface has a point on top from the Full Crease function.

Figure 9.39 Carefully select four evenly spaced points from the bottom of the surface. It helps to tumble around the camera to be sure the right points are selected.

Figure 9.40 The points are moved down, and proportionally scaling them moves them out from the center. They now form the legs of a simple rocket ship.

To add a full crease to vertices:

1. From the Create menu, select Subdiv Primitives > Cylinder.

2. Scale the surface along the Y axis so that it's about three times the original length.

3. Right-click the surface of the cylinder and select Vertex from the Marking menu.

4. Select the point in the middle of the top and move it up.

5. From the Subdiv Surfaces menu, select Full Crease Edge/Vertex.

   The top point becomes sharp (**Figure 9.38**).

6. Marquee-select the bottom row of points and scale them in.

7. With those points still selected, right-click the surface; select Refine from the Marking menu.

8. Select four evenly spaced points on the bottom of the surface (**Figure 9.39**).

9. From the Subdiv Surfaces menu, select Full Crease Edge/Vertex.

10. Move the points down and scale them out.

    You have created a simple rocket ship (**Figure 9.40**).

To add a full crease to edges:

1. Using the rocket in the previous task, "To add a full crease to vertices" (**Figure 9.41**), right-click the surface and select Edge from the Marking menu.

2. Right-click the surface and select Display Level > 0.

3. Right-click the surface and select Edge from the marking menu that appears.

4. Select all of the vertical edges.

   To avoid selecting horizontal edges, marquee-select the vertical edges at the bottom, then Shift-select those at the middle, and finally Shift-select those at the top (**Figure 9.42**).

5. From the Subdiv Surfaces menu, select Full Crease Edge/Vertex.

   Your rocket now has sharp edges (**Figure 9.43**).

✔ Tip

- You can remove a crease by selecting the edge that the crease is on and choosing Uncrease Edge/Vertex from the Subdiv Surfaces menu.

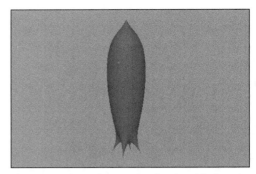

Figure 9.41 This is the completed rocket ship from the previous task.

Figure 9.42 By Shift-selecting the vertical edges one bunch at a time, you can avoid selecting the horizontal edges.

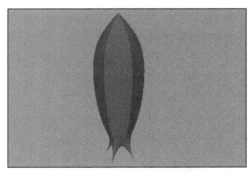

Figure 9.43 The edges of the rocket ship are sharp, giving it a more interesting shape.

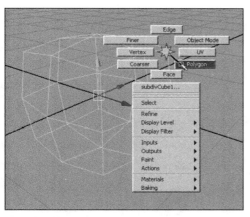

Figure 9.44 Select Polygon from the Marking menu.

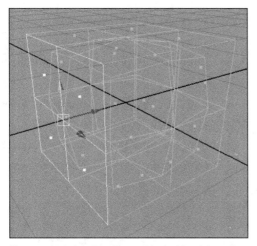

Figure 9.45 Select four faces on one side of the cube.

Mirroring Subdiv Services

When you are making symmetrical models, you can use the Mirror command to copy and flip the subdiv surface.

To mirror a subdiv surface:

1. From the Create menu, select Polygon Primitives > Cube.

2. Right-click the cube and select Polygon from the Marking menu (**Figure 9.44**).

3. Press F8 to switch to component mode.

4. Click the Faces icon ⬦ and select all four faces on one side of the cube (**Figure 9.45**).

continues on next page

5. Press [Delete] to remove the faces.

The subdiv surface will now be open on one end (**Figure 9.46**).

6. Select the Subdiv Surface and then select the box next to Mirror in the Subdiv Surfaces menu.

The Subdiv Mirror Options dialog box opens (**Figure 9.47**).

7. Select X to mirror the object across that axis and click Apply.

A flipped copy of the surface is created (**Figure 9.48**).

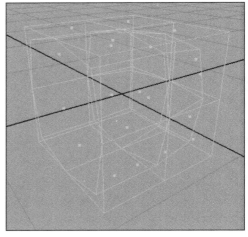

Figure 9.46 The deleted faces create an open-ended subdiv surface.

Figure 9.47 For Mirror, choose X in the Subdiv Mirror Options dialog box.

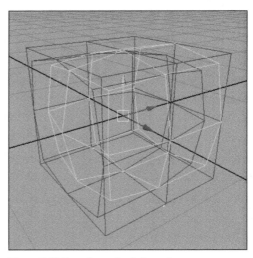

Figure 9.48 The mirrored subdiv surface.

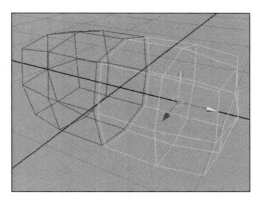

Figure 9.49 Place the openings of the surfaces that you want to attach near one another.

Figure 9.50 Set the Threshold to 5 in the Subdiv Attach Options dialog box.

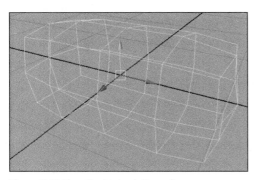

Figure 9.51 The attached subdiv surface.

When your model is made up of many separate pieces, you can use the Attach command to join them as one piece. However, any edges you attach must have the same number of vertices.

To attach two subdiv surfaces:

1. Arrange the surfaces from the previous task, "To mirror a subdiv surface," so that their openings are near one another (**Figure 9.49**).

2. Select both surfaces.

3. From the Subdiv Surfaces menu, select the box next to Attach.

   The Subdiv Attach Options dialog box opens (**Figure 9.50**).

4. Set the Threshold amount to 5 to close the gap between the surfaces.

5. Click Apply.

   The two surfaces become one surface (**Figure 9.51**).

Collapsing the Hierarchy

As you model, you start off simple, add details until your model is more complex, then collapse the mesh and start on the next level of complexity. Collapsing lets you convert your subdivision changes to polygonal components that can be edited in polygon mode with the polygon tool set. By collapsing the mesh, your model becomes more complex, but you get more editing possibilities.

The Collapse Hierarchy command reduces the number of levels in a subdiv surface. Collapse Hierarchy lets you specify the number of levels you wish to collapse and moves the edits from those levels to the level above.

To collapse subdiv hierarchy:

1. From the Create menu, select Polygon Primitives > Cube.

2. Right-click the cube and select Face from the Marking Menu (**Figure 9.52**).

3. Select a face on one side of the cube (**Figure 9.53**).

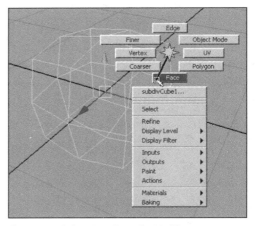

Figure 9.52 Select Face from the Marking menu.

Figure 9.53 Select a face.

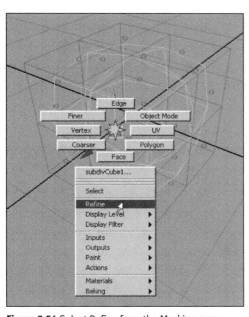

Figure 9.54 Select Refine from the Marking menu.

4. Right-click the cube and select Refine from the Marking menu (**Figure 9.54**).

This adds a level-1 to the mesh (**Figure 9.55**).

5. Right-click and select Polygon from the Marking menu.

Notice that the polygon cage does not show the detail that was created by adding level-1 (**Figure 9.56**).

continues on next page

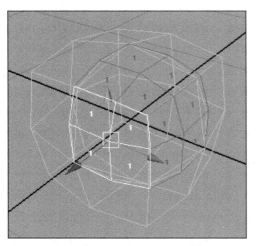

Figure 9.55 By refining the face, you've added a level to the model.

Figure 9.56 Polygon mode does not show the added detail of level-1.

COLLAPSING THE HIERARCHY

6. From the Subdiv Surfaces menu, select the box next to Collapse Hierarchy.

The Subdiv Collapse Options dialog box opens (**Figure 9.57**).

7. Set the Number of Levels to *1* and click Apply.

A collapsed copy of the selected surface is made (**Figure 9.58**).

8. Right-click the cube and select Polygon from the Marking menu (**Figure 9.59**).

Notice that the polygon cage now shows the detail that was created by adding level-1 and that the overall cage is much more dense (**Figure 9.60**).

✔ Tip

■ Maya's Mental Ray Renderer only renders Subdiv Surfaces that are quadralateral. This means that all the faces involved in the mesh may only have four sides. Maya's renderer, however, will render non-quadralateral subdiv surfaces. Collapse Hierarchy will fix non-quad subdivs so that Mental Ray will render them.

Figure 9.57 Set the Number of Levels to *1* in the Subdiv Collapse Options dialog box.

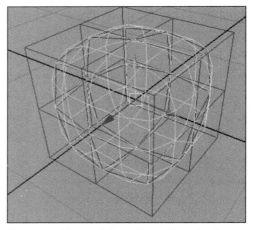

Figure 9.58 After applying Collapse Hierarchy, the surface now has the level-1 detail in level-0.

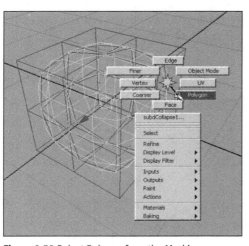

Figure 9.59 Select Polygon from the Marking menu.

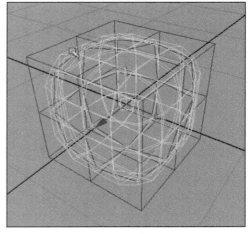

Figure 9.60 The new surface allows the detail that was in level-1 to be edited in polygon mode.

SKELETONS AND INVERSE KINEMATICS

Once you model a character, you need to place a skeleton inside it in order to animate it. The skeleton is built as a hierarchy of individual joints connected by bones.

In general, nature serves as the best template for placing joints: Use pictures of skeletons, human or animal (**Figure 10.1**). A shoulder joint should go at the shoulder; an elbow joint should go at the elbow; and so on. However, you don't need to be too literal. For example, although the human foot has 26 bones, you can animate a shoe with three bones. Wherever you want something to bend, that's where you need a joint.

Figure 10.1 Inside this eyeball character you can see the skeleton, which is used to pose and animate the character.

Joints are hierarchical—that is, the joints at the top of the hierarchy will move those beneath them. The first joint you place will be at the top of the hierarchy and is often referred to as the *root joint*. This is the joint that moves the whole skeleton. Because the knee, ankle, and foot joints are below the hip joint, the rest of the leg moves when the hip joint is rotated. Animating in this fashion is called *forward kinematics* (FK) (**Figure 10.2**).

Inverse kinematics, or IK, refers to animating from the bottom of the hierarchy up. In this type of animation, if you moved the foot around, the knee and hip would rotate accordingly (**Figure 10.3**).

Figure 10.2 Illustrating the principle of forward kinematics, when the hip joint is rotated, all of the joints below rotate with it.

Figure 10.3 The foot is moved using an IK handle. Some animators avoid IK because it tends to move limbs in straight lines rather than natural arcs.

FK or IK?

New animators always wonder which is better—FK or IK? The answer is that they both have advantages and weaknesses.

Forward kinematics allows for very precise and mechanical motion but require more effort from the animator because each joint in a chain has to be animated.

Inverse kinematics is great for bipedal and quad pedal creatures like humans or dogs because you can place the hand, foot, or paw of the character by animating the handle rather than adjusting each joint in the skeleton. However, IK handles can flip and getting precise movement out of the intermediate joints can be difficult.

Spline IKs (discussed later in this chapter) are good for tentacles and spinal columns or any skeleton that has many joints that need to move in a fluid, organic manner.

A complex character will employ all of these methods to give the animator the greatest amount of freedom and control.

SKELETONS AND INVERSE KINEMATICS

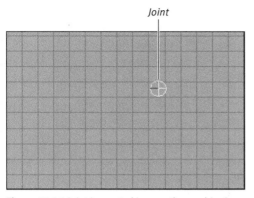

Joint

Figure 10.4 A joint is created in an orthographic view by selecting Skeleton > Joint Tool.

Figure 10.5 The second joint is created. A bone appears between the two joints, demonstrating that they are parented together. The bone is thicker at the parent joint than at the child joint.

About Joints

When you create joints, the bones appear automatically between the joints. The order in which you create joints is important: The first joint that's created resides at the top of the hierarchy; the second joint is parented to the first (making it a child of that joint and forcing it to follow the parent's movement); the third is parented to the second; and so on down the line.

A joint is like a pivot point in a hierarchy. You can't take a joint's pivot point away; the joint always remains with its pivot point. A joint's position in the hierarchy determines which joints will rotate with it: The joints below it rotate with that joint; the joints above it are not affected by that joint's movements. Don't confuse this hierarchy with joints that are above or below each other *physically:* One joint can be above another in the *Y* direction but below it within the hierarchy.

To create joints:

1. From the Skeleton menu, select Joint Tool.

2. In the Side view, click to place the joint.
   You should generally use an orthographic view when you create joints (**Figure 10.4**).

3. Click where you want the next joint to be placed.
   A bone appears between the two joints (**Figure 10.5**).

4. Click and drag to place the third joint. When you release the mouse button, the joint will be placed.

5. Press (Enter).
   The skeleton is complete, and you're no longer in the Joint tool. The top joint of the hierarchy is selected, which causes the whole skeleton to be highlighted.

continues on next page

ABOUT JOINTS

✔ Tips

- It's often a good idea to build a skeleton with grid snap turned on so that all your joints are securely aligned. A convenient way to do this is by holding down $\boxed{\text{X}}$ when you place joints.

- You can make the joints appear bigger or smaller by selecting Display > Joint Size and choosing a size from the list.

- To delete a joint, select the joint and then press $\boxed{\text{Del}}$. That joint will be deleted, along with any joints below it in the hierarchy.

Often you'll want to branch off from a joint in the hierarchy. For example, both arms branch off from the chest joint.

To branch off from an existing skeleton:

1. Using the skeleton from the previous task, "To create joints," click the Joint tool icon .

2. Click the joint from which you want to branch off.

    This will *select* the joint, not create a new one.

3. Click where you want the new joint to be placed.

    A new joint appears with the bone branched off from the original skeleton (**Figure 10.6**).

4. From the Window menu, select Hypergraph to view the resulting hierarchy.

    Note that two joints are at the same level in the hierarchy, both parented under the same joint (**Figure 10.7**).

Figure 10.6 A new joint branches off from the existing joints.

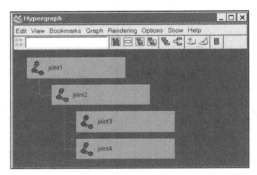

Figure 10.7 Joint3 and joint4 are both children of joint2. That means that if joint2 is rotated, joint3 and joint4 will rotate with it.

Figure 10.8 This is a typical leg skeleton. Starting from the top, the joints are named hip, knee, ankle, ball, and toe. If the character is wearing shoes, you don't need bones for each toe; one bone is sufficient to rotate the front of the shoe.

Figure 10.9 A spine joint is created from the bottom up. This makes the bottom joint the parent of the rest of the spine. The rest of the joints are beneath it in the hierarchy even though they are above it in space.

Figure 10.10 The leg has been parented to the spine. Now the bottom joint of the skeleton is the root joint for the whole character. When this joint is moved, the whole character moves.

You can think of bones as a visual representation of your skeleton's joint hierarchy. When you parent one joint to another, a bone appears. If you unparent a joint, the bone disappears. Sometimes it's easier to create separate hierarchies and then place them inside a single skeleton by parenting them.

To parent joints:

1. Create the skeleton of a leg and foot out of five joints in the Side view (**Figure 10.8**).

   Press (Enter) to complete the creation.

2. As a separate hierarchy, create spine joints in the Side view, starting from the bottom and working your way up (**Figure 10.9**).

3. In the Front view, move the leg to the side.

4. Select the top joint of the leg and then (Shift)-select the bottom joint of the spine. Now press (p).

   A bone appears between the leg and the spine. It is now one hierarchy (**Figure 10.10**).

✔ Tip

- You can similarly unparent joints. Select the joint you want to unparent and press (Shift) (p). The joint becomes unparented, and the bone disappears.

To save time, once you create a leg or arm, you can mirror the joint, which makes a duplicate leg or arm appear on the other side of the body.

To mirror joints:

1. Using the leg from the previous task, "To parent joints," select the hip joint (**Figure 10.11**).

2. From the Skeleton menu, select the box next to Mirror Joint.

   The Mirror Joint Options dialog box opens.

3. For Mirror Across, select YZ (**Figure 10.12**).

4. Click Mirror.

   A new leg appears on the other side (**Figure 10.13**).

✔ Tips

■ If the leg was built in the Side view, you should mirror it across the *YZ* plane. To figure out which plane you should use, look at the view axis in the corner of the panel and imagine two of the axes forming a plane that you want to mirror across. If the new leg does not appear in the correct location, undo the mirror joint and try choosing a different plane to mirror across in the Mirror Joint Options dialog box.

■ Don't mirror a joint that falls on the center line of the body: If you do, you'll end up with two joints on top of each other.

Figure 10.11 The hip joint is selected so that the leg can be mirrored over to the other side.

Figure 10.12 The YZ option is chosen so that the leg will mirror across the *YZ* plane.

Figure 10.13 The opposite leg is created using the Mirror Joint Options dialog box from the Skeleton menu.

Figure 10.14 The knee joint of the leg has been selected so that it can be moved.

Figure 10.15 As the knee is moved back, the foot bones move with it. Note that the bone between the hip and the knee becomes longer.

Figure 10.16 When the knee joint is moved in pivot move mode, the foot, which is below it in the hierarchy, stays put.

When you move a joint to position it, all of the joints beneath it in the hierarchy move along with it. You can move a joint *independently* of its position in the hierarchy by using pivot move mode.

To move a joint:

1. Create a skeleton like the one from the previous tasks.

2. Select the knee joint (**Figure 10.14**).

3. Press w.

4. Move the knee backward.
   The rest of the leg moves with it (**Figure 10.15**).

5. Press z to undo the last move.

6. Press Insert/Home on the keyboard.
   You are now in pivot move mode.

7. Move the knee forward.
   The rest of the leg does not move with it (**Figure 10.16**).

8. Press z to undo the last move. Press Insert/Home again to get out of pivot move mode.

To insert a joint:

1. Create a skeleton of several joints (**Figure 10.17**).

2. From the Skeleton menu, select Insert Joint Tool.

3. Click on a joint and drag out the new joint.

   The new joint will be inserted between the joint you clicked and the joint beneath it in the hierarchy. It is easiest to do this in an orthographic view (**Figure 10.18**).

4. Press Enter to finish, and exit the tool.

Figure 10.17 A skeleton of several joints is created in an orthographic view.

Figure 10.18 A new joint is created between two existing joints. It is positioned between the joints both physically and in the hierarchy.

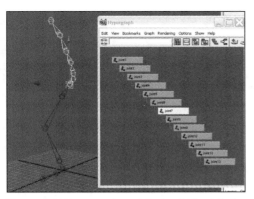

Figure 10.19 You can select a joint by clicking it in the modeling window, or by clicking the corresponding joint node in the Hypergraph.

Figure 10.20 Select Remove Joint from the Skeleton menu.

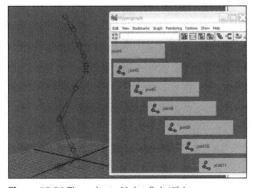

Figure 10.21 The selected joint (joint7) is now completely deleted from the scene and cannot be viewed in the Hypergraph.

Occasionally you may find that you've created more joints than you need. If so, you can select the joint and remove it from the hierarchy without deleting any additional nodes, like simply deleting the joint would do.

To remove a joint from the hierarchy:

1. Click the joint you would like to remove (**Figure 10.19**).

2. From the Skeleton menu, select Remove Joint (**Figure 10.20**).

   The joint is removed from the hierarchy and deleted from the scene. Now that the selected joint has been removed, the bone from its parent ends at the selected joint's child (**Figure 10.21**).

Sometimes you'll want to disconnect a portion of a previously created skeleton to use it in a new character. Say for a *half-human* character that uses a human joint system—with human-like arms but nonhuman-like legs. By disconnecting the center joint, you could use the upper half of the human skeleton on the human half of the new character.

To disconnect a joint from the hierarchy:

1. Click the joint you would like to disconnect from the hierarchy (**Figure 10.22**).

2. From the Skeleton menu, select Disconnect Joint (**Figure 10.23**).

   The selected joint and its children are disconnected from the original hierarchy.

3. From the Window menu, select Hypergraph.

   The Hypergraph opens in a new window.

4. Press [a] to focus all of the joints in the Hypergraph window.

   The skeleton is now split into two hierarchies that can be selected and moved independently of each other (**Figure 10.24**).

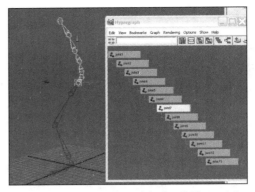

Figure 10.22 You can select a joint by clicking on it in the modeling window, or by clicking the corresponding joint node in the Hypergraph.

Figure 10.23 Select Disconnect Joint from the Skeleton menu.

Figure 10.24 Although in the modeling view the skeleton still appears to be one, you can see in the Hypergaph that there are now two separate hierarchies.

Figure 10.25 On the left, an IK handle moves the foot. On the right, both the hip and ankle are rotated to move the foot.

Figure 10.26 The top of the leg is moving, but the ankle is staying put because it has an IK handle, which is keyframed. Note that this foot also has an IK handle going from the ankle to the ball and from the ball to the toe. These IK handles keep the rest of the foot in place.

Figure 10.27 This is a typical leg skeleton. Sometimes a heel joint is added, but it is used merely as a placeholder since the ankle joint bends but the foot does not bend at the heel.

About IK Handles and Solvers

Inverse kinematics makes animation easier in many situations. For example, to put a foot in a certain position using forward kinematics, you would need to rotate the hip and the knee. However, by using an IK handle on the ankle, you can simply move the ankle into position, and the hip and knee will rotate accordingly (**Figure 10.25**).

You can also use an IK handle to make a foot or hand stick in one spot. When your character is walking and you want one foot to remain planted on the ground, IK handles make it much easier to keep that foot in place (because multiple rotations in the joints connected to the IK handle help to keep it that way) (**Figure 10.26**). Once it is keyframed, the foot will do its best to stay where it is even though the joints in the IK chain are rotating. The same goes for arms and hands. If your character is climbing a ladder or leaning against a wall, an IK handle will help keep it in place.

To add an IK handle:

1. Create a leg out of five joints (**Figure 10.27**).

2. From the Skeleton menu, select IK Handle Tool.

3. Click the hip joint.

4. Click the ankle joint.
   An IK handle is created.

continues on next page

5. Move the IK handle around
(**Figure 10.28**).

6. Select Twist in the Channel Box.

7. With the middle mouse button, drag
from left to right in the Perspective view.
The leg rotates around the IK chain
(**Figure 10.29**).

The Twist attribute only works on a Rotate
Plane (RP) type of IK handle. By default, a
Rotate Plane solver is created when you make
an IK handle. If you move the IK handle too
high, however, the leg flips around, and the
knee points in the opposite direction (**Figure
10.30**). You can solve this problem by
adjusting the Pole Vector attributes, which
are in the Channel Box for the IK handle.

Another alternative is to create a Single
Chain solver. Although it doesn't permit the
Twist attribute like the Rotate Plane solver
does, the Single Chain solver doesn't have
the same flipping problem that Rotate Plane
has. When using a Single Chain solver, you
can rotate the limb by rotating the IK handle.
However, the Rotate Plane solver is considered more predictable because it's not affected
by the rotation of the IK handle.

Figure 10.28 The IK handle is moved around, allowing
for easy placement of the foot.

Figure 10.29 The leg is rotated via the Twist attribute.

Figure 10.30 When lifted too high, a leg can flip over if
you're using an RP IK handle.

Figure 10.31 This is the basic skeleton for a leg.

Figure 10.32 In the Tool Settings dialog box, choose ikSCsolver. This type of IK handle won't cause the flipping problem that an RP handle can cause.

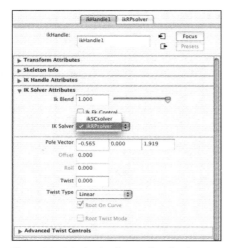

Figure 10.33 In the Attribute Editor for the IK handle, you can change the type of solver after it is created.

To create a Single Chain IK handle:

1. Create a leg out of five joints (**Figure 10.31**).

2. From the Skeleton menu, select the box next to IK Handle Tool.
   This opens the Tool Settings dialog box.

3. Select ikSCsolver from the Current Solver pop-up menu (**Figure 10.32**).

4. Click the hip joint.

5. Click the ankle joint.
   An IK handle is created with a Single Chain solver.

6. Rotate the IK handle.
   The limb rotates.

✔ Tips

■ You can also change the type of solver after you've created the IK handle: Select the IK handle and open the Attribute Editor. If you click IK Solver Attributes, you'll be able to choose the solver type from the pop-up menu (**Figure 10.33**).

■ IK handles can also flip when a character turns 180 or 360 degrees. To avoid this problem, you can constrain the orientation of the Pole Vector of an IK handle to the joint above it. For more about constraints, see Chapter 12, "Animation."

ABOUT IK HANDLES AND SOLVERS

About Spline IK

Spline IK gives you a way of controlling many joints using a curve rather than by rotating them directly. This is especially useful when you have many joints in a continuous chain (such as in a spine or a tail), because you can move the skeleton quickly into the shape you desire without rotating each individual joint (**Figure 10.34**).

To create a Spline IK:

1. Create a spine skeleton, starting from the bottom and working your way up (**Figure 10.35**).

2. From the Skeleton menu, select IK_Spline Handle Tool.

3. Click the top joint of the skeleton.

4. Click the second joint from the bottom of the skeleton.

   Two things are created, the Spline IK handle and a curve. By default, the curve is automatically parented to the joints.

5. Select Twist in the Channel Box.

6. With the middle mouse button, drag from left to right.

   The bones rotate around.

Figure 10.34 By creating an IK spline on these joints, you can animate a spine skeleton by moving just one point. Keyframing the rotation of each joint to achieve the same effect would be much more difficult.

Figure 10.35 The human spine has a natural curve. When creating a spine for a character, it's helpful to match the shape of the character's back.

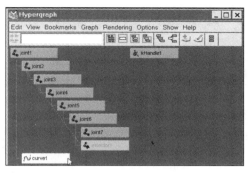

Figure 10.36 It's easier to select the curve in the Hypergraph because the icon can be isolated.

Figure 10.37 When the CV is moved, the spine bends to form the shape of the control curve.

7. From the Hypergraph select the curve you just created (**Figure 10.36**).

8. In the Pick mask, select component mode. You can now see the CVs of the curve.

9. Select and move a CV (**Figure 10.37**). The joints rotate in response and stick to the shape of the control curve.

✔ Tip

■ In general, you don't want to use the root joint of the skeleton as part of your Spline IK chain. If you do, when you move the CVs, the whole skeleton will rotate. To avoid this, choose one joint above the root joint of the skeleton as the base of your Spline IK.

ABOUT SPLINE IK

When you are using Spline IK to animate your character, you move and keyframe CVs. However, CVs don't have their own node: Since they're components, they don't show up in the Hypergraph or Outliner as a node that can be animated. It can be helpful to make a cluster for each CV of the curve so that there *is* a node you can keep track of when animating. A cluster can also aid in the selection process since you can move a cluster handle away from the spline curve, making it easier to select.

To create clusters for a Spline IK's CVs:

1. Using the Spline IK created in the previous task, select one of the CVs of the control curve.

   Be sure that the root joint of the skeleton is not included in the IK chain.

2. From the Deform menu select the box next to Create Cluster. The Cluster Options dialog box opens.

3. Check the box next to Relative (**Figure 10.38**).

   Checking this box will make the cluster move in relation to the curve. If you don't check Relative, the cluster will do a *double transform*, which means it will move twice as much when the root joint is moved.

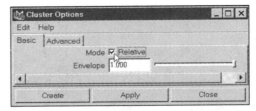

Figure 10.38 In the Cluster Options dialog box, Relative is checked.

The Assassin (kick) by Loïc "e338" Zimmermann (www.e338.com). Main image created in Maya, then composited in Adobe Photoshop with photograph taken by the artist.

Kaya Pose #2 by Alceu Baptistão (www.vetorzero.com.br). Main image created in Maya, then composited on photographic background taken by the artist.

LEGO Hub by Eric Hanson (www.visuraimaging.com). Image (rendered in Maya 5.0) from a special-venue stereoscopic film, "Racers 4D," which is installed at Legoland theme parks.

Mother Nature by Meats Meier (www.3dArtSpace.com). Main image created in Maya, then composited in Adobe Photoshop with photograph taken by the artist.

Gas Mask by Meats Meier (www.3dArtSpace.com). Image created and rendered in Maya.

Cathedral Entrance by Martin Mayer (www.waterworthvfx.com). Main image created in Maya, then composited and color-corrected in Discreet Combustion.

generated city VIII by Matt Daly (www.luxwork.com). City created with a custom MEL script and rendered with Mental Ray.

The Horde by Balazs Kiss (www.3dluvr.com/ward). Elephants and siege machines modeled and textured in Maya, rendered with Mental Ray, and composited into a matte painting background in Photoshop.

Los Focos by Jorge Adorni (www.dreamsofnimrod.com.ar). Main image modeled and rendered in Maya with minor color and contrast corrections done in Adobe Photoshop; photographic background by Paul Debevec.

Tamara by Sebastien Legrain (http://sebleg.free.fr). Image created and rendered in Maya, then colorized with Adobe Photoshop.

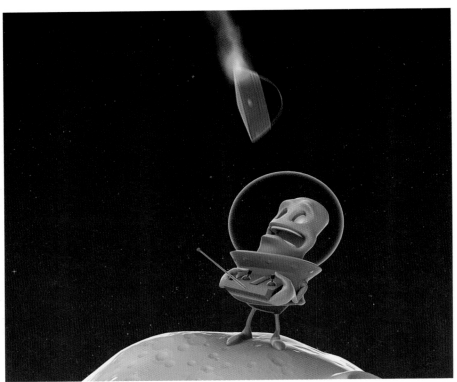

Spaceman In Trouble by Niels Jansson (www.kay-kay.com). Main 3D images animated and rendered in Maya using Mental Ray; composited background created by artist in Adobe Photoshop.

Figure 10.39 A *C* (for *cluster*) appears where the CV is. The cluster controls the CV.

Figure 10.40 The *C*s are used as selection tools for the spine's rotation.

4. Click Create.

The cluster is created and is represented as a *C* (**Figure 10.39**).

5. Shift-select the root joint of the skeleton.

6. Press p.

The cluster is now parented to the root joint so that it will move with the whole skeleton.

7. Repeat Steps 2 through 7 for all but the bottom CV of the control curve.

There are now clusters for each of the CVs, which you can easily select and animate (**Figure 10.40**).

✔ Tip

- When you're making clusters out of the CVs of the curve for an IK spline, don't make a cluster for the bottom CV of the curve. Moving this CV will stretch out the bone—often undesirable because the entire body moves out of place.

Understanding the Hypergraph and Skeletons

When you're creating characters, the Hypergraph plays an important role in hierarchy order and selection. In fact, it's the best tool Maya offers to help you understand the way hierarchies are formed as well as how Maya's various elements relate to one another.

The Hypergraph provides two layout options: Freeform and Automatic, with Automatic being the default. If you choose the Automatic option, Maya lays out the Hypergraph for you, with the root node at the top of the hierarchy and each child indented below its parent with a line connecting child and parent. In addition, nodes are locked in place so that the hierarchies remain visually consistent and organized.

In contrast, if you select Freeform from the Options > Layout menu, you can move the nodes around and organize them to your liking. In addition, you can import an image of your character into the background of the Hypergraph so that you can align its joints to their proper positions on top of the image, making it much easier to select individual joints. In a simple hierarchy this may not be necessary, but when you have hundreds of joints and surfaces, selection can become quite cumbersome without this aid.

The Hypergraph displays each of your joints with a blue joint icon 👟. When a single joint is selected in the view pane, all of its children are highlighted to indicate their relationship to the selected joint. As children of the joint, they will be affected if the selected joint is rotated. Be aware that although the children are highlighted in the view pane, they haven't been *individually* selected.

Select a joint and open the Hypergraph. The joint you clicked is selected (yellow), but the joints underneath it (its children) are not. Because the parent is selected, the children will follow. If in the Hypergraph you Shift-select the children and then rotate the joints, you will see that each joint will rotate. Although you will rarely select the joints in this fashion, it's important to understand what is and is not selected in a hierarchy.

You can move joints from one hierarchy to another or disconnect them from a hierarchy—all from within the Hypergraph. You use the middle mouse button to move joints in and out of hierarchies. To move a joint (and its children) into another hierarchy, simply drag the joint (using the middle mouse button) onto the node you want to serve as its parent. Once you do this, you will see that the selected node (and its children) are connected to the new hierarchy.

To remove a joint (and its children) from a hierarchy, select its node with the middle mouse button and drag it away from the hierarchy (releasing the mouse when the node has been moved away from the hierarchy). This technique also works well for removing objects from a group within the Hypergraph.

ABOUT SPLINE IK

PARENTING AND BINDING TO A SKELETON

PARENTING AND BINDING TO A SKELETON

Figure 11.1 For the leg to bend at the knee, it needs to be bound to a skeleton.

Figure 11.2 When the elbow joint is rotated, only the forearm rotates with it.

Once you've created a skeleton, you need to either parent or bind the surfaces to the joints in order for the surfaces to move with the skeleton. Anything that doesn't need to bend, like a hat, glasses, or eyeballs, can be *parented* to the joints. Anything that does need to bend, like an arm, leg, or torso, must be *bound* to the skeleton (**Figure 11.1**).

Parenting to joints works much like parenting to anything else. The bone is the parent, and the surface is the child, so the surface rotates and moves when the bone is rotated.

Binding, however, is a bit different. When a surface is bound to a skeleton, only a portion of that surface will move with a bone. For example, an arm has a shoulder joint and an elbow joint. However, only the forearm should move when the elbow is rotated; the shoulder and biceps should remain in place (**Figure 11.2**). When you bind the arm geometry to the skeleton, you make the forearm part of the arm (attached at the elbow joint) and the shoulder and biceps part of the arm as well (attached to the shoulder joint).

At the heart of binding are *clusters*. A cluster is like a set of points that have weight. Weight represents the amount of influence a cluster wields over each point in the set. Understanding clusters and weight is an important step in understanding binding. In this chapter, we'll take a close look at clusters and their effect on surfaces.

There are two kinds of binding—*rigid bind* and *smooth bind*. Rigid bind works well for things like arms, legs, and fingers—things that bend clearly at a joint and are rigid in between. Smooth bind works well for things like torsos, tails, and snakes—things that bend gradually along a surface (**Figure 11.3**). Either can be used for any kind of surface, and in some cases it just boils down to a matter of personal preference.

The surface of a simple character, such as a robot, can sometimes be parented, rather than bound, to a skeleton—for example, if all the parts are made out of metal and don't bend. Parenting a character that does not have bending joints is a good way to create your first character since it's easy to set up and quick to animate.

Figure 11.3 These two objects have identical geometry and the same joints, which are rotated equally. However, the one on the left is smooth bound, and the one on the right is rigid bound. The surface on the left bends more smoothly; the one on the right bends more abruptly and is straighter between joints.

Figure 11.4 This character is built from simple shapes. As a robot, he's made of steel and thus does not bend, making him a good candidate for having his surfaces parented (rather than bound) to joints.

Figure 11.5 A skeleton is built into the character. The root joint, which is at the top of the hierarchy, is at the waist.

Figure 11.6 Once all the surfaces have been parented to the appropriate joints, you can pose or animate the character.

To parent surfaces to joints:

1. Create the surfaces of a character (**Figure 11.4**). (See Chapter 9, "Subdiv Surfaces," for more information.)

2. Create a skeleton (**Figure 11.5**). (See Chapter 10, "Skeletons and Inverse Kinematics," for more information.)

3. Select a surface.

4. (Shift)-select the joint to which it will be parented.

5. Press (p).

   Now when you select and rotate that joint, the surface will rotate with it.

6. Repeat Steps 3 through 5 for all of the other surfaces.

   Now when any joint is rotated, the parented surface will move with it (**Figure 11.6**).

✔ Tip

■ Because parented geometry is the fastest way to animate with a character, it will often have a segmented "stand-in" model made of non-bending pieces parented to the skeleton, as well as a bound model that can bend. You can use the stand-in while you're creating your animations and hide the other in a display layer until you're ready to use it in the finished work. For more information on display layers, see Chapter 16, "Cameras and Rendering."

About Clusters and Weights

A cluster provides a means of controlling a set of points as a group. The points can be NURBS control vertices (CVs), polygon vertices, or lattice points. (For more information on these elements, see Chapter 4, "Selection Modes, Hiding, and Templating.")

Points that are members of a cluster have weight. As mentioned earlier, weight represents the amount of influence the cluster has over the points it contains. Weight is generally set between 0 and 1. A point with a weight of 0 will not move with the cluster. A point with a weight of 1 will move exactly as much as the cluster itself. Anything in between will make the point move a fraction of how much the cluster moves.

For example, suppose a CV in a cluster had a weight of 0.5. If the cluster was moved up two grid units in the Y direction, the CV would move only one unit (**Figure 11.7**). Simply multiply the weight by the distance the cluster moves, and you'll get the distance the point moves.

Clusters represent a convenient way of animating portions of a surface. For example, if you wanted to animate the movement of a character's fat belly, you could make a cluster out of the points that form his belly, add different weights to the points on his belly, and then animate that cluster (**Figure 11.8**).

Understanding clusters is also the key to understanding binding. What binding does, in the background, is create clusters of portions of your surface and then parent those clusters to the joints. Once the surface has been bound, you can adjust the weight of the points to get the surface to deform the way you desire. When you understand parenting, clusters, and weight, binding will no longer seem mysterious.

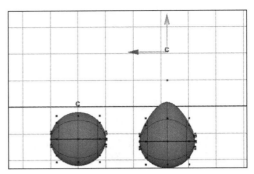

Figure 11.7 A cluster is made with one CV whose weight is set to 0.5—which means the point moves only half the distance of the cluster (right).

Figure 11.8 The points that make up the belly are included in a cluster. That cluster is parented to the belly and animated to make it bouncy.

Figure 11.9 When you click makeNurbPlane1 in the Channel Box, it will expand these options.

Figure 11.10 At the bottom is the plane before the patches were increased. At the top is the plane after the patches have been increased.

Figure 11.11 The plane is dense, so it has many points. The CVs in the center have been selected so that they can be made into a cluster.

To create a cluster:

1. From the Create menu, select NURBS Primitives > Plane.

2. Select makeNurbPlane1 from the Inputs section of the Channel Box (**Figure 11.9**).

3. Increase Patches U and Patches V to *30*. The plane becomes more dense (**Figure 11.10**).

4. Press (F8) to switch to component mode.

5. Select some points in the center of the plane (**Figure 11.11**).

6. From the Deform menu, select Create Cluster.

   A *C* appears in the middle of the selected points.

7. Press (w) to activate the Move tool and then click and drag to move the cluster. The CVs move with it (**Figure 11.12**).

Figure 11.12 The cluster, which is represented by a *C*, has been moved up. The CVs, which are members of the cluster, move with it, forming a plateau.

To weight the points of a cluster using the Component Editor:

1. Using the cluster created in the previous task, "To create a cluster," select some of the CVs that are included in the cluster (**Figure 11.13**).

2. From the Window menu, select General Editors > Component Editor.

   The Component Editor dialog box appears.

3. Select the Weighted Deformers Tab in the Component Editor (**Figure 11.14**).

4. Click the top numeric field and drag down to highlight all of the weights.

5. Type *.5* in the field, and press Enter.

   All of the weights in that column become 0.5 (**Figure 11.15**).

   or

   Click and drag a range of CVs and use the slider at the bottom of the Component Editor to change the weights interactively.

Figure 11.13 Some of the CVs on the side of the cluster have been selected so that their weights can be changed.

Figure 11.14 In the Component Editor, a cluster is referred to as a Weighted Deformer. The weights of the selected points show up when this tab is selected.

Figure 11.15 On the right, the Component Editor shows that the weights of the selected points have been reduced to 0.5. On the left, the selected points are only moved up half the distance of the cluster because of their lower weight.

Figure 11.16 The Paint Attributes tool can be used to interactively change the weights of points. The options shown here control how the weight is changed.

About the Paint Attributes tool

Another way of adjusting the weights of a cluster is by using the Paint Attributes tool. Especially handy for working with dense surfaces, this tool includes several options for interactively changing the weight of points (**Figure 11.16**).

There are four settings for Paint Operations:

◆ **Replace**—When Paint Operation is set to Replace, the current weight of the painted points will change to whatever number is set in the Value field.

◆ **Add**—When Paint Operation is set to Add, the value will be added to the weight of the painted points. This is useful for incrementally increasing the weights of points.

◆ **Scale**—When Paint Operation is set to Scale, the current weight of a point will be multiplied by the value when it is painted. If you have a value of 0.9, you can incrementally decrease the weight of a point.

◆ **Smooth**—This averages the weights of the adjacent points to make the area smoother.

The Flood button can speed work considerably, because rather than have to paint on an effect, you can have the Paint Attributes tool's settings affect all of the points simultaneously by pressing Flood. This is useful when you're setting all points to the same weight or smoothing all points.

To edit cluster weights using the Paint Attributes tool:

1. Create a cluster and move it up, as in the previous tasks.

2. Select the surface.

3. Right-click the surface, and select Paint > cluster > cluster1-weights from the Marketing menu (**Figure 11.17**).

   This activates the Paint Attributes tool, which should provide color feedback in shaded mode. The area of the surface that includes CVs in the cluster turns white; the rest appears black.

4. Hold down b and drag the mouse from right to left to shrink the brush size (**Figure 11.18**).

5. Double-click the Paint Attributes tool in the toolbox.

   The Tool Settings dialog box for the Paint Attributes tool appears.

6. Change Value to *0.5*.

   Paint Operation should already be set to Replace (**Figure 11.19**).

7. Click and drag on the surface.

   The painted portion moves down because the weight of the points has been changed to 0.5.

8. Change Paint Operation to Smooth.

9. Click Flood several times.

   The lump becomes smooth (**Figure 11.20**).

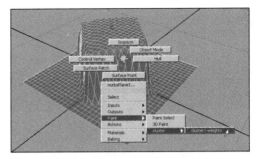

Figure 11.17 Using the Marking Menu, which pops up when you right-click the surface, is the most convenient way to access the Paint Attributes tool.

Figure 11.18 The brush size started out much too big for this small surface. Here we see the progression as the brush size gets smaller.

Figure 11.19 Using Replace with a value of 0.5 will bring about the same result as if you had typed it in as the weight in the Component Editor.

ABOUT CLUSTERS AND WEIGHTS

Figure 11.20 Flood will apply the current Paint Operation setting to all members of the cluster. In this case, it's set to Smooth so that all the points are smoothed simultaneously when you click Flood, which is quicker than having to paint the surface.

Figure 11.21 Adjusting a joint's cluster weights can modify the amount of influence a joint has on a CV. The less influence the joint has, the less movement the CV has, in turn lessening the crease around the joint area.

Figure 11.22 The cylinder on the left has been smooth bound. The weights of the selected points show up in the Component Editor. Their weight is spread among the three joints; however, they are primarily influenced by joint2.

About Binding

When you bind skin, you make the surfaces move with the bones. In the beginning the process may seem mysterious; however, it's really little more than a combination of actions you already know.

We've learned that when you parent a surface to a joint, it rotates with that joint. We also know that a cluster is a set of points that have weight. Binding skin creates a cluster composed of the points nearest to a bone, and then parents that cluster to the bone. After this is done, you can adjust the weight to make the points rotate more or less with a specific joint (**Figure 11.21**).

As mentioned earlier, there are two kinds of binding—rigid and smooth. When you use rigid bind, each point can be a member of only one joint. When you use smooth bind, each point is a member of more than one joint. Its weight is spread out among two or more joints, but the total weight always adds up to 1 (**Figure 11.22**).

To bind skin using rigid bind:

1. From the Create menu, select NURBS Primitives > Cylinder.

2. Increase Scale Y to *8* (**Figure 11.23**).

3. In the Channel Box, select makeNurbCylinder1.

4. Increase Spans to *8* (**Figure 11.24**).

   Bound surfaces require extra detail, particularly in the areas where they bend.

5. Create three joints in the surface (**Figure 11.25**).

6. Select the joints, and [Shift]-select the surface.

7. From the Skin menu select the box next to Bind Skin > Rigid Bind.

   The Rigid Bind Skin Options dialog box opens.

Figure 11.23 On the left is the cylinder with a Y Scale of 8; on the right is the Channel Box, which provides a convenient place to change the scale to a precise number.

Figure 11.24 On the left is a cylinder with eight spans; on the right is the Channel Box with attributes for this cylinder.

Figure 11.25 Three joints are placed inside the cylinder, which produces two bones.

Figure 11.26 The Rigid Bind Skin Options dialog box is set to Bind to Complete Skeleton and Color Joints.

Figure 11.27 Only the lower half of the surface rotates with the middle joint.

8. Select Complete Skeleton in the "Bind to" menu, and check Color Joints next to Coloring (**Figure 11.26**).

Complete Skeleton means that the skin will be bound to every joint in the hierarchy (as opposed to just the selected ones). Color Joints means that the joints and the points that become members of those joints will be color-coded the same once the skin is bound.

9. Click the Bind Skin button.

10. Select the middle joint and rotate it. The lower half of the surface moves with the bone (**Figure 11.27**).

✔ Tips

■ Any kind of surface can be bound to a skeleton—NURBS, polygon, or subdivision. You can also bind a lattice, or just a selection of points.

■ You can bind a whole character with multiple surfaces at once. To do this, select the root joint of the skeleton and all of the surfaces involved, then bind the skin.

ABOUT BINDING

A point becomes a member of a specific joint when you use rigid bind; however, sometimes it can become a member of the *wrong* joint. The Edit Membership tool allows you to change the joint that the point belongs to.

To edit the membership of a point:

1. Using the bound cylinder from the previous task, "To bind skin using rigid bind," select the middle joint.

2. From the Deform menu, select Edit Membership Tool.

   The cursor changes.

3. Click the middle joint.

   The points that are members of that joint are selected.

4. [Shift]-select the middle row of points (**Figure 11.28**).

   This adds points to the membership of the middle joint, and they, too, are selected. If you do not hold down [Shift], this will not work.

5. Select and rotate the middle joint.

   The points that were just added now rotate with the joint (**Figure 11.29**).

✔ Tips

- If you [Ctrl]/[Control]-select points while using the Edit Membership tool, they will be removed from the joint's membership. However, if they are not added to a joint, the points will be left behind when the character moves.

- The Edit Membership tool can be used for any deformer, such as a lattice or a blend shape.

Figure 11.28 The Edit Membership tool allows you to change which joint the points are members of. Here, some of the points that were not members of the middle joint are being added to that joint.

Figure 11.29 When a joint is rotated, all the points that are members of that joint rotate with it. Therefore, the points we just added rotate along with the joint as well.

Figure 11.30 Some of the CVs of the surface are being selected so that their weight can be changed. Be sure you're in component mode when you try to select CVs.

Figure 11.31 In the Component Editor, click and drag to select all the weights in the column. This allows you to conveniently change all of their weights at once.

Figure 11.32 The selected points of the cylinder on top have not yet been changed—they still have a weight of 1. On the bottom cylinder, the selected points have a weight of 0.5.

To edit the weights of rigid-bound points:

1. Using the the bound cylinder from the previous tasks, select the row of points in the middle joint (**Figure 11.30**).

2. From the Window menu, select General Editors > Component Editor.

3. In the Component Editor, click the Rigid Skins tab.

4. Click the top numeric field and drag down to highlight all of the weights.

   In this case the column is labeled joint2Cluster1. The column is highlighted (**Figure 11.31**).

5. Type .5 in the field.

   All of the weights for the selected points become 0.5. The points now rotate half the distance of the joint, creating a smoother shape around the joint (**Figure 11.32**).

Sometimes the area where a surface bends will seem too rounded and you'll want it to be more angular, as with an elbow. A *flexor* provides an easy way to adjust the rounding and creasing that occurs on a surface near a joint.

To create a flexor:

1. Using the rigid-bound cylinder from the previous tasks, select the middle joint.

   Make sure that the joint to which you want to add the flexor is straight—that is, its rotations are set to zero.

2. From the Skin menu, select Edit Rigid Skin > Create Flexor.

3. Click Create.

   A lattice is created around the joint (**Figure 11.33**).

4. Rotate the joint about 90 degrees (**Figure 11.34**).

   When the joint is rotated, the flexor reshapes the surface automatically to prevent creasing.

5. Select the lattice that appeared when the flexor was created.

6. In the Channel Box, click Rounding.

7. With the middle mouse button, drag from left to right in the panel until the bent area of the surface is more angular and elbow-shaped (**Figure 11.35**).

✔ Tip

- If you check Position the Flexor in the Create Flexor Options window, it will select the group that the lattice and lattice base are in. This allows you to reshape the lattice by moving and scaling the group without having it affect the shape of the surface. Once you deselect this group, the lattice will go back to deforming the surface.

Figure 11.33 Create Flexor makes a lattice appear around the selected joint. It has special attributes that other lattices do not have, such as Creasing and Rounding used to form an elbow or knee. Be sure to add a flexor only when the joint is straight; otherwise, you'll get undesirable results.

Figure 11.34 A flexor has been put on the middle joint. As the joint is rotated, the flexor improves the shape of the surface where it is bent.

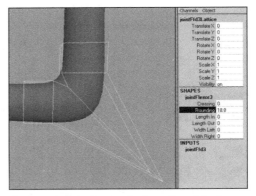

Figure 11.35 By adjusting the Rounding attribute, you can make the bent portion more angular. This is commonly used on things like elbows, knees, and finger joints. When the joint is rotated to straight again, the surface returns to its original shape.

ABOUT BINDING

Figure 11.36 Five joints are placed inside the cylinder. Smooth bind lends itself to parts of characters that have many joints and need to bend smoothly.

Figure 11.37 This is a smooth bound cylinder.

To bind skin using smooth bind:

1. From the Create menu, select NURBS Primitives > Cylinder.

2. In the Channel box, increase Scale Y to *8*.

3. Select makeNurbCylinder1.

4. Increase Spans to *16*.

   Bound surfaces require extra detail, particularly in the area where they bend.

5. Create five joints in the cylinder (**Figure 11.36**).

6. Select the surface, and Shift-select the root joint.

7. From the Skin menu, select Bind Skin > Smooth Bind.

8. Select the top joints, and then Shift-select the rest of the joints one by one.

9. Rotate all the joints simultaneously.

   The surface moves with the joints and bends smoothly (**Figure 11.37**).

About Binding

285

To paint skin weights on a smooth-bound surface:

1. Create a polygon shape from a cubeby scaling it with Extrude Face, and then from the Polygon menu, select Smooth (**Figure 11.38**). (See Chapter 8, "Polygons.")

   The shape roughly represents an arm extending from a torso.

2. Create four joints in the surface (**Figure 11.39**).

3. Select the root joint, and [Shift]-select the surface.

4. From the Skin menu, select Bind Skin > Smooth Bind.

5. Select and rotate the second joint.

   It bends too much of the torso portion of the surface (**Figure 11.40**).

6. Select the surface.

7. Right-click the surface and select Paint > skinCluster > skinCluster1 - paintWeights from the Marking menu (**Figure 11.41**).

   The Paint Skin Weights Tool is activated.

Figure 11.38 Here are four stages in creating the surface. First, create a polygon cube and scale it. Extrude the side face and scale, and move it to the start point of the arm. Extrude again and pull the arm out. Finally, smooth the surface with divisions set to 3 and continuity set to 0.35.

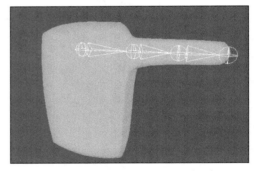

Figure 11.39 Starting from the center of the chest, four joints are placed inside the surface.

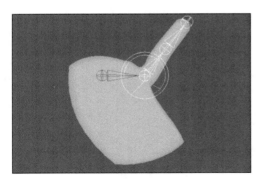

Figure 11.40 When the shoulder is rotated, it affects too much of the torso. Had there been more joints placed in the torso, this would not have been as much of a problem because the points would stick to the joints they were near. It's common practice to place rib joints in a character for this purpose.

Figure 11.41 Right-click to open the Marking menu and select the Paint Skin Weights tool.

Figure 11.42 The options shown are the default settings for the Paint Skin Weights tool; they also happen to be what we need in this instance.

8. Double-click the Paint Skin Weights tool button in the toolbox ⬛.

This opens the Tool Settings window for Paint Skin Weights. Under Influence, joint1 should be selected. Under Paint Weights, Replace should be the Paint Operation and Value should be 1.0000 (**Figure 11.42**).

9. Adjust the brush size by holding down ⓑ and dragging from right to left with the middle mouse button.

10. Paint all over the surface of the torso (**Figure 11.43**).

The torso moves back to its original shape and turns white. This is because all of the weight is being placed on joint1 and taken away from joint2.

11. Change Paint Operation to Smooth.

12. Click Flood several times.

The area where the surface bends is smoothed (**Figure 11.44**).

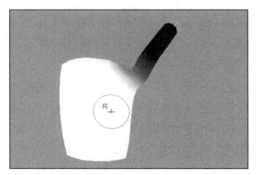

Figure 11.43 When the surface is painted, the points get a weight of 1 with the first joint, so they do not move with the shoulder joint. Be sure to get all around the surface with the brush.

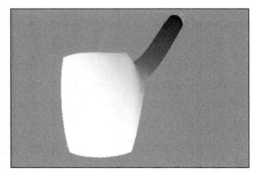

Figure 11.44 Flooding with Smooth creates a smoother connection at the shoulder.

To detach a surface from joints:

1. Create a bound skeleton (see "To bind skin using rigid bind," earlier in this chapter).

2. Select the geometry that you want to detach from the skeleton (**Figure 11.45**).

3. From the Skin menu, select Detach Skin (**Figure 11.46**).

   The geometry becomes detached from the skeleton.

4. Select the middle joint and rotate it.

   The joint moves but the surface remains in place (**Figure 11.47**).

Figure 11.45 Select only the surface, not the joint, for the Detach Skin command to work correctly.

Figure 11.46 Select Detach Skin to separate the surfaces from the bones.

Figure 11.47 Once detached from the surface, joints no longer affect the geometry.

Figure 11.48 Select the joint that you want to reset to its bind pose.

Figure 11.49 The selected joint returns to its original rotation amount.

When you bind geometry to a skeleton, Maya remembers the joints' rotation at the time of binding: This rotation is referred to as the *bind pose*. When animating, there will be times when you want the joints to align with the original rotation—that is, the rotation that existed when you bound the geometry to the skeleton. You can reset joints back to this rotation by setting the joint(s) back to the bind pose.

To set a rotated joint back to its bind pose:

1. Select the joint you want to set to the bind pose (**Figure 11.48**).

2. From the Skin menu, select Go to Bind Pose.

   The joint is set to the same rotation as it was when it was bound to the skeleton (**Figure 11.49**).

ABOUT BINDING

Parenting vs. Binding

There are two ways to connect surfaces to geometry: parenting and binding.

If you plan ahead when creating your character, you can save a lot of time by designing a *segmented* character, meaning a character that does not need to bend at the elbows or other major bending joints. A simple example would be a character wearing knee and elbow pads: You can individually parent each surface (the upper leg, bottom leg, and knee pad). Each of these objects can move individually without having to bend or deform, only rotate.

By parenting geometry to a skeleton, you avoid having to create clusters and weigh individual points because the surfaces don't bend and deform with the character.

If, however, your character requires realistic deformations in its joints, you must bind it to the skeleton to create that effect. And this poses all sorts of extra character-setup challenges. Take, for example, a character's armpit: Because the geometry near the outside of the breast and under the arm are so close to one another, Maya must guess which bone each point should be attached to—and often its choice will differ from yours. This means you'll spend extra time separating the points that are moving with the wrong joint, and moving them onto the correct joints.

12

ANIMATION

Figure 12.1 Toby Marvin animated the shape of this monkey's face to change his expression from happy to angry.

Maya was built for animation. Almost anything you encounter can be animated, such as a color, a texture, an object's shape, or the intensity of a light (**Figure 12.1**).

Most animation is accomplished by setting keyframes. The term *keyframe* has its origin in traditional hand-drawn animation, in which a lead animator creates key poses of a character—drawings at the beginning and end and other key points of an action—and an assistant then draws the in-between frames, making the final result a smooth motion. When using Maya, you are the lead animator and the program is your assistant. To animate, you set keyframes—that is, you tell an object or attribute where to be at certain points in time—and the program does the in-betweening for you.

Animations are easy to tweak: You can change the timing or distance covered by existing keyframes, you can add or remove keyframes, and you can adjust the acceleration between keyframes by tweaking the animation curve between them.

Animation Controls

The Time and Range sliders are Maya's primary controls for creating and fine-tuning your animation (**Figure 12.2**).

◆ **Time slider**—The Time slider determines your position in time. It is the area at the bottom of the screen that includes the playback buttons and timeline (**Figure 12.3**). You can click any frame to go to that point in time, or you can click and drag to preview a region of animation. You also use the Time slider to select, move, and scale keyframes.

◆ **Current Time indicator**—This indicator shows the present position in time (**Figure 12.4**).

◆ **Current Time field**—This field also shows the current position in time. You can type a number in this field to change the current time (**Figure 12.5**).

◆ **Start Time/End Time fields**—These values show the time span for the entire animation. The numbers establish the length of time within which the Range slider can move (**Figure 12.6**).

◆ **Range slider**—This slider controls the portion of time you're viewing (**Figure 12.7**). It allows you to quickly adjust which portion of the animation shows up in the timeline. You can use the buttons on the ends to change the playback start and end times, or you can drag the range forward or backward as a whole. This is helpful when you want to work on only small portions of an animation. The smaller the range, the easier it is to pick individual frames.

Figure 12.2 The Time and Range sliders allow you to play back animation, control your position in time, and choose the portion of the animation you're looking at.

Figure 12.3 Click any point in the timeline to go to that time.

Figure 12.4 The Current Time indicator shows what frame you are on. If you want to cut, copy, or delete a frame in the timeline, the Current Time indicator must be over that frame.

Figure 12.5 The Current Time field also tells you where you are in time. You can type any time here (even one that's not included in the playback range) and go to that time.

Figure 12.6 The number fields on the far left and far right show the start and end times. You should generally set these to the start and end of your entire animation. They can be changed at any time.

Figure 12.7 The Range slider provides a convenient means of changing which portion of the animation is currently in the timeline.

Figure 12.8 The playback start and end times appear in the fields on the left and right. You can type the times to change the beginning and end of your timeline.

Figure 12.9 From left to right, the playback buttons do the following: go to the start of the playback range, step back one frame, step back one key, play backward, play forward, step forward one key, step forward one frame, go to the end of the playback range.

Figure 12.10 The Auto Keyframe function is on when the button looks like this.

Figure 12.11 This is the Animation Preferences button.

Figure 12.12 You can create and choose character sets here.

◆ **Playback Start Time/Playback End Time fields**—These values control the range of animation that will play back, much like the Range slider (**Figure 12.8**).

◆ **Playback buttons**—These controls are like the buttons on a CD player (**Figure 12.9**). The Rewind and Fast Forward buttons change the current time to the start or end of the playback range. You can step forward one frame at a time or move to the next or previous keyframe. There is a Play button to go forward or backward; it toggles to a Stop button during playback.

◆ **Auto Keyframe toggle**—This button turns Auto Keyframing on and off (**Figure 12.10**). If it is on, any attribute that is already keyframed will be automatically keyframed again when you change its value.

◆ **Animation Preferences button**—This button opens a window to set animation preferences (**Figure 12.11**). It also provides a convenient way to access all general preferences in Maya.

◆ **Current Character Set menu**—This sets which character in a scene you're currently working on (**Figure 12.12**). When working with more than one character, it's helpful to be able to access individual characters' attributes.

ANIMATION CONTROLS

About Setting Keyframes

Keyframes are at the heart of animation in Maya. Setting a keyframe means that you want a certain attribute to have a specific value at a point in time. For example, a ball could begin at –2 along the X axis at frame 1, and end at a Translate X of 2 at frame 10. Between those frames, it would gradually move across the screen (**Figure 12.13**).

There are many ways to set keyframes and adjust them once they've been set. When you set a keyframe, a couple of things happen: The channels that were keyframed are highlighted orange in the Channel Box. In addition, you'll see key ticks in the time-line—thin, red lines indicating where each keyframe is (**Figure 12.14**). Keyframes also show up in the Graph Editor and the Dope Sheet, discussed later in this chapter.

The following section covers most of the ways to set a keyframe.

To set a keyframe:

1. From the Create menu, select NURBS Primitives > Sphere.

2. Press (Shift)(w).

   This keyframes the translates only. Press (Shift)(E) to keyframe the rotates and (Shift)(R) to keyframe the scales. These correspond to the hotkeys for the Move, Rotate, and Scale tools.

3. In the Channel Box, select Rotate X and (Shift)-select Rotate Y and Rotate Z (**Figure 12.15**).

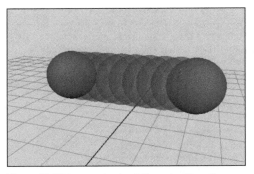

Figure 12.13 As you play back the animation, the sphere moves across the panel.

Figure 12.14 The thin line near the 10 is a key tick. It lets you know there is a keyframe for the selected object at that time.

Channels	Object	
nurbsSphere1		
Translate X		0
Translate Y		0
Translate Z		0
Rotate X		0
Rotate Y		0
Rotate Z		0
Scale X		1
Scale Y		1
Scale Z		1
Visibility		on

Figure 12.15 Rotate X, Y, and Z are selected in the Channel Box so that they can be keyframed. You can easily select multiple attributes in the Channel Box by dragging the names.

Figure 12.16 When you click in the Channel Box with the right mouse button, you can keyframe the selected attributes.

Figure 12.17 You can change the current time to 20 by typing this value in the field. When you have a particularly long playback range, entering a frame number can be easier than clicking it in the timeline.

4. Right-click the Channel Box and choose Key Selected from the Marking menu that appears (**Figure 12.16**).

Any channels that are selected (in this case, the rotate channels) are keyframed.

5. Go to frame 10 by clicking that number in the timeline.

6. Move and rotate the sphere.

7. Press (s).

All attributes in the Channel Box are keyframed.

8. Turn on Auto Keyframe ⬛.

The button will look pressed down and become highlighted.

9. Type *20* in the Current Time field to change the time in the timeline; then press (Enter) (**Figure 12.17**).

10. Move the sphere.

A new keyframe appears: when Auto Keyframe is turned on, it sets a keyframe any time an attribute is changed.

✔ Tip

■ You can set keyframes on an object only when that object is selected. Likewise, you can see the key ticks in the timeline only when the keyframed object is selected.

While much of the advanced editing of keyframes can be done in the Graph Editor and Dope Sheet windows (discussed later in this chapter), you can access the most frequently used editing tools directly from the timeline.

To edit keyframes in the timeline:

1. From the Create menu, select NURBS Primitives > Sphere.

2. Change the playback start time to *1* and the playback end time to *30*.

3. Set keyframes on the sphere every five frames, starting with the first frame.

4. Move the sphere and change the current time each time you set a keyframe. If Auto Keyframe is still on, you can press ⟨Shift⟩⟨w⟩ in the first frame and all of the other frames will automatically be keyed (**Figure 12.18**).

5. Click a frame in the timeline where there is a key tick. With the right mouse button, click the timeline; select Delete from the pop-up menu (**Figure 12.19**).

   The keyframe is removed.

6. Hold down ⟨Shift⟩ and drag over the range of two key ticks in the timeline.

   A red area should appear with two small arrows near the middle and two small arrows at the edges (**Figure 12.20**).

7. Drag from left to right on the two small arrows in the center of the selected area.

   The keyframes move together without being scaled. You can do this with an individual keyframe as well.

Figure 12.18 This is an example of some simple motion you can add to an object. Select the sphere and press ⟨Shift⟩⟨w⟩ to keyframe it With Auto Keyframe turned on, Maya will automatically keyframe the sphere every time you move it.

Figure 12.19 Clicking the timeline with the right mouse button gives you access to a variety of convenient commands.

Figure 12.20 The highlighted section of the timeline is selected. The outside arrows allow you to scale the time, and the inside arrows allow you to move several keyframes at once.

Figure 12.21 Double-clicking the timeline is a convenient way to select all of the keyframes in the playback range.

8. Double-click the timeline.

All of the keyframes in the playback range are selected. However, the arrows used for scaling end up just outside the playback range, so you must change the playback end time to access them.

9. Change the playback end time to *31*.

An arrow appears at the end of the selected range (**Figure 12.21**).

10. Drag the arrow to the left.

The animation is scaled down, which makes the sphere move faster. Note that the key ticks do not fall on whole-number frames anymore.

11. With the right mouse button, click the timeline; select Snap from the Marking menu that appears.

The keyframes are moved to the nearest whole-number frame.

✔ Tips

■ If you want to ensure that the timeline is sitting on a keyframe, use the back and forward arrows with the red marks on them in the animation controls. These jump the timeline to the preceding and next keyframes, respectively.

■ When you're working on the timing of your animation, it's often fastest, and easiest, to select, move, and scale keyframes in the timeline.

ABOUT SETTING KEYFRAMES

Setting Animation Preferences

There are a few animation preferences that are essential to set. They affect the way your animation is played back and how you see and work with the timeline.

When a scene gets extremely complicated, with many animated surfaces, Maya may not be able to play back every frame of the animation at full speed. This leaves you with two choices: You can either play back at full speed or play every frame. In some cases, you'll want to see the detail in the motion; other times, you'll want to see the overall pace. For a simple scene, however, you can have your cake and eat it, too—that is, you can play back at full speed and see every frame of animation.

Maya is used to make animations for films, television, games, and the Internet. Films run at 24 frames per second (fps); television runs at 30 fps; and animation on the Internet often runs at 15 fps. It is important to set the playback speed before you start animating: If you don't, the final animation may be incorrectly paced.

To set animation playback speed:

1. Click the Animation Preferences button , which is near the lower-right corner of the interface.

   The Preferences window opens (**Figure 12.22**).

2. Select Real-time in the pop-up menu next to Playback Speed inside the timeline category.

3. Select Settings from the Categories column.

Figure 12.22 It is important to set Playback Speed before you start animating. Choosing the wrong playback speed can cause the audio to go out of sync with the animation when it's rendered.

Figure 12.23 NTSC (30 fps) is a fairly standard setting for video.

4. Select your frame rate from the pop-up menu next to Time (**Figure 12.23**).

5. Click Save so that these settings will be recalled the next time you open Maya.

Key ticks are the red lines that appear on the timeline when you set a keyframe. Set them to appear only for the selected channels if you want to make changes to some attributes and not others in the timeline.

To change key ticks options:

1. Keyframe an object.

2. Click the Animation Preferences button ▣ in the lower-right corner of the interface.

3. In the Preferences window, for Key Ticks select Channel Box.

Any key ticks in the timeline disappear.

4. Select any keyframed channels in the Channel Box.

The key ticks for those channels appear.

5. Open the Preferences window again, change the Key Ticks setting back to Active, and click Save.

✔ Tips

■ Click the Animation Preferences button to access many of Maya's preferences. Once the window is open, try selecting different categories.

■ If the Key Ticks options are set to Channel Box, only the attributes selected will be affected when you edit them. If you keyframe both an object's scale and rotate attributes, you could move the keyframes of the scale alone by selecting those attributes in the Channel Box and moving the key ticks. The rotate keyframes would be left behind.

SETTING ANIMATION PREFERENCES

Importing Sound Files

Maya lets you import a sound file so you can animate to dialog or to the beat of a song. The file must be in AIFF or WAV format.

To import a sound file:

1. From the File menu, select Import (**Figure 12.24**).

2. Navigate to the sound file you want to use and click Import.

   The sound file does not automatically appear in the timeline.

3. To hear the sound file and see the waveform, right-click the timeline, select Sound, and select your imported file (**Figure 12.25**).

   The waveform should now be visible in the timeline.

4. Click Play to hear the sound file.

   If the sound file doesn't play back, the animation preferences may need to be adjusted.

5. Click the Animation Preferences button near the lower-right corner of the interface.

6. Check to make sure that Playback Speed is set to Real-time. If it is not, select Real-time from the pull-down menu and then click Save (**Figure 12.26**).

   You should now be able to play back the sound. By default, Maya imports the sound file at frame 0 of the timeline.

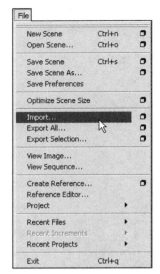

Figure 12.24 Importing sound using the File menu.

Figure 12.25 Change the current sound file, or adjust the setting by right-clicking in the timeline.

Figure 12.26 For playback, the animation settings must be set to Real-time playback speed.

Figure 12.27 You can change the height of the timeline in the animation Preferences window.

Figure 12.28 This is a timeline at the height of 4x. Increase the height only if you need to see the audio more clearly, because the extra height takes up valuable real estate.

7. To change where the sound file begins to play, right-click the timeline, select Sound, and open the options box next to your sound file.

8. Adjust the Offset value to move the beginning of the sound file that number of frames; positive or negative.

✔ Tip

■ You can also import a file by dragging it directly onto the timeline, where it will appear immediately.

You can see the sound waves better if you increase the timeline's height.

To set preferences for timeline height:

1. Click the Animation Preferences button ▨ near the lower-right corner of the interface.

2. Click 2× or 4× next to Height (**Figure 12.27**).

The timeline gets taller (**Figure 12.28**).

3. Click 1× to return the timeline to the normal height.

4. Click Save to keep these preferences.

About the Graph Editor

The Graph Editor is a window that shows a graphic representation of your animation. It has points that represent the time and position in which a keyframe was set, and curves between the keyframes, which show the acceleration (**Figure 12.29**).

By changing the distance between keyframes, you can change an object's speed. However, you must adjust the curve that represents its motion between keyframes to change its acceleration.

You can use the tangent types in the Graph Editor to quickly change the shapes of the curves (**Figure 12.30**). By default, the keyframes you set will be spline tangents. You can also manually adjust the shapes of the tangents. The Graph Editor is helpful for editing, copying, and looping animation.

Tangent types

There are six tangent types, all of which you can set by selecting a keyframe or an animation curve and choosing from the Tangent menu in the Graph Editor. You can also change which tangent type is automatically assigned to keyframes before they are set, in the Keys section of the Preferences window.

◆ **Spline**—Keyframes with spline tangents have smooth curves between and through them (**Figure 12.31**). When animating a fish through water, you might use a spline tangent.

◆ **Linear**—This tangent type simply draws a straight line from one keyframe to the next. It creates jerky movement with sudden changes, which might be good for some-thing mechanical (**Figure 12.32**).

Figure 12.29 Use the Graph Editor to fine-tune your animation once you get the basic timing down.

Figure 12.30 From left to right, these tangent types are spline, linear, and flat.

Figure 12.31 These keyframes are set to the spline tangent type. Note that while the values at frames 1 and 12 are the same, there is still a curve between those points because the keyframes are not set flat. This causes drifting, which can be problematic if you want an object to stay still.

Figure 12.32 These keyframes are set to the linear tangent type.

Figure 12.33 These keyframes are set to the clamped tangent type. This tangent type is similar to the spline tangent except that the drifting problem between frames 1 and 12 has been removed.

Figure 12.34 These keyframes are set to the stepped tangent type.

◆ **Clamped**—This is the default tangent type. Keyframes with clamped tangents act just like spline tangents with one very useful exception: If two keyframes are set at the same value at different points in time, it acts like a linear tangent. It prevents the problem that sometimes occurs with spline tangents, which is that an object you want to be still will drift slightly (**Figure 12.33**).

◆ **Stepped**—This tangent type ensures that a value remains the same until it gets to the next keyframe, when it jumps to that position. It makes the curve look like a step—hence, the name (**Figure 12.34**). One use for this tangent is for producing camera cuts. If you want a camera to hold in one position and then cut to another position, keyframe using a stepped tangent.

◆ **Flat**—The tangent itself becomes horizontal when using this tangent type. Flat tangents typically create "slow-in slow-out"—which means that the animation gradually accelerates between keyframes, goes quickly in the middle of the curve, and then gradually decelerates as it moves to the next keyframe (**Figure 12.35**).

◆ **Fixed**—The tangent doesn't change when you edit the keyframe.

Figure 12.35 These keyframes are set to the flat tangent type.

ABOUT THE GRAPH EDITOR

Creating a bouncing-ball animation is a good way to learn some of the functions of the Graph Editor.

To use the Graph Editor to change tangent types:

1. From the Create menu, select NURBS Primitives > Sphere.

2. Move the sphere up 10 grid units.

   An easy way to do this is to type *10* in the field next to Translate Y in the Channel Box.

3. Make sure you're at frame 1 in the time-line and that Auto Keyframe is turned on.

   The key icon should appear red and pressed down.

4. Press Shift W to keyframe only the translate attributes.

5. Go to frame 15 and translate the sphere down to *1* along the *Y* axis.

   The ball will be keyframed once it is moved, because Auto Keyframe is on.

6. Go to frame 30 and translate the sphere back up to *10* along the *Y* axis.

   Rewind and play back the animation. The ball's bounce is not convincing.

7. From the Window menu, select Animation Editors > Graph Editor.

   The Graph Editor window opens. The curve for the sphere's animation should appear as long as the sphere is still selected.

8. Marquee-select the two keyframes at the top of the graph (**Figure 12.36**).

9. Click the Flat Tangents button in the Graph Editor window.

Figure 12.36 The keyframes at the top of the curve are being selected. The ball is at its highest between these points, and it needs to slow down on the way in and out of them—a perfect use for the flat tangent type.

ABOUT THE GRAPH EDITOR

Figure 12.37 This keyframe is at the point when the ball hits the ground. As it is now, the ball doesn't seem to bounce; it just kisses the ground.

Figure 12.38 Now that the tangents have been adjusted, the ball will appear to really bounce.

10. Select the keyframe at the bottom of the curve (**Figure 12.37**).

Since you're trying to click on such a small point, it helps if you marquee-select, even when you're only selecting one keyframe.

11. Click the Break Tangents button ▼.

This allows you to move the tangents on either side individually.

12. Select the tangent on the left of the keyframe; then Shift-select the tangent on the right.

13. Click the Move Nearest Picked Key Tool button, which is at the top-left corner of the Graph Editor ▣.

14. With the middle mouse button, drag the tangents and move them up one at a time to form a V shape (**Figure 12.38**).

Play back the animation. It should now look more like a real bouncing ball.

ABOUT THE GRAPH EDITOR

Perhaps you want your ball to bounce again. One easy way to accomplish this is to copy and paste keyframes in the timeline.

To copy and paste in the timeline:

1. Animate the bouncing ball as described in the previous task.

2. Make sure that the playback end time is set to at least 60.

   You can do this by typing *60* in the Playback End Time field.

3. Hold down (Shift) and drag in the timeline from 1 to at least 31 (**Figure 12.39**).

4. Right-click the timeline; select Copy from the pop-up menu (**Figure 12.40**).

5. Click frame 30.

   The frame you are on when you paste sets the time when the range of keyframes you paste will begin.

6. From the Edit menu, select Keys and then select the option box next to Paste.

   The Paste Keys Options dialog box opens.

7. In the Paste Method section, click Merge (**Figure 12.41**) to paste the keyframe at the current frame without moving any adjacent keyframes.

8. Click Apply.

   A new keyframe marker appears on the timeline.

9. Rewind and play the animation.

   The ball now bounces twice.

Figure 12.39 You can (Shift)-click and drag the keyframes you want to copy from. If you stop at frame 30 in your selection, the selection will not include the keyframe at 30, so you must go one frame beyond it.

Figure 12.40 Copy the keyframes from the convenient pop-up menu.

Figure 12.41 In the Paste Keys Options dialog box, click Merge to place the keyframe at the current frame without offsetting any adjacent frames.

ABOUT THE GRAPH EDITOR

Figure 12.42 Be sure that the current time is at the point where you want to begin the paste operation. Otherwise, when you paste, the keyframes will end up wherever the current time indicator happens to be and overwrite the frames that were there.

Figure 12.43 Using the Paste Keys options, you can conveniently make several copies at once.

Figure 12.44 This is the result of the paste operation. The ball bounces four times instead of just once.

Sometimes you want an animation to repeat several times. You can use the Graph Editor to perform multiple paste operations at once.

To copy and paste in the Graph Editor:

1. Animate a bouncing ball.

2. Make sure that the timeline goes to at least 120.

   You can do this by typing *120* in the Playback End Time field.

3. From the Window menu, select Animation Editors > Graph Editor.

   The curve for the sphere's animation should appear. If it does not, select the sphere.

4. From the Edit menu in the Graph Editor, select Copy.

5. Hold down $\boxed{k}$ and drag in the Graph Editor window until the red line, which is the time indicator, is at the end of the curve (**Figure 12.42**).

6. From the Edit menu in the Graph Editor, select the box next to Paste.

   The Paste Keys Options window opens.

7. In the Copies field, type *3* (**Figure 12.43**).

8. While the mouse is in the Graph Editor, press $\boxed{f}$.

   The entire animation curve now fits within the window. There are now three additional bounces (**Figure 12.44**).

9. Rewind and play the animation.

   The ball bounces four times.

   If you want to speed up or slow down your animation, you can scale the time in the Graph Editor. A longer time for the same distance means slower movement, and vice versa.

ABOUT THE GRAPH EDITOR

You can also scale values. Perhaps all of your bounces are too high, or none of your arm swings extends far enough. Scaling a value is just as easy as scaling an object's size.

To scale in the Graph Editor:

1. Create a bouncing ball with four bounces, as in the previous task.

2. From the Window menu, select Animation Editors > Graph Editor.

3. From the column on the left, select Translate Y.

   This isolates the Y translate curve.

4. Marquee-select the whole curve.

5. Press [r] to switch to scale mode.

6. Move the mouse over the first keyframe on the left side of the curve (**Figure 12.45**).

   The mouse's location when you begin to scale serves as the scale's pivot point.

7. With the middle mouse button, drag to the left.

8. Move the mouse over one of the low points of the bounces (**Figure 12.46**).

9. With the middle mouse button, drag down.

   The bounces get shorter (**Figure 12.47**).

✔ Tip

■ You can also scale just a portion of a curve by selecting only those keyframes you want to scale. You can likewise scale multiple animated objects at the same time, which is often desirable so that their actions remain synchronized.

Figure 12.45 It is important to have the mouse at the correct position when you start to scale keyframes in the Graph Editor. Wherever you begin to scale is where the pivot point of the scale will be.

Figure 12.46 Here the time has been scaled down so that the ball bounces faster. The mouse has been carefully placed at the bottom of the bounce, so that position will be the pivot point of the scale.

Figure 12.47 Now the value has been scaled down—that is, the bounces don't go as high as they did. Because the pivot point was at the bottom of the curve, the position at which it bounces hasn't changed—which means that the ball will still appear to be bouncing on the ground, not above or below it.

Figure 12.48 The Dope Sheet is especially helpful when working on the timing of a large number of objects.

Figure 12.49
Four joints used
to represent a tail.

Figure 12.50 The first three joints rotated –40 degrees on the Z axis.

About the Dope Sheet

The Dope Sheet is another window used for editing keyframes. You can move, scale, cut, copy, paste, and delete in it, much as you can in the timeline and the Graph Editor. It has the advantage of offering a simple, clear way to move the keyframes of multiple objects in time. For this reason, it's most helpful for adjusting the timing of many objects simultaneously (**Figure 12.48**).

The Dope Sheet can also be useful in creating offset animation. If you set keyframes on a number of objects on the same frame, you can open the Dope Sheet and select those keys easily per object and move them together. In this example, you will create joints and animation for a wagging tail, offset the keys, and cycle the animation.

To create a cycled animation in the Dope Sheet:

1. Create four joints in the front view. Start at the center of the grid and place them one grid unit apart in the positive Y direction (**Figure 12.49**).

2. At frame 0, select the first three joints and set a key by pressing $\boxed{s}$.

3. Move to frame 10 and rotate the three joints –40 degrees along the Z axis (**Figure 12.50**). Press $\boxed{s}$.

4. Move to frame 20 and rotate the three joints back to 0 along the Z axis. Press $\boxed{s}$.

5. Move to frame 30 and rotate the three joints 40 degrees along the Z axis. Press $\boxed{s}$.

continues on next page

ABOUT THE DOPE SHEET

6. Move to frame 40 and rotate the three joints back to 0 along the *Z* axis. Press ⑤.

Now offset the keyframes for each joint so that the second and third joints start to rotate slightly later than the first.

7. Select Window > Animation Editors > Dope Sheet (**Figure 12.51**).

You see the three joints and the block representation of the keyframes we have created.

8. Click joint2 on the left side of the Dope Sheet.

The keyframes for joint2 are highlighted in the right panel of the Dope Sheet.

9. With the middle mouse button, move the keyframes to the right three frames (**Figure 12.52**).

10. Click joint3 on the left side of the Dope Sheet.

11. With the middle mouse button, move the keyframes to the right six frames.

12. Select all three joints on the left side of the Dope Sheet.

13. Select Curves > Pre Infinity > Cycle (**Figure 12.53**).

14. Select Curves > Post Infinity > Cycle.

You now have a cycled and offset tail wag animation.

15. Click Play to see the resulting animation.

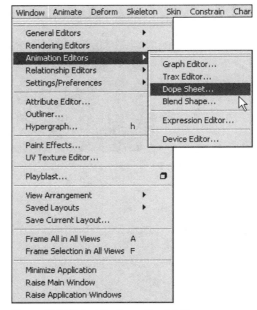

Figure 12.51 Select the Dope Sheet Editor.

Figure 12.52 The keyframes for joint2 can be moved using the middle mouse button.

Figure 12.53 Select Pre Infinity or Post Infinity and then Cycle to cycle the animation before or after the keyframed animation.

ABOUT THE DOPE SHEET

About Constraints

Constraints in Maya connect attributes of objects together so they behave in the same way. This can be useful when you want one object to rotate exactly like another, but you don't want the translate values to change. You can use a constraint to connect the rotate values from one object to another, leaving all other attributes unchanged. Constraints can also be animated and turned on and off, allowing you to connect attributes temporarily.

Constraint Types

Maya offers the following constraint types:

♦ **Point**—A point constraint connects the translate values of one object to another.

♦ **Orient**—An orient constraint connects the rotate values of one object to another.

♦ **Scale**—A scale constraint connects the scale values of one object to another.

♦ **Aim**—An aim constraint aims one object at another object. This type of constraint can be useful for controlling where a character is looking, for example.

♦ **Parent**—The parent constraint works similar to the parent function in Maya but allows you to offset the child object from the parent. You can also turn the constraint on and off and choose which attributes are being affected, which you can't do with the parent function.

♦ **Geometry**—A geometry constraint constrains the position of one object to the surface of another object. The pivot point of the constrained object determines where the constrained object sits on the surface.

continues on next page

◆ **Normal**—A normal constraint constrains an object's orientation values so that they align with the normals of another surface.

◆ **Tangent**—A tangent constraint constrains an object's orientation in the direction of a curve. If the constrained object is attached to a path, a tangent constraint ensures that the object always points in the direction of the path curve.

◆ **Pole Vector**—A pole vector constraint allows you to use an object to control the pole vector value of an IK Rotate Plane handle.

To create a point constraint:

1. Create a NURBS sphere and a polygon cube.

2. Translate the cube a few units away from the sphere.

3. Select the sphere and (Shift)-select the cube.

4. From the Constrain menu, select the box next to Point (**Figure 12.54**).

5. Turn on Maintain Offset (**Figure 12.55**). This ensures that the initial position of the cube remains the same.

6. Click Apply.

   The cube's wireframe becomes pink when the sphere is selected. This means that the sphere is influencing the cube in some way.

7. Select the sphere and translate it in any direction using the Move tool.

   The cube will translate in the exact same way automatically.

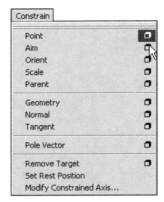

Figure 12.54 Select the Point Constraint options.

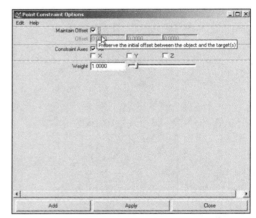

Figure 12.55 Set the Maintain Offset option to keep the object at its current position.

✔ Tips

■ Try adding an orient constraint using the same method as described in the preceding task. Then when you rotate the sphere, the cube will rotate in the same manner.

■ Which object gets constrained is determined by which object is selected first. If you want the cube to control the sphere, you would select the cube first and Shift-select the sphere before creating the constraint.

Muting animation channels

The Mute Animation Channel function lets you temporarily turn off specified animation curves for an object, making it easier to focus on a particular aspect of the animation. For example, if you have a ball bouncing from the left side of the screen to the right, it might be difficult to focus your attention on the up-and-down motion due to the left-to-right motion. If you mute the left-to-right motion, you can see the up-and-down motion more clearly. When you have adjusted the up-and-down motion as you want, you can unmute the left-to-right motion.

To mute an animation channel:

1. Create a NURBS sphere.

2. Change the playback start time to *1* and the playback end time to *50*.

3. At frame 1, select the sphere and set a keyframe.

4. Move to frame 40 and translate the sphere in the front view *20* units to the right. Set another keyframe.

5. Move to frame 20 and set another keyframe.

continues on next page

ABOUT CONSTRAINTS

6. Move to frame 10 and translate the sphere up *10* units. Set a keyframe.

7. Move to frame 30 and translate the sphere up *10* units. Set a keyframe.

You should now have a ball that moves across the screen and bounces up and down.

Now to see only the up-and-down motion, you need to mute the Translate X channel in the Channel Box.

8. With the sphere selected, select Translate X in the Channel Box. Right-click the highlighted word and choose Mute Selected (**Figure 12.56**).

The channel turns brown, and as you drag through the timeline, the ball moves only up and down.

9. To unmute the channel, select Translate X in the Channel Box. Right-click the highlighted word and choose Unmute Selected.

Figure 12.56 Select a channel to mute, right-click, and choose Mute Selected to temporarily disable the animation.

ABOUT CONSTRAINTS

Figure 12.57
Choose Ghost Selected to see the position of your object before and after the current frame.

Figure 12.58 The original sphere in the middle is ghosted, showing its position before and after its current frame.

Figure 12.59
Open the Ghost Options dialog box to adjust the display.

Ghosting

Another way to see problem areas in your animation is to apply ghosting to an object. Ghosting leaves a trail showing where your object is going and where it came from. Some animators find ghosting very useful because it can provide a snapshot of an entire animation.

To ghost an object:

1. Create a sphere.

2. Go to frame 0 in the timeline and key the sphere by pressing $\boxed{s}$.

3. Go to frame 40, translate the sphere *40* units in the *X* direction, and set another keyframe.

4. From the Animate menu, choose Ghost Selected (**Figure 12.57**).

   You should now see multiple spheres. The blue spheres represent where the object was, and the orange spheres represent where it's going (**Figure 12.58**).

5. To change the display of the ghosting, return to the Animate menu and select the options box next to Ghost Selected (**Figure 12.59**).

   The Ghost Options dialog box opens.

continues on next page

GHOSTING

315

6. Change Type of Ghosting to Custom Frame Steps (**Figure 12.60**).

7. Change Steps before Current Frame to *4*.

8. Change Steps after Current Frame to *4*.

9. Change Step Size to *4*.

The step size refers to the number of frames that are skipped between display of a ghost object. If the step size were 1, a ghost of the object would be displayed on every frame.

10. Click Ghost.

Motion Trail is another preview function similar to ghosting. When you apply motion trail to an animated object, a line traces where the object has been and is going.

To create a motion trail:

1. Create a sphere.

2. Go to frame 0 in the timeline and press ⟨s⟩ to create a keyframe.

3. Go to frame 40, translate the sphere *10* units in the *X* direction, and set another keyframe.

4. Go to frame 20, translate the sphere *5* units in the *Y* direction, and set another keyframe.

5. From the Animate menu, select the option box next Motion Trail.

The Motion Trail Options dialog box opens.

6. Set the Increment to *5* and set the Draw Style to *Line* (**Figure 12.61**).

7. Click Apply.

You should now see a line that traces the path that the sphere travels (**Figure 12.62**).

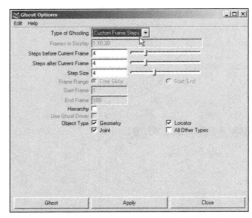

Figure 12.60 Custom settings for the ghosting display.

Figure 12.61 Set the Increment to *5* and the Draw Style to *Line*.

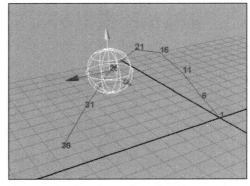

Figure 12.62 A line shows where the object travels and the keyframes at different points on the path.

GHOSTING

Figure 12.63 This curve is drawn in the top view.

INPUTS	
motionPath1	
makeNurbCone1	
U Value	0
Front Twist	0
Up Twist	0
Side Twist	-90

Figure 12.64
The different twists are needed to orient the cone. You cannot simply rotate the cone because its rotate attributes are controlled by the path animation.

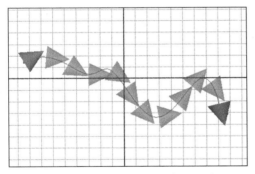

Figure 12.65 This is the resulting path animation.

Path Animation

It could be difficult to animate the flight of an airplane just by setting keyframes because of the number of keyframes that would be required to simulate the detail of the rotation and direction of the plane. Sometimes you'll want to establish the path first and then simply send the object along that path. Maya can even make an object automatically bank around turns and point in the direction of the path.

To animate along a path:

1. Create a curve in the Top view (**Figure 12.63**). (See Chapter 7 for more on creating curves.)

2. From the Create menu, select NURBS Primitives > Cone.

3. Select the cone; then (Shift)-select the curve.

4. From the Animate menu, select Motion Paths > Attach to Motion Path.

   The cone jumps to the beginning of the curve, and when the animation is played back, it moves along the curve.

5. With the cone still selected, click motionPath1 in the Channel Box.

6. Enter −90 in the Side Twist field so that the cone points down the path (**Figure 12.64**).

   When the animation is played back now, you can see how the rotation of the cone follows the path (**Figure 12.65**).

About the Trax Editor

The Trax Editor is another useful animation editor in Maya, incorporating a nonlinear approach to animation. Nonlinear animation allows you to create clips of animation and arrange them in any manner you wish. For example, if you have a ball in your scene, you could have a bouncing clip, a rolling clip, and a deflating clip. You can then blend, rearrange, add, duplicate, or delete these clips, making new animations without touching a keyframe.

At the heart of the Trax Editor is the character set. The character set defines a set of keyframable attributes. What those attributes are is up to you. A character set is not necessarily a complex, rigged character; it could just simply be a sphere.

The character set can be all the keyable attributes of a number of objects. When you create a keyframe for any one of those objects, all of the attributes in that character set will be keyed.

To create a character set:

1. Create a NURBS sphere and a polygon cube.

2. Translate the cube *1.5* units above the sphere.

   This is going to be your character.

3. To create the character set, select the sphere and the cube.

4. From the Character menu, select the box next to Create Character Set (**Figure 12.66**).

5. Change the name of the character set to *All* (**Figure 12.67**).

Figure 12.66
Open the Create Character Set options.

Figure 12.67 Set the options for the character, including what will be keyable.

Figure 12.68
Display the options for creating a subcharacter set.

Figure 12.69 Set the options for the subcharacter set.

Figure 12.70 Use the menu in the bottom right corner or the interface to select the character set you are working with.

6. Click Create Character Set.

   This creates a character set that includes your two objects. Next you will create subcharacter sets for the sphere and cube individually.

7. Select the sphere.

8. From the Character menu, select the box next to Create Subcharacter (**Figure 12.68**).

9. Change the name to *Ball* and click Create Subcharacter (**Figure 12.69**).

10. Select the cube.

11. From the Character menu, select the box next to Create Subcharacter.

12. Change the name to *Box* and click Create Subcharacter.

13. Navigate to current character set menu below the playback controls.

14. Click the arrow and select All (**Figure 12.70**).

   This is where you choose the character or subcharacter you will be working with.

To create a clip:

1. With *All* selected in the current character set menu, go to frame 0 in the timeline.

2. Select the sphere and the cube and press [s].

3. Move to frame 10 in the timeline.

4. Translate the sphere *1* unit up in the *Y* direction.

continues on next page

5. Translate the cube *0.5* unit up in the *Y* direction; press ⑤.

This keyframes the sphere and the cube because they are both in the selected character set. When you keyframe any object in a character set, all objects are keyframed automatically.

6. Move to frame 20 in the timeline.

7. Translate the sphere back down *1* unit so it is back in its original position.

8. Translate the cube back to its original position and press ⑤.

Both the sphere and cube should move up and back down as you drag through the timeline.

9. From the Window menu, select Animation Editors > Trax Editor.

The Trax Editor opens.

10. Click the Load selected Characters icon 🔳.

Two tracks appear, representing your characters.

11. From the Create menu in the Trax Editor, select the box next to Clip (**Figure 12.71**).

12. Change the name to *Bounce* and click Create Clip (**Figure 12.72**).

Two clips now appear in the Trax time-line: Bounce and Bounce1. One clip is assigned to the box and one to the ball.

Figure 12.71 Clips contain all of the keyframes for all of the objects in your character set's animation. The clips can then be manipulated in the Trax Editor.

Figure 12.72 In the Create Clip Options dialog box, you can give the clip a unique name and set specific options for the length and content of the clip.

Figure 12.73 Collapsing the All character set allows you to work with clips under the main character set. You will see one clip as opposed to two subcharacter clips.

Figure 12.74 Scaling the clip.

Figure 12.75 Click the arrow next to your main character set to reveal the subcharacter clips.

To manipulate a clip:

1. Hold (Shift) and select both clips (**Figure 12.73**).

   Arrows appear on both sides of the selected clips, indicating that they can be manipulated together.

2. Scale the clip by clicking the arrow near the right end of the clip then drag the clip to scale it (**Figure 12.74**).

3. Click the middle of the clip and drag to move it in the timeline.

4. Click the All character set to deselect the two clips (**Figure 12.75**).

5. Position the cursor over the upper right corner of the Balls Bounce clip until you see a double-headed arrow with a line in the middle (**Figure 12.76**). Drag the clip to the left until it becomes smaller.

   This cuts off the animation in that clip at that point.

   or

   Position the Current Time indicator at the point in the clip that you would like to trim it to and click the Trim clip after current time icon ☒.

Figure 12.76 Cutting the clip off at a certain point will not destroy the original animation. You can adjust this at any time in the Trax Editor.

ABOUT THE TRAX EDITOR

6. Right-click the Bounce clip and select Duplicate. (**Figure 12.77**).

This inserts the same clip at the position of the cursor in the timeline.

7. Drag the Bounce2 clip to the left so that it overlaps the Bounce clip.

The Trax editor creates a new track for Bounce2 (**Figure 12.78**).

8. Select Bounce2 and Bounce and click the Create Blend icon ▦.

This blends the two animation clips together to create a smooth transition between the clips (**Figure 12.79**).

9. Select Bounce2 and drag it to the right so that it no longer overlaps with Bounce (**Figure 12.80**).

There is currently no translation between the two clips, even though a blend has been assigned, because Bounce2 is currently set to a Relative Offset.

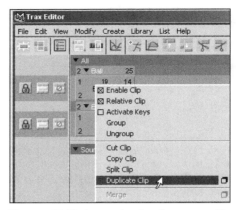

Figure 12.77 All of your animation clips are stored in the library for easy access when you import them.

Figure 12.78 Drag Bounce2 to the left so that it overlaps Bounce. The Trax editor creates a new track for Bounce2.

Figure 12.79 The Blend function creates a spline curve between the last frame of one clip and the first frame of another clip.

Figure 12.80 Drag Bounce2 to the right so that it does not overlap Bounce. Currently there is no nterpolation between the two clips because the Offset of Bounce2 is set to relative.

Figure 12.81 The Trax Editor allows you to have multiple tracks for each character or subcharacter. By using multiple tracks, you can have more than one clip playing at the same time for the same character.

Figure 12.82 The same clip can be imported and moved to a new track. There it can be placed to overlap the original clip, adding to the motion of the original animation.

10. Select Bounce2 and in the Channel Box, click in the field next to Offset and select Absolute.

Now the blend interpolates between the end position of the last clip and the next clip.

11. Right-click the Bounce1 in the Box track and select Duplicate.

12. Select the new clip and position the Current Time indicator so that it is halfway through the clip and click the Trim clip after current time icon (**Figure 12.81**).

This trims the clip so that the Box goes up but does not come down.

13. Right-click the new clip and select duplicate. Repeat this several times to get several instances of the shortened clip on the track. (**Figure 12.82**).

You now have several clips of the same animation one after each other for the Box subcharacter. The Bounce2 clip will have an additive affect because the Offset on each clip is set to Relative, and the box should bounce higher and higher.

The Trax Editor is a powerful tool, with many functions and controls. Here is a list of other commonly used functions:

◆ **Cut, Copy, Paste, Duplicate**—Select the clip you want to edit; then from the Edit menu, select Cut, Copy, Paste, or Duplicate.

◆ **Attribute Editor**—The clip's Attribute Editor allows you to adjust the scale, offset, and cycling of the clip you've selected. To see the Attribute Editor, select the clip; then from the Modify menu, select Attribute Editor.

◆ **Animation Curves**—To see and adjust the original animation curves in the graph editor, select the clip; then click the Graph Anim Curves icon .

ABOUT THE TRAX EDITOR

323

About Blend Shapes

Blend Shapes are deformers that let you blend the shape of one object into another. This feature is particularly useful for facial animation and muscle deformation and to fix badly deformed geometry. For example, if you wanted to make a character smile, you could simply duplicate the head, change the shape of the mouth into a smile, and apply the smiling head as a Blend Shape. The one restriction of Blend Shape is that both objects must have the same topology, or surface construction.

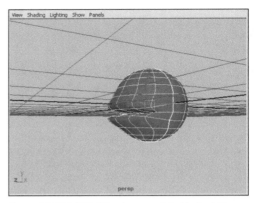

Figure 12.83 A NURBS sphere modeled to look like a head with a mouth.

To apply a Blend Shape:

1. Create a NURBS sphere.

   You may need to add more spans to the sphere to get more detail. I've used 14 sections and 14 spans.

2. Change the shape of the sphere by moving CVs so that it looks like it has a mouth (**Figure 12.83**).

3. Duplicate the sphere and move it away from the original.

4. Change the shape of the new sphere by moving the CVs so that it looks like it is smiling (**Figure 12.84**).

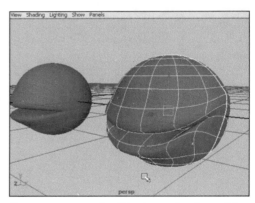

Figure 12.84 By moving CVs, change the shape of the mouth to a smile.

5. Duplicate the original sphere again, move it aside, and change its shape so that it looks like it is frowning (**Figure 12.85**).

6. (Shift)-select, in this order; the smile, the frown, and the original head.

7. From the Deform menu, select Create Blend Shape (**Figure 12.86**).

   This applies the two new shapes to the original head.

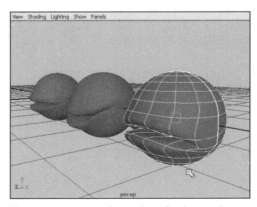

Figure 12.85 Create a frown shape for the mouth.

Figure 12.86 Create a Blend Shape from the Deform menu.

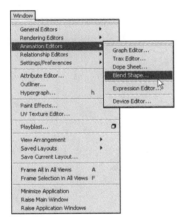

Figure 12.87 Open the Blend Shape controls from the Animation Editors menu.

8. From the Window menu select Animation Editors > Blend Shape (**Figure 12.87**).

9. In the Blend Shape window adjust the two sliders to see the effect on the original head.

10. At frame 1, click the Key All button (**Figure 12.88**).

11. Go to frame 10 and move the first slider all the way up (**Figure 12.89**).

12. Click the Key All button.

13. Go to frame 20 and move the first slider down and the second slider up.

14. Click the Key All button again.

Now when you play back the animation, the original head changes its shape from a neutral look to a smile and then to a frown.

✔ Tip

■ The key ticks do not show up automatically in the timeline for Blend Shapes. To show the key ticks click the Select button in the Blend Shape editor.

Figure 12.88 Sliders are used to adjust how much the original shape is deformed.

Figure 12.89 The blend shapes can be keyframed over time to create facial animation.

Previewing Your Animation

When you want to preview an animation, you can play it back in the timeline. However, a complex scene won't play smoothly at full speed. In addition, you'll often want to output your animations. For this, Maya provides Playblast, which produces screen snapshots of your animation and turns it into an AVI on the PC or a Quicktime on the Mac file or a series of numbered images.

To create a Playblast preview:

1. Create an animation.

2. From the Windows menu, select the box next to Playblast to open the Playblast Options window (**Figure 12.90**).

3. Choose the time range for the movie file you want to create.

   The Time slider will use your current playback start and end times. The Start Time and End Time fields allow you to enter your own times.

4. Adjust the resolution of the movie.

   If Display Size is set to From Window, the movie will use whichever view panel is currently active as the basis for the size. If you change Display Size to Custom, you can enter whatever resolution you want.

5. Select Save to File if you want Playblast to automatically save your series of numbered frames after you create it.

   If Save to File is checked, you can click Browse to choose where you want the files saved. In Windows, you can make a Movieplayer file instead of a series of numbered frames.

6. Click the Playblast button.

   You will see your animation play back a frame at a time. A moment later, the FCheck window, where you can watch your animation, will pop up.

Figure 12.90 You set the Playblast options in this window. If you don't click Save to File and you close your movie player after you watch your animation, you will have to repeat the Playblast procedure on the animation.

DEFORMERS

Wrinkles, waves, and folds are just a few of the things you can create using Maya's deformer tools and a few simple mouse clicks. You can use these versatile tools to manipulate surfaces with the greatest of precision, as well as to simplify the selection and transformation of complex surfaces. Whether you're creating a twisted logo or a water droplet in a glass, you can find a deformer that fits the bill and makes the task a breeze.

Say, for example, you wanted to create a model of an elderly person: You could use the Wire deformer to create the fine folds and wrinkles of the face, and the Sculpt deformer for the areas of the face that you want to be more rounded.

Deformers can also speed modeling tasks by creating a simplified cage (called a *lattice*) around a complex surface. You use this lattice to select and manipulate the surface with a minimal amount of points—as opposed to selecting all of the fine detail on the surface of a model. You can use a lattice to create the point of an elbow or add emotion to a cartoon character's eye. The following describes Maya's deformers and how to use them.

Nonlinear Deformers

You can use nonlinear deformers to quickly bend, twist, flare, or even squash a surface, greatly speeding tasks that would otherwise require multiple CV selections, rotations, scales, and transformations. Create a spiral staircase out of a cube with the Twist deformer. Bend a steel spoon with ease using a Bend deformer, or create bell-bottom pants using the Flare deformer. Each of the nonlinear deformers performs a specific task related directly to its name. Nonlinear deformers include Bend, Flare, Sine, Squash, Twist, and Wave (**Figure 13.1**).

Figure 13.1 The nonlinear deformers (from left): Bend, Flare, Wave, Twist, Sine, and Squash.

The two most common options for the nonlinear deformer tools include the following:

◆ **Envelope**—You use this option to specify the scale factor of the deformation. You can select values from 0 to 1, and you can enter values from −2 to 2. A value of 2 doubles the overall deformation effect; a negative value inverts the effect. The default value is 1.

◆ **Low and High Bound (all nonlinear deformers except Wave)**—Adjust the Low and High Bound when you want part of the surface to remain unaffected by the deformer.

In addition, each of the nonlinear deformer tools has its own distinct options, discussed in the sections that follow.

Figure 13.2 From the Deform menu select Create Nonlinear › Bend.

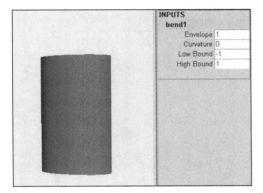

Figure 13.3 The Bend properties control how much an object is deformed.

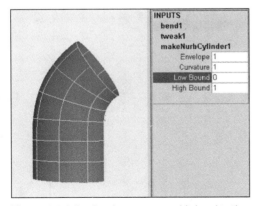

Figure 13.4 Adjusting the curvature adds bend to the object; adjusting the Low Bound controls the start point of the Bend from the bottom of the object. With a Low Bound of 0, half of the cylinder remains undeformed (shown); with a Low Bound of –1, the entire lower half is deformed.

Bend deformer

The Bend deformer can be a great time saver when you need to bend geometry but don't want to take the time to move each CV individually. Once a Bend deformer is added to a surface, the user can control the amount of surface arc, thus making the surface appear to bend. The more isoparms (the lines that define the NURBS geometry) that you add to a surface before adding the Bend deformer, the smoother the arc will appear.

An additional option for the Bend deformer is Curvature, which determines the amount the object bends.

To use the Bend deformer:

1. Select the object to be deformed.

2. From the Deform menu, select Create Nonlinear > Bend (**Figure 13.2**).

   The Bend deformer is added to the selected surface.

3. Click the bend1 title under the Inputs section of the Channel Box to view the Bend properties (**Figure 13.3**).

4. Set Curvature to *1*.

   The object is now bent around its center.

5. Set Low Bound to *0*.

   The object's bend still starts at its center, but only the top of the object is bent (**Figure 13.4**).

✔ Tip

■ You can translate or rotate deformers through the objects to get different effects.

NONLINEAR DEFORMERS

Flare deformer

You can attach this deformer to a surface to taper or flare selected geometry—useful on surfaces like jugs, bellies, and bell-bottoms.

Additional options for the Flare deformer include the following:

◆ **Start Flare X and Z**—Determines the amount of flare at the start of the Low Bound along the specified axis.

◆ **End Flare X and Z**—Determines the amount of flare at the start of the High Bound along the specified axis.

◆ **Curve**—Determines the amount of curvature between the Low and High Bound.

To use the Flare deformer:

1. Select the object to be deformed.

2. From the Deform menu, select Create Nonlinear > Flare.

   A Flare deformer is added to the selected surface (**Figure 13.5**).

3. Click the flare1 title under the Inputs section of the Channel Box to view the Flare properties.

4. Click Start Flare X (**Figure 13.6**).

5. Click and drag with the middle mouse button in the Perspective view to flare the base of the object until Start Flare equals 3.

   or

   If you don't have a three-button mouse, you can type the desired value in the Start Flare X field.

   The object is flared along the *x* axis (**Figure 13.7**).

✔ Tip

■ Have your surface geometry ready with the desired amount of CVs and isoparms before adding a deformer to a surface. Adding geometry after a deformer is applied may cause undesirable results, such as the surface ignoring the deformer or over-emphasizing the deformation.

Deformer   Cylinder

Figure 13.5 When a nonlinear deformer is added to a surface (Flare is shown here), a special manipulator is created to control the look of the deformation. The original cylinder is gray, the deformer is white.

Figure 13.6 The Flare parameters.

Figure 13.7 The object becomes stretched by the Flare deformer.

Figure 13.8 Select Sine to add the deformer to the geometry.

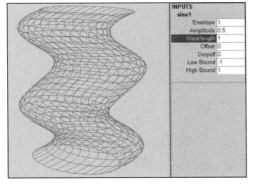

Figure 13.9 The Sine deformer causes the object to appear wavy.

Sine deformer

The Sine deformer changes the shape of an object along a specified sine wave, which is a scribble-like line that looks similar to the way a heart monitor line displays a normal heartbeat. Added Sine options include:

◆ **Amplitude**—Determines the maximum wave amount.

◆ **Wavelength**—Decreasing Wavelength greatens the frequency; increasing it lessens the frequency.

◆ **Offset**—Determines the location of the sine wave relative to the center of the deformer handle.

◆ **Dropoff**—Determines how the amplitude of the sine wave decays. Negative values decay toward the center of the deformer handle; positive values decay away from the center of the deformer handle.

To use the Sine deformer:

1. Select the object to be deformed.

2. From the Deform menu, select Create Nonlinear > Sine (**Figure 13.8**).

   A Sine deformer is added to the selected surface.

3. Click the Sine(n) title under the Inputs section of the Channel Box to view the sine properties.

4. Click Amplitude.

5. Click and drag with the middle mouse button in the Perspective view until Amplitude equals 0.5 or type *0.5* in the Amplitude field.

   The surface begins to have a wavy shape.

6. Click Wavelength.

7. To add more curve to the object's shape, click and drag with the middle mouse button in the Perspective view until Wavelength equals 1 or type *1* in the Wavelength field (**Figure 13.9**).

NONLINEAR DEFORMERS

Wave deformer

The Wave deformer is perfect for creating water-droplet rings and small waves over a surface. This deformer works best on highly detailed flat surfaces. Additional Wave options include:

◆ **Amplitude**—Determines the maximum wave amount.

◆ **Wavelength**—Decreasing Wavelength greatens the frequency; increasing it lessens the frequency.

◆ **Offset**—Determines the location of the sine wave relative to the center of the deformer handle. Animating the Offset will make the surface ripple outward.

◆ **Dropoff**—Determines how the amplitude of the sine wave decays. Negative values decay towards the center of the deformer handle; positive values decay away from the center of the deformer handle.

◆ **Dropoff Position**—Determines the start and end position of the amplitude of the sine wave.

◆ **Min and Max Radius**—Determines the minimum and maximum radius of the circular sine wave.

To use the Wave deformer:

1. Create a NURBS primitive plane.

2. In the Channel Box, change patches U and patches V to *10*.

3. From the Deform menu, select Create Nonlinear > Wave.

   A Wave deformer is added to the selected surface (**Figure 13.10**).

4. Click the Wave(n) title under the Inputs section of the Channel Box to view Wave properties.

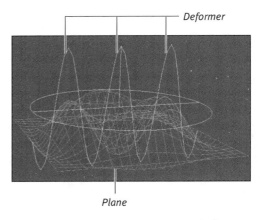

Figure 13.10 The Wave manipulator controls the Wave deformer's parameters. Deformer is white, plane is gray.

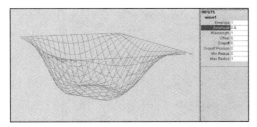

Figure 13.11 The Amplitude setting determines the maximum wave amount.

Figures 13.12 By increasing Wavelength to 1.4, we decrease wave frequency.

5. Set Amplitude to *0.6*.

The object becomes wavy (**Figure 13.11**).

6. Set Wavelength to *1.4*.

Fewer waves now define the object's shape (**Figure 13.12**).

The Squash deformer

The Squash deformer gives the user precise control over a surface's volume when it's being squashed. If you scale a surface vertically along one axis without scaling the other axes horizontally, you create a surface with less physical volume, breaking the illusion of real objects, which keep the same volume when they are squashed. If you want your objects to appear realistic, it's important to keep the volume of the object the same when adding squash and stretch. Additional Squash options include the following:

◆ **Factor**—Determines the amount an object can be squashed or stretched.

◆ **Expand**—Determines how much an object will expand (in volume) outward while squashing, or inward while stretching.

◆ **Start and End Smoothness**— Determines the amount of smoothing (similar to Dropoff) near the low-bound position (Start Smoothness), or near the high-bound (End Smoothness). In a cylinder the high-bound and low-bound position would be the top and bottom of the cylinder, respectively. So if Start Smoothness is altered, the point at the bottom of the cylinder will have a smoother transition into the squash.

NONLINEAR DEFORMERS

To use the Squash deformer:

1. Create a NURBS primitive cylinder to be deformed.

2. From the Deform menu, select Create Nonlinear > Squash (**Figure 13.13**).

   A Squash deformer is added to the selected surface.

3. Click the Squash(n) title under the Inputs section of the Channel Box to view the Squash properties.

4. Set Factor to *–0.7*.

   The object is squashed vertically (**Figure 13.14**).

5. Set Expand to *1.7*.

   The object expands to add volume to the shape (**Figure 13.15**).

✔ Tip

■ The Squash deformer can be keyframed to squash and stretch an object or character.

Figure 13.13 Select Deform > Create Nonlinear > Squash.

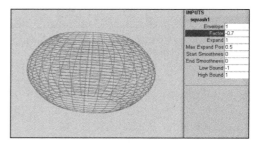

Figure 13.14 A negative Factor setting squashes the object; a positive Factor setting stretches it.

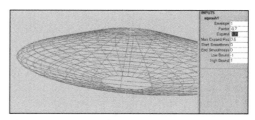

Figure 13.15 If you squash an object, you should expand it to make sure it retains its volume.

NONLINEAR DEFORMERS

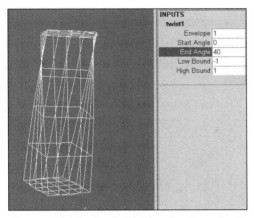

Figure 13.16 Adjusting End Angle twists the surface's shape.

Figure 13.17 Adjusting Low Bound to *0* forces the twisting to begin halfway up the deformed surface.

Twist deformer

The Twist deformer is often used to twist a cube into a cartoon-style building or to quickly create a twisted metal sculpture. The higher the density of the geometry, the smoother the twist will appear.

The Twist deformer includes one option, the Start and End Angle, which determines the degree of twisting from the Low or High Bound position.

To use the Twist deformer:

1. Create a primitive polygonal cube.

2. From the Deform menu, select Create Nonlinear > Twist.

   A Twist deformer is added to the selected surface.

3. Click the Twist(n) title under the Inputs section of the Channel Box to view the Twist properties.

4. Set End Angle to *40*.

   The entire object twists around the center of the deformer (**Figure 13.16**).

5. Set Low Bound to *0*.

   The twist now starts halfway up the object (**Figure 13.17**).

NONLINEAR DEFORMERS

The Lattice

The Lattice is one of Maya's most used, and most functional, deformers. You can use it to simplify CV selection on a complex surface, to create the point of a character's elbow, or to provide added control to surface areas prone to creasing (for example, elbows and knees).

Lattice deformers surround deformable objects with a box-like shape called a *lattice* (**Figure 13.18**). The lattice is then used to select and deform the surface by moving, rotating, or scaling the lattice structure (**Figure 13.19**). Lattices are also deformable objects, which means you can add other deformers to deform the lattice (and the object it's deforming).

An important option of the Lattice deformer is Divisions, found under the Lattice's Shape node in the Channel Box; A lattice is one of the few Maya objects that have options under its Shape node. Adding more divisions to a lattice indirectly adds more lattice points for future selection. A lattice point is created at every lattice crossing.

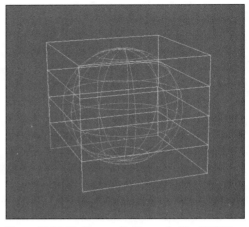

Figure 13.18 A lattice applied to a primitive NURBS sphere.

Figure 13.19 By moving lattice points you deform the surface.

Figure 13.20 Select Create Lattice to apply a lattice to the surface.

Figure 13.21 Set the Pick Mask selection type to "Select by component type" to show the lattice points.

Lattice ——————— Sphere

Lattice points

Figure 13.22 Lattice points appear at each of the lattice cross-sections.

To use a Lattice to deform a surface:

1. Create a NURBS primitive sphere.

2. From the Deform menu, select Create Lattice (**Figure 13.20**).

   A Lattice deformer is added to the selected surface.

3. Set the Pick Mask selection type to "Select by component type" (**Figure 13.21**).

   Lattice points appear on the corners of the lattice.

4. Select a corner lattice point (**Figure 13.22**).

5. Move the lattice point away from the surface (**Figure 13.23**).

   The original surface is now deformed by the change in the lattice shape.

Figure 13.23 Moving one lattice point moves multiple CVs on the surface.

THE LATTICE

Wire and Sculpt Deformers

The Wire and Sculpt deformers use objects and curves to manipulate and deform a selected surface.

Wire deformers use one or more NURBS curves, called *wires,* to deform the selected surface (**Figure 13.24**). You can use additional curves, called *holders*, to limit the influence of the Wire deformer. This gives you the precise control you need to create subtle surface deformations.

Sculpt deformers use a spherical influence object (a deform manipulator that is shaped like a sphere), called a *sculpt sphere,* to deform a surface (**Figure 13.25**). Sculpt deformers are great for creating rounded surface effects like the tip of a nose or chin. Switching the deformer's mode between flip, project, and stretch can produce different surface effects.

Figure 13.24 One wire is used here to deform a flat plane.

Plane ─────────┐   ┌──────── Deformer

Figure 13.25 A flat plane is deformed by the Sculpt deformer's influence. Deformer is white, plane is gray.

Figure 13.26 A NURBS plane that has 10 patches added in the *U* and *V* directions. The more patches you add to a surface, the smoother the deformation will be.

Figure 13.27 Although the wire doesn't need to overlap the deformed surface, it helps clarify the area to be deformed.

Figure 13.28 Select Wire Tool to select the surface to be deformed and the deforming wire.

To create a Wire deformer without a holder:

1. Create a NURBS plane and, in the Channel Box options, set patches U and patches V to *10* (**Figure 13.26**).

2. Create a NURBS curve that overlaps the plane (**Figure 13.27**).

   This curve will be used as the influence wire (a deform manipulator shaped like a wire; a curve is used for our wire shape).

3. From the Deform menu, select Wire Tool (**Figure 13.28**).

4. Select the plane and press Enter.

5. Select the CV curve and press Enter.

6. Move the CV curve along the *Y* axis.

   The plane deforms along the contour of the CV curve (**Figure 13.29**).

✔ Tips

- The curve's CVs can be manipulated along any axis to further control the deformation of the surface.

- If you want the curve to affect less surface area, lower the value of the Dropoff Distance.

Figure 13.29 The shape of the curve is reflected in the way the surface becomes deformed.

To create a Wire deformer *with* a holder:

1. Follow steps 1 and 2 in the previous task, "To create a Wire deformer without a holder."

2. Create a NURBS circle that overlaps the plane (**Figure 13.30**).

    The circle will be your holder.

3. From the Deform menu, select the Wire Tool options box.

4. Select the Holders check box (**Figure 13.31**).

5. Click Close.

6. Select the plane and press (Enter).

7. Select the CV curve and press (Enter).

8. Select the NURBS circle and press (Enter).

9. Move the CV curve along the *y* axis.

    The plane deforms along the contour of the CV curve but not past the circle object (**Figure 13.32**).

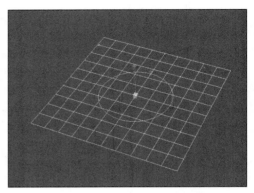

Figure 13.30 Scale the circle until it overlaps most of the plane.

Figure 13.31 If Holders is checked, you can use an additional curve to stop the Wire deformer's influence.

Figure 13.32 The plane deforms along the contour of the CV curve but not past the circle object.

WIRE AND SCULPT DEFORMERS

Figure 13.33 The Sculpt deformer pushes the surface geometry around its spherical shape, deforming the plane much like the way mud would look if a heavy ball was dropped onto it.

Figure 13.34 The surface wraps around the Sculpt deformer's influence sphere.

To create a Sculpt deformer:

1. Create a NURBS plane, and in the Channel Box, set U and V patches to *10*.

2. Set the X, Y, and Z scale to *5*.

   Scaling the plane ensures the deformer will not be larger than the plane.

3. From the Deform menu, select Create Sculpt Deformer.

   A Sculpt object is applied to the object (**Figure 13.33**).

4. Select the Sculpt object and move it in the positive *Y* direction.

   The Sculpt object causes the original geometry to expand (**Figure 13.34**).

✔ Tip

■ You can select and move the locator (crosshairs) to move the geometry over the Sculpt object.

Jiggle Deformers

Unlike the other deformers we have discussed, Jiggle deformers are dynamic because they deform geometry in reaction to motion. When a rubbery or fleshy surface object stops moving, the surface jiggles and eventually settles.

To create a Jiggle deformer:

1. Create a NURBS primitive cylinder, and in the Channel Box, set the Y scale to *4*.

2. In the Inputs section of the Channel Box, click makeNurbCylinder1 to display more options and set Spans to *10* (**Figure 13.35**).

3. In the timeline, create a keyframe (press ⒮) at frame 1.

4. Go to frame 30, press ⓦ and use the Move tool to click and drag the object to a new location.

5. Press ⒮ to create another keyframe. The faster the object moves, the more the deformer will jiggle.

6. Set the last frame at 300 in the timeline to give the jiggle time to settle after the object stops (**Figure 13.36**).

7. Select the cylinder and then choose Deform > Create Jiggle Deformer.

   Several nodes are added to the cylinder in the Inputs section of the Channel Box (**Figure 13.37**).

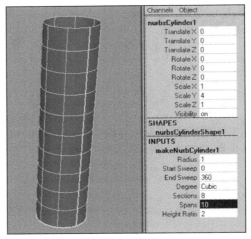

Figure 13.35 Add ten Spans to a NURBS cylinder.

Figure 13.36 Set the end of playback to 300 in the timeline.

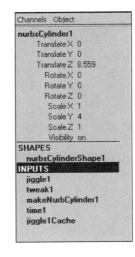

Figure 13.37 A Jiggle node is added to the Inputs section of the Channel Box.

INPUTS
jiggle1
tweak1
makeNurbCylinder1
time1
jiggle1Cache

Envelope	1
Enable	Enable
Ignore Transform	off
Force Along Normal	1
Force On Tangent	1
Motion Multiplier	20
Stiffness	0.5
Damping	0.5
Jiggle Weight	1
Direction Bias	0

Figure 13.38 Set the Motion Multiplier of the Jiggle node to *20* to amplify the effect of movement.

Figure 13.39 You can apply a jiggle to just one part of an object using the Attribute Editor for the Paint Jiggle Weights tool.

Figure 13.40 Replace the current weights to *0*.

8. Click jiggle1 to display more options and set Motion Multiplier to *20* (**Figure 13.38**).

A higher value will exaggerate the effect that the motion has on the jiggle relative to the scale of the object.

9. Set Stiffness and Damping to *0.1*.

A low Stiffness value will cause the jiggle to be more stretchy and rubbery, whereas a low Damping value causes the jiggle to take longer to settle.

10. In the timeline, press Play ▶ to view the animation and then press Stop ■.

When the object stops, it moves back and forth as if it was dangling from a rubber band.

To apply a Jiggle deformer to part of an object:

1. Follow all the steps in the previous task, "To create a Jiggle deformer."

2. From the Deform menu, select the box next to Paint Jiggle Weights tool.

The Attribute Editor for the Paint Jiggle Weights tool opens. The cursor changes to a paintbrush, indicating that the Paint Jiggle Weights tool is active, and the object turns white, indicating that the deformer has equal control over the entire surface (**Figure 13.39**).

3. In the Paint Attributes section, select Replace next to Paint Operations.

4. Set the Value slider to *0* and click Flood.

The object turns black, indicating that the deformer has no control on the surface so that the jiggle has no effect (**Figure 13.40**).

continue on next page

JIGGLE DEFORMERS

5. Set the Value slider to *1*.

The areas painted with 1 will be the most effected by the Jiggle deformer and will jiggle freely, while the areas with lower values painted on them will move less or not at all.

6. With the brush, paint white all the way around the middle of the cylinder (**Figure 13.41**).

7. In the Paint Attributes section, select Smooth next to Paint Operations and then click Flood several times to spread out the effect more evenly.

8. Click Play ▶.

Now when the object stops, only the mid-section of the cylinder wobbles like a bowl full of jelly (**Figure 13.42**).

Figure 13.41 Make the middle of the cylinder soft by painting a value of *1* around the middle.

Figure 13.42 The middle of the cylinder now jiggles when it comes to a stop.

JIGGLE DEFORMERS

Figure 13.43 The first object selected will be Wrap deformed to the second object.

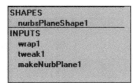

Figure 13.44 A wrap node is added under Inputs section of the Channel Box.

Figure 13.45 Moving the influence object moves the second object as well.

Figure 13.46 When the Max Distance value is set to *0*, it gives the influence object infinite control over a surface.

Figure 13.47 A Max Distance value of *1* causes part of the first object to stick to the influence object.

Wrap Deformers

Wrap deformers use an object to deform other objects so that part of one surface sticks to the other surface. You'll often use Wrap deformers in character rigging. Using a low-res poly cage bound to a skeleton, you can deform a high-res NURBS patch model. However, that takes a lot of memory and can be difficult to work with. Instead, many animators prefer to use the low-res poly cage of a Smooth Proxy Polygon model or the level-0 of a Subdiv model to deform the higher detail of the other levels.

To create a Wrap deformer:

1. Select two objects.

   The first object selected (the plane) will be deformed by the second (the cross) (**Figure 13.43**).

2. Select Deform > Create Wrap.

   A wrap1 node is added to the Channel Box in the Inputs section of the first object you selected (**Figure 13.44**).

3. Select the first object and press ⓦ to activate the Move tool, then click and drag the object up (**Figure 13.45**).

   Both objects move because the Max Distance of the first object (otherwise known as the influence object) is set at *0* by default. This value gives the influence object (the cross) infinite control over the other object (the plane).

4. With the influence object selected, click wrap1 in the Outputs section of the Channel Box (**Figure 13.46**).

5. Set the Max Distance to *1*.

   Now the object being deformed will return to it's original position with the areas that were nearest the influence object sticking to it (**Figure 13.47**).

WRAP DEFORMERS

Deforming Particles

In all the previous examples we have shown you how to deform surfaces, but you can also deform particles. With deformers, you can control particles in ways that would be difficult—even physically impossible, in some cases—using dynamics.

To deform particles:

1. Select a particle object (**Figure 13.48**).

   For more information on creating parti-cle systems, see Chapter 18, "Dynamics."

2. From the Deform menu, select the box next to Create Lattice.

   The Lattice Options dialog box opens (**Figure 13.49**).

3. Set Divisions to *4-2-2* (**Figure 13.50**).

4. From the Outside Lattice pull-down menu, choose Transform All Points (**Figure 13.51**).

   This option applies the effect to particles or geometry that move outside of the lat-tice. Otherwise, there would be an abrupt change in the effect on the particle or surface.

Figure 13.48 Select a particle object to deform.

Figure 13.49 Open the Lattice Options dialog box.

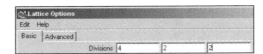

Figure 13.50 Set the Divisions for the lattice to *4*, *2*, and *2*.

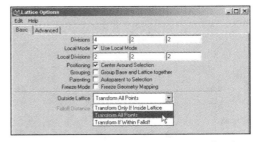

Figure 13.51 Choose Transform All Points so that the deformation continues even if the particles go outside the lattice.

DEFORMING PARTICLES

Figure 13.52 Uncheck Use Local Mode to make the lattice look smooth and curvy.

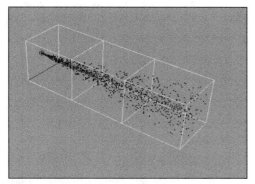

Figure 13.53 A lattice appears around the particle object.

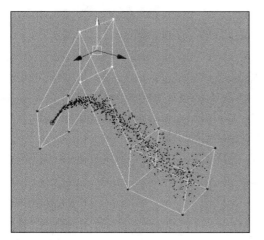

Figure 13.54 Move selected points in the lattice to deform the particle object.

5. Uncheck Use Local Mode (**Figure 13.52**).

Use Local Mode forces the deformation to be strictly based on the number of divisions in the lattice and the result often looks angular and unnatural. Unchecking this option results in a smooth, curvy deformation that appears more organic.

6. Click Apply.

A lattice appears around the particles (**Figure 13.53**).

7. Press F8 to switch to component mode and click the Points icon ▪.

8. Select points in the lattice, then press w and use the Move tool to drag them (**Figure 13.54**).

9. Press Play ▶ to see the effect of the lattice on the moving particles (**Figure 13.55**).

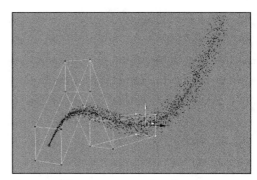

Figure 13.55 Press Play to see the effect the lattice has on the particles in motion.

Hiding, Showing, and Deleting Deformers

To delete a deformer:

1. Select the deformer handle of the deformer you wish to delete (**Figure 13.56**).

2. Select Edit > Delete, or press ⌷Bksp⌷.

To delete a deformer but keep the deformations on the surface:

1. Select the object with the deformer you wish to delete (**Figure 13.57**).

2. Select Edit > Delete by Type > History. The deformer is deleted but the object is locked into its deformed state.

To show all deformers:

◆ From the Display menu select Show > Show Deformers > All (**Figure 13.58**).

To hide all deformers:

◆ From the Display menu select Hide > Hide Deformers > All (**Figure 13.59**).

✔ Tip

■ In addition to showing all of the deformers, you can individually show many object types such as lattices, sculpt objects, cluster handles, and nonlinear deformer handles.

Figure 13.56 The surface wraps around the Sculpt deformer's influence sphere.

Figure 13.57 The Taper deformer handle connected to a cylinder is selected.

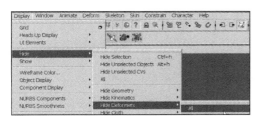

Figure 13.59 All of the deformers are hidden.

Figure 13.58 All of the hidden deformers are shown.

CREATING LIGHTS

Figure 14.1 Adding an area of focus strengthens the scene.

Figure 14.2 An object can be accented through the correct use of light.

Light and shadow are essential in creating a three-dimensional, realistic scene. Lighting is a crucial element in setting the mood and feeling of a scene. Too much light can flatten out a scene, leaving the viewer unengaged and uninterested in the imagery. However, the right light intensity and placement can draw the eye around the scene. You can use lights to focus a viewer's attention on a particular place in your scene (**Figure 14.1**) or on an object you don't want the viewer to miss (**Figure 14.2**). Light can be used to draw spectators into the scene, as if they were participants, or to leave them feeling like onlookers, outside the action.

For centuries, artists have used *chiaroscuro*—the play of light and dark—to invoke emotions and to draw viewers into their paintings. Leonardo da Vinci, Gerrit Van Honthorst, and the master of painting with light, Caravaggio, all experimented with light in their paintings. More recently, we've seen filmmakers use similar techniques in their movies. *Blade Runner, The Godfather*, and *The Blair Witch Project* are all great examples: As these movies unfold, their action is supported with lighting through various colors, intensity, and placement.

Controlling light, however, can be tricky. In this chapter, we'll look at the attributes and techniques used to control lights in a Maya scene.

Setting the Scene's Mood

One of the first things to consider in lighting your scene is the time of day. A good exercise to demonstrate how much difference lighting can make is to create and light the same scene in three or four different lighting scenarios. You can set up one scene to have a scary and luminous quality (**Figure 14.3**), and then relight the scene for a bright summer day (**Figure 14.4**). You will quickly see how essential lighting is to a well-produced scene.

The following describes the various qualities of light found at different times of the day (from an artistic point of view):

◆ **Dawn**—Most of the sky is filled with a light glow, soft and diffused, leaving objects in the room dimly lit. Highlights and reflections become visible first, then everything else slowly comes into view. Dawn has a very subtle light, requiring some time for the human eye to adjust.

◆ **Sunrise**—Light pours into the room as a new day begins. Long shadows and light patterns are projected on the wall through the window, splashing light around the room. As the sunrise progresses, the day's shadows become more transparent and shorter, leading into the sharp midday sun.

◆ **Sunset**—Orange, red, and pink sunset colors fill the clouds and the sky, bringing a feeling of tranquility and closure to the day. Mountains and trees are silhouetted against the sun at the horizon, and long shadows lay along the ground.

◆ **Evening**—Peaceful silvery-blue light fills the room, illuminating it softly. The room is lit with candles and ceiling lights that quickly fall off into the darkness. The only light coming in from outside is the moon glowing through the haze around it, creating ominous bluish highlights throughout the scene.

Figure 14.3 You can use light to create specific moods—for example, ominous and scary, as shown here.

Figure 14.4 Light can be used to brighten an entire scene.

Figure 14.5 The Hypershade.

Figure 14.6
The Create bar.

About the Hypershade

The Hypershade is a window where you can create, delete, view, and enhance lights as well as materials, textures, and utilities (**Figure 14.5**).

To open the Hypershade:

◆ Select Panel > Panels > Hypershade.

or

◆ Click the Hypershade/Persp button right below the toolbar at the left of the layout.

or

◆ Select Window > Rendering Editors > Hypershade.

When you first open the Hypershade, you'll see a panel on its left side called the Create bar (**Figure 14.6**). This is where the different texture- and light-related nodes are housed. You can create a new node by using the middle mouse button to drag the icon into the work area to the right of the Create bar.

continues on next page

You can see the node types you want to create by expanding the category you need in the Create bar. For example, you can expand Lights to have the Create bar show the light types (**Figure 14.7**).

The rest of the Hypershade provides tabs for viewing already-created node types: Materials, Textures, Utilities, Lights, Cameras, and Projects. Any created node will be visible under its respective tab or drop-down menu. For instance, if you create a directional light and a point light in your scene, you can view them both by clicking the Lights tab in the Hypershade (**Figure 14.8**).

Under the pane containing the node-type tabs is a pane containing the Work Area and Shader Library tabs. In the Work Area panel you can connect attributes, view all of the connections, and isolate a light or texture for fine-tuning. The Shader Library tab holds all of the pre-made, ready-to-use shaders, including ones for buildings, food, glass, and other common objects. (The Shader Library must be installed separately from the Maya installation CD.) These shaders often provide a good starting point for creating new shaders.

In this chapter we'll explore the lighting section of the Hypershade and Create bar.

Figure 14.7
The Create bar with an expanded Lights section.

Figure 14.8 The Lights panel shows the two lights created and the work area below them.

Figure 14.9 Streamline your setup with the Hypershade/Render/Persp in the Marking menu.

Figure 14.10 The Hypershade on top, the Render View pane on the bottom left, and the Perspective view on the bottom right pane.

Setting Up for a Render

Maya provides many ways to create the same result. In this section we'll go over some different setups for streamlining your workflow.

Three essential windows are used to create a final render: the Hypershade, the Render View, and a camera view (Front, Top, Side, Perspective, or a camera you create). One way to streamline the render's setup is to use Hypershade/Render/Persp in the Marking menu in the north region of the Hotbox (**Figure 14.9**). This sets the Layout window to three panes. The top will become a Hypershade; the bottom-left pane will become a Render View; and the bottom-right pane will become a Perspective view (**Figure 14.10**). This is a good way to set up a scene for a render because you can tap the (Spacebar) to enlarge any of the panes, temporarily hiding the other two. This layout also gives you access to the most common texturing and lighting windows.

continues on next page

Another way to set up a render is to open each window separately as needed. To open the Hypershade or Render View in its own window, select the window you want in the Window > Rendering Editors menu (**Figure 14.11**). This opens a new window with the view inside it (**Figure 14.12**).

Since most of the light attributes can be edited in the Attribute Editor, you may want to temporarily change the Channel Box (on the right side of the Maya window) to an Attribute Editor (**Figure 14.13**). You do this by clicking in the east region of the Hotbox and selecting Attributes > Attribute Editor or clicking the icon in the upper-right corner of the Maya window. The Render View holds many of the tools needed to produce an effective render. We'll touch on the Render View throughout this chapter; for a more complete discussion of it, see Chapter 16, "Cameras and Rendering."

Figure 14.11 The Window > Rendering Editors menu.

Figure 14.12 The Render View in its own pop-up window.

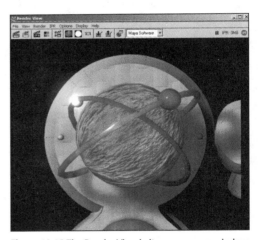

Figure 14.13 The Attribute Editor is docked beside the Front view, replacing the Channel Box.

Figure 14.14
The Ambient Light icon.

Figure 14.15
The Area Light icon.

Figure 14.16
The Directional Light icon.

About Lights

There are six light types in Maya: *ambient, area, directional, point, spot,* and *volume.* You can combine these light types to produce just about any lighting scenario. A Maya scene may use one or all of the above light types, depending on the mood and art direction of the scene.

The following describes the different light types and some of their common uses:

◆ **Ambient**—Produces a uniform light throughout the scene. You should keep this type of light to a minimum, because the more you use it, the flatter and more devoid of contrast the scene will appear (**Figure 14.14**).

Examples of ambient light include the following:

▲ Light that allows you to see in a room or closet without having an actual light on

▲ Light that doesn't originate from an obvious source

◆ **Area**—Two-dimensional, rectangular light source that emits light from the entire rectangle in the direction of the line perpendicular to the rectangle (**Figure 14.15**).

Examples of area light include the following:

▲ Illuminated ceiling panels

▲ Rectangular light reflections on walls

◆ **Directional**—Parallel light rays that wash light across the scene in one specific direction (**Figure 14.16**).

Examples of directional light include sunlight and moonlight.

continues on next page

ABOUT LIGHTS

355

◆ **Point**—Radiates light out from its center in all directions. The farther an object is from this light, the less it is illuminated (**Figure 14.17**).

Examples of point light include:

▲ Light bulbs

▲ LEDs

▲ Torches

◆ **Spot**—Lights an area within a cone shape. The light comes from the center point and travels in a specified direction (**Figure 14.18**).

Examples of spotlight include:

▲ Flashlights

▲ Street lamps

▲ Headlights

▲ Spotlights

◆ **Volume**—Lights an area within a user-defined volume (**Figure 14.19**). Examples of volume light include light around a lit candle or torch.

Light types have the following common attributes (**Figure 14.20**):

◆ **Type**—Sets the kind of light: ambient, area, directional, point, spot, or volume. You can change this attribute at any time—for example, from a point to a spot.

◆ **Color**—Sets the foundation color of the light. Image maps may be added to vary the color of the light.

Figure 14.17
The Point Light icon.

Figure 14.18
The Spot Light icon.

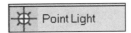

Figure 14.19
The Volume Light icon.

Figure 14.20 Common light attributes: type, color, intensity, and decay rate.

ABOUT LIGHTS

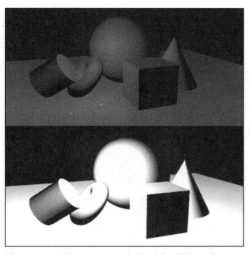

Figure 14.21 The top scene is lit with a light at low intensity; the bottom scene is lit with the same light at a high-intensity setting.

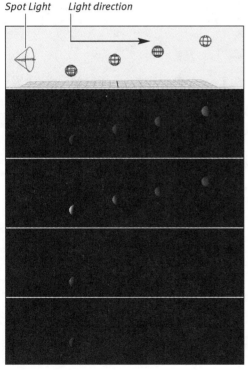

Figure 14.22 Decay rates top to bottom: wireframe, no decay, linear, quadratic, and cubic.

◆ **Intensity**—Sets the brightness and darkness of the light. For best results, start low and work your way up (**Figure 14.21**).

◆ **Decay Rate**—Controls how quickly the light's intensity decreases over distance. When you change this setting, you must also raise or lower the intensity of the light to make up for the decay-rate change. This is not an attribute of the ambient, directional, or volume lights (**Figure 14.22**).

▲ *No Decay*—Light will have the same intensity regardless of distance.

▲ *Linear Decay*—The light's intensity diminishes with distance less abruptly than with Quadratic and Cubic decay.

▲ *Quadratic Decay*—The light's intensity diminishes at a rate between Linear and Cubic decay. This setting is closest to real-world light decay.

▲ *Cubic Decay*—The light's intensity diminishes most abruptly, substantially more abruptly than with Linear and Quadratic decay.

ABOUT LIGHTS

357

Ambient light

Ambient light is light that is still present even when you turn the lights out; it's the light your eyes see once they adjust to the darkness, without an obvious light source. Using ambient light gives you a quick way to see how things render without having to set up a bunch of lights. In general, however, you should use ambient light sparingly because it can quickly flatten out a scene.

First, let's create a practice scene.

To create a practice scene:

1. Choose File > New Scene to create a new scene.

2. Create five or six primitives in the scene, and move them around randomly, with the bottom of each sitting on the grid (**Figure 14.23**).

3. From the Create menu, select NURBS Primitive > Plane to create a plane at the origin.

4. Scale the plane larger than the objects in your scene (**Figure 14.24**).

5. Save the practice scene as a file called practice.mb.

To create an ambient light:

1. Open the practice.mb file.

2. Choose Create > Lights, and in the submenu select the box next to Ambient Light (**Figure 14.25**).

Figure 14.23 Create five or six primitives in the scene, and place them randomly.

Figure 14.24 The plane is scaled larger than the objects in the scene.

Figure 14.25 Select the box next to Ambient Light.

Figure 14.26 Click the swatch beside the Color attribute.

Figure 14.27 Select a color from the color wheel, which in Maya looks more like a color block.

Figure 14.28 Select Render > Render > persp in the Render View to render the scene.

3. In the Options dialog box that opens, click the swatch beside the Color attribute (**Figure 14.26**).

The color wheel opens when you click the swatch.

4. Click in the color wheel to select a color for the light (**Figure 14.27**).

5. Click Apply to lock in the color.

6. Click Create to make the ambient light.

The ambient light is placed at the origin of the scene.

7. In the Hotbox's north-region Marking menu, select Hypershade/Render/persp to split your window layout into these three panes.

8. In the Render View pane, select Render > Render > persp to render the Perspective view (**Figure 14.28**).

✔ Tip

■ Don't use more than one ambient light per scene unless absolutely necessary. Ambient light can quickly flatten the 3D effect of a scene.

ABOUT LIGHTS

The Ambient Shade attribute inside the ambient light affects the direction of the light source. If Ambient Shade is set to 0, light comes from all directions (**Figure 14.29**). If it's set to 1, light comes from the source itself, acting similarly to a point light (**Figure 14.30**). You must be careful when adjusting this attribute because the lower the number, the flatter the image will appear.

To change an ambient light's Ambient Shade attribute:

1. With an ambient light selected, open the Attribute Editor by selecting Window > Attribute Editor, or pressing [Ctrl]/[Control][a].

2. Set the Ambient Shade attribute to *0* (**Figure 14.31**).

   The 0 value sends light evenly over the entire scene.

3. Render the Perspective view.

   Because Ambient Shade is 0, the objects blend together flatly, as in Figure 14.29.

4. With the light still selected, go to the Attribute Editor and change the Ambient Shade attribute to *.7*.

   The .7 value makes the ambient light act similarly to a point light, so that its intensity fades slightly as the distance from the light source increases.

5. Click the Redo Previous Render icon in the Render View.

   Because Ambient Shade is higher, the scene has more depth, similar to Figure 14.30.

6. In the Attribute Editor, set Intensity to *.25* (**Figure 14.32**).

   This brings down the intensity of the ambient light and keeps the flattening of the scene to a minimum.

7. Click the Redo Previous Render icon in the Render View.

   The scene will be very dark.

Figure 14.29 The Ambient Shade attribute is set to *0*, flattening the scene.

Figure 14.30 The Ambient Shade attribute is set to *1*, making the light similar to a point light.

Figure 14.31 Set the Ambient Shade attribute to *0*.

Figure 14.32 Set the intensity to *.25*.

Figure 14.33 Select Area Light in the Lights section of the Create bar.

Figure 14.34 Point the surface normal at the area you want to light.

Figure 14.35 Select Render > Render > persp to render the Perspective view.

Area lights

Area lights are best for situations that call for rectangular lighting—for example, florescent lighting. Another great use for an area light is to backlight a character. However, using area lights extensively in a scene can slow rendering.

To create an area light:

1. Open the practice.mb file.

2. In the Hypershade, right-click the black triangle below the Create Tab and select Create All Nodes.

   A list of nodes appears in the Create bar.

3. Select Area Light in the Lights section of the Create bar (**Figure 14.33**).

4. Scale the light to the size you want the area light to be.

5. Move and rotate the light around the scene until the surface normal points at the object or area you want to light (**Figure 14.34**).

6. Select the light, and press Ctrl/Control a to open the Attribute Editor.

7. In the Attribute Editor, click the swatch beside Color.

8. Click in the color wheel to select a color for the light.

9. Click Accept to lock in the color.

10. Move the Intensity slider in the Attribute Editor to set the light's brightness.

11. Close the Attribute Editor.

12. From the Hotbox's north-region Marking menu, select Hypershade/Render/persp to split your panel layout into these three panes.

13. Render the Perspective view (**Figure 14.35**).

ABOUT LIGHTS

361

Directional lights

Directional lights work great for representing sunlight and moonlight.

To create a directional light:

1. Open the practice.mb file.

2. From the Create menu, select Lights > Directional Light.

   A directional light is created at the origin of the scene. The default direction points down the Z axis in the negative direction (**Figure 14.36**). The perpendicular light rays follow a horizontal direction by default (**Figure 14.37**).

3. Select the directional light by clicking it. Rotate the light around the axes until the arrows point in the direction you want the light to follow (**Figure 14.38**).

4. With the light still selected, choose a new intensity setting for the light in the Channel Box.

5. From the Window menu, select Rendering Editors > Render View (**Figure 14.39**).

   The Render View opens in a new window.

6. Render the Perspective view.

✔ Tip

- Translating a directional light has no effect on how it lights the scene; however, it could help you find or select that light later.

Point lights

Point lights are great for lamps and torches. They're also great for adding a little light to a dark corner, removing light from an overlit area, or faking reflected light on an object.

To create a point light:

1. Open the practice.mb file.

Figure 14.36 The default position of the directional light.

Figure 14.37 The perpendicular light rays of the directional light follow a horizontal direction by default.

Figure 14.38 Point the arrows in the direction you want the light to follow.

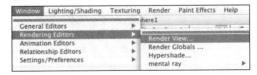
Figure 14.39 Select Rendering Editors › Render View to open the Render View in a new window.

Figure 14.40 Scroll down to the Lights section of the Create Bar in the Hypershade to select the Point Light.

Figure 14.41 Click the Point Light icon to create a new light to work with in Hypershade's Work Area panel.

Figure 14.42 Move the light above the ground plane.

2. In the Hypershade, click the Point Light icon in the Lights section of the Create bar (**Figure 14.40**).

The Point Light appears in the Work Area of the Hypershade window (**Figure 14.41**).

3. Double-click the Point Light icon in the Work Area to open the Attribute Editor.

4. Set the Color and Intensity attributes, then close the Attribute Editor.

5. Click the light to select it, and move it above the ground plane to keep it from being obstructed by the plane (**Figure 14.42**).

6. From the Hotbox's north-region Marking menu, select Hypershade/Render/persp to split your panel layout into these three panes.

7. Render the Perspective view (**Figure 14.43**).

✔ Tip

■ Setting the intensity attribute to a negative number will subtract light from the area around it.

Figure 14.43 The final rendering in the Perspective view.

ABOUT LIGHTS

Spotlights

Spotlights are great for areas where you want to focus light. You can use them as stage or theater spotlights, headlights, or any cone-shaped light source.

To create a spotlight:

1. Open the practice.mb file.

2. Click the Spot Light icon ▩ in the Rendering shelf to create a spotlight at the origin of the scene.

3. Set the Object Pick mask to select lights only, and swipe across the Spot Light icon at the origin to select it (**Figure 14.44**).

   If the Object Pick mask is selected correctly, only the light will be selected.

4. Select the Show Manipulator Tool by pressing ⊤ or selecting its icon ▧ in the toolbar.

5. Pull up the *Y* axis translation manipulator on the spotlight to raise it above the ground (**Figure 14.45**).

   Notice when you're in the Show Manipulator tool that the end of the spotlight stays in its original position, forcing the light to point at it.

6. Select the center square of the end manipulator, and move it to the position where you would like the light to point (**Figure 14.46**).

Figure 14.44 Set the Object Pick mask to select lights only.

Figure 14.45 Pull up the *Y*-axis translation manipulator on the spotlight to raise it above ground.

Figure 14.46 Move the end manipulator into a new position.

Figure 14.47 Select Render > Render > Persp to render the Perspective view.

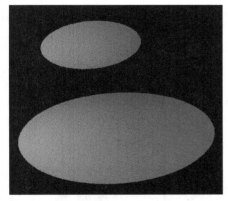

Figure 14.48 The default cone angle on top; the same light position but with a larger cone angle on the bottom.

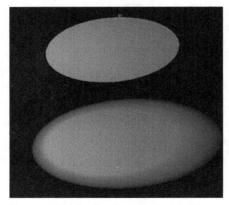

Figure 14.49 Adjusting the penumbra angle blurs the edge of the spotlight. The top light has a setting of 0; the bottom light has a setting of 7.

7. From the Hotbox's north-region Marking menu, select Hypershade/Render/Persp to split your panel layout into these three panes.

8. Render the Perspective view (**Figure 14.47**).

A spotlight has a number of attributes that you can change. Below are definitions of some of these attributes.

Spotlight attributes

◆ **Cone Angle**—The larger the number you input here, the wider the cone (and thus the illuminated area) will be (**Figure 14.48**).

◆ **Penumbra Angle**—Adjusting the penumbra angle softens the edge of the spotlight by blurring it. A negative number blurs inside the edge of the cone; a positive number blurs outside the edge of the cone (**Figure 14.49**).

◆ **Dropoff**—Adjusts the intensity of the light from its center out to its edge. Raising the value of this attribute results in a soft gradation from the center to the edge (**Figure 14.50**).

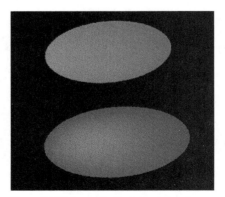

Figure 14.50 Dropoff adjusts the intensity of the light from its center out to its edge. The light at the top has a default setting of 0; the light at the bottom has a setting of 8.

Many light attributes can have an image added to them to affect the light in additional ways. An example would be adding an image into the color attribute of a light. This projects the image through the light—similar to having light filtered through a stained-glass window project a pattern onto the floor (**Figure 14.51**). This technique is also helpful for creating light shapes that aren't round.

Volume light

Volume lights are great for illuminating multiple objects that are placed in the same proximity to each other because you can illuminate all objects within the area of the volume lights icon.

To create a volume light:

1. Open the practice.mb file.

2. From the Create menu, select Lights > Volume Light (**Figure 14.52**).

3. Scale the Volume Light icon until it surrounds the objects you want to illuminate (**Figure 14.53**).

4. From the Window menu, select Attribute Editor.
    The Attribute Editor opens.

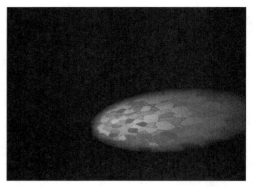

Figure 14.51 A light with an image mapped into it.

Figure 14.52 Select Lights > Volume Light from the Create menu to create a volume light at the scene's origin.

Figure 14.53 The Volume Light icon is similar to a sphere and should be placed around the objects you want to illuminate.

ABOUT LIGHTS

Figure 14.54 Set Color and Intensity to achieve the desired brightness and color for the scene.

Figure 14.55 The Render drop-down menu allows you to select which view, or camera, you would like rendered.

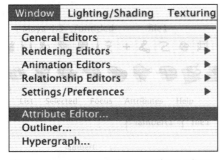

Figure 14.56 Select Window > Attribute Editor.

5. Set the Color and Intensity attributes, then close the Attribute Editor (**Figure 14.54**).

6. From the Hotbox's north-region Marking menu, select Hypershade/Render/Persp to split your panel layout into these three panes.

7. Render the Perspective view (**Figure 14.55**).

To add an image map to a light's Color attribute:

1. Click a spotlight to select it.

2. With the light selected, select Window > Attribute Editor (**Figure 14.56**).

3. In the Attribute Editor, select the map icon next to the Color slider to open the Create Render Node panel.

continues on next page

ABOUT LIGHTS

4. In the Create Render Node panel, select the Textures tab and then click File in the 2D Textures section (**Figure 14.57**).

This creates a File node and also opens the Attribute Editor.

5. In the Attribute Editor, select the File icon ▣ next to the Image Name attribute.

The Open dialog box appears.

6. In the Open dialog box, browse to the folder containing the image you want to use, then select it and click Open.

The icon at the top of the Attributes Editor, updates with the image you selected.

7. From the Hotbox's north-region Marking menu, select Hypershade/Render/Persp to split your panel layout into these three panes.

8. Render the Perspective view (**Figure 14.58**).

Figure 14.57 From the Create Render Node panel, select the Textures tab, and in the 2D Textures section, select File.

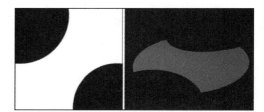

Figure 14.58 The image used is on the left, and the final render of light with the image mapped into it is on the right.

Figure 14.59 Look Through Selected can be chosen from any pane menu or the Hot Box.

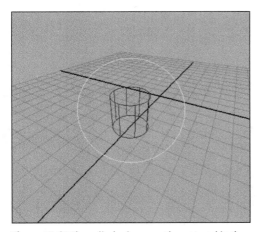

Figure 14.60 The cylinder is currently centered in the spotlight's view. The circle around the object defines the spotlight's view.

Looking Through a Light

Pointing a light at just the right area of a scene can be difficult, but Maya makes it a little easier by allowing you to look through the light as you position it. As you look at the scene through the light, you can pan and dolly around until the light is pointing at the precise area of the scene you want to illuminate.

To look through a light:

1. Select the light through which you want to view the scene.

2. Inside a pane, select Panels > Look Through Selected (**Figure 14.59**).

   The view of the scene is now from the light's point of view (**Figure 14.60**).

✔ Tip

- If there is an object you would like to focus the light on, select the object and from inside a pane select View > Look at Selection.

Light Linking

Light linking is Maya's way of giving you endless flexibility when it comes to lighting your scene. It lets you define a surface to be lit by only specific lights, or you can define a light to hit only certain surfaces, both of which let you isolate and control the lighting of a specific area of your scene. Light linking works particularly well for character lighting when you want some lights to illuminate the character but not the rest of the scene. In addition, it speeds rendering times because Maya does not need to examine the entire scene to see which surface is being hit by each light and by how much.

Figure 14.61 Create a simple scene to use for light linking.

To link a light to an object:

1. Start a new scene with two spotlights and three primitives aligned as in **Figure 14.61**; save this scene for later use.

2. From the Lighting/Shading menu, select Light Linking > Light-Centric (**Figure 14.62**).
   The Relationship Editor opens.

3. On the left side of the Relationship Editor, select the light for which you want to specify objects.

4. On the right side, select the objects you want the light to hit, and, if necessary, deselect any objects you do not want the light to hit (**Figure 14.63**).

5. Repeat steps 3 and 4 for each light to which you want to link objects.

6. Render the scene to see the results.

✔ Tip

■ You can click and drag across the object names in the Relationship Editor to select objects quickly.

Figure 14.62 Choose Light-Centric to control the linking of one light to multiple objects.

Figure 14.63 Spotlight1 will illuminate only nurbsCylinder1.

LIGHT LINKING

Figure 14.64 Select nurbsSphere1 on the left side and the lights you want to illuminate nurbsSphere1 on the right side. Here spotlight2 will be the only light hitting nurbsSphere1.

Figure 14.65 The lights in this scene are linked to specific objects, so no light is hitting the plane below.

To link an object to a light:

1. Open the scene created for the previous task, "To link a light to an object."

2. From the Lighting/Shading menu, select Light Linking > Object-Centric.
   The Relationship Editor opens.

3. On the left side of the Relationship Editor, select the object for which you want to define lighting (**Figure 14.64**).

4. On the right side, select the lights you want to hit the object, and, if necessary, deselect any lights you don't want to light the object.

5. Repeat steps 3 and 4 for each object to which you want to link lights.

6. Render the scene to see the results (**Figure 14.65**).

About Shadows

Shadows are an important scene element because they visually plant objects on the ground, as well as make it easier for us to tell how far apart objects are spaced (**Figure 14.66**). Shadows add realism that would often be difficult to achieve in a scene without them.

A real-world shadow is the complementary color of the light source: The sun is yellow; therefore, the shadows it casts are purple—in essence, there are no black shadows in the real world, only very dark representations of a particular color. Keep this in mind as you create both realistic and artistic shadows: If you apply this principle to your 3D work, you'll produce deeper, richer imagery.

A real shadow is darkest close to an object, fading and blurring as it gets farther away. Many times, shadows that people create appear too bold, and are thus unrealistic. You'll do much to bring your scenes to life by remembering that the core, or darkest area, of a shadow is located slightly away from the object's edge, near the base of the shadow (**Figure 14.67**).

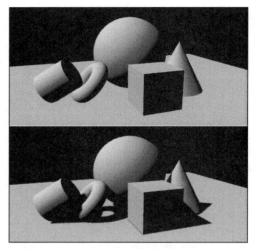

Figure 14.66 Shadows help to visually plant objects on the ground.

Figure 14.67 A real shadow's darkest area is slightly away from the object's edge, near the base of the shadow.

Figure 14.68 Depth-map shadow.

Figure 14.69 Raytraced shadow.

Creating shadows

Shadows are turned off on all lights by default. To see shadows in a render, you must turn them on, not only in the light but in the object as well. An individual object will not cast a shadow if shadow casting is turned off on the object, regardless of whether shadow casting is turned on in the light. This gives Maya users an incredible amount of control over each shadow.

There are two types of shadows in Maya: *depth map* (**Figure 14.68**) and *raytraced* (**Figure 14.69**). Both methods can produce realistic shadows, through raytracing often produces *more* realistic shadow with less effort and tweaking. However, raytraced shadows can take much longer to render than depth-map shadows, so the choice is really a trade-off. It's a constant battle to produce good-looking shadows while keeping rendering time to a minimum for each scene.

Depth-map shadows attempt to simulate real-world shadows without adding major amounts of rendering time but at the cost of using more RAM. A depth map is an image file that contains a depth channel (a grayscale representation of how far objects are from the camera, the lights, and each other) rendered from a light's point of view. Maya uses the depth map to determine which surfaces have light hitting them and which surfaces are in shadow. Think of the depth map as a pre-drawn shadow brought into the scene just before it's rendered. This image becomes a replacement for a real shadow in the scene, saving Maya the time it would take to calculate the real shadow. These depth-map image files can be reused, saving even more rendering time.

continues on next page

ABOUT SHADOWS

In most scenarios, raytraced shadows produce great-looking, realistic images—results you wouldn't be able to achieve with depth-map shadows. One example of this would be a transparent shadow cast from a partially transparent object (**Figure 14.70**).

Raytraced shadows do, however, have some restrictions, as well. For one, they won't show up if rendered with interactive photo-realistic rendering (IPR) (see Chapter 16)—because IPR does not allow raytracing. This represents an additional speed cost because you can use IPR to see depth-map shadows, making depth-map shadow adjustment much faster. You can also preview light placement and depth map shadows using the shaded mode in any view.

Depth-map shadows—which are available in all but ambient light—can produce relatively realistic shadows without greatly affecting rendering time.

To create a depth-map shadow:

1. Select the light from which you want to produce a shadow.

2. Open the Attribute Editor.

3. Click the arrow next to the Shadows heading to expand the shadow options.

4. Select the box next to Use Depth Map Shadows under the Depth Map Shadow Attributes heading (**Figure 14.71**).

5. In the Shadows section (above Depth Map Shadow Attributes), click the swatch next to the Shadow Color attribute to open the Color Chooser (**Figure 14.72**).

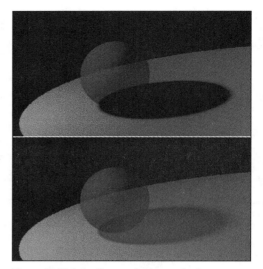

Figure 14.70 A depth-map shadow can't show an object's transparency within the shadow (top); a raytraced shadow, however, can (bottom).

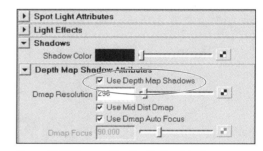

Figure 14.71 Turn on Use Depth Map Shadows.

Figure 14.72 Click the swatch next to the Shadow Color attribute to open the Color Chooser.

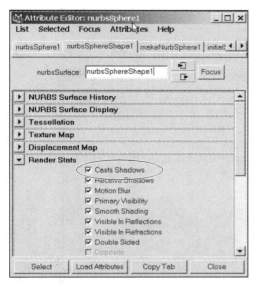

Figure 14.73 Turn on Casts Shadows in the Render Stats section of the Attribute Editor.

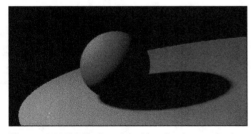

Figure 14.74 The final render with a depth-map shadow.

6. In the Color Chooser, select a shadow color from the color wheel.

7. Click Accept to lock in the color.

8. Select the surface you want to cast shadows.

9. In the Render Stats section of the surface's Attribute Editor, make sure that Casts Shadows (the default option) is on (**Figure 14.73**).

10. From the Hotbox's north-region Marking menu, select Hypershade/ Render/persp to split your panel layout into these three panes.

11. Test-render the scene by selecting Render > Render > persp in the Render View pane.

The render shows a depth-map shadow (**Figure 14.74**).

To preview depth-map shadows:

1. Continuing from the previous task, "To create a depth-map shadow," click in the persp pane.

   A blue box around the Perspective view indicates that it is the active pane.

2. Press ⑤ to switch to shaded mode.

3. Press ⑦ to enable Use All Lights in the Perspective view.

4. Select Lighting > Shadows to display depth-map shadows (**Figure 14.75**).

   The camera can now be moved and animation can be played with a good approximation of what the final lighting will look like (**Figure 14.76**). If the lights are set to raytraced shadows, then the shadows will not appear in the view.

5. Select Shading > High Quality Rendering (**Figure 14.77**).

   The overall shading quality and especially the shadow edges should be greatly improved, giving an even more accurate preview of what the final shading will look like (**Figure 14.78**).

Figure 14.75 Select Lighting › Shadows to display depth-map shadows.

Figure 14.76 Theses depth-map shadows are a good approximation of the final rendering.

Figure 14.77 Select Shading › High Quality Rendering to display depth-map shadows.

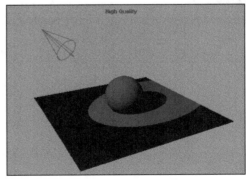

Figure 14.78 The overall shading quality is improved, especially the depth-map shadow edges.

Figure 14.79 Shadow edges appear pixilated if the resolution is too low.

Figure 14.80 Dmap filter size controls the softness of the shadow's edges.

Common depth-map shadow attributes

◆ **Dmap Resolution**—This is the resolution of the depth-map shadow file. Shadow edges will appear pixilated if the resolution is too low (**Figure 14.79**). However, you will want to use the lowest possible setting that still produces acceptable results, since this attribute is extremely memory intensive.

◆ **Dmap Filter Size**—Works in unison with Dmap resolution to control the softness of the shadow's edges (**Figure 14.80**). Try to maintain a setting of 3 or less to avoid adding excessive render time.

◆ **Dmap Bias**—Moves the map closer to or away from the light. You will only need to use this attribute in the following circumstances:

▲ If a shadow appears detached from the shadow-casting surface, gradually decrease the Dmap bias value until the shadow looks correct.

▲ If dark spots or streaks appear on illuminated surfaces, gradually increase the Dmap bias value until the spots or streaks disappear.

Raytraced shadows can create highly realistic shadows but also add expensive rendering time. To produce raytraced shadows, you must check three things:

◆ Use Raytraced Shadows must be selected in the light's Attribute Editor.

◆ Casts Shadows must be selected in the Render Stats section of the Attribute Editor of each object you want to cast a shadow.

◆ Raytracing must be checked in the Raytracing Quality section of the Render Globals window (see Chapter 15, "Shaders, Materials, and Mapping").

ABOUT SHADOWS

To create a raytraced shadow:

1. Select the light from which you want to produce a shadow.

2. In the Raytrace Shadow Attributes section of the light's Attribute Editor, select Use Ray Trace Shadows (**Figure 14.81**).

3. Above the Raytrace Shadows Attributes, open the Shadows section and click the swatch beside the Shadow Color attribute to open the Color Chooser.

4. Click in the color wheel to select a shadow color.

5. Click Accept to lock in the color.

6. Select the surface you want to cast shadows.

7. In the Render Stats section of the surface's Attribute Editor, select Casts Shadows.

Figure 14.81 Select Use Ray Trace Shadows in the light's Attribute Editor.

Figure 14.82 Select Window > Rendering Editors > Render Globals to open the Render Globals panel.

Figure 14.83 Select Raytracing in the Render Globals panel.

8. To open the Render Globals panel (**Figure 14.82**), select Window > Rendering Editors > Render Globals (Windows) or Window > Render Globals (Mac), or click the Render Globals icon in the Render View.

9. Select Raytracing in the Raytracing Quality section of the Render Globals panel (**Figure 14.83**).

10. Test-render the scene by selecting Render > Render > persp in the Render View window.

Common raytraced shadow attributes

◆ **Light Radius**—Sets the softness of the shadow's edge relative to the size of the light. For example, smaller light values produce crisper shadows, and greater light values create softer shadows (**Figure 14.84**).

◆ **Shadow Rays**—Sets the amount of grain visible along soft shadow edges (**Figure 14.85**). Increasing this attribute increases rendering time, so keep it as low as possible.

◆ **Ray Depth Limit**—If a light bounces off multiple mirrors before it hits your object, the Ray Depth Limit number determines whether that light will still cast a shadow.

Figure 14.84 A default raytraced shadow (top), and a shadow with the Light Radius attribute turned up (bottom).

Figure 14.85 Changing the Shadow Rays attribute can cut down on grainy shadows.

SHADERS, MATERIALS, AND MAPPING

Figure 15.1 The objects at left and the objects at right have the same geometry. However, they've been assigned different shaders, which make them look like they're made from different substances.

Objects in Maya start out a drab, gray color. By assigning a *shader* to a surface, you give it a color or a texture map (an image that's mapped onto the surface).

Achieving realistic-looking surfaces, however, is about more than just color. You can make a surface's default gray color look like chrome (if it's shiny and reflective), or you can make it look like rocks (if it's bumpy with a matte finish) (**Figure 15.1**).

continues on next page

Whether a surface is shiny or matte is determined by how it reflects light. A *material* in Maya is the part of a shader that controls an object's shininess and color (in addition to a number of other attributes). There are several Maya material types—all of which deal with reflection differently. One important aspect of how shiny a surface is, is the *specular highlight*, which is the portion of the surface that appears brightest from reflecting the light. By working with the specular highlight, you can achieve the look of different substances. For instance, an eyeball has a tiny, tight, specular highlight, and a plastic surface has a wide, fuzzy specular highlight (**Figure 15.2**).

A light bulb is neither shiny nor reflective, and coloring it yellow is not going to make it look realistic. However, you can add incandescence to a bulb's shader, making it appear to have its own source of light. You can also place glow on an object like a light bulb to surround it with something resembling a halo. By combining incandescence and glow, you can get a realistic-looking light bulb (**Figure 15.3**).

Mapping controls how a texture is placed on a surface. Some surfaces, like NURBS, have built-in UV coordinates for textures. Primitive polygonal and subdiv surfaces have UV coordinates, too, but when those types of surfaces are more complicated, you must manually edit the UV mappings. Editing is largely done in the UV editor, but Maya also features special mapping tools for polygons and subdivs.

Figure 15.2 Much of what distinguishes different substances is how they reflect light. Light is reflected differently depending on what material you assign to a surface.

Figure 15.3 This light bulb is created when its material is given some incandescence and glow.

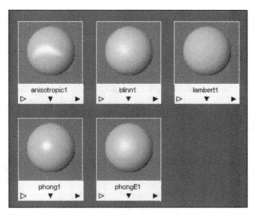

Figure 15.4 These are the basic materials that are available in the Hypershade.

Figure 15.5 The sphere on the left has a fractal texture, which is a procedural texture. The sphere on the right has an image texture.

About the Hypershade

The Hypershade is the window in which you will do much of your work with shaders. In it you will find materials, textures, lights, and utilities.

A *material* is a node that contains most of the controls that determine the look of the object. The kind of material you use also affects the look of the object and which controls are available to it (**Figure 15.4**).

A *texture* is an image, often mapped to the color of an object. However, you can also map a texture to the bump of an object. A bump map makes a surface appear bumpy rather than smooth. The value of the image determines the height of the bumps. A texture can also determine which areas of a surface are transparent or shiny, as well as lighten portions of the surface.

There are two basic texture categories: *image* and *procedural*. An image texture can be something as simple as a scanned photo. A procedural texture is also an image; however, it's calculated based on a mathematical formula. A fractal is one example of a procedural texture (**Figure 15.5**).

Utilities are another kind of node you can find in the Hypershade. Different Maya utilities adjust shaders in various ways. A couple of common utilities are the bump2d utility, which allows for the creation of a bump map, and the 2d placement utility, which allows for the positioning of a texture on a surface.

Using the Hypershade

The Hypershade is split into three areas: the Create and Bins bars, the Hypershade tabs, and the work-area tabs.

◆ To use the Create bar, click the black triangle below the Create tab and select Create Maya Nodes from the pull-down menu.It reveals a long list of nodes you can use for creating shaders (**Figure 15.6**). The nodes you will need most often are: Surface, 2D Textures, 3D Textures, and Other Textures.

◆ Beside the Create tab in the Hypershade is a Bins tab. Click the Bins tab to reveal the Bins bar. Here you can create virtual folders to organize your project's shaders and other nodes. When you click a bin, the shaders or nodes stored within are displayed in the top part of the Hypershade under the relevant tab (**Figure 15.7**). Using bins to store your shaders makes it much easier to work with projects that require a large numbers of shaders.

◆ The Hypershade tabs allow you to see all of your materials, textures, utilities, lights, or cameras. If you create any of these nodes, they will show up under the appropriate tab. For example, if you create a material like Blinn by clicking it in the Create bar, it will show up under the Materials tab (**Figure 15.8**). You can make custom tabs to display any node type you specify or even display related files on the hard drive.

ABOUT THE HYPERSHADE

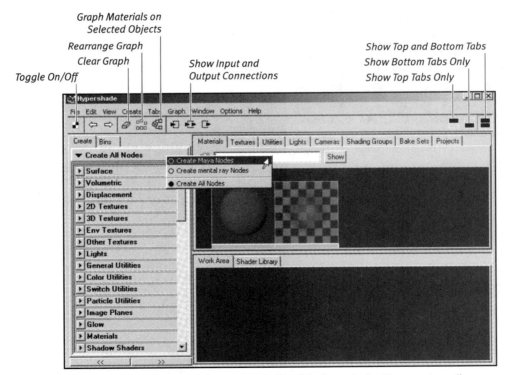

Figure 15.6 The Create bar, which is on the left side of the Hypershade, allows you to easily create a variety of different nodes.

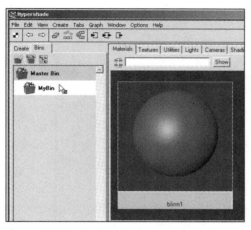

Figure 15.7 The Bins bar lets you organize shaders and other node types into bins.

Figure 15.8 The Hypershade tabs allow you to access all of the different nodes, separated by category.

Figure 15.9 The work area is the part of the Hypershade where you can drag other nodes to make connections. Here a ramp texture is connected to the color of a Blinn material.

◆ The work area is a place to work on your materials and textures. When you make a new node from the Create bar, it also shows up here. You can middle mouse button–drag nodes from the Hypershade tabs down to the work area. Once they are there, you can make connections. An example of this is assigning a texture to the color of a material. If you use the middle mouse button to drag a texture onto a material and choose color from the Marking menu that appears, the color of the texture will be connected to the color of the material (**Figure 15.9**).

◆ The Toggle On/Off Create bar button allows you to hide or show the Create bar. Hiding it will give you more room to work with other nodes (see Figure 15.6).

◆ The Clear Graph button clears out any nodes in the work area. It doesn't delete them; it just clears the area.

◆ The Rearrange Graph button cleans up the work area, which tends to get cluttered when you create new nodes.

◆ The Graph Materials on Selected Objects button provides a quick way to find out what material is assigned to a specific object. Just select the object, then click this button, and the material and everything connected to it will show up in the work area.

◆ The Show Input and Output Connections button shows everything connected to a node. For example, if you select a material and then click this button, the material will show up in the work area with all of its connections.

◆ These buttons let you isolate the Hypershade tabs or the work area. On the left is Show Top Tabs Only. In the middle, Show Bottom Tabs Only. On the right, Show Top and Bottom Tabs.

ABOUT THE HYPERSHADE

To create your own bins:

1. From the Window menu, select
   Rendering Editors > Hypershade.

2. Click the Create tab and expand the
   Surface category (**Figure 15.10**).

3. Click the Blinn icon four times.

   Four blinn shaders appear in the
   work area and in the Materials tab.
   (**Figure 15.11**).

4. Click the Bins tab to reveal the Bins bar
   (**Figure 15.12**).

Figure 15.10 The Create
tab contains a catego-
rized list of nodes to use
in creating materials.

Figure 15.11 Four blinn shaders are displayed in the
work area.

Figure 15.12
Click the Bins tab to
reveal the Bins bar.

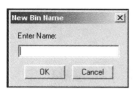

Figure 15.13 Enter a name for the custom bin using the New Bin Name dialog box.

Figure 15.14 A bin called MyBin appears below the Master Bin in the Bin bar.

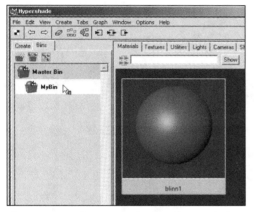

Figure 15.15 Clicking MyBin displays blinn1, which is currently the only node stored in MyBin.

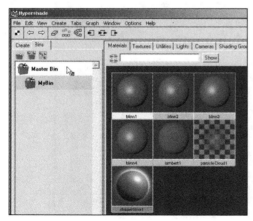

Figure 15.16 Clicking the Master Bin displays all the shaders in the scene.

5. Click the Create Empty Bin icon ▧ at the top of the Bins bar.

The New Bin Name dialog box appears (**Figure 15.13**).

6. Enter a name for the new bin (MyBin) and click OK.

A new bin called MyBin appears below the Master Bin (**Figure 15.14**).

7. Using the middle mouse button, click and drag blinn1 to MyBin.

8. Click MyBin.

The Materials tab displays blinn1 alone (**Figure 15.15**).

9. Click Master Bin.

All the shaders are shown in the Materials tab (**Figure 15.16**).

10. Select blinn2, then right-click MyBin and choose Add Selected from the pull-down menu (**Figure 15.17**).

continues on next page

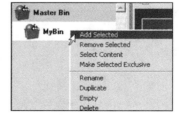

Figure 15.17 Right-click MyBin and select Add Selected.

ABOUT THE HYPERSHADE

11. Right-click MyBin and choose Select Content (**Figure 15.18**).

Both blinn1 and blinn2 are selected.

12. Select blinn3, then click the Create Bin from Selected icon ![icon] at the top of the Bins bar.

The New Bin Name dialog box appears.

13. Enter a new name (MyBin2) and click OK.

A new bin called MyBin2 appears below the Master Bin and MyBin.

14. Click MyBin2.

The Materials tab displays blinn3 alone (**Figure 15.19**).

15. Click Master Bin.

All the shaders are shown in the Materials tab.

16. Click the Select Unsorted Content icon ![icon] to the right of the Bins bar.

All the shaders that had not previously been assigned to a custom folder are selected.

To create your own Tabs:

1. Open the Hypershade (Window > Rendering Editors > Hypershade).

2. From the Tabs menu, select Create New Tab (**Figure 15.20**).

The Create New Tab dialog opens (**Figure 15.21**).

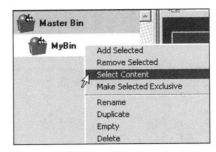

Figure 15.18 Right-click MyBin and select Select Content.

Figure 15.19 Clicking MyBin2 displays blinn3.

Figure 15.20 Select Create New Tab from the Tabs menu in the Hypershade to create a new tab.

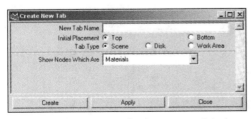

Figure 15.21 Enter a name for the custom tab in the Create New Tab dialog box.

Figure 15.22 The Browse for Folder window opens to the current project directory.

Figure 15.23 Select a folder that contains images or folder of images.

Figure 15.24 Type a name into the New Tab Name field.

3. For Tab Type, select Disk to display files on the hard drive

4. Click the folder icon next to Root Directory.

   The Browse for Folder window opens (**Figure 15.22**).

5. Select a folder that contains image or folders of images and click OK (**Figure 15.23**).

   The path to the selected directory is displayed next to Root Directory.

6. Enter a name (we used Universal Images) for the Tab into New Tab Name and click Apply (**Figure 15.24**).

   The new tab appears in the top half of the Hypershade (**Figure 15.25**).

7. Click one of the subfolders in your image directory or click the folder icon next to the Root Directory path.

   Icons of the images stored in the directory are created and displayed (**Figure 15.26**).

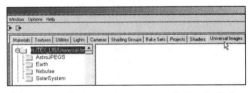

Figure 15.25 The new tab appears in the top half of the Hypershade window.

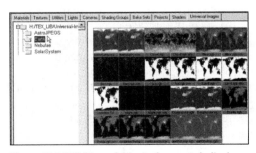

Figure 15.26 Clicking a folder in the new tab displays icons of images stored on the hard drive.

About Materials

Maya offers several types of materials, including Lambert, Blinn, Phong, Layered, Ocean, Ramp, and Anisotropic. Each material type has its own options and reflects light in a unique fashion. Lambert, for example, has no specular highlight, so it's matte, while Blinn and Phong both look shiny. Anisotropic is also shiny, but unlike Blinn and Phong, it reflects specular light unevenly (**Figure 15.27**). Maya also includes two specialty materials—Ramp and Layered—which we'll cover in this chapter. And finally, the Ocean material, which relates closely to fluid dynamics, is covered in Chapter 16, "Cameras and Rendering."

There are several controls that are common to the basic materials. They include *color, transparency, ambient color, incandescence,* and *bump mapping*. You can map images to all of these, and most of them can have a color or luminance value assigned to them as well. All are accessible from the Attribute Editor for the corresponding material (**Figure 15.28**).

Common material attributes

◆ Color simply determines the color of an object. You can pick a color using the Color Chooser, or you can map an image to the color.

◆ Transparency allows you to make a surface see-through. You can use the slider to make the surface more or less transparent, or you can map an image to make part of the surface transparent and part of it opaque. This attribute only recognizes luminance—that is, how light or dark an image is. White is transparent; black is opaque (**Figure 15.29**).

Figure 15.27 Each banana has a different material assigned to it (from left to right): Anisotropic, Blinn, Lambert, Phong, and Phong E.

Figure 15.28 This is the Attribute Editor for a Blinn material. It holds most of the controls that determine the look of the surface.

Figure 15.29 The node in the lower-right corner is the texture, which was mapped to the plane as a transparency map. The parts of the image that are white determine the parts of the plane that are transparent.

Figure 15.30 The node in the lower-right corner is the texture, which was mapped to the plane as a bump map. The white areas are higher; the dark areas are lower. Render to see the results of a bump map.

Figure 15.31 This is a portion of the Hypershade. When the Lambert button is clicked, a new material node, called lambert2, appears.

Figure 15.32 This is the Attribute Editor for the material that was just created in the Hypershade.

◆ Ambient color allows you to lighten the color of the material. You can lighten the whole surface evenly by using the slider, or you can map an image to the ambient color to lighten only certain parts of a surface.

◆ Incandescence gives a material the appearance of having its own light. In general, you need to have a light in a scene for anything to render out. However, if an object has a material on it with the ambient color turned up, it will render out without any lights in the scene.

◆ Bump mapping makes a surface appear bumpy. To work, this attribute must have an image mapped to it. The whitest parts of the image will cause the tallest bumps; the black parts of the image will cause the lowest bumps; 50 percent gray will cause no bumps (**Figure 15.30**).

To change the color of an object:

1. Open the Hypershade and select Create Maya Nodes (if it's not already selected) from the pull-down menu in the Create bar.

2. Click Lambert in the Surface section (**Figure 15.31**).

   A new material appears in the work area (the lower half of the window).

3. Double-click the new material.

   The Attribute Editor for this material appears (**Figure 15.32**).

   continues on next page

ABOUT MATERIALS

4. Click the field next to Color.

The Color Chooser opens (**Figure 15.33**).

5. Choose a color by clicking one of the color swatches at the top of the window or by clicking in the color wheel.

6. Click Accept.

The Color Chooser window closes.

7. With the middle mouse button, drag the material from the Hypershade onto the surface.

or

Select the surface, right-click the material to open the Marking menu, and select Assign initialShadingGroup To Selection (**Figure 15.34**).

✔ Tip

■ If you assign a shader to a surface by using the middle mouse button to drag it from the Hypershade, be sure that the view you drag it into is in shaded mode. If it were in wireframe mode, you would need to drag it precisely onto an isoparm or edge of the surface, which is more difficult. However the drag method of assigning textures will only allow you to assign a shader to one object at a time. In most cases it's easier to use the Marking menu since it allows you to assign a shader to many objects or groups.

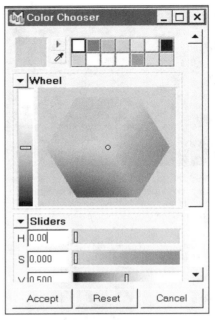

Figure 15.33 The Color Chooser lets you select a color from the swatches at the top or from the color wheel.

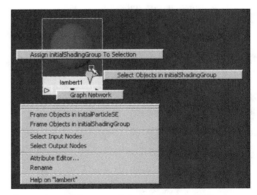

Figure 15.34 When you right-click a material in the Hypershade, a Marking menu appears that allows you to assign that material to the selected surface. This is a particularly convenient method if you're assigning shaders to multiple surfaces simultaneously.

ABOUT MATERIALS

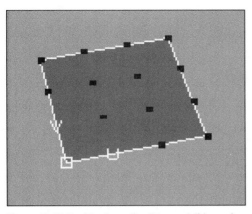

Figure 15.35 On this plane, the CVs are visible, and you can easily see the U and V directions. The square at lower left is the start point; the U is to the right of it, and the V is above it. This means that the U direction goes from left to right, and the V direction runs from bottom to top.

Figure 15.36 The same image is assigned to different NURBS surfaces. It gets wrapped around the surface, and its orientation depends on the U and V directions of the surface.

About texture-mapping NURBS surfaces

A NURBS surface is always four-sided. Even a sphere is four-sided—it's pinched at the top and bottom, and the other two sides meet. NURBS surfaces have U and V directions. In a plane, the U direction extends from left to right, and the V direction extends from bottom to top. This makes the lower-left corner the start point (**Figure 15.35**).

Any image you bring in is also four-sided since image files are square or rectangular. The lower-left corner of the image is placed at the start point of the surface. The bottom of the image is mapped on the surface along the U direction, and the left side of the image is wrapped along the V direction (**Figure 15.36**).

Once the image has been placed on the surface, you can move, rotate, and repeat it. If you want to place one image over two or more surfaces, you must use a *projection map*—which is a bit like pointing a slide projector at a surface.

Maya comes with several textures, but you can also use your own images. Maya can accept many different image formats, including JPEG, TIFF, and Maya's own format, IFF.

To assign an image map from the Shader Library to a NURBS object:

1. From the Create menu, select NURBS Primitive > Plane.

2. From the Panel menu in any pane, select Panel > Panel > Hypershade to open the Hypershade in the current pane instead of as a free-floating window.

3. Click Lambert in the Create bar of the Hypershade to create a new material.

   A new Lambert material appears in the Hypershade.

4. Assign the material to the plane by using the middle mouse button to drag it onto the surface.

5. Click the Shader Library tab, in the lower half of the Hypershade window.

6. Click the Textures folder, in the lower half of the Hypershade.

   Several textures appear to the right (**Figure 15.37**).

7. With the middle mouse button, drag a brick texture onto your new Lambert (probably called lambert2), which is in the top half of the Hypershade.

8. From the Marking menu that appears, select "color" (**Figure 15.38**).

   The brick texture appears on the Lambert node and is mapped to the Lambert's color channel.

Figure 15.37 The Shader Library provides several textures—all of which are repeatable, which means that if they're tiled on a surface, there will be no seams.

Figure 15.38 When a texture is dragged onto a material, a Marking menu appears that allows you to choose which attribute you want to map the texture to.

ABOUT MATERIALS

Figure 15.39 The brick texture appears on the plane. It's only visible when you're in textured mode.

A

B

C

D

9. Click in the Perspective view, and press 6 to switch to textured mode.

The brick texture shows up on the surface to which it was assigned (**Figure 15.39**).

✔ Tip

- If you don't have a three-button mouse, you can use the Marking menu, but this workaround is a little complicated. Following step 7 in the previous task, click the brick texture so that it appears in the work area. Click the triangle in the lower right corner of the brick texture icon, and from the Marking menu that appears, choose outColor > outColor (**Figure 15.40A**). A line connects the brick texture to the cursor (**B**). Now click the triangle in the lower left corner of the lambert2 shader, and from the Marking menu that appears, select color (**C**). The brick texture appears on the Lambert node, indicating that it is connected to the Lambert's color channel (**D**).

Figure 15.40 (A-D) Click the lower right-hand corner of the brick texture and select outColor from the menu that appears (A). A line from the texture to the cursor indicates that it is ready to be connected to an input (B). Select color by right-clicking the lower left-hand corner of the lambert2 shader (C). The icon of the Lambert shader updates, indicating that the brick texture has been connected (D).

To assign your own image map to a NURBS object:

1. From the Create menu, select NURBS Primitive > Plane.

2. Open the Hypershade and click Lambert to create a new material.

   A new Lambert material appears in the Hypershade.

3. Double-click the new Lambert you just created in the Hypershade.

   The Attribute Editor for the Lambert opens.

4. Click the Map icon, which is to the right of the Color slider (**Figure 15.41**).

   The Create Render Node window opens.

5. Make sure the Normal radio button is selected, and then click File in the Create Render Node window (**Figure 15.42**).

   The Attribute Editor for the File node opens.

6. Click the Browse button 🔲 next to Image Name.

7. Browse for and open your own image file.

8. With the middle mouse button, drag the Lambert you created from the Hypershade onto your surface.

9. Click in the Perspective view, and press ⑥ to switch to textured mode.

   The image you chose is now color-mapped to your surface (**Figure 15.43**).

✔ Tips

- You can similarly map an image to any of the common material attributes.

Figure 15.41 By clicking the Map icon, which is the little checkerboard to the right of the slider, you can map a texture to the color.

Figure 15.42 In the Create Render Node window, you can choose which texture you want to map to an attribute of a material.

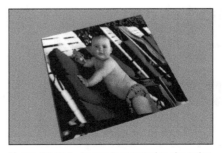

Figure 15.43 An image is mapped to the color of the plane.

ABOUT MATERIALS

Figure 15.44 The file texture in the Hypershade is being dragged with the middle mouse button to the color in the Attribute Editor of a material. This provides a quick and convenient way to make connections.

Figure 15.45 In the work area of the Hypershade, we can see all of the nodes that are associated with this material.

Figure 15.46 The position of the texture is moved via interactive placement. Compare the bricks' position after they've been moved (lower right) with their original position (upper left).

■ You can also map an image by dragging an existing texture onto the name of an attribute in a material's Attribute Editor (**Figure 15.44**).

■ You can find your textures more quickly if you place them in the source images folder of your project directory. Maya will default to this directory whenever you use an Open dialog box to assign an image file.

When you first map an image on a NURBS surface, it may not be oriented correctly. You can use the place2dTexture node to rotate, move, and scale the image on the surface.

To use place2dTexture:

1. Map a brick texture to a NURBS plane as you did when assigning an image map to a NURBS object from the Shader Library above.

2. Select the surface.

3. Open the Hypershade and click the Graph Materials on Selected Objects icon 🔳.

   The entire shading network and its connections show up in the work area of the Hypershade (**Figure 15.45**).

4. Double-click the place2dTexture node, on the left side of the work area.

   The Attribute Editor for the place2dTexture node appears.

5. Click the Interactive Placement button in the Attribute Editor for the place2dTexture node. A red square with a dot in the middle appears on the surface.

6. Drag with the middle mouse button, starting from the center point of the interactive placement icon on the object's surface.

   The texture moves on the surface (**Figure 15.46**).

continues on next page

397

7. With the middle mouse button, drag at the corners of the red square. The texture rotates (**Figure 15.47**).

8. Click in the field next to Repeat UV, and type *4*. Press (Enter).

The bricks are repeated four times in the *U* direction. The column on the left is for *U* values; the column on the right is for *V* values.

9. In the field two columns to the right of Repeat UV, type *4*. Press (Enter).

The bricks are now also repeated four times in the *V* direction (**Figure 15.48**).

Procedural textures are built into Maya; they do not rely on an image file. Their color and luminance are determined mathematically. One commonly used procedural texture is a ramp, which is like a gradient.

To assign a ramp texture to a surface:

1. From the Create menu select NURBS Primitive > Sphere.

2. In the Channel Box, type *90* in the field next to Rotate X, and press (Enter).

3. Open the Hypershade and click Phong E.

A Phong E material shows up in the work area.

4. Double-click the Phong E material in the Hypershade.

The Attribute Editor for the Phong E material appears.

5. In the Attribute Editor for the Phong E, material, click the Map button next to the Color slider [.].

The Create Render Node window opens.

6. Click the Ramp button (**Figure 15.49**).

The Attribute Editor for the ramp appears. A ramp texture node also appears in the Hypershade.

Figure 15.47 The interactive placement was used to rotate the brick texture.

Figure 15.48 By increasing Repeat UV of the place2dTexture to *4* (in the Attribute Editor on the left), you can make the brick texture repeat many times on the surface.

Figure 15.49 When you click Ramp in the Create Render Node window, a new ramp texture is created and mapped to a material.

ABOUT MATERIALS

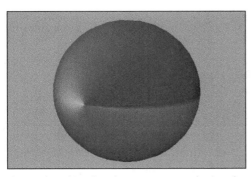

Figure 15.50 This sphere has a ramp textured to its color.

Figure 15.51 The Attribute Editor for the ramp holds the controls for determining the look of the gradient it produces. Position indicators are the circles to the left of the ramp. They determine where a color is positioned within the gradient.

Figure 15.52 When you click in the middle of the ramp, a new position indicator is created. By clicking the square with the *X* in it to the right of the ramp, you can delete a position indicator.

7. With the middle mouse button, drag the Phong E from the Hypershade onto the sphere to assign the shader.

If you have trouble finding the Phong E material, click the work area of the Hypershade and press ⓐ. This will frame all of the nodes.

8. Click the Perspective view and press ⑥ to see the texture (**Figure 15.50**).

To make the ramp texture look like an eyeball:

1. Create a material with a ramp texture, and assign it to a sphere as in the previous section.

2. Open the Hypershade, and in the work area, double-click on the ramp texture.

The Attribute Editor for the ramp appears.

3. In the Attribute Editor for the ramp, change the type to U Ramp.

4. Click and drag the top position indicator down slightly (**Figure 15.51**).

5. Change its color to black by dragging the Selected Color slider all the way to the left.

6. Click and drag the middle position indicator, which is green by default, to just below the top one.

7. Click on the ramp about one-fifth of the way down from the top.

A new position indicator appears (**Figure 15.52**).

8. Click and drag the bottom position indicator up to just below the new one.

continues on next page

ABOUT MATERIALS

399

9. With the bottom position indicator still selected, click the color swatch next to Selected Color.

The Color Chooser opens.

10. Click the white swatch at the top of the Color Chooser (**Figure 15.53**).

The sphere is now textured like an eyeball (**Figure 15.54**).

In addition to the 2D ramp texture available in past versions, Maya now includes a shader—called a *Ramp shader*—similar to the 2D ramp texture. Like the 2D ramp texture, the Ramp material shader can be used to create more exotic textures such as cartoon shading, which involves creating a shader that renders like a flat 2d cartoon, instead of rendering with the appearance of 3d surfaces, and advanced gradient effects. You can also use the new Ramp shader to produce the same type of eyeball effect as we created in the steps above, making it a worthy addition to your texturing toolset.

To create a simple cartoon look on a surface:

1. From the Create menu select NURBS Primitives > Sphere.

2. Open the Hypershade, and under the Create Maya Nodes menu, click Ramp Shader in the Surface section to create a ramp shader (**Figure 15.55**).

3. Double-click the Ramp Shader material in the Hypershade.

The Attribute Editor for the Ramp Shader material appears.

4. Click the Selected Color swatch to open the Color Chooser.

5. Select a color for the shadow area of the sphere.

6. Click Accept to close the Color Chooser.

Figure 15.53 The white swatch is selected in the Color Chooser, causing the selected position indicator and the ramp below it to become white.

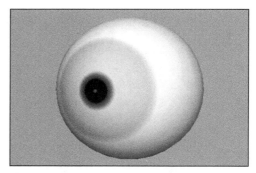

Figure 15.54 The eyeball is complete with a pupil and iris.

Figure 15.55 You can create a ramp shader from the Create Maya Nodes drop-down menu.

Figure 15.56 Each time you click in the Color slider you create a new color.

Figure 15.57 The ramp will remain a gradient until you set Interpolation to None.

Figure 15.58 Set Interpolation to None to limit the Color slider to only two colors, no gradients.

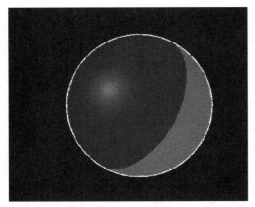

Figure 15.59 A cartoon-style rendering.

7. Click once in the Color slider beside Selected Color.

A new color is added to the slider (**Figure 15.56**).

8. Click the Selected Color swatch and adjust the Value (V) slider to *1*.

9. Click Accept to close the Color Chooser.

10. Set the Color Interpolation drop-down menu to None.

The None setting changes the gradient between the selected colors to two flat colors with no gradient in-between (**Figure 15.57**).

11. Set Color Input to Brightness.

The Brightness setting flattens out the sphere's color to give the surface a flatter, more cartoon-like appearance.

12. Create two colors in the slider beside the Selected Color section of the Incandescence area. Make the left one white and the right one black (**Figure 15.58**).

13. Set Incandescence Interpolation to None.

14. Apply the material to the surface.

The surface now appears to have flat color inside and a white outline (**Figure 15.59**).

✔ Tip

■ For best results, use different shades of the same colors when adding colors to the color sliders. Using shades of color helps to better form the object because when using similar colors, your eye reads those colors as the same surface; whereas using completely different colors makes your eyes jump from color to color.

To create a layered shader:

1. From the Create menu select NURBS Primitives > Sphere.

2. Create two Blinn materials; color one red and one blue.

3. Open the Hypershade and double-click the blue Blinn material.

4. Click the Map icon ⬚ next to the Transparency slider.

5. Click Fractal in the Textures tab of the Create Render Node window (**Figure 15.60**).

6. Under the Create Maya Nodes menu in the Hypershade, click Layered Shader in the Surface section (**Figure 15.61**).

7. Double-click the Layered Shader material in the Hypershade.

   The Attribute Editor for the Layered Shader material appears.

8. With the middle mouse button, drag the red and blue materials from the Hypershade into the red square under Layered Shader Attributes (**Figure 15.62**).

Figure 15.60 We're adding a fractal to the Transparency channel so that we can see our red shader through our blue shader.

Figure 15.61 You can click Layered Shader once to create it, or you can use the middle mouse button to drag the icon into the Hypershade to create it.

Figure 15.62 You can drag multiple shaders into your layered shader to create layered effects using the transparency of each layer.

Figure 15.63 The small *x* at the bottom of each square is used to remove shaders from your layered shader.

Figure 15.64 The rendered layered shader has both red and blue coloring.

9. Click the *x* under the original green square to delete it (**Figure 15.63**).

   You should now have two squares in the red square under Layered Shader Attributes.

10. Apply the layered shader to the sphere.

11. From the Window menu, select Rendering Editors > Render View.

12. In the Render view, click the Redo Previous Render icon 🖳.

    The sphere is now red and blue. The red can be seen through the blue because we added a fractal to its transparency channel (**Figure 15.64**).

✔ Tip

- You must have transparency in the top shader in the layered shader if any of the bottom shader is to be visible. The first shader on the left is the top shader.

To assign a bump map to a surface:

1. From the Create menu select NURBS Primitives > Plane.

2. Open the Hypershade and create a Lambert.

3. Assign the Lambert to the plane by using the middle mouse button to drag it from the Hypershade to the plane.

4. Double-click the Lambert in the Hypershade.

   The Attribute Editor for the Lambert appears.

5. Click the Map button next to Bump Mapping [.].

   The Create Render Node window appears.

6. Click Bulge (**Figure 15.65**).

   The bulge shows up in the work area of the Hypershade. We'll need to render it to see the resulting bump.

7. From the Create menu, select Lights > Directional Light.

   Bump maps show up better with a directional source of light than with ambient light.

8. Rotate the light so that it points diagonally at the plane (**Figure 15.66**).

9. Click the Render icon [🖼], which is near the top right of the interface.

   The image renders out into a new window. The bulge is visible on the surface (**Figure 15.67**).

✔ Tip

- The Interactive Photorealistic Renderer can be very useful for tuning shaders. For more more information on IPR, see Chapter 16.

Figure 15.65 Clicking Bulge in the Create Render Node window creates a bulge texture that is mapped to the bump of a material.

Figure 15.66 A directional light is created and rotated diagonally to the plane. Directional lights make bumps stand out in greater contrast because the light is only coming from one side.

Figure 15.67 This is a rendered image of a plane with a bulge texture mapped to its bump. Render to see the bump—it does not show up in the Perspective view.

Figure 15.68 All of the nodes associated with the material are visible in the work area of the Hypershade. The utility that controls the height of the bump is in the middle.

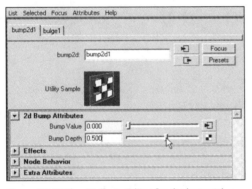

Figure 15.69 The Attribute Editor for the bump2d node contains the Bump Depth attribute. Bump depth controls the overall height of the bump.

Figure 15.70 The plane on the left has a bump depth of 1; the plane the right has a bump depth of 0.5.

To adjust the height of a bump map:

1. Create a plane with a bump map, as in the previous task, "To assign a bump map to a surface."

2. Select the plane.

3. Open the Hypershade and click the Graph Materials on Selected Objects button ![icon].

   The material with all its connections appears in the work area of the Hypershade (**Figure 15.68**).

4. Double-click the bump2d node.

   The Attribute Editor for the bump2d node appears.

5. Change the bump depth by moving the slider or typing in a number (**Figure 15.69**).

6. Click the Render icon ![icon].

   The bumps are smaller than in the previous bump map (**Figure 15.70**).

About Projection Maps

Sometimes you'll want to map one image across two or more surfaces. For that you can use a projection map. The default projection type is *planar*, which acts like a slide projector pointed at a surface. Other projection types include *spherical* and *cylindrical*, which project an image from a shape that surrounds the surface (**Figure 15.71**).

Figure 15.71 A checkered texture is mapped to spheres using three different projection types: (left to right) cylindrical, planar, and spherical.

To map a texture as projection:

1. Open the Hypershade, create a Lambert material, and assign it to a NURBS plane and a NURBS sphere (**Figure 15.72**).

2. Double-click the Lambert in the Hypershade.

   The Attribute Editor for the Lambert opens.

3. In the Attribute Editor for the Lambert, click the Map button next to the Color slider 🔳.

   The Create Render Node window appears.

4. Click the radio button next to "As projection" (**Figure 15.73**).

5. Click the File button.

   The Attribute Editor for the projection appears. A place3dTexture node appears in the Perspective view.

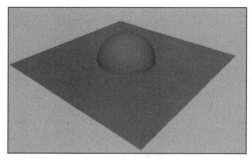

Figure 15.72 A NURBS sphere and a plane.

Figure 15.73 The "As projection" radio button has been selected in the Create Render Node window.

Figure 15.74 The planar projection is projecting the image across the two surfaces from the side. This causes the image to be stretched along the plane.

6. Click the file1 tab at the top of the Attribute Editor.

   The Attribute Editor changes to show the options for the file texture.

7. Click the Folder icon next to Image Name.

   The file browser appears.

8. Browse for and open an image of your own.

9. Click the Perspective view, and press ⑥ to switch to textured mode.

   The place3dTexture node is visible in the Perspective view. The image is visible on the surface, but it is stretched out because it is being projected on from the side (**Figure 15.74**).

✔ Tip

■ If you move a surface with a projection texture mapped to it, the surface will appear to be moving through its texture when it is rendered out. To solve this problem, select the surface, and then from the Texturing menu select Create Texture Reference Object.

ABOUT PROJECTION MAPS

To adjust a projection:

1. Projection-map a texture onto a plane as in the previous task, "To map a texture as projection."

2. Select the place3dTexture utility in the Perspective view (**Figure 15.75**).

   The line coming out from the center indicates the projection direction—in this case, on the side of the plane—and we want it to project on the top.

3. Rotate the plane –90 degrees in the X axis.

   The image is no longer stretched; however, it doesn't fit precisely on the surface.

4. With the place3dTexture still selected, press [Ctrl]/[Control][A] to open the Attribute Editor.

   The Attribute Editor for the place3dTexture node opens.

5. Click the "Fit to group box" button.

   The place3dTexture is automatically resized to that of the plane, and the image now fits (**Figure 15.76**).

✔ Tip

■ If you move or rotate the place3dTexture, the image on the surface will move or rotate. If you scale it up, the image will scale up. If you scale it down, the image will scale down and be tiled (**Figure 15.77**).

Figure 15.75 The place3dTexture utility has been selected in the Perspective view. You can move, rotate, and scale this node the same way you would for any object.

Figure 15.76 Now that the place3dTexture utility is oriented to the surface, the image is projected across the two surfaces.

Figure 15.77 The place3dTexture utility has been scaled down, rotated, and moved.

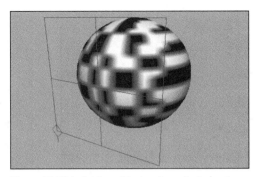

Figure 15.78 A checkered texture is projected onto a sphere. It appears very blurry and does not accurately represent how it will look when it is rendered.

Figure 15.79 Hardware Texturing options are visible in the Attribute Editor for a material. By increasing the "Texture quality" setting to High, the checkers will become clear.

Figure 15.80 The checker texture is much sharper now that the texture quality for Hardware Texturing has been increased.

Textures, especially projected ones, often appear blurry in the view even though they render clearly. However, you often need the image to appear sharper in order to place the texture.

To improve the quality of a texture image in a view:

1. Following the steps in the previous tasks, projection-map a checkered texture onto a sphere (**Figure 15.78**).

   The texture on the surface will appear very blurry.

2. Select the sphere.

3. Open the Hypershade and click the Graph Materials on Selected Objects icon 🖧.

   The material with all of its connections appears in the work area of the Hypershade.

4. Double-click the material in the Hypershade.

   The Attribute Editor for the material appears.

5. Under Hardware Texturing in the Attribute Editor, click the arrow to expand the options (**Figure 15.79**).

6. Change the "Texture quality" setting to High.

   The blurry checkers on the sphere become sharper (**Figure 15.80**).

✔ Tip

■ Making the texture quality high will slow down Maya's interactivity, especially with a high-resolution image. Once you've finished placing the texture, it's a good idea to reset it to low quality.

ABOUT PROJECTION MAPS

About the 3D Paint tool

The 3D Paint tool allows you to paint directly on a surface. You can create a new texture image from scratch with this method, and Maya will create a new image file.

It's important to make sure you've set your project (File > Project > Set) before you begin painting, because the current project will determine where this image ends up. When you save the scene after painting, a folder named after your scene is created in the 3dPaintTextures folder of the project you're currently set to. Any images that were created by painting will be put in that folder.

You can also paint on a surface that already has an image file textured on it—for example, to add dirt or other details to an existing image.

To paint directly on a surface:

1. Open the Hypershade, create a Lambert material, and assign it to a NURBS sphere.

2. Select the sphere.

3. From the Texturing menu, select the box next to 3D Paint Tool.

   The 3D Paint Tool Settings window opens (**Figure 15.81**).

4. Scroll down until you see File Textures (**Figure 15.82**).

   If necessary, you can change the image format that will be created.

5. Click the Assign Textures button.

   The Assign File Textures window appears. You can increase the resolution of the texture here if you need a highly detailed texture. The default of 256 by 256 will suffice for now (**Figure 15.83**).

Figure 15.81 The 3D Paint Tool Settings window includes many controls that determine the look of your brush strokes.

Figure 15.82 Under File Textures in the 3D Paint Tool Settings window, you can assign a texture to the material for a selected object. You cannot paint on a surface that does not have a file mapped to its color.

Figure 15.83 Once you click Assign/Edit Textures, you can paint, because a file texture has been connected to the material for the object you want to paint.

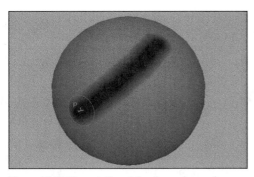

Figure 15.84 The paintbrush has been dragged across the sphere, producing this black mark.

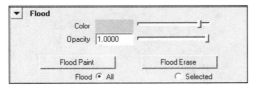

Figure 15.85 You can choose a color to flood the whole object with by clicking the Color swatch.

Figure 15.86 A smiley face has been painted on the sphere with three brush strokes.

6. Click Assign Textures.

   A file texture has now been connected to the material so you can paint.

7. Click in the Perspective view, hold down b, and then using the middle mouse button drag from right to left to get the brush down to size.

   The red circle, which represents brush size, should shrink.

8. Click and drag on the surface to paint on it.

   A mark appears on the surface (**Figure 15.84**).

To use the 3D Paint tool:

1. Continue with the sphere from the previous section.

   If the paintbrush is not visible or the tool options are no longer open, select the sphere, and then from the Texturing menu select the box next to 3D Paint Tool.

2. Click the swatch next to Color in the 3D Paint Tool Settings window under the Flood section (**Figure 15.85**).

   The Color Chooser appears.

3. Choose the yellow swatch at the top of the Color Chooser, and click Accept.

4. Click Flood Paint.

   The sphere turns yellow.

5. Paint a smiley face by clicking and dragging on the surface (**Figure 15.86**.

6. Click the Get Brush button ▓, which is to the right of Paint Effects in the 3D Paint Tool Options window.

   The Visor window opens.

continues on next page

ABOUT PROJECTION MAPS

7. Scroll down in the Visor, and click the Hair folder.

Several hair types appear (**Figure 15.87**).

8. Click on the hair of your choice.

9. Paint some hair on your smiley-face sphere (**Figure 15.88**).

10. Clear the surface texture by clicking the Flood Erase button under the Flood section.

The texture is cleared, and the original gray surface is ready to be repainted.

✔ Tips

■ After using a Paint Effects brush, you can return to a normal brush by clicking one of the Brush Profile buttons next to Artisan in the 3D Paint Tool Settings window (**Figure 15.89**).

■ By decreasing the opacity in the 3D Paint Tool settings, you can paint on a surface but still see the color beneath your brush strokes—helpful if you're trying to make a surface appear dirty.

■ You can use this tool to paint areas roughly to mark the different parts of a surface. You can then open the image file (which is created once you save the scene) in Adobe Photoshop and paint the details there.

■ These same steps can be used for other attributes, such as Transparency and Displacement. Just select the desired attribute from the dropdown menu under File Textures.

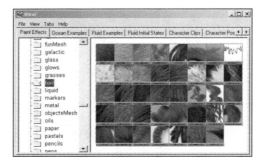

Figure 15.87 You can choose from a variety of brushes to use with the 3D Paint tool in the Visor. Here we see the brushes in the Hair folder.

Figure 15.88 Hair has been painted on the sphere by using one of the Paint Effects brushes.

Figure 15.89 To return to a normal brush, choose from one of the profiles of the Artisan brushes.

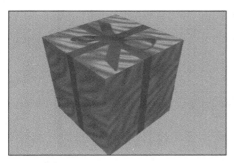

Figure 15.90 A wrapped-gift texture has been mapped to a cube.

Figure 15.91 The white lines in the UV Texture Editor represent the edges of the cube. You can see how the cube has been "unwrapped." The image beneath these lines is what the actual image file that's mapped to the surface looks like.

Figure 15.92 Four different textures have been mapped to different parts of the same polygon sphere by assigning them to specific faces of the sphere.

About Texturing Polygons

All of the techniques covered thus far work on polygon primitives. They will not, however, necessarily work on any polygon surfaces you've modeled. While NURBS surfaces are always four-sided, polygon surfaces are made up of many small faces—which means that applying textures to them is not as simple as it is on NURBS surfaces.

Think of a wrapped present. Imagine carefully removing the wrapping paper and flattening it out. Once the paper has been flattened, you can easily paint a new image on it (**Figure 15.90**).

This is essentially what you need to do to add texture to a polygon surface. Before you can successfully texture-map it, you need to "unwrap" the surface. To do this, you create a UV map, which you can see in the UV Texture Editor (**Figure 15.91**).

The UV maps for complicated characters can be confusing to look at, and require a lot of work to use effectively. However, you don't need to create them for polygon primitives because they come with them.

One distinct advantage of polygons over NURBS is that you can assign shading groups to individual faces of a polygon surface, while a NURBS surface can have only one shading group assigned to it. You do this by selecting polygon faces and assigning the materials to *them*, not to the object as a whole (**Figure 15.92**).

To create automatic mapping for a polygon texture:

1. Create a polygon telephone (**Figure 15.93**).

   For a detailed instruction of how to do this, see "To model a Subdiv telephone receiver, starting with a polygon" in Chapter 9, "Subdiv Surfaces." However, do not convert it to subdivision surfaces. Instead, smooth the polygon with a subdivision level of *3* and a continuity of *0.35*. Save this model for later use.

2. Create a Blinn material, and assign it to the surface.

3. Open the Hypershade and double-click the Blinn material.

   The Attribute Editor for the Blinn material opens.

4. Click the Map button ■ next to the Color slider in the Attribute Editor.

   The Create Render Node window appears.

5. Make sure that the radio button next to Normal is selected, and then click File.

   The Attribute Editor for the file node opens.

6. Click the Browse button ■ next to Image Name.

7. Browse for and open your own image file.

   This one was created especially for the phone, but any image will do. The image will look messed up and stretched out on the phone in the Perspective view (**Figure 15.94**).

8. Select the surface.

9. From the Edit Polygons menu, select Texture > Automatic Mapping.

   Now the image is not stretched out as much, but the different elements are not in place (**Figure 15.95**).

Figure 15.93 By using Extrude Face and Smooth, a phone can be modeled from a cube in a few easy steps.

Figure 15.94 On the left is the file texture that is mapped to the phone. On the right, the texture on the phone is stretched out and in the wrong places.

Figure 15.95 Now that a UV map has been created using automatic mapping, the texture is placed on all parts of the surface, but not in the right places.

Figure 15.96 One UV point has been selected from the center of the earpiece of the phone.

Figure 15.97 In the UV Texture Editor, you can see how the different parts of the surface have been laid out over the image map. The UV point that was selected in the Perspective view is also selected here and is seen with move manipulators on it. This makes it easy to recognize which shell is the phone's earpiece.

You navigate the UV Texture Editor just as you would any panel. You can track and dolly the same way you do in any view panel. And the Move, Rotate, and Scale tools work just as they do in the rest of the program.

The image that is mapped to the surface is tiled in the UV Texture Editor. This allows you to move up different parts of the surface onto the part of the image you want without a lot of messy overlapping.

To use the UV Texture Editor:

1. Continue using the phone from the previous task.

2. Right-click the surface and select UV from the Marking menu.

3. Choose one UV point from the center of the earpiece of the telephone (**Figure 15.96**).

4. From the Window menu select UV Texture Editor.

   The UV Texture Editor opens. You can see the image that was assigned to the surface, and on top of that is the wireframe of the different parts of the surface (shells) that have been separated. The one point you picked on the surface is visible and is easy to find because of the transform manipulator on it (**Figure 15.97**).

continues on next page

ABOUT TEXTURING POLYGONS

5. Right-click the shell, and from the Marking menu, choose Select > Select Shell (**Figure 15.98**).

All the UVs of the shell are selected.

6. Move, scale, and rotate the shell over a recognizable part of the image.

You can watch the image on the selected area of the phone change interactively in the Perspective view (**Figure 15.99**).

7. Repeat Steps 3 through 6 for other parts of the phone.

Because the surface is in many separate pieces (shells) in the UV Texture View, there are seams on the surface (**Figure 15.100**). We can combine two shells and get rid of the seam by using Move and Sew UVs.

Figure 15.98 Rather than having to carefully select each UV of the shell, you can select the whole shell at once by clicking with the right mouse button and choosing Select › Select Shell from the Marking menu.

Figure 15.99 While placing the UVs in the Texture view (right), you can see their effect on the surface simultaneously (left).

Figure 15.100 A seam in the texture is apparent along the side of the phone.

Figure 15.101 All of the polygon edges along the edge of the seam have been carefully selected.

Figure 15.102 The edges of two shells are selected because they are, in fact, one edge shared by both shells.

To eliminate a seam in a texture using Move and Sew UVs:

1. Continue using the phone from the previous tasks.

2. In the Perspective view, carefully select all of the edges along the seam (**Figure 15.101**).

   The corresponding edges are automatically selected in the UV Texture Editor when you select them on the object (**Figure 15.102**).

3. From the Edit Polygons menu select Texture > Move and Sew UVs.

   The seam on the object disappears in the Perspective view (**Figure 15.103**). In the UV Texture Editor, two shells have been combined along that edge (**Figure 15.104**).

Figure 15.103 The seam is now gone because the edges of the two shells have been sewn together, allowing the texture image to extend across both.

Figure 15.104 What was once two separate shells is now one bigger shell covering a larger portion of the phone.

Using the UV Texture Editor toolbar

The UV Texture Editor toolbar holds shortcuts to many of the actions in the UV Texture Editor menus. The toolbar is divided into four main sections: UV position buttons, Isolate Selection buttons, View buttons, and UV edit buttons. They provide the following functions:

◆ **UV position buttons**—This section holds shortcuts to many of the UV position tools, including Flipping, Rotating, Sewing, and Aligning UVs (**Figure 15.105**).

◆ **Isolate Selection buttons**—This section holds shortcuts to adding, removing, and toggling isolation tools (**Figure 15.106**).

◆ **View buttons**—This section holds snaps, toggles, and border menu shortcuts (**Figure 15.107**).

◆ **UV edit buttons**—This section holds UV coordinate input fields as well as UV copying and pasting features (**Figure 15.108**).

Figure 15.105 The UV position buttons section of the UV Texture Editor toolbar.

Figure 15.106 The Isolate Selection buttons section of the UV Texture Editor toolbar.

Figure 15.107 The View buttons section of the UV Texture Editor toolbar.

Figure 15.108 The UV edit buttons section of the UV Texture Editor toolbar.

Setting material attributes via the Channel Box

You can adjust many of the material attributes using the Channel Box, which spares you having to search through the Attribute Editor for the right command.

To set material attributes using the Channel Box:

1. Create a NURBS primitive sphere.

2. Open the Hypershade and create a new Blinn and assign it to the sphere.

3. Select the Blinn in the work area.

   Many of the Blinn attributes are now available in the Channel Box. For this example, we'll change the transparency.

4. In the Channel Box, change the Transparency R, B, and G attributes to .5.

   The Sphere is now transparent.

Avoiding swimming textures

Swimming textures is an undesirable effect that can occur when you animate an object that has a 3D texture applied to it; the animated object moves, but the assigned texture stays in the same place. To avoid swimming textures, you can parent the placement node to the object or set the texture to local. But if the object deforms, you need to convert the 3D texture to a file-based texture by using the Convert to File Texture command.

To convert a 3D texture to a file texture:

1. Create a NURBS primitive sphere.

2. Open the Hypershade, create a new Blinn, and assign it to the sphere.

3. Double-click the Blinn to open the Attribute Editor.

4. Click the map button for Color.

5. Select the 3D texture wood.

continues on next page

ABOUT TEXTURING POLYGONS

6. In the modeling window select the
sphere, and in the Hypershade (Shift)-
select the Blinn.

7. From the Edit menu in the Hypershade,
select Convert to File Texture.

A new Blinn is assigned to the sphere.

About projecting UV maps

Earlier in this chapter you were shown how
to project a texture; you can also project UV
maps. One main difference is that a projected UV map sticks to the object even if it
deforms, whereas a deforming object will
"swim" through a projected texture.

To create a planar UV map for a polygon object:

1. Open the model of the polygon telephone
made in the first step of the task "To
create automatic mapping for a polygon
texture" earlier in this chapter.

2. Open the Hypershade, create a Blinn
material, and assign it to the surface.

3. Double-click the Blinn material in
the Hypershade.

The Attribute Editor for the Blinn
material opens.

4. Click the Map button 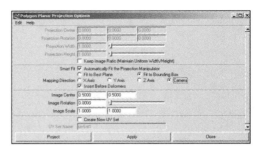 next to the
Color slider in the Attribute Editor.

The Create Render Node window appears.

5. Make sure that Normal is selected, and
then click File to open.

6. Select the phone surface, choose Edit
Polygons > Texture and select the box
next to Planar Mapping.

The Polygon Planar Mapping Options
dialog box opens (**Figure 15.109**).

7. For Mapping Direction, click Camera and
click Apply.

A projected mapping manipulator appears
around the object (**Figure 15.110**).

Figure 15.109 Use the Polygon Planar Mapping Options
dialog box to control how the object is mapped.

Figure 15.110
The projected
mapping
manipulator
appears
around the
object.

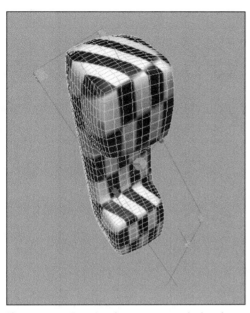

Figure 15.111 Rotating the camera reveals that the texture was projected from the camera's previous POV (point of view).

8. Rotate the camera by pressing [Alt] while you click and drag in the 3d view.

The texture stretches across the object from the camera's previous position (**Figure 15.111**).

9. In the Polygon Planar Mapping Options dialog box, click Apply again.

The projected mapping manipulator changes position to match the camera's current direction (**Figure 15.112**).

Using the camera option forces the projection to be created from the camera's current view.

10. In the Mapping Direction section of the Polygon Planar Mapping Options dialog box, click Y Axis and click Apply.

The projected mapping manipulator changes position so that it projects directly down the *Y* axis (**Figure 15.113**).

continues on next page

Figure 15.112 The projected mapping manipulator updates to match the current camera POV.

Figure 15.113 The projected mapping manipulator projects down the *Y* axis.

11. Repeat step 10, but click the Z Axis button to project down the *Z* axis (**Figure 15.114**) or click the X Axis button to project down the *X* axis (**Figure 15.115**).

12. Click and drag the green box on the texture projection manipulator.

This scales the manipulator and allows additional control over the placement of a UV projection (**Figure 15.116**).

13. Switch to Selection by Hierarchy mode and select the phone.

14. From the Deform menu, select Create Nonlinear > Bend.

This applies a bend deformer to the object.

Figure 15.114 Projecting down the *Z* axis.

Figure 15.116 Drag the handles on the projected mapping manipulator to change its scale and position.

Figure 15.115 Projecting down the *X* axis.

Figure 15.117 Apply a bend deformer and then expand the bend1 options under the Inputs section of the Channel Box.

15. In the Inputs section of the Channel Box, click bend1 to reveal the bend controls (**Figure 15. 117**).

16. Using the middle mouse button, click and drag Curvature back in forth in the 3D view to set it to .5.

or

In the numeric entry field, set Curvature to .5.

This deforms the object so that the texture to stick to it (**Figure 15.118**).

17. Uncheck Insert Before Deformers and click Apply again.

The mapping changes to reflect the deformation of the object (**Figure 15.119**).

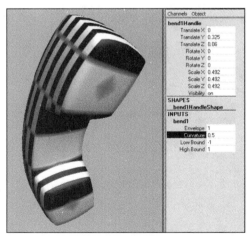

Figure 15.118 The object deforms and the texture sticks to it.

Figure 15.119 Uncheck Insert Before Deformers to allow the mapping to be applied to the object in its current deformed shape.

To create a cylindrical UV map for a polygon object:

1. Repeat steps 1–5 from the previous task, "To create a planar UV map for a polygon object."

2. Select the phone surface, choose Edit Polygons > Texture and select the box next to Cylindrical Mapping.

   The Polygon Cylindrical Projection Options dialog box opens (**Figure 15.120**).

3. Click Apply to accept the default values and update mapping on the surface (**Figure 15.121**).

4. In the first numeric entry field, set Image Scale to .5 click Apply (**Figure 15.122**).

   The mapping updates so that the texture around the object is larger.

Figure 15.120 The Polygon Cylindrical Projection Options dialog box.

Figure 15.121 The mapping on the object updates and the projected mapping manipulator appears.

Figure 15.122 Type a lower value into Image Scale to force the texture to be larger in relationship to the object.

Figure 15.123 Drag the handles on the projected mapping manipulator to control the position and scale of the projection in relationship to the object.

5. Click and drag the red box on the texture projection manipulator to make the texture around the object larger or smaller (**Figure 15.123**).

To create a spherical UV map for a polygon object:

1. Repeat steps 1–5 from the task "To create a p!anar UV map for a polygon object," earlier in this chapter.

2. Select the phone surface, choose Edit Polygons > Texture and select the box next to Spherical Mapping.

The Polygon Spherical Projection Options dialog box opens (**Figure 15.124**).

continues on next page

Figure 15.124 The Polygon Spherical Projection Options dialog box.

Figure 15.125 The mapping on the object updates and the projected mapping manipulator appears.

3. Click Apply to accept the default values and update mapping on the surface (**Figure 15.125**).

4. Click and drag the blue box on the texture projection manipulator to make the texture around the object smaller (**Figure 15.126**) or larger (**Figure 15.127**).

Texturing Subdivs

Texturing subdiv surfaces is very similar to texturing polygons and under some circumstances it can be done exactly the same way.

Say you want to create automatic mapping for a subdiv object (like the telephone you made in Chapter 9, "Subdiv Surfaces"). You can follow the same steps in "To create a planar UV map for a polygon object," earlier in this chapter, but choose Subdiv Surfaces > Texture > Automatic Mapping to open the Automatic Mapping Options dialog box. Or, to create a planar UV map for your subdiv phone, choose Subdiv Surfaces > Texture > Planar Mapping to open the Planar Mapping Options dialog box. Then continue with the steps in "To use the UV Texture Editor," earlier in this chapter.

However, you cannot edit the UV mapping of a subdiv by switching to polygon mode. Instead, choose Modify > Convert > Convert to Subdiv Options to open the Convert to Subdiv Options dialog box. Then select Proxy Object Subdivision Surface Mode and when you edit the UV mapping on the polygon cage and it will update UV mapping on the subdiv surface.

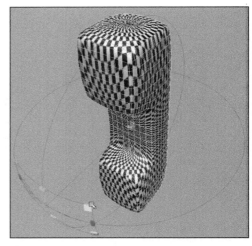

Figure 15.126 Drag the handles on the projected mapping manipulator to scale the projection and make it smaller...

Figure 15.127 ...or larger.

Figure 15.128 Use the Create PSD Texture Options dialog box to create layered Photoshop image files to use as textures.

Figure 15.129 Select color and transparency and click the right arrow (>) to add them to Selected Attributes.

Using Adobe Photoshop

In Maya, you can create layered PSD (Photoshop Document) files or use PSD image files with layers from Adobe Photoshop for textures. Being able to use layered files makes it simpler to manage complex textures that require individual image maps for one or more channels in a single shader.

To create layered PSD in Maya:

1. Select an object and, from the Texturing menu, select Create PSD Texture.

   The Create PSD Texture Options dialog box opens (**Figure 15.128**).

2. In the Attributes section, select color and transparency and click the right arrow (>) to add them to Selected Attributes (**Figure 15.129**).

3. Click Create.

   The dialog box closes and Maya saves the PSD to the sourceimages folder in your current project directory.

4. Open the PSD in Adobe Photoshop (**Figure 15.130**).

   The layered image file has a layer called UVSnapShot that you can use as a reference while painting in PS (Photoshop). The file also has layer sets named after the channels that were selected in the Create PSD Texture Options.

   continues on next page

Figure 15.130 Open the PSD file that Maya created in Photoshop.

ABOUT TEXTURING POLYGONS

427

5. Paint several strokes on the layer in the lambert1.transparency layer set (**Figure 15.131**).

White is fully transparent and black is fully opaque.

6. Click the eye icon 👁 next to the lambert1.transparency layer set and the Uvsnapshot layer so that they are hidden.

7. Paint some colorful strokes on the layer in the lambert1.color layer set (**Figure 15.132**).

8. Save the PSD file and switch back to Maya.

9. In the active view, choose Shading > Hardware Texturing.

The hardware shaded view can display texture maps assigned to surfaces.

10. Select the object that for which the PSD texture was originally created and choose Texturing > Update PSD Textures.

The surface updates, displaying the color map that was created in Photoshop (**Figure 15.133**).

Figure 15.131 Paint some strokes on the layer contained in the lambert1.transparency layer set.

Figure 15.132 Paint some colors on the layer.

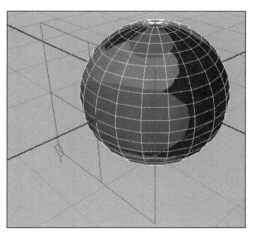

Figure 15.133 The surface displays the color map.

Figure 15.134 The surface updates show the color map that was created in Photoshop.

Figure 15.135 Render the view so that all the channels used for a shader can be seen.

11. From the Render menu, select Render Current Frame.

The Render View dialog box opens and renders the current view, showing the color channel and transparency channels that were painted (**Figure 15.134**).

✔ Tip

■ If you have an existing PSD with layer sets that you wish to import into Maya, you can do so using the PSD File Texture node.

To use an existing layered PSD in Maya:

1. Open the Hypershade and, in the Create bar, expand 2D Textures.

2. Click Normal, then click the PSD File icon (**Figure 15.135**).

A PSD File node appears as psdFileTex1 in the work area (**Figure 15.136**).

3. Double-click the psdFileTex1 node to open its Attribute Editor.

continues on next page

Figure 15.136 A PSD File node appears as psdFileTex1 in the work area.

ABOUT TEXTURING POLYGONS

4. Click the Folder icon [icon] next to Image Name.

The Open dialog box appears (**Figure 15.137**).

5. Select a PSD file from the hard drive and click Open.

The Open dialog box closes and the texture sample of the psdFileTex1 updates with the PSD file that was selected (**Figure 15.138**).

6. From the pull-down menu next to Link To Layer Set, choose Composite (**Figure 15.139**).

This pull-down menu lists each layer set in the image. If the image has no layer sets, then Composite is the only item in the list. Composite is a "flattened" combination of all the visible layers in the PSD file.

7. In the Hypershade, create a Blinn shader, and assign it to the surface.

The blinn shader appears in the work area next to the psdFileTex1 node.

8. With the middle mouse button, click and drag the psdFileTex1 node onto the blinn1 icon.

9. From the Marking menu that appears, select "color" (**Figure 15.140**).

The icon of the blinn1 shader updates with the new texture.

Figure 15.137 The Open dialog box appears and defaults to the current project directory.

Figure 15.138 The texture sample updates with an image of the file that was selected.

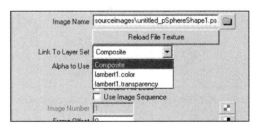

Figure 15.139 Choose Composite from the Link to Layer Set pull-down menu.

Figure 15.140 Middle-click and drag the psdFileTex1 node onto blinn1 to open the Marking menu.

Figure 15.141 Right-click the psdFileTex and select Convert to Layered Texture from the Marking menu.

Figure 15.142 Convert to Layered Texture creates psdFileTex nodes for each layer set in the PSD file and connects them to a layeredTexture node.

Maya provides a one-click method to convert a PSD File node into a layered texture. The Convert to Layered Texture command creates a separate PSD file node for each layer set and connects them to a Layered Texture node.

This command is also useful if you need to connect the layer sets to the channels of a shader. Convert to Layered Texture automatically creates additional PSD File nodes for each layer set and selects them in the Link To Layer Set section of the PSD File node attributes. Then you can use the middle mouse button to connect each PSD File node to the appropriate channel in the shader.

To create layered texture from a PSD File node:

1. Follow steps 1–6 from the previous task.

2. Right-click the psdFileTex node and select Convert To Layered Texture from the Marking menu that appears (**Figure 15.141**).

   Several new nodes appear in the work area. For each layer set in the PSD file, a new psdFileTex node is created (**Figure 15.142**).

   continues on next page

3. Click and drag the nodes so they do not overlap (**Figure 15.143**).

4. Right-click the layeredTexture node and select Graph Network from the Marking menu (**Figure 15.144**).

The work area updates showing how the psdFileTex nodes are connected to the layeredTexture node (**Figure 15.145**).

5. With the middle mouse button, click and drag the layeredTexture node to any channel input of a shader.

6. Repeat step 5 with the individual psdFileTex nodes.

Figure 15.143 Click and drag the nodes to rearrange them.

Figure 15.144 Right-click layeredTexture and select Graph Network from the Marking menu.

Figure 15.145 The graph of the psdFileTex nodes connect to the layeredTexture.

CAMERAS AND RENDERING

16

Figure 16.1 Compare a hardware render of a tractor (left) with a software render (right). The software render has a bump map that forms the tire treads and a transparency map that creates the grill in the front.

Figure 16.2 These renderings were created with Maya's rendering technologies: Mental Ray (upper left), Hardware Renderer (upper right), Software Renderer (lower left), Vector Renderer (lower right).

Creating quality images in Maya, whether for print or video, depends on rendering—the process of creating an image (or sequence of images) from a scene. When you render, you create a two-dimensional image from a specified three-dimensional view of your scene. Maya makes intensive mathematical calculations and applies the laws of physics to realistically create lighting, shadows, reflections, and textures. With a few settings, you can take even a very simple scene and make it look realistic by rendering it.

Rendering lights, shadows, and textures is performed using software rendering. Maya also performs hardware rendering, which is essentially what you see in your Perspective view and is greatly enhanced by your computer's display card. When you press ⑦ for hardware lighting, you are using hardware rendering. Maya's Playblast, Hardware Render Buffer, and Hardware Renderer will take a series of screen snapshots and export the images for you (**Figure 16.1**).

Maya has a unified Render Globals window to help set render qualities for the Hardware Renderer, Vector Renderer, and Mental Ray Renderer, as well as the Software Renderer. These rendering technologies, combined with the unified Render Globals window, makes Maya a powerful rendering and animation program (**Figure 16.2**).

About Cameras

An essential part of rendering is determining the point of view for your scene. Any time you view a scene in Maya, you're looking through a camera. The four views—Top, Front, Side, and Perspective—are actually four different cameras. Most often you render using the Perspective view; however, you can use the other views as well.

Cameras determine both your view of the scene and the view that is rendered. When you're tumbling and tracking in the Perspective view, you're really just moving and rotating that camera. You can't delete any of the four default cameras, but you can create new ones (**Figure 16.3**).

You can also animate a camera, just as you would any other object. You can simulate the camera motion used in real-world film, such as crane, helicopter, and dolly shots. And by animating a camera, you can even simulate a fly-through, which is often used for architectural visualization. You can also simulate camera cuts, where the camera remains at one view for a while and then jumps to another view.

Cameras include some useful attributes. Focal length allows you to adjust the zoom of the lens just as you would on a real camera (this is different from the dolly feature). You can set the center of interest to specify the point where you want the camera to look. And an image plane will place an image in the background of the camera view, regardless of how the camera is moved.

Figure 16.3 The icon that looks like a camera represents the Perspective view. The orthographic views (top, front, and side) are represented by squares with a line extending from the middle.

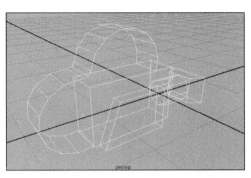

Figure 16.4 When a new camera is created, it appears at the origin.

Figure 16.5 The camera itself has been moved, and its center of interest is moved separately; the camera continues to aim at it.

Figure 16.6 The view through the camera you just created. The manipulator you see is the camera's own center of interest (still visible because the camera remains selected).

To create and adjust a camera:

1. From the Create menu, select Cameras > Camera.

   A new camera appears in the Perspective view (**Figure 16.4**).

2. With the camera still selected, press ⊤ for the Show Manipulator tool.

   A move manipulator appears on the camera and another appears in front of it. The one in front is called the center of interest.

3. Move the camera and the center of interest around.

   The camera follows the center of interest—that is, it remains aimed at it (**Figure 16.5**).

4. From the Panels menu in the Perspective view, select Look Through Selected.

   You are now looking through the camera that was just created. Note that the camera name at the bottom of the screen has changed from persp to camera1 (**Figure 16.6**).

✔ Tips

- You can also choose the camera you are looking through from the Panels menu in the Perspective view. To find the list of available cameras, select Panels > Perspective (**Figure 16.7**).

- You can rotate a camera—useful when you want the camera to pan.

- Scaling a camera does not affect its view; however, it can make the camera easier to select.

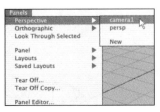

Figure 16.7 The Panels › Perspective menu provides camera views.

There is a subtle but important difference between creating a regular camera and creating a camera and aim control. The camera and aim control have an additional node, which can be keyframed or parented to an object.

To create and adjust a camera and aim:

1. From the Create menu, select Cameras > Camera and Aim.

   A new camera appears in the Perspective view. The dot in front of the camera is the aim (**Figure 16.8**).

2. From the Window menu, select Hypergraph.

   You can see the various nodes associated with the camera group (**Figure 16.9**).

3. From the Hypergraph, select the group node of the camera (probably called camera1_group).

4. Move the camera around.

   The aim and camera move together.

5. In the Perspective view, select and then move the aim.

   The camera remains aimed at the dot.

6. In the Perspective view, select and then move the camera.

   The camera moves but continues to point at the aim (**Figure 16.10**).

Figure 16.8 A camera and aim has been created. Note that the aim is represented by a small circle with a dot in the middle.

Figure 16.9 A camera and aim as represented in the Hypergraph. It has three nodes for added flexibility.

Figure 16.10 The camera has been moved up and away from the origin, but it continues to focus on the aim.

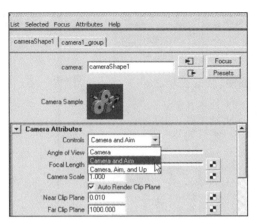

Figure 16.11 If you decide that you want a different camera type after you've created one, you can change the type here, in the Attribute Editor.

Figure 16.12 At the bottom of the pane, you can see the name of the camera you're looking through—in this case, persp (short for perspective). However, note that the camera that's selected is *not* the perspective (persp) camera.

Figure 16.13 In the Channel Box, you can see the name of the camera selected. When you create a new camera, it is named camera1 by default.

✔ Tips

- You can also create a camera aim and up control. Similar to the camera and aim control, the camera aim and up control has an additional node that controls the tilt of the camera.

- You can change whether the camera has an aim and up control after the camera has been created. The Attribute Editor for the camera provides a Controls option, under Camera Attributes, where you can choose among the three types of cameras (**Figure 16.11**).

Animating the camera

Animating a camera is, in essence, the same as animating anything else: You select it, keyframe it, change the current time, move it, and keyframe it again. However, there are a number of things you do differently when animating a camera.

You may, for example, want to use camera cuts, where the camera remains still, then jumps to the next position. Or you might want the aim of the camera to follow an object as it passes through a scene. Cameras can also be animated along a path—useful for creating a fly-through of a scene.

One point you need to understand before you begin animating is that the selected camera isn't necessarily the one you're looking through. At the bottom of the view, you can see the name of the camera you're currently looking through (**Figure 16.12**). In the Channel Box, you can see the name of the currently selected camera (**Figure 16.13**). One common mistake is to move the view and set keyframes without having the camera you're looking through selected. If you make this mistake, you won't end up with any camera animation.

An easy way to animate the camera is to use tumble, track, and dolly, which you've been using all along to see different parts of your scene.

To animate the camera using tumble, track, and dolly:

1. Create some objects and move them around the scene so you have something to look at.

2. From the View menu in the Perspective view, choose Select Camera (**Figure 16.14**).

   You can see that the camera is selected because the name of the camera, persp, appears at the top of the Channel Box.

3. Press ⓢ to keyframe the camera.

4. In the Time slider, change the current time to *30* by clicking the number 30.

5. Tumble, track, and dolly the camera to change the point of view.

   (See Chapter 2 for more on how to tumble, track, and dolly.)

6. Press ⓢ to keyframe the camera again.

7. Rewind and play back the animation by using the playback control buttons in the timeline (**Figure 16.15**).

   Because the camera's motion is animated, the view changes as you play back the animation (**Figure 16.16**).

To make the aim of the camera follow an object:

1. From the Create menu, select NURBS Primitives > Sphere.

2. With the sphere still selected, press ⓢ to keyframe the sphere.

3. Change the current time in the timeline to *30*.

Figure 16.14 From the View menu in the Perspective view, choose Select Camera. This selects the camera you're currently looking through.

Figure 16.15 The playback controls. On the far left is the Rewind button. The large triangle pointing to the right is the Play button.

Figure 16.16 This image shows what you would see through the camera once it's animated.

ABOUT CAMERAS

Figure 16.17 The aim of the camera is put at the center of an animated sphere and then parented to it.

Figure 16.18 The camera follows the sphere as it is animated across the screen.

4. Move the sphere; then press ⓢ to keyframe it again.

The sphere is now animated.

5. From the Create menu, select Cameras > Camera and Aim.

6. Select and move the aim of the camera to the center of the sphere (**Figure 16.17**).

7. With the aim still selected, Ⓢⓗⓘⓕⓣ-select the sphere. Press ⓟ to parent the aim to the sphere.

8. Rewind and play back the animation.

The camera follows the sphere (**Figure 16.18**).

9. Select the camera, and from the Panels menu in the Perspective view, choose Look Through Selected.

The view changes to the camera you just created.

10. Rewind and play back the animation.

You can see the camera following the sphere from the point of view of the camera.

When modelers want to show off their models, they often create a turntable animation. One way to do this is to place the model at the center of the scene and rotate the camera around it.

To rotate the camera around an object:

1. Place any object at the origin.

2. From the Create menu, select Cameras > Camera.

A new camera appears in the Perspective view.

3. Move the camera back from the origin.

4. Press ⓦ; then press Ⓘⓝⓢⓔⓡⓣ/Ⓗⓞⓜⓔ to go into Pivot Move mode.

continues on next page

ABOUT CAMERAS

5. Move the pivot point to the origin (**Figure 16.19**). Press [Insert]/[Home] again to get out of Pivot Move mode.

6. Select the camera and press [s] to keyframe it.

7. Change the current time in the timeline to *30*.

8. In the Channel Box, type *360* in the field next to Rotate Y and press [Enter].

9. Press [s] to keyframe the camera again.

   If you play back the animation now, you will see the camera rotating around the object (**Figure 16.20**).

10. Select the camera, and from the Panels menu in the Perspective view, choose Panels > Look Through Selected.

    You are now seeing through the view of the camera. When the animation is played back, it will look like a turntable animation.

✔ Tip

■ To move the pivot point to the exact origin of the scene, hold down [x] to snap the pivot point to the grid.

Figure 16.19 The pivot point of a camera is put at the center of an object so the camera can rotate around that object.

Figure 16.20 The camera is animated to rotate around the object.

Figure 16.21 A curve is created that weaves through some cones, seen from the Top view.

Figure 16.22 The camera is attached to a motion path, so it jumps to the beginning of the curve. However, it is facing the wrong way.

Figure 16.23 The camera, now oriented correctly, follows the curve as the animation is played back.

To animate a camera along a path:

1. Create a row of cones.

2. In the top view, create a NURBS curve that weaves through the cones (**Figure 16.21**).

3. From the Create menu, select Cameras > Camera.

   A new camera appears in the Perspective view.

4. With the camera still selected, Shift-select the curve.

5. From the Animate menu, select Motion Paths > Attach to Motion Path.

   The camera jumps to the beginning of the path, but it might not be pointing in the right direction (**Figure 16.22**).

6. With the camera still selected, click motionPath1 in the Channel Box.

   Four attributes of the motion path appear.

7. If the camera is not pointing in the right direction, click Up Twist in the Channel Box and then, using the middle mouse button, drag in the Perspective view until the camera is pointing down the path correctly.

8. Rewind and play back the animation.

   The camera travels down the path (**Figure 16.23**).

Focal length

The Focal Length attribute is similar to the zoom on a real camera. When you increase the focal length, you zoom in. An object appears closer, but zooming in also has the effect of flattening distance. When you decrease focal length, you zoom out. Distances seem exaggerated with a short focal length, and you get a fisheye-lens effect.

To adjust the focal length of the camera:

1. Place any surface at the origin (**Figure 16.24**).

2. From the View menu in the Perspective view, choose Select Camera.

   The perspective camera becomes selected.

3. In the Channel Box, change Focal Length to 6.

   The object seems farther away (**Figure 16.25**).

4. Dolly the camera in close to the object. (For more information on dollying, see Chapter 2, "Navigating and Changing the Interface.")

   The object is distorted like it would be with a fisheye lens on a real camera (**Figure 16.26**).

Figure 16.24 A robot character has been placed at the origin. The camera's focal length is set to the default of 35.

Figure 16.25 With the focal length set to 6, the robot seems very far away, even though the camera hasn't moved.

Figure 16.26 The camera has been moved close to the robot with the focal length still set to 6. The effect is similar to that provided by a fisheye lens—distances are exaggerated.

Figure 16.27 Select Image Plane > Import Image to assign an image plane to the camera.

Figure 16.28 The sunrise image appears in the background of the scene. This image will stay in the same place relative to the camera even if you tumble, track, or dolly.

Image planes

An image plane is a component of the camera that remains in the background of the view regardless of where the camera is moved. Since it's always oriented to the camera and can have an attached image, an image plane can come in handy when you want to use an image as a template for modeling a character. You can also use an image plane as a backdrop to a scene; it is rendered with the rest of the scene.

To create an image plane:

1. From the View menu of the Perspective view, select Image Plane > Import Image.

   An Open dialog box appears (**Figure 16.27**).

2. Browse for your image and click open.

   The image now appears on the image plane (**Figure 16.28**).

✔ Tips

- To select the image plane, you must set the pick mask to Select by Component Type ▣. You must also select the Miscellaneous icon ▣.

- Once you've selected the image plane, you can move it by changing the Center X, Y, and Z settings in the Channel Box. You can delete it by pressing ⟨Backspace⟩/⟨Delete⟩.

- A quick way to hide an image plane is to uncheck Cameras on the Show menu of the view pane you're in. Since the image plane is a component of the camera and you're hiding the camera, the image plane is also hidden.

About Rendering

Rendering is how you output images once you finish modeling, animating, lighting, and texturing your scene. There are many options to set—all of which you'll find in the Render Globals window.

First, you must decide what your output will be. The resolution of an image is its size in pixels. The size you choose depends on the medium your images will end up on.

If you're creating a small image for a Web site, you might use the default resolution of 320 by 240. If you plan to put the images on NTSC video, you'll probably use 720 by 486 (**Figure 16.29**).

For decent-quality printing, you need a much higher resolution. Printing at 300 dots per inch (dpi) will produce a sharp image. If you want to print an 8-by-10-inch image, you will need a resolution of 2,400 by 3,300 pixels—which will take a long time to render.

You can set resolution quality in the Render Globals window. Lower-quality images will render faster, making them good for tests. Higher-quality settings will produce a cleaner, better-looking image and should be used for final output (**Figure 16.30**).

Before you render your scene, you need to save it and set your project. Taking these steps will help you avoid losing images when you render because if the project is set, the renders will automatically be sent to the correct folder.

Figure 16.29 The same scene rendered in a variety of resolutions.

Figure 16.30 Compare production quality (left) with preview quality (right). The image on the right renders much more quickly but looks worse.

Figure 16.31 These renderings were created with Maya's rendering technologies: Mental Ray (upper left), Hardware Renderer (upper right), Software Renderer (lower left), Vector Renderer (lower right).

Figure 16.32 The Common tab holds the attributes common to all rendering technologies.

Figure 16.33 Choose a name and frame extension for your file.

Maya provides four ways to render your scene from the Render Globals window: using Maya Software, Maya Hardware, Maya Vector, and Mental Ray (**Figure 16.31**). These are all accessible from the unified Render Globals window. The Render Globals window provides users with a tab-based render settings system that includes one always-accessible Common tab for setting a file name, resolution, and other attributes common to all four Render technologies. The settings on the Common tab will not be reset when the render technology is changed, saving setup time when multiple rendering technologies are used on the same file. Each of the Maya rendering technologies is discussed in the remainder of this chapter.

To set the Common attributes to render a single image:

1. In the Render View, click the Render Globals button ▦, or from the Options menu, select Render Globals.

   The Render Globals window appears (**Figure 16.32**).

2. Click the Common tab to open the common settings.

3. Click the triangle next to Image File Output to expand the options; in the File Name Prefix field, type a file name for the render.

4. Click the Frame/Animation Ext drop-down menu and select name.ext (Single Frame) (**Figure 16.33**).

   The rendered file name will now read as the file name typed in the File Name Prefix and will have the extension of the selected Image Format.

   continues on next page

5. Choose an image format.

Maya IFF is the default, but files with this format won't necessarily open in other programs. You might want to choose something more common, like TIFF or Targa.

6. Choose the camera view you want to render from (**Figure 16.34**).

Even if you've created new cameras, Perspective is still the default camera in the Render Globals window. It's a common mistake to overlook this and render the wrong camera view.

7. Click the triangle next to Resolution. The Resolution options are expanded.

8. From the Presets menu, choose CCIR 601/Quantel NTSC (**Figure 16.35**).

This is a good choice if your image is going to end up on NTSC video.9.

9. Specify the appropriate settings for the desired render technology.

See "About the Software Renderer," "About the Hardware Renderer," "About the Vector Renderer," or "About Mental Ray" later in this chapter.

To set the Common attributes to render a series of images:

1. In the Render Globals window, set the camera, anti-aliasing quality, resolution, and image-format options as in the previous section.

2. Change the file name if you want the images to be named something other than the name of the scene file.

When a new name is entered, the example file name at the top of the window reflects this change (**Figure 16.36**).

Figure 16.34 Select a camera to render from the Camera menu.

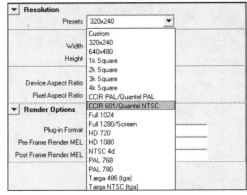

Figure 16.35 NTSC is the standard U.S. video size; select this option to set your file to 720 by 486.

Figure 16.36 The file name at the top of the Render Globals window changes when a different file name is entered.

```
Path: D:/andrew/maya/projects/book/images/
File Name: billyTheRobot.1.tga
To:        billyTheRobot.10.tga
```

Figure 16.37 The path name and file name appear at the top of the Render Globals window.

3. Choose name.#.ext from the Frame/Animation Ext menu.

The example name changes to reflect this update. You must choose an option that includes the pound sign (#) to be able to render animation as opposed to rendering single frames.

The name.#.ext option is a good choice for most programs and operating systems. The choice mostly depends on the software into which you plan to bring the images. Each type of software uses a different naming convention, but Maya gives more than one choice for naming schemes to accommodate the differences. For example, an output with name.#.ext would output happy.1.tga, happy.2.tga, happy.3.tga, and an output with name.# would output happy.1, happy.2, and happy.3.

4. Set the start and end frames of your animation.

These should be set to the range of time you want to render.

5. Change Frame Padding to *4* and close the Render Globals window.

This will put zeros in front of the numbers in the image name so that the numbers are four digits long. This is helpful because your images will be listed in order when sorted by name (**Figure 16.37**).

6. Specify the appropriate settings for the desired render technology.

See "About the Software Renderer," "About the Hardware Renderer," "About the Vector Renderer," or "About Mental Ray" later in this chapter.

About the Software Renderer

Maya includes two basic categories of software rendering: the default (known as A-buffer, or raycasting) and raytracing. The default Software Renderer can create high-quality images with lighting, shadows, texture, and motion blur. However, for added realism, you may need reflections and refractions (See "About Raytracing" later in this chapter). This is where raytracing comes in. If you want to make a wineglass look real, you need to raytrace it (**Figure 16.38**).

Figure 16.38 Raytracing can help bring realism to the scene.

To render a scene using Maya Software Renderer:

1. Open or create a scene to software render.

2. Open the Render Globals window and set Render Using to Maya Software (**Figure 16.39**).

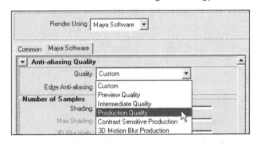

Figure 16.39 The Render Using menu changes the Render Global tabs and rendering technology.

3. Specify the Common settings as you did in "To set the Common attributes to render a single image" earlier in this chapter.

4. On the Maya Software tab, click the triangle next to Anti-Aliasing Quality to expand the options.

5. From the Quality menu, choose Production Quality (**Figure 16.40**).

   This automatically sets several of the options and is a good choice for most high-quality renders.

Figure 16.40 The Quality presets can save time by automatically setting the Render Globals options to standard values.

6. From the Render menu, select Batch Render.

   The render begins.

7. Click the Script Editor icon 🗉 in the lower-right corner of the interface.

   The Script Editor opens. You can watch the progress of the render here (**Figure 16.41**).

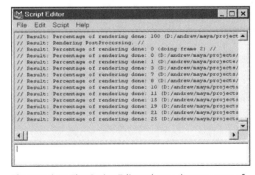

Figure 16.41 The Script Editor shows the progress of your render.

Figure 16.42 Since the batch render is still in process, the progress of the current frame shows up in FCheck. This view will not be updated as the render continues.

Figure 16.43 You can open an animation in the FCheck window that can play back all of the frames you've rendered.

✔ Tip

- In the Render Globals window, on the Maya Software tab, turn on Motion Blur to blur moving surfaces slightly. This makes them look better because they more closely resemble moving objects captured by a real camera.

Maya's FCheck program provides an easy way to view images and animations.

To view a render:

1. From the Render menu, select Show Batch Render.

   While rendering, the progress of the current frame opens in FCheck (**Figure 16.42**). If finished the last frame opens FCheck.

2. From the File menu in the FCheck window, select Open Animation (Windows) or Open Sequence (Mac) (**Figure 16.43**). A file-browsing window opens.

3. Browse for your rendered image files in the Images folder of the project folder you are currently using.

4. Open the first image in the series.

   The animation will load slowly and play back at full speed, unless it includes lots of images or the resolution is high. Animation speed also depends on your computer's hardware.

5. Drag from left to right to scroll through the animation.

✔ Tip

- FCheck includes the following hotkeys:

   (Spacebar) starts and stops the animation's playback.

   (a) goes back one frame.

   (b) goes forward one frame.

Using the Hardware Render Buffer

Software rendering can take a long time. If you want to make a preview of your animation without having to software render it, you can hardware render it instead. This provides a kind of a middle ground between a playblast and a software render. Hardware rendering is essentially a series of screen snapshots of your scene.

Hardware rendering does a few things that playblast cannot. It can anti-alias the edges of your surfaces and create motion blur so that the animation looks smoother. It can also create an alpha channel, so that you can easily composite with other images (**Figure 16.44**). One approach is to hardware render some elements of your scene and composite them with a software-rendered background.

There are also a number of things that hardware rendering doesn't do that software rendering does. Hardware rendering cannot create shadows, reflections, or refractions. And it doesn't do as good a job with textures and lights. Special effects like glow don't work, and you can't see bump maps. In general, hardware renders are great for scenes that have minimal textures, and/or have hardware-rendered particle effects that you may want to layer into a high-res file later (**Figure 16.45**).

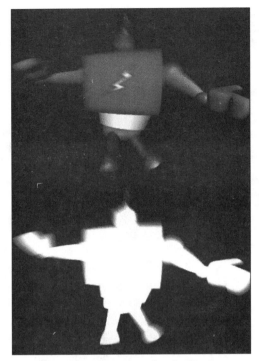

Figure 16.44 The robot was rendered using the Hardware Render Buffer with Motion Blur turned on. At the bottom, you can see the alpha channel created for this image; you can use it for compositing.

Figure 16.45 This robot was software rendered. Note the bump map on the arms, the glow on the visor, and the reflectivity of the robot's chest.

Figure 16.46 Choose a camera view from the Cameras menu in the Hardware Render Buffer.

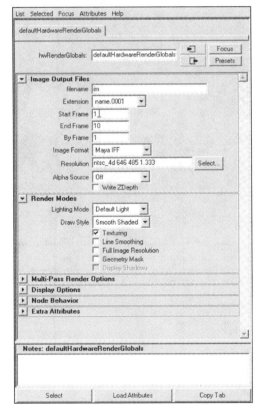

Figure 16.47 The Hardware Render Globals window is where you indicate the file name, resolution, range of frames, and numerous other attributes for the render.

To use the Hardware Render Buffer:

1. Open or create a scene that includes animation.

2. From the Window menu, select Rendering Editors > Hardware Render Buffer.

   The Hardware Render Buffer appears.

3. From the Cameras menu in the Hardware Render Buffer, select the camera view you want to render (**Figure 16.46**).

   To adjust the view, you can tumble, track, and dolly inside the Hardware Render Buffer.

4. From the Render menu in the Hardware Render Buffer, select Attributes.

   The Attribute Editor for the Hardware Render Globals window opens (**Figure 16.47**). The Hardware Render Globals window contains a collection of settings for outputting your image files using the Hardware Render Buffer. Note that this is not the same as the Render Globals window, which is used to set the render attributes for Maya's Hardware Renderer feature. See "About the Hardware Renderer" later in this chapter.

5. Set the file name, extension, start frame, end frame, image format, and resolution as desired.

6. From the Render menu in the Hardware Render Buffer, select Render Sequence.

   The sequence quickly renders. The image files are put in the Images folder of the project you are currently using.

To adjust the Hardware Render Buffer's render quality:

1. From the Window menu, select Rendering Editors > Hardware Render Buffer.

   The Hardware Render Buffer appears.

2. Set up the hardware-render attributes as in the preceding task.

3. Scroll down to Multi-Pass Render Options. Select Multi Pass Rendering and Anti Alias Polygons (**Figure 16.48**).

4. Click the Test Render button in the Hardware Render Buffer to see the result.

   Three passes of the image are created and then composited together automatically. The edges of the surfaces are anti-aliased.

5. Change Render Passes to 5 and Motion Blur to 1.

6. Click the Test Render button in the Hardware Render Buffer to see the result.

7. Five passes of the image are completed. With Motion Blur set to 1, the passes occur over the duration of one frame (**Figure 16.49**).

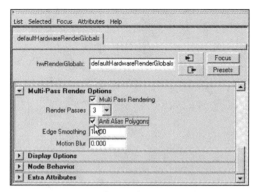

Figure 16.48 Turning on Multi Pass Rendering and Anti Alias Polygons will improve the look of your render by smoothing aliased (stair-stepped) edges.

Figure 16.49 Since the banana was animated and Motion Blur was turned on in the Hardware Render Globals settings, you can see some blur in the resulting image.

Figure 16.50 This scene is made up exclusively of spheres. The spheres reflect one another because Raytracing is turned on.

Figure 16.51 Each transparent sphere has a different refraction index: left 1.0, middle 1.333, right 2.0.

About raytracing

Achieving realistic renders often requires reflections and refractions. To achieve these effects, you must turn on raytracing. Although renders can take significantly longer with raytracing on, they look much more realistic.

When you can see other objects in an object's reflection, the light rays are bouncing off one surface and then bouncing off another surface and into your eyes or a camera lens. You need other objects in the scene in order to see a reflection of them; the object has to have something to reflect (**Figure 16.50**).

Refraction is the bending of light as it travels through a dense, transparent material such as glass or liquid. Without it, glass doesn't look real. You can set a refraction index, which controls how much the light bends as it passes through the surface (**Figure 16.51**).

You can see a good example of refraction when you're standing in a lake and see a fish under water: If you were to reach in the water and try to grab that fish, you would miss it because refraction bends the image of the fish so that from your point of view it appears to be in a position other than its actual one. You must compensate for the bending of light to catch the fish.

To create reflections:

1. Create a scene with a large plane, a sphere, many cubes, and some lights (**Figure 16.52**).

2. For the cubes, assign a red Phong material; for the plane, assign a checkered Phong material, and for the sphere, assign a reflective Phong material.

3. Open the Render Globals window and set Render Using to Maya Software.

4. Change the Anti-Aliasing Quality Preset to Production Quality.

5. Scroll down and click the triangle next to Raytracing Quality.

   The Raytracing Quality options are expanded.

6. Select Raytracing to activate Raytracing (**Figure 16.53**).

7. Frame the sphere in the Perspective view; then click the Render button 🎬.

   The Render View appears, and the image is rendered with reflections (**Figure 16.54**).

✔ Tip

■ Objects can be visible or invisible in reflections. To change an object's reflection state, select the object and open the Attribute Editor, expand the Render Stats section, and uncheck Visible in Reflections to make the object not visible in reflections.

Figure 16.52 This scene has a plane, a sphere surrounded by many cubes, a directional light, and an area light.

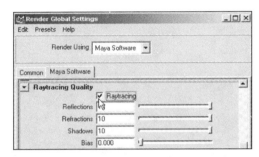

Figure 16.53 Raytracing is turned on in the Render Globals window. Reflections and refractions are not rendered unless this option is selected.

Figure 16.54 When the scene is rendered, you can see the cubes reflected in the sphere.

Figure 16.55 The Transparency slider is dragged to the right, which makes the color field white. White is transparent, and black is opaque in Maya.

Figure 16.56 Refractions are turned on, and the Refractive Index is set to *1.333*. If you do not do this, reflections will render but refractions will not.

Figure 16.57 The transparent sphere is rendered and refracts light. It is dark because the scene surrounding it is dark.

To create refraction:

1. Continue with the scene in the previous task; select the sphere.

2. Click the Graph Materials on Selected Items button in the Hypershade ⬚.

   The material for the sphere appears in the work area of the Hypershade.

3. Double-click the Phong material assigned to the sphere.

   The Attribute Editor for the Phong material opens.

4. Drag the Transparency slider all the way to the right.

   The color field next to Transparency becomes white (**Figure 16.55**).

5. Scroll down in the Attribute Editor and click the arrow next to Raytrace Options.

   The Raytrace Options are expanded.

6. Select Refractions.

7. Change Refractive Index to *1.333* (**Figure 16.56**).

8. Click the Render button ⬚.

   The Render View window appears, and the scene is rendered. The sphere refracts the light, which causes the objects seen through it to appear warped (**Figure 16.57**).

✔ Tip

- Objects can be visible or invisible in refractions. To change an object's refraction state, select the object and open the Attribute Editor, expand the Render Stats section, and uncheck Visible in Refractions to make the object not visible in refractions.

About Interactive Photorealistic Rendering

Every time you make a change to a material or a light, you need to render it again. This makes tweaking elements like lights or bump maps time consuming because of the wait for the rendering.

To address this problem, Maya offers Interactive Photorealistic Rendering, or IPR. If you render using IPR, you can select a region of the render, and the changes you make will update interactively (**Figure 16.58**).

IPR, however, has some limits. It won't update the positions of objects or changes to the camera. It won't update the position of a shadow. It doesn't do any raytracing, which means no reflections or refractions. And it always performs low-quality anti-aliasing.

However, IPR will update most changes to materials and lights—and that capability alone can save you a great deal of time. A good workflow is to use IPR rendering while you're setting up and tweaking your objects' color and lighting and then use software rendering for your final images and tweaks.

To use IPR:

1. Create a plane, assign a material with a bump map to it, and create a directional light pointed diagonal to the plane (**Figure 16.59**).

   See "To assign a bump map to a surface" in Chapter 15, "Shaders, Materials, and Mappings," for more on bump maps.

2. Click the IPR button ⛶.

   The Render View appears, and the scene is rendered. You will see the prompt "Select a region to begin tuning" at the bottom of the Render View.

3. Marquee-select a region in the Render View (**Figure 16.60**).

Figure 16.58 A bump map is tweaked in IPR. The selected area updates when the bump depth for this surface is changed from 1.0 to *0.1*.

Figure 16.59 A plane with a bump map and a directional light pointed at it.

Figure 16.60 After being prompted in the Render View, select a region. Only this region will update when you make changes, but you can select the whole image as the region if you want.

Figure 16.61 When the bump depth is changed, the selected region updates interactively in the Render View.

4. Select the plane.

5. Click the Graph Materials on Selected Objects button in the Hypershade 🖼.

The nodes for the shader appear in the work area of the Hypershade.

6. Double-click the bump2d utility in the Hypershade.

The Attribute Editor for bump2d opens.

7. Change Bump Depth to 2.

The selected region of the Render View updates the change quickly (**Figure 16.61**). Try updating other elements, such as the intensity and color of lights or the color or type of material.

✔ Tip

■ If IPR is not updating, it may be because Raytracing for the Maya Software Renderer is turned on. Turn off Raytracing in the Render Globals window and try IPR again.

About the Hardware Renderer

Maya's Hardware Renderer takes advantage of the next-generation graphics card's power and speed. In addition to being integrated with the Unified Render Globals, the new Hardware Renderer produces higher-quality images than the Hardware Render Buffer (see "Using the Hardware Render Buffer" earlier in this chapter). The Hardware Renderer helps the user produce broadcast-quality images in significantly less time than the Software Renderer.

As with the Hardware Render Buffer, the new Hardware Renderer is great for producing animation previews, hardware-rendered particles, and object render passes, all of which can later be integrated with higher-resolution layers in the compositing stage of

continues on next page

ABOUT RENDERING

the animation, cutting down on overall rendering time. One advantage that the Hardware Renderer has over the Hardware Render Buffer is the ability to batch render. The current Hardware Render Buffer uses a screen-capture technology that can be interrupted when other application windows open over your render; this can now be avoided by batch rendering using the new Hardware Renderer.

To render an image using the Hardware Renderer:

1. Open or create a scene to software render.

2. Open the Render Globals window and set Render Using to Maya Hardware (**Figure 16.62**).

3. Set the Common settings by following the steps in "To set the Common attributes to render a single image" earlier in this chapter.

4. On the Maya Hardware tab, click the triangle next to Quality to expand the options.

5. From the Quality menu, choose Preview Quality (**Figure 16.63**).

   This will automatically set several of the options and is a good choice for quick render tests. For high-quality renders, choose Production Quality.

6. From the Render menu, select Batch Render.

   The rendering begins.

7. Click the Script Editor icon in the lower-right corner of the interface.

   The Script Editor opens. You can watch the progress of the render here (**Figure 16.64**).

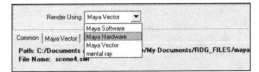

Figure 16.62 Choose Render Using Maya Hardware.

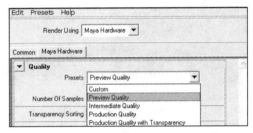

Figure 16.63 Preview Quality is great for quick feedback on your renders when high quality is not needed.

Figure 16.64 The Script Editor displays the progress of your rendering.

Figure 16.65 One-color Vector Render (top); and Include Edges turned on to show the wireframe of an object (bottom).

About the Vector Renderer

The Vector Renderer is unlike the other Maya renderers—Software Renderer, Hardware Renderer, and Mental Ray—because they render each image as a bitmap. If you scale a rendered bitmap larger, the image blurs and degrades. Vectors, on the other hand, are mathematical curves that can be scaled larger or smaller without loss of image quality. Maya's Vector Renderer can be used to render SWF files for Macromedia Flash, AI files for Adobe Illustrator, Encapsulated Postscript (EPS) files, and Scalable Vector Graphics (SVG), covering all of the most common vector formats.

Rendered vector files can be imported into Adobe Illustrator to create 3D logos, brought into Flash files to add 3D animation and graphics to a Web site, or imported into a Photoshop collage to add depth and interest, to name just a few of the Vector Renderer's applications. You can use the Vector Renderer to render just the flat color of a character or object or to render the entire wireframe of the character or object (**Figure 16.65**). Maya gives you the option of filling the wireframe with color or simply rendering the lines of the wireframe to produce the final image. With all of Maya's vector rendering options, you have solid control over how much of the scene is rendered and how large or small the file size.

In the following task, we will render our vector file in SWF format. When a rendered SWF file has animation and is imported into Flash, each frame is rendered and will appear in the Flash timeline, ready for further editing or symbol creation.

To render an image as vectors:

1. Open or create a scene to render as vectors.

2. Open the Render Globals window and set Render Using to Maya Vector.

3. On the Common tab in the Render Globals window, name your file, select name.ext (Vector Multi Frame) for Frame/Animation Ext, and select Macromedia SWF (swf) for Image Format. You can set the resolution to a small size, 320×240, for example, because the vector file can be scaled without degrading.

4. On the Maya Vector tab in the Image Format Options (swf) area, set the frame rate to the desired Flash frame rate; for example, choose *12*. (Be aware that the larger the frame rate, the larger the overall file size.) Set the Flash version; here, we will use the default Flash 5 (**Figure 16.66**).

5. In the Fill Options area, turn on Fill Objects, set the radio button to Single Color, and turn on Show Back Faces (**Figure 16.67**).

6. Click the Render the Current Frame button in the Status Bar.

   The scene is rendered in the Render View. Each color assigned to an object is rendered flat because Single Color is selected in the Fill Options area (**Figure 16.68**).

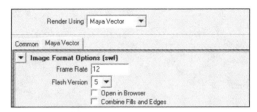

Figure 16.66 Set Frame Rate and Flash Version for your SWF file.

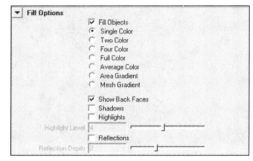

Figure 16.67 The settings in the Fill Options area control the amount of color and the color styles, as well as shadows and highlights.

Figure 16.68 The one-color setting will create flat color for each surface material assigned to a surface.

Figure 16.69 The more colors, the more detail in a surface and the larger the file size.

Figure 16.70 The edges outline the colored areas with the stroke color you choose.

Figure 16.71 Including edges and fills can increase the render file size.

7. In the Fill Options area, select Four Color.

8. Click the Render the Current Frame button in the Status Bar.

The scene is rendered in the Render View. Each color assigned to an object is rendered with four versions of the color because Four Color is selected in the Fill Options area (**Figure 16.69**).

9. Below the Fill Options area is the Edge Options area. Open the Edge Options panel and turn on Include Edges.

10. Click the Render the Current Frame button.

The scene is rendered in the Render View. You can now see outlines on the object (they're most noticeable on the wheels in the figure) because Include Edges is turned on in the Edge Options area (**Figure 16.70**).

11. In the Edge Options area, turn on Edge Detail and set Min Edge Angle to *1*.

12. Click the Render the Current Frame button.

The scene is rendered in the Render View. You now see outlines on the object, and some of the wireframe is visible because Edge Detail is turned on and Min Edge Angle is turned down in the Edge Options area (**Figure 16.71**).

continues on next page

ABOUT RENDERING

13. In the Edge Options area, change Edge Color to bright red and turn off Fill Objects (**Figure 16.72**).

14. Click the Render the Current Frame button.

The scene is rendered in the Render View. Now only the wireframe is rendered (**Figure 16.73**).

✔ Tip

■ Lights are not required to see a vector rendering, but point lights provide a good way to control the distribution of color across a surface.

About Mental Ray

Mental Ray is similar to Maya's Software Render, but adds advanced rendering features such as caustic light patterns and global illumination. Caustics and global illumination can help produce advanced lighting effects, which can produce more realistic renders.

Caustics are light patterns similar to those created at the bottom of a pool on a bright day. Caustics are created due to the refraction of light and are created when light illuminates a diffuse surface from specular reflections. These patterns cannot be produced with normal raytracing. To overcome the standard raytracing shortcomings, Mental Ray uses photon maps, which store the global illumination information and can be invoked during standard raytracing.

When standard raytracing is used to render a scene, light rays illuminate only the directly hit objects in the scene. Mental Ray's Global Illumination allows light to reflect around the scene, partially illuminating objects that are not directly hit with a light source.

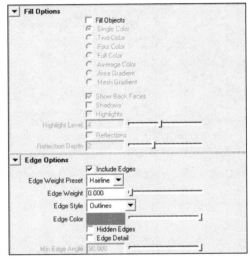

Figure 16.72 The Include Edges option controls the outlines and wireframes of objects.

Figure 16.73 Setting the Vector Renderer to render wireframes only can reduce your render file size because the shapes don't need to be filled.

ABOUT RENDERING

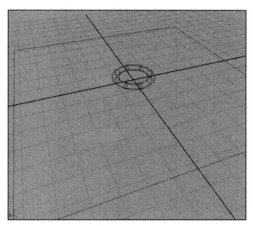

Figure 16.74 We will use a ring-like surface to reflect our caustic patterns.

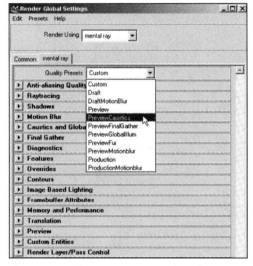

Figure 16.75 Select PreviewCaustics from the Quality menu to set Render Globals to the caustics presets.

The Final Gather option creates very realistic shading effects by bouncing an object's color onto other objects, as in real life. When Final Gather is turned on, light rays are cast from the light; then when the light ray hits an object, additional rays are projected from the object used to calculate the amount of energy that is coming from the surrounding objects, in turn producing the effect of bounced light and color. To a point, final gather turns every object into a type of light source.

Mental Ray can produce very photorealistic renders, but the realism requires long rendering time. Be aware that using Global Illumination or Final Gather in Mental Ray can give fantastic results, but often it is more efficient to find another way to achieve the advanced photorealism and to use the faster, scanline (non raytracing) Maya Software Renderer or Mental Ray to render your scenes.

Mental Ray has many options and rendering capabilities; for more advanced information about Mental Ray, see the Maya Help files.

To create caustics:

1. Create a NURBS primitive plane.

2. Create a NURBS primitive torus, set the height ratio to *.2*, and move the torus up so it sits on the plane (**Figure 16.74**).

3. Open the Render Globals window and set Render Using to Mental Ray.

4. Specify the Common settings by following the steps in "To set the Common attributes to render a single image" earlier in this chapter.

5. On the Mental Ray tab, from the Quality menu, choose PreviewCaustics (**Figure 16.75**).

   Caustics is now on in the Caustics and Global Illumination section.

   continues on next page

6. In the Caustics and Global Illumination section, set Caustic Accuracy to *64*.

Setting Caustic Accuracy to 64 or less reduces spotting.

7. Create a spotlight and point it at the torus (**Figure 16.76**).

8. Open the spotlight's Attribute Editor and set the intensity to *13*, the decay rate to Quadratic, and the cone angle to *80*.

9. In the Mental Ray Caustic and Global Illumination section inside the light, turn on Emit Photons (**Figure 16.77**).

Using a higher number of photons increases rendering time, but increasing energy values does not increase rendering time. We are using the default settings here. The light will now emit photons, used to reflect light around the scene.

10. In the Hypershade, create a Phong material and assign it to the torus.

11. Open the Phong's Attribute Editor, change the color to bright yellow, and set the Diffuse attribute to *0.3* (**Figure 16.78**).

The caustics-casting object should have a low diffuse shader assigned to it, like our Phong set to 0.3.

12. Create a Lambert material and assign it to the plane.

13. Open the Lambert's Attribute Editor, change the color to light gray, and set the Diffuse attribute to *0.8*.

The caustics-receiving object should have a highly diffuse material assigned to it, like our Lambert set to 0.8.

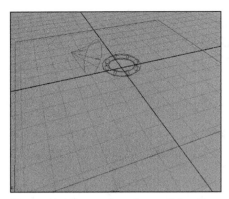

Figure 16.76 The rays from the spotlight will produce the reflected caustics on the plane.

Figure 16.77 Emit Photons around the scene to help reflect light around the scene.

Figure 16.78 Set the Diffuse attribute to *0.3* to turn the diffusion down.

Figure 16.79 The caustic reflections appear on the plane's surface.

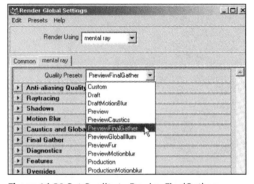

Figure 16.80 Set Quality to PreviewFinalGather.

Figure 16.81 The Final Gather render reflects the yellow color of the ring onto the plane.

14. Click the Render the Current Frame button.

The scene is rendered in the Render View (**Figure 16.79**). Be aware that the rendering may take quite a few minutes.

✔ Tips

- Turn off Photon Map Rebuild in final renders to reduce rendering time.

- To show caustics, the light can be any of the Maya lights.

- To specify whether the object is casting caustics or receiving caustics, select the object and open its Attribute Editor. In the Attribute Editor, expand the Mental Ray section and turn off DeriveFromMaya. Set the caustic flag to Cast Only or Receive Only.

To turn on Final Gather:

1. Continue with the previous scene; open the Render Globals window.

2. Under the Mental Ray tab, set the Quality menu to PreviewFinalGather (**Figure 16.80**).

Final Gather is now on in the Final Gather section.

3. Set the number of Final Gather Rays desired.

The higher the number the longer the render. We will use the default of 1000 here.

The Min and Max Radius values also have an impact on how long the scene will take to render. Using the default setting of 0 forces Maya to estimate this for you. Usually the Min value is 10% of the Max value.

4. Click the Render the Current Frame button.

The scene is rendered in the Render View (**Figure 16.81**). Be aware that the rendering may take quite a few minutes.

ABOUT RENDERING

To create a raytraced practice scene:

1. Create a new scene similar to the one in **Figure 16.82**.

   Be sure to leave the door-like shape on the left wall open for the light to come through.

2. Open the Render Globals window, set Render Using to Maya Software, and set Quality to Production Quality; then turn on Raytracing in the Raytracing Quality section.

   We will first create a raytraced render to compare to our Mental Ray rendered scene.

3. Set the Common settings by following the steps in the task "To set the Common attributes to render a single image" earlier in this chapter.

4. Create a spotlight and point it into the room from the outside (**Figure 16.83**).

5. Open the spotlight's Attribute Editor and set the intensity to 1000, the decay rate to Quadratic, and the cone angle to 80 (**Figure 16.84**).

6. Click the Shadows arrow in the spotlight's Attribute Editor to open the shadow options; turn on Use Ray Trace Shadows.

   The light will now cast raytraced shadows.

Figure 16.82 Create the scene using a floor, ceiling, and two side walls.

Figure 16.83 Make sure the light is outside the room and pointing in.

Figure 16.84 Turn up the intensity when you set the decay rate to Quadratic to make up for the extremely light decay.

Figure 16.85 A standard raytraced scene; notice that only areas hit with direct light are illuminated.

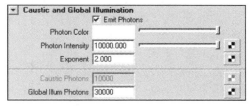

Figure 16.86 Protons are emitted throughout the scene to reflect the light around the scene.

Figure 16.87 The final Mental Ray rendering lights areas of the room that are not directly hit with direct light.

7. Click the Render the Current Frame button.

The scene is rendered in the Render View (**Figure 16.85**).

To add global illumination:

1. Follow the steps in the previous task, "To create a raytraced practice scene."

2. On the Mental Ray tab in the Render Globals window, choose PreviewGlobal-Illum from the Quality menu.

Global Illumination is now on in the Caustics and Global Illumination section.

3. In the Caustics and Global Illumination section, set Global Illum Accuracy to *6000*, Global Illum Radius to *35*, and Photon Volume Accuracy to *5000*.

4. Select the spotlight; then open the spotlight's Attribute Editor.

5. In the Mental Ray Caustic and Global Illumination section inside the light, turn on Emit Photons and set Photon Intensity to *10000*.

6. Set Global Illum Photons to *30000* (**Figure 16.86**).

7. In the Hypershade, create a Phong material and assign it to the sphere and cubes (not the walls).

8. Open the Phong's Attribute Editor and change the color to bright yellow and set the Diffuse attribute to *.3*.

9. Click the Render the Current Frame button.

The scene is rendered in the Render View (**Figure 16.87**). Be aware that the rendering may take quite a while.

ABOUT RENDERING

Image-based lighting, or IBL, is a complimentary feature to both Global Illumination and Final Gather. IBL uses an image to create the overall lighting for a scene. This is especially useful if you are trying to match lighting for 3D objects to the lighting of a live action set. IBL also simulates outdoor lighting very well because it typically uses a round "dome" to encompass the objects being lit.

To add image-based lighting:

1. Create a new scene similar to the one in **Figure 16.88**.

2. Open the Render Globals window and click the Mental Ray tab; then select PreviewFinalGather from the Quality Presets pull-down menu to turn on Final Gather.

3. In the Image Based Lighting section, click Create (**Figure 16.89**).

   A sphere appears in the scene (**Figure 16.90**).

Figure 16.88 Create a scene similar to the one pictured.

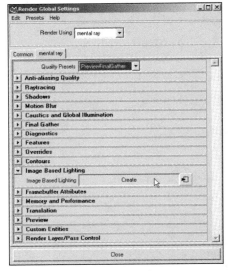

Figure 16.89 Click Create in the Image Based Lighting section of the Render Globals window.

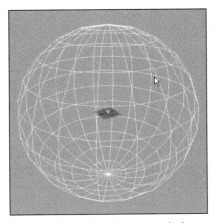

Figure 16.90 A sphere that surrounds the objects appears in the scene.

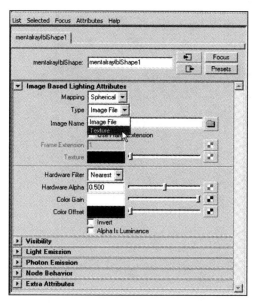

Figure 16.91 In the sphere's Attribute Editor, you can assign a texture or an image file to use for the source of the IBL.

4. If the sphere does not fit around all the objects in the scene, click r to activate the Scale tool and scale the sphere until it fits.

5. In the sphere's Attribute Editor, which is automatically activated when you create an IBL sphere, select Texture from the Type pull-down menu (**Figure 16.91**).
The Texture option becomes available.

6. Click the map icon next to the Texture option.
The Create Render Node window appears.

7. In the 2D Textures section, select Normal (**Figure 16.92**).

8. Click the Ramp button (**Figure 16.93**).
A ramp appears in the Attribute Editor.

continues on next page

Figure 16.93 A ramp appears in the Attributes Editor.

Figure 16.92 Click Normal in the Create Render Node window.

9. In the scene, position the camera so that it is inside the sphere (**Figure 16.94**).

10. Select Render > Render the Current Frame.

The scene is rendered in the Render View. The objects are lit by the colors in the ramp assigned to the IBL sphere (**Figure 16.95**).

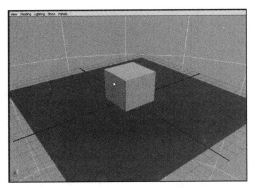

Figure 16.94 Position the camera so that it is inside the IBL sphere.

Figure 16.95 Render the scene to observe the effect of IBL lighting.

Compositing

For complex scenes, it is often necessary to render in passes or sections. This not only allows the renderer to use smaller amounts of RAM but also gives the artist more control if revisions are necessary.

Say you've got a scene with a complex background where the camera does not move. You could easily speed things up by rendering one frame of the background and then compositing the character or other foreground objects on top. To facilitate this, Maya uses Render Layers, which tell the renderer to only render specific objects and save them to a separate image file.

Maya also uses Render Passes, which separate Beauty, Color, Shadow, Diffuse, and Specular values into separate files. This way, you can make fast changes in the compositing program rather than having to re-render the entire 3D scene. If the shadows in your scene are too dark, for example, it may take days to re-render the entire scene in 3D; but in composite, it can take just a matter of a few minutes to make the shadows lighter.

If you're interested in learning more about compositing, Adobe After Effects, Apple Shake, Discreet Combustion, and Eyeon Digital Fusion are all popular programs.

ABOUT RENDERING

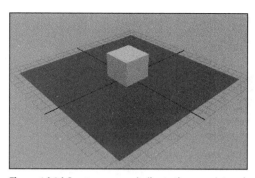

Figure 16.96 Create a scene similar to the one pictured.

Figure 16.97 Choose Render to access the Render Layers.

Figure 16.98 Right-click the new layer and select Add Selected Objects.

To use render layers:

1. Create a new scene similar to the one in **Figure 16.96**.

2. From the pull-down menu in the Layer Editor, select Render to access the Render Layers (**Figure 16.97**).

3. Select one of the objects and click Create a New Layer 🖳.

   A new Render Layer appears in the Layer Editor.

4. Right-click the new render layer and select Add Selected Objects from the pull-down menu that appears (**Figure 16.98**).

   The selected object is now in layer1.

5. Repeats steps 3 and 4 for the other object.

6. Open the Render Globals window and select the Maya Software renderer.

7. In the Maya Software tab, click Render Layer/Pass Control to display more options below (**Figure 16.99**).

continues on next page

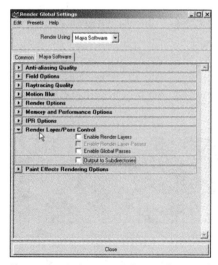

Figure 16.99 In the Maya Software tab, expand the Render Layer/Pass Control section.

8. Click Enable Render Layers to display a list of available render layers (**Figure 16.100**).

9. In the defaultRender field, type *off* (**Figure 16.101**).

By default, Maya creates a render layer for any objects that have not been assigned a render layer. Since we have assigned layers for each of the objects in the scene, we can disable this feature.

10. From the Render menu, select Batch Render to render the scene.

When the render is complete, the images folder of your project directory will contain a separate image for each render layer (**Figure 16.102**).

To use render passes:

1. Create a polygonal sphere and assign a blinn shader to it.

See Chapter 3, "Creating Primitives and Text," for more information

2. Open the Render Globals window and select the Maya Software renderer.

3. In the Maya Software tab, click Render Layer/Pass Control to display more options.

4. Click Enable Global Passes to display the Beauty, Color, Shadow, Diffuse, and Specular render passes (**Figure 16.103**).

Figure 16.100 A list of created layers appears.

Figure 16.101 Turn off defaultRender.

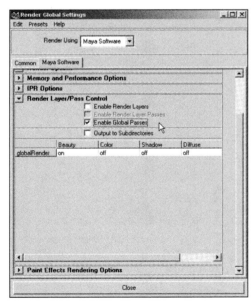

Figure 16.103 Click the Enable Global Passes check box.

Figure 16.102 Launch a Batch Render of the scene to create two images in your project directory; when composited, these will create the whole image.

Figure 16.104 Turn on Diffuse and Specular.

Figure 16.105 Render the scene in the Render View to see what the image looks like.

5. In the Beauty field, type *off*; in the Diffuse and Specular fields, type *on* (**Figure 16.104**).

6. Render the scene in the Render View (**Figure 16.105**).

The scene renders and displays the combined render passes.

7. Render the scene using Render > Batch Render.

When the render is complete, the images folder of your project directory will contain a separate image for each render pass (**Figure 16.106**). When these images are combined in a compositing program they will resemble Figure 16.105.

✔ Tip

■ For larger scenes, you will need as much RAM as possible. To reduce memory usage, close all open programs, including Maya.

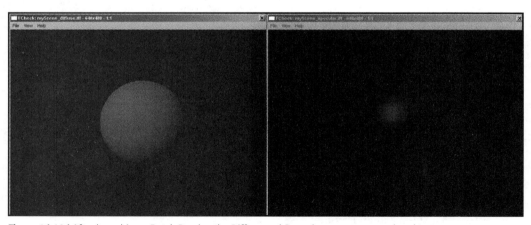

Figure 16.106 After launching a Batch Render, the Diffuse and Specular passes are rendered to your project directory.

Launching Renders with Scripts

To launch a render for Maya, use the operating system's command line. On Windows, the Command Prompt can be found in the Start menu (All Programs > Accessories). On the Mac, open the Terminal window located under Applications > Utilities. Both of these commands execute a Maya render using the parameters stored in the Render Globals window.

To render a scene from the desktop:

◆ On Windows, you can right-click a scene file and select "render" from the pull-down menu that appears (**Figure 16.107**).

To render from the command line:

1. From the Windows Start menu, select All Programs > Accessories > Command Prompt.

   The Command Prompt window opens (**Figure 16.108**).

2. Type render -h into the Command Prompt and press [Enter].

   A long list of parameters is printed for the render command (**Figure 16.109**).

3. Type render myscene.mb into the Command Prompt to render your scene.

   This assumes that the parameters in the Render Globals window do not need to be changed. Your scene file must either be in the current directory or in the directory that the command prompt has open.

Figure 16.107 Right-click a scene file in Windows and select "render" to launch a render outside of the Maya GUI.

Figure 16.108 The Windows Command Prompt.

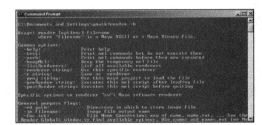

Figure 16.109 Type render -h to display all the parameters for the render command.

Figure 16.110 Windows uses backslashes(\) to separate folders in path names.

Figure 16.111 The Mac uses forward slashes(/) to separate folders in path names.

4. On Windows, specify the full path of where your scene file is stored using the following script (**Figure 16.110**):

```
render C:\myproject\scenes\myscene.mb
```

or

On the Mac, specify the path as in **Figure 16.111** using the following script:

```
render /Users/username/myproject/
→ scenes/myscene.mb
```

Avoid any blank spaces in the file path because they will cause problems.

5. Add the start and end frame flags to the render command in the Command Prompt:

```
Render –s 1 –e 100 myscene.mb
```

This command will render frames 1 through 100.

✔ Tip

- The render flag dontReplaceRendering (**–rep**) tells the renderer not to write over a frame if it is already in the output directory.

```
Render –rep –s 1 –e 100 myscene.mb
```

This allows several computers to render the same scene to the same directory and effectively create a simple distributed rendering network. For more information, see the Network Rendering sidebar below.

LAUNCHING RENDERS WITH SCRIPTS

When executing several renders, one after the other, it is much easier to launch them using some form of scripting. On Windows, you need to create a `bat` (batch) file that uses `NTscript`. This is basically a text file that contains one render command after another. On Mac OS X, you will create a `shell` script instead, which is only slightly different from a bat file.

To create a Windows bat script:

1. In a Windows directory, right-click and choose New > Text Document from the pull-down menu that appears (**Figure 16.112**).

   A text file appears with its name highlighted, indicating that it can be renamed.

2. Enter the name *myscript.bat* and press Enter (**Figure 16.113**).

   You can name the file anything you like, as long as it ends with `.bat`.

3. Right-click the file and select Edit from the pull-down menu that appears (**Figure 16.114**).

   The script opens in Notepad.

4. Using the syntax from the step 4 of the previous task, "To render from the command line," enter a render command for each scene you need to render.

5. Add the `pause` command to the end of the script so that you can see the results of the commands after they are executed (**Figure 16.115**).

6. Save the file and double-click it to execute it.

   The render command is executed and the progress is printed in the command prompt.

Figure 16.112 Create a text file to use as a `bat` (batch) file.

Figure 16.113 Rename the file `myscript.bat`.

Figure 16.114 Right-click the file and select edit from the menu.

Figure 16.115 Add `pause` to the end of the script so that it will not close when it's done.

Figure 16.116 Select Make Plain Text from the Format menu to remove the unnecessary Rich Text Styles that will prevent the script from running normally.

Figure 16.117 Enter a render command for each scene you need to render.

Figure 16.118 Open the Mac OSX Terminal window to launch a render without Maya being open.

Figure 16.119 The Mac OS X Terminal window opens with a text prompt where you can enter commands.

To create a Mac OS X `shell` script:

1. From the Applications menu, choose Utilities and double-click TextEdit to create a new document.

2. From the Format menu, choose Make Plain Text to switch from Rich Text Format (RTF) to Plain Text Format (**Figure 16.116**).

   RTF files store a lot of extra information, like font, size, and type, which we don't need.

3. Using the syntax from step 4 of the task "To render from the command line," enter a render command for each scene you need to render (**Figure 16.117**).

4. From the File menu, choose Save As and enter the name *myrenderscript.command* in the dialog box that appears.

5. Click Save to save the script to your hard drive, and in the Warning dialog box that appears, click Don't Append.

6. From the Applications menu, choose Utilities and double-click Terminal (**Figure 16.118**).

   The Mac OS X Terminal window opens with a text prompt where you can enter commands (**Figure 16.119**).

continues on next page

LAUNCHING RENDERS WITH SCRIPTS

7. Type `ls -l` and press <kbd>Enter</kbd>.

A list of scripts appears on the screen, giving you the permissions for all the files in that directory (**Figure16.120**).

8. From the Mac OS X Terminal window, run the command `chmod` on your script to make it executable.

`chmod +x myrenderscript.command;` (**Figure 16.121**).

9. Type `ls -l` again and you will now see an x at the end of the permissions section of your files (**Figure 16.122**).

This changes the permissions on the script so that it executes when the name of the file is typed into the Mac OS X Terminal window or double-clicked in a directory.

Figure 16.120 Typing `ls -l` into the Terminal window list the contents of the current directory.

Figure 16.121 Running the `chmod +x` command on the script makes it executable.

Figure 16.122 Running `ls -l` again reveals that the script has been made executable.

Networking Rendering

Larger projects will require many hours to render. Using several computers to render a single animation will greatly speed up the process. The Windows and Mac versions of Maya do not come with network rendering software. However, there are several commercial and free applications that make it easy to render across multiple computers.

In order to use several computers in a rendering network, you will need a 100 baseT (or faster) network with a network switch as opposed to a hub. If you're only using two different software products, you can use a crossover cable.

You'll also need to have Maya installed on each computer or have it properly installed on a server. You do not need additional licenses to use the Maya Software, Vector, or Hardware renderers on multiple systems. However, for the Hardware renderer, each system should have the same display card installed; otherwise, there may be differences between the frames that each system renders. Mental Ray requires a license for each system, and any plug-ins will need to be installed and properly licensed.

The path to the project directory also needs to be same between each system. On Windows, this can be accomplished by assigning the network drive a common letter between all the systems. On the Mac, create a common link on each computer pointing to the same drive on the network. Then, using network rendering software, packets of frames can be rendered by each computer to the common project directory.

Finally, here's a list of products and URLs that can help you get off to the right start.

Commercial distributed rendering programs for Windows and Mac OSX:

- Rush (http://seriss.com/rush/)
- Muster (http://www.vvertex.com)
- Lemon Pro (http://martin.ice.org/lemon_pro.html)

Commercial distributed rendering programs for Windows:

- Smedge2 (http://www.uberware.net/)
- Rendermax (http://www.rendercorp.com/)

Free distributed rendering programs for Mac OSX:

- Farm Manager by Dave Schmitz (http://www.schmitzware.org/indexFarmManager.html)

Free distributed rendering programs for Windows:

- Spider (http://groups.yahoo.com/group/SXSpider)

LAUNCHING RENDERS WITH SCRIPTS

MEL AND EXPRESSIONS PRIMER

In Maya, many repetitive tasks can be made easier with MEL (Maya Embedded Language) or expressions. MEL is a scripting language, so if you have any experience with Perl or Javascript, MEL should seem familiar to you. MEL can be used for a wide range of tasks. The Maya interface is built out of numerous MEL scripts, allowing it to be very customizable and flexible.

Expressions are scripts, too, and they even use MEL, but they work a little differently. You can enter expressions into any node's parameters, instead of keyframing, and you can assign expressions to an object's parameters, rather than using a variable. In this way, expressions let you make connections between nodes more directly and efficiently. Expressions are usually executed at each frame in a sequence and tend to execute faster, so they're very useful for creating animation, character rigs, and particle systems.

About the Script Editor

You'll edit and execute MEL scripts in the Script Editor, and whenever you perform a command in Maya, the associated MEL scripts are printed in the Script Editor. In many cases, you can copy and paste commands printed in the Script Editor and save them on a shelf for easy reuse.

MEL has an extensive list of commands that are listed in the Maya Help files. Press F1 to launch Maya Help and go to MEL commands in the Developer Resources section. These commands are listed alphabetically and categorically.

MEL scripts are text files and can be stored in several ways. You may write scripts that are used one time, save them to a shelf, or save them to a script folder on the hard drive. You can load a script into the editor for further development or even edit a script in an external text editor.

The Script Editor is divided into two areas. In the top pane, the results of any executed commands are reported. In the bottom pane, scripts can be typed and executed (**Figure 17.1**).

To use the Script Editor:

1. Click the Script Editor icon ▣ in the lower right area of the Maya interface.

   The Script Editor opens.

2. Create a cube by selecting Polygon Primitives > Cube from the Create menu.

   The MEL command used to create the cube is printed in the top pane of the Script Editor (**Figure 17.2**).

   ```
   polyCube -w 1 -h 1 -d 1 -sx 1 -sy
   → 1 -sz 1 -ax 0 1 0 -tx 1 -ch 1;
   // Result: pCube1 polyCube1 //
   ```

The top pane   *The bottom pane*

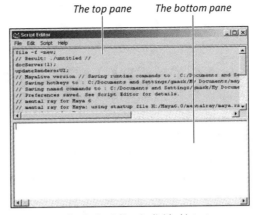

Figure 17.1 The Script Editor is divided into two main areas.

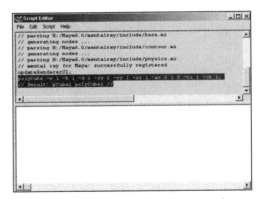

Figure 17.2 The MEL command used to create the cube is printed in the top pane of the script editor.

Figure 17.3 Select the line containing the polyCube MEL command in the Script Editor.

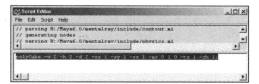

Figure 17.4 Select all of the script in the lower section of the Script Editor and press (Enter) on the numeric keypad to execute the script.

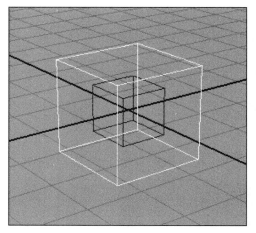

Figure 17.5 A cube twice the size of the first one appears at the world origin.

3. Select the line containing the polyCube MEL command (**Figure 17.3**) and click and drag it to the lower pane.

4. Edit the command's parameters for –w 1, –h 1 and –d 1 to –w 2 –h 2 and –d 2.

5. Select the entire line of MEL script and press (Enter) on the numeric keypad to execute the script (**Figure 17.4**).

   A cube twice the size of the first one appears at the world origin (**Figure 17.5**).

6. Select the script and click and drag it to a Shelf to save it for later use (**Figure 17.6**).

   An icon for the MEL script appears in the Shelf (**Figure 17.7**).

7. Select the two cubes that were created in the view and press (Del).

8. Click the MEL script icon that was created.

   A new cube twice the size of the first one appears in the view.

continues on next page

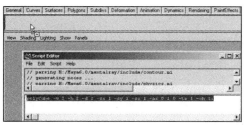

Figure 17.6 Select the entire script in the Script Editor and drag it to a Shelf for later use.

Figure 17.7 A default icon for the MEL script appears in the shelf.

In the previous example, the parameters of the polyCube command were manually edited to make a large cube. Instead of manually typing in value for parameters, MEL can use variables to assign those values. This allows the script to modify those values over time or interactively based on any number of events or conditions that the user defines.

There are several kinds of variables. The ones you will use most are floats, integers, and strings. A float variable stores a value that has a decimal point in it such as 1.001. An integer variable stores whole numbers 1, 5, or 1007. A string variable stores lines of text (such as "hello world"). If you assign a value that has a decimal point in it to an integer variable, the value past the decimal will be lost.

Each of those variable types can also be an array. An array is a variable that can contain several individual and separate values. You can then use all of the values stored in an array or specify an index number you wish to use.

In the next example, a random value will be stored in a float variable and used to create a cube. Then we will use a string array to randomly move the cube.

To use random variables:

1. Create a float variable called $R by typing
   `float $R;` into the bottom pane of the Script Editor.

   Variables always begin with a dollar sign.

2. Assign a random number to $R using the rand( ) command by typing
   `$R=rand(10);` after the previous line of script.

3. Edit the polyCube command to use the value of $R for the value -w, -h, and -d.

   ```
   polyCube -w $R -h $R -d $R -sx 1 -sy
   ⇥ 1 -sz 1 -ax 0 1 0 -tx 1 -ch 1;
   ```

ABOUT THE SCRIPT EDITOR

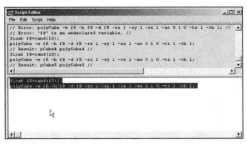

Figure 17.8 Select all of the script in the lower section of the Script Editor and press [Enter] on the numeric keypad to execute the script.

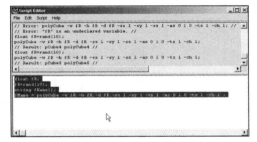

Figure 17.9 The script should look like this.

4. Select all the lines of script and press [Enter] on the numeric keypad (**Figure 17.8**).

```
float $R=rand(10);
polyCube -w $R -h $R -d $R -sx 1 -sy
→ 1 -sz 1 -ax 0 1 0 -tx 1 -ch 1;
```

A cube with a randomly chosen size appears in the view. To make this script more useful, the cubes should not only be random in scale but in position.

5. Create a string array variable called `$Name` by typing `string $Name[];` into the Script Editor before the `polyCube` command.

6. Modify the line with the `polyCube` command by putting `$Name` = in front of it.

This will store the name of the cube created by `polyCube`.

7. Encapsulate the `polyCube` command and its parameters with single open quotes [`].

The script so far should look like **Figure 17.9**.

8. Create a new set of variables that will be used to randomly place the cubes in the scene by typing the following lines at the end of the script:

```
$Gx=gauss(10);
$Gy=gauss(10);
$Gz=gauss(10);
```

The `gauss` command is like `rand` in that it creates random numbers that are positive and negative and uses a more natural method to calculate the numbers.

continues on next page

9. Add the following line of script to move the cube to a new random position:

```
move $Gx $Gy $Gz $Name;
```

The move command moves the named object three values for x, y, and z. The x,y, and z values are stored in $Gx, $Gy, and $Gz. The name of the object created with the polyCube command is stored in the $Name string variable.

10. Highlight the entire script in the Script Editor and press (Enter) on the numeric keypad several times (**Figure 17.10**).

```
float $R;
$R=rand(10);
string $Name[];
$Name ='polyCube -w $R -h $R -d $R -
→ sx 1 -sy 1 -sz 1 -ax 0 1 0 -tx
→ 1 -ch 1`;

$Gx=gauss(10);
$Gy=gauss(10);
$Gz=gauss(10);

move $Gx $Gy $Gz $Name;
```

An interesting formation of cubes appears (**Figure 17.11**).

✔ Tip

- You can use any word you like to name variables as long as it begins with a dollar sign. You cannot, however, put numbers directly after the dollar sign. The name **$4** will not work but **$var4** will.

In the previous script, we created an interesting formation of cubes with a simple script. But executing the script over and over again is tedious. To automate this, we need a conditional control statement, such as while. Other conditional statements include if and for.

While loops wait for the the condition to become true and then stop executing the lines of script contained in in between brackets { }.

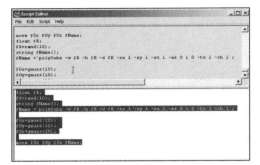

Figure 17.10 Select all of the script in the lower section of the Script Editor and press (Enter) on the numeric keypad several times.

Figure 17.11 An interesting formation of cubes appears in the scene.

To use a while loop:

1. Using the script from the previous task, "To use random variables," add a new integer variable at the beginning:

```
int $x=1;
```

This variable is used to count off how many times the script has been executed.

2. Add the `while` statement to control the flow of the script:

```
while($x<10){
```

As long as `$x` is less than (<) the value of 10, the script will repeat. You could create another variable instead of the "hardcoded" value of 10, or simply change 10 to a higher value, as needed. We will need to add the closing bracket (}) in order to have a functioning script.

3. Type `$x++;` at the end of the script to increment the value of `$x`.

The script will count up to equal the value of 10 and stop the script from continuing to execute. However, if the count value never equals the value given in the `while` statement, there will be no simple way to stop the program.

continues on next page

ABOUT THE SCRIPT EDITOR

4. Type the closing backet (}) at the very end of the script to close the `while` loop. The script should look like **Figure 17.12**.

```
int $x=1;

while($x<10)
{

float $R;

$R=rand(10);

string $Name[];

$Name =`polyCube -w $R -h $R -d $R -
→ sx 1
-sy 1 -sz 1 -ax 0 1 0 -tx 1 -ch 1`;

$Gx=gauss(10);
$Gy=gauss(10);
$Gz=gauss(10);

move $Gx $Gy $Gz $Name;

$x++;
}
```

5. Highlight the script and drag it to the Shelf, then double-click it to see the results in the Perspective view.

Sometimes you may have objects that look too orderly. By repositioning them in a random fashion, you can make the composition look more natural.

That's a good time to use a `for` loop. Create an array to store the names of the objects you want to move. The `for` statement steps through each object and moves them.

Use the `ls` command to retrieve the names of the objects you wish to move. This command lists objects and nodes in a Maya scene based on the parameters you specify. The `ls -sl` command will only list objects that are currently selected.

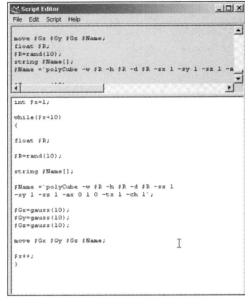

Figure 17.12 Now the script should look like this.

Figure 17.13 After step 6, the script should look like this.

To use a for-in loop:

1. In the Script Editor, select Edit > Clear Input.

2. Select the cubes created in the previous task, "To use a while loop."

3. Type for($cube in `ls -sl`){ into the Script Editor.

4. Type $x=gauss(1); $y=gauss(1); $z=gauss(1); into the Script Editor.

   This variable will be used to randomly move the cubes.

5. Type move -r $x $y $z $cube; into the Script Editor to add a new parameter to the move command.

   The –r flag stands for relative, which means that the specified values are passed to the current position of the object. By default, the object moves to the absolute position of the value passed to it.

6. Close the for statement by adding a closing bracket (});

   The script should look like **Figure 17.13**.

   ```
   for($cube in `ls -sl`){

   $x=gauss(1);
   $y=gauss(1);
   $z=gauss(1);
   move -r $x $y $z $cube;
   }
   ```

7. Highlight all of the script in the Script Editor and press [Enter] on the numeric keypad.

   The cubes shuffle from their original positions. The ls –sl command is like a six pack of sodas with several bottles. The for statement takes one of those bottles and pours it into a cup called $cube. Each time the for statement is executed, it will take one value in the list of values created by `ls –sl` and store it in the variable $cube. The list of values in this case is the names of the objects selected.

ABOUT THE SCRIPT EDITOR

To use the if command:

1. Using the script from step 6 of the previous task, "To use a for loop," add the following after the move statement.

   if ($y > 1) { scale -r 2 2 2 $cube; }

   If the value the $y variable is more than 1, the cube will be scaled to twice its original size.

2. Highlight the entire script and press [Enter] on the numeric keypad.

   The script should look like **Figure 17.14** and some of the cubes will randomly become larger than the others (**Figure 17.15**).

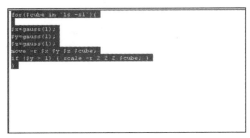

Figure 17.14 Select all of the script in the lower section of the Script Editor and press [Enter] on the numeric keypad.

Figure 17.15 The script scales the cubes larger when the variable $y is greater than 1.

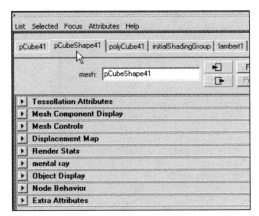

List Selected Focus Attributes Help

pCube41 | pCubeShape41 | polyCube41 | initialShadingGroup | lambert1 |

mesh: pCubeShape41

- ► **Tessellation Attributes**
- ► **Mesh Component Display**
- ► **Mesh Controls**
- ► **Displacement Map**
- ► **Render Stats**
- ► **mental ray**
- ► **Object Display**
- ► **Node Behavior**
- ► **Extra Attributes**

Figure 17.16 Click the pCubeShape tab in the Attribute Editor.

▼ **Render Stats**
☐ Casts Shadows
☑ Receive Shadows
☑ Motion Blur
☑ Primary Visibility
☑ Smooth Shading
☑ Visible In Reflections
☑ Visible In Refractions
☑ Double Sided
☐ Opposite

☐ Geometry Anti-aliasing Override
Antialiasing Level 1

☐ Shading Samples Override
Shading Samples 1
Max Shading Samples 1

Figure 17.17 Uncheck Cast Shadows in the Render Stats section of the cube's Attribute Editor.

Script Editor
File Edit Script Help

```
move -r $x $y $z $cube;
if ($y > 1) { scale -r 2 2 2 $cube; }
};
for($cube in `ls -sl`){

$x=gauss(1);
$y=gauss(1);
$z=gauss(1);
move -r $x $y $z $cube;
if ($y > 1) { scale -r 2 2 2 $cube; }
};
setAttr "pCubeShape41.castsShadows" 0;
```

Figure 17.18 The Script Editor displays the MEL script for turning off the cube's ability to cast shadows.

The `setAttr` command is very useful in MEL scripting because it allows you to assign values to nodes attributes without using the attribute editor spreadsheet. Adding `setAttr` to looping scripts like the one in the previous task can make repetitive tasks simple. Next, we'll turn off the shadows cast by the cubes.

To use the `setAttr` command:

1. Select one of the cubes and press Ctrl/Control a to open the Attribute Editor.

2. Click the pCubeShape tab (**Figure 17.16**) and in the Render Stats section, uncheck Cast Shadows (**Figure 17.17**). The following is printed in the Script Editor (**Figure 17.18**).

   ```
   setAttr "pCubeShape57.castsShadows" 0;
   ```

3. Using the script from the previous task, "To use the `if` command," replace the lines of script between the brackets ({}) with `setAttr ($cube+".castsShadows") 0;`

4. To add an attribute to an object stored in the `$cube` variable, put a plus sign (+) between them. Since you are combining these values and passing them to the `setAttr` command, put them in parentheses.

5. The script should look like this:

   ```
   for($cube in `ls -sl`){
   setAttr ($cube+".castsShadows") 0;
   }
   ```

6. From the Windows menu, select General Editors> Attribute Spread Sheet to open the Attribute Spread Sheet.

   continues on next page

ABOUT THE SCRIPT EDITOR

7. Click the Render tab (**Figure 17.19**).

In the Casts Shadows column, notice that all the selected objects currently have Casts Shadows turned on. Keep this window open so that later we can see the effect of the script.

8. Select the cubes, then select the script and press (Enter) on the numeric keypad.

The Casts Shadows column of the Attribute Spread Sheet updates to indicate that the cubes can no longer cast shadows (**Figure 17.20**).

9. Select the script and drag it to a Shelf for later use.

10. In the Script Editor, change the 0 to a 1 at the end of the script to enable shadow casting again.

```
setAttr ($cube+".castsShadows") 1;
```

11. Select script and drag it to a Shelf.

Now you can toggle on or off shadow casting for all the selected objects with a single click.

Once you have started adding scripts to the Shelf, it becomes difficult to tell them apart. In some cases, you can hold the cursor over the MEL icon to reveal a snippet of the script. Add a comment to the beginning of the script to make this feature more useful.

To add a comment:

1. Add the following line to the beginning of the script from the previous task, "To use the setAttr command":

```
//disable shadow casting
```

MEL will ignore any line of script that comes after two forward slashes.

2. Select and drag the script back to the Shelf.

3. Hold the cursor over the MEL icon to reveal the comment in the Tooltips (**Figure 17.21**).

Figure 17.19 Click the Render tab and locate the Casts Shadows column.

Figure 17.20 The values in the Cast Shadows column update, indicating that they are off.

Figure 17.21 Hold your cursor over an icon in the Shelf to reveal its Tooltip.

ABOUT THE SCRIPT EDITOR

Figure 17.22 Click the arrow next to the Shelf and select Shelf Editor from the menu.

Figure 17.23 The Shelves dialog box appears with the current shelf selected for editing.

Figure 17.24 Select the script that you would like to edit in the upper portion of the shelf editor.

About the Shelf Editor

The Shelf Editor lets you add icon names as well as icons to make it easier to identify scripts.

To add an icon name and icon:

1. Click the downward pointing arrow next the Shelf and select Shelf Editor from the pull-down menu that appears (**Figure 17.22**).

   The Shelves dialog box opens with the current shelf automatically selected (**Figure 17.23**).

2. Click the script to which you'd like to add a text note (**Figure 17.24**).

3. In the Icon Name field, type *CS1* to enable cast shadows and press Enter.

   The icon name updates in the Shelf (**Figure 17.25**). Keep the name short so that it can fit into the space provided.

continues on next page

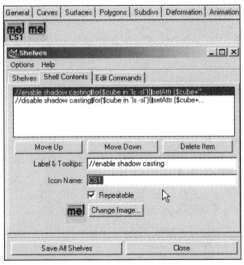

Figure 17.25 The icon name updates in the Shelf after you press Enter.

4. Click Change Image to change the icon from the default MEL icon.

The Open dialog box appears (**Figure 17.26**).

5. Select an icon and click Open.

The icon appears next to the Change Image button and updates in the Shelf (**Figure 17.27**).

7. In the Label & Tooltips field, add a comment and press (Enter).

When you roll your mouse over the script's icon in the Shelf, this comment will appear as the Tooltip.

8. Click Save All Shelves. The shelves are saved to the Shelves folder in your user/prefs/maya directory. On Windows, the path will look like this:

```
C:\Documents and Settings\adrian\
→ My Documents\maya\6.0\prefs\shelves
```

On Mac, the path will look like this:

```
OSX\Users\gregb\Library\Preferences\
→ Alias\maya\scripts
```

✔ Tip

■ You can also create your own 32x32 pixel BMP (Windows) or XMP (Mac) image to use as an icon for your script.

Now that you have learned a little bit about creating your own MEL scripts, it is important to know how to use other people's MEL scripts. You'll find a wealth of free MEL scripts for Maya at Web sites such as *www.highend3d.com*.

Many scripts will have information about how to install and use the script in the header (or beginning) of the script itself. They may also include a readme.txt file or even an html file.

Some scripts are simply a single MEL script file, while others may have several files that

Figure 17.26 By default, the Open dialog box displays the location where Maya stores icons.

Figure 17.27 Select the icon and click Open. The icon updates next to the Change Image button and updates in the Shelf.

ABOUT THE SHELF EDITOR

need to go into several locations, as well as icons or shelves. The scripts with several parts will often be stored in zip files, a common file archive format.

Many scripts will work regardless of which platform you are using (Windows, Mac, Linux, or Irix). Most of the scripts available at *www.highend3d.com* indicate which platforms they have been tested with and which version of Maya they were created for, though most will work with any version of Maya.

For this next task, download a basic script called MEX from *www.gmaskfx.com/mel.*

To install a MEL script:

1. Open the script to read the usage instructions.

```
// MEX (MultiEXtrude) by Adrian
→ Dimond www.gmask.com 2001
// Select a curve to extrude along
→ multiple paths.
// Then add the curves that you want
→ to use as paths.
// Then type mex into the commandline

global proc mex( )
{
string $select[] = `ls -sl`;

string $profile;
string $path;
$profile = $select[0];
$path = $select[1];

for ( $node in $select ) // process
→ each selection
{
extrude -ch true -rn false -po 0 -et
→ 2 -ucp 1 -fpt 1 -upn 1 -rotation
→ 0 -scale 1 -rsp 1 $profile $node;
}
}
```

continues on next page

ABOUT THE SHELF EDITOR

2. Download the mex script to the script's directory located in C:\Documents and Settings\gmask\My Documents\maya\ 6.0\scripts\ (Windows) or OSX\Users\ username\Library\Preferences\Alias\ maya\scripts (Mac).

Each time Maya is launched, it will scan this directory for scripts. If Maya is already open when you add the script, you will need to source the script in the Script Editor in order to use the script right away.

3. Launch Maya and create a primitive NURBS circle and several CV curves (**Figure 17.28**).

4. Select the circle and (Shift)-select the curves.

5. Type mex; into the Command Line and press (Enter) (**Figure 17.29**).

The script extrudes the circle over both curves (**Figure 17.30**).

6. Type mex; into the Script Editor, then select the script and drag it to the Shelf for later use.

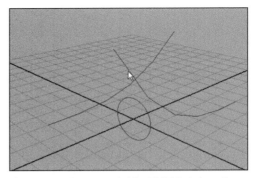

Figure 17.28 Create a primitive NURBS circle and several CV curves.

Figure 17.29 Type mex; and press (Enter).

Figure 17.30 The script extrudes the circle over both curves.

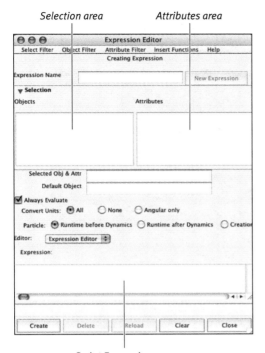

Selection area   Attributes area

Script Expression area

Figure 17.31 You can you create and edit scripts and expressions in the Expression Editor.

Using Expressions

Expressions are MEL scripts that are executed on a per frame basis. That means that any parameter with an expression assigned to it will execute that expression for each frame in a sequence.

Using expressions lets you animate objects easily and realistically using a few simple commands.

About the Expression Editor

You'll use the Expression Editor to create and edit expressions (**Figure 17.31**). It is divided into several areas. In the bottom area, scripts are displayed and edited; above, objects, expressions, or script nodes are displayed.

When you select an expression or script job in the selection area, the statements are displayed in the lower section. When an object is selected, you must also select the attribute that the expression is assigned to in order for it to be displayed in the bottom area.

The following task includes a simple expression that uses the sin function to move a sphere up and down. sin is short for sine as in sinewave. sin creates an oscillating value based on the input. The input has to be incremented at every frame in order for it to animate. If sin has the same value at every frame, there would be no animation, so you need to use the time node. The time node is easily accessible to expressions and not to MEL scripts executed from the Script Editor or elsewhere.

Another unique attribute of expressions is that you use an attribute of an object or node like you would with a variable. This is not only convenient but is faster to execute. Adding expressions like this can create simulated movement for butterflies, blinking eyes, or heaving chests.

To create an expression:

1. Create a sphere and press Ctrl/Control a to open its Attribute Editor (**Figure 17.32**).

2. In the Transform Attributes section, type =sin(time) in the middle Translate field and press Enter (**Figure 17.33**).

   The field turns a violet color, indicating that it is controlled by an expression (**Figure 17.34**).

Figure 17.32 Press Ctrl/Control A to open the sphere's Attribute Editor.

Figure 17.33 Click in the middle Translate field and type =sin(time).

Figure 17.34 The field turns violet, indicating that it is controlled by an expression.

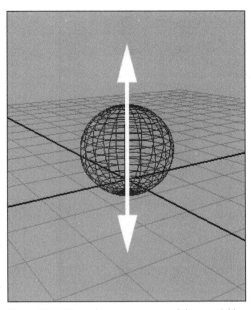

Figure 17.35 The sphere moves up and down quickly.

3. Press Play ▶.

The sphere moves up and down quickly (**Figure 17.35**).

4. Right-click the violet-colored field and select Edit Expression from the pull-down menu that appears (**Figure 17.36**).

The Expression Editor opens with the object and its assigned attribute already selected (**Figure 17.37**).

5. To speed up the movement of the sphere, edit the line of script as follows:

```
pSphere1.translateY=sin(time*10);
```

6. Click Edit, then press Play ▶ on the timeline.

Multiplying the value of the time node by 10 will cause the object to move much faster.

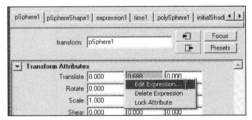

Figure 17.36 Right-click the violet colored field and select Edit Expression from the menu that appears.

Figure 17.37 The Expression Editor opens with the object and the attribute already selected.

To gain more control over an expression, you may wish to keyframe the values that you input into them. To do so, you need to add an attribute to the object. You can then use the value of the attribute in the expression instead of hardcoding the value into the expression.

To add an attribute:

1. Select the sphere from the previous task, "To create an expression."

2. From the Modify menu, select Add Attribute to open the Add Attribute dialog box (**Figure 17.38**).

3. In the Attribute Name field, type *Height* (**Figure 17.39**).

4. For Data Type, click Float (**Figure 17.40**).

5. Click OK to add the Attribute to the sphere.

   In the Channel Box, the attribute's Height appears (**Figure 17.41**).

Figure 17.38 Select Add Attribute from the Modify menu to open the Add Attribute dialog box.

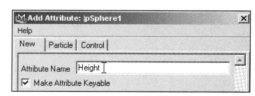

Figure 17.39 Type *Height* into the Attribute Name field.

Figure 17.41 The new Height attribute appears in the Channel Box.

Figure 17.40 For Data Type, choose Float.

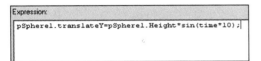

Figure 17.42 Select Translate Y in the Channel Box; then right-click and select Expressions from the menu that appears.

Expression:
pSphere1.translateY=pSphere1.Height*sin(time*10);

Figure 17.43 Edit the expression to use the attribute.

Figure 17.44 Right-click the Height attribute and select Key Selected from the menu that appears.

6. In the Channel Box, right-click Translate Y and select Expressions from the pull-down menu (**Figure 17.42**).

The Expression Editor opens.

7. Edit the expression as follows (**Figure 17.43**).

:pSphere1.translateY=pSphere1.Height*
→ sin(time*10);

The expression is now relying on input from the Height Attribute to determine how high or low to move up and down.

8. In the timeline, click frame 1 to go to the first frame.

9. In the Channel Box, right-click the Height attribute and choose Key Selected from the pull-down menu (**Figure 17.44**).

10. Go to frame 100 in the timeline and type *10* into the Height attribute in the Channel Box.

11. Right-click the Height attribute and select Key Selected from the pull-down menu.

continues on next page

12. From the Windows menu, select Animation Editors to open the Graph Editor.

The Graph Editor opens and displays the animated attributes of the sphere (**Figure 17.45**).

13. From the View menu, select Show Results (**Figure 17.46**) to see the curve created by the sin function and the height curve.

The curve moves up and down and its height follows the Height curve exactly. You can edit the Height curve and see the results update in the graph editor (**Figure 17.47**).

14. Press Play ▶ on the timeline.

The sphere starts out moving up and down a little bit and as the Height increases, the sphere moves up and down much more.

Figure 17.45 The Graph Editor displays the selected object and the attributes that are animated.

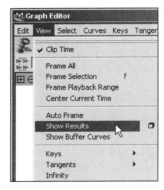

Figure 17.46 Select Show Results from the View menu of the Graph Editor to view curves created by the sin function.

Figure 17.47 Edit the Hieght curve in the Graph Editor to show the effect it has on the sin function.

USING EXPRESSIONS

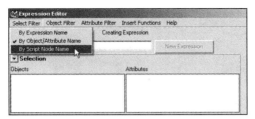

Figure 17.48 Select By Script Node Name from the Select Filter menu.

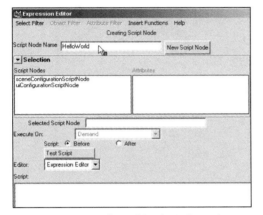

Figure 17.49 Type *HelloWorld* in the Script Node Name field.

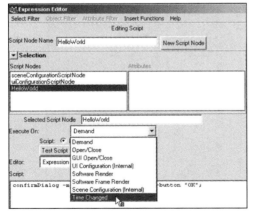

Figure 17.50 Select Time Changed from the Execute On menu.

About script nodes

Expressions are stored in the Maya scene file, but MEL scripts that you create are not stored on a per scene basis. In order to store MEL scripts in a scene file, you can create a script node.

Script nodes are specialized in that they execute in response to certain events, such as opening a scene file or rendering a frame. One example of how you might use this feature is to make sure that a special interface or dialog box is open whenever the scene file is opened.

To create a script node:

1. From the Windows menu, select Animation Editors to open the Expression Editor.

2. From the Select Filter menu, select By Script Node Name (**Figure 17.48**).

   The top portion of the Expression Editor switches to Script Node mode.

3. In the Script Node Name field, type *HelloWorld* (**Figure 17.49**).

4. In the Script field, enter the following script:

   ```
   confirmDialog -message "Hello World"
   → -button "OK";
   ```

5. Click Create.

   The HelloWorld script appears in the Script Nodes section of the Expression Editor.

6. From the Execute On menu, select Time Changed (**Figure 17.50**).

   You do not need to click Edit since this setting will automatically be saved for the Script Node.

continues on next page

USING EXPRESSIONS

503

7. Move to a new frame in the timeline.

When the current frame is changed, it triggers the HelloWorld script and a confirmation dialog box appears (**Figure 17.51**).

Figure 17.51 Move to a new frame on the timeline to trigger the HelloWorld script node.

8. Click OK.

To delete a script node:

1. Open the Expression Editor.

2. From the Select Filter menu, select By Script Node Name.

3. In the Script Nodes section, click the name of the script node you would like to delete.

4. Click Delete.

The name of the script node disappears from the Script Nodes section.

DYNAMICS

Figure 18.1 Rocket trails created using particle effects.

As you build your scenes in Maya, you'll likely encounter effects or situations that would be difficult to create or animate using traditional keyframing. Leaves blowing across the landscape, for example, or a glass shattering as it hits the ground can take hours to animate by hand—and the scene still may not end up looking realistic.

You can use Maya's Dynamics menus to simplify these tasks by simulating the motion of an object being affected by different physical forces (**Figure 18.1**). For example, with just a few mouse clicks (and without setting a single keyframe), you can make a leaf appear to be pushed along by the wind as it simultaneously collides with and rolls along the ground.

While using the Dynamics menu set can be fun, it can also be frustrating: Hundreds of options are available for most dynamic simulations. In this chapter, we'll concentrate on the basics so that you can get up and running quickly.

Particles

Particle dynamics can be used to create myriad effects, including fire, fog, dust, explosions, mud, and even a swarm of bees.

A particle is a point in 3D space that can be affected by simulated physical forces, which are displayed as a number of items, including spheres, clouds, images, and blobby surfaces—even specified objects like leaves or spaceships.

You can draw particles in a scene by using the Particle tool, or you can create them with an emitter, which emits particles automatically in a number of ways, depending on the effect desired.

Let's begin by creating a simple particle object and changing the size in the Attribute Editor.

To create a particle object:

1. Switch to the Dynamics menus by choosing Dynamics from the pop-up menu in the top-left corner of the Maya interface.

2. From the Particles menu, select Particle Tool (**Figure 18.2**).

3. Click in the Top view to place particles in the scene. Each click creates one particle (**Figure 18.3**).

   You can use any view you want, and the particles will be placed on the grid. As you place the particles, they will be displayed as crosshairs.

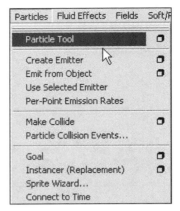

Figure 18.2 From the Particles menu, select Particle Tool.

Figure 18.3 Create particles by clicking in the Top view.

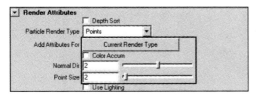

Figure 18.4 Use the Render Attributes section to change the look of the particle.

4. Place as many particles as you like. When you have finished, press (Enter) to complete the particle object.

A particle object is a group of individual particles. Each individual particle is a component of the particle object.

5. With the particle object selected, open the Attribute Editor by pressing (Ctrl)/(Control)(a).

6. Scroll down to the Render Attributes section of the Attribute Editor.

7. Click Add Attributes For Current Render Type.

Additional attributes are now available for you to adjust (**Figure 18.4**).

8. Change the value of Point Size to make the particles bigger or smaller.

This will change the size in the display as well as in the render.

✔ Tip

■ By default, you create particles by clicking in the View pane. In the options for the Particle tool, you can turn on the Sketch option to draw particles on the grid.

PARTICLES

Particles can also be produced by an emitter, which emits particles in a particular speed and direction. There are three main types of emitters:

◆ **Omni**—Emits particles in all directions (**Figure 18.5**).

◆ **Directional**—Emits particles in one user-specified direction (**Figure 18.6**).

◆ **Volume**—Emits particles from a primitive shape such as a cube, cone, or cylinder (**Figure 18.7**).

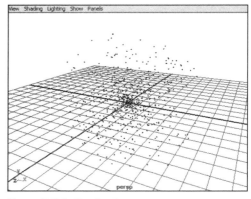

Figure 18.5 An Omni emitter.

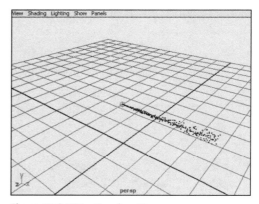

Figure 18.6 A Directional emitter.

Figure 18.7 A cylindrical Volume emitter.

PARTICLES

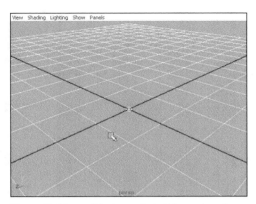

Figure 18.8 An emitter is created at the center of the grid.

Figure 18.9 Particles emit in all directions from an Omni emitter.

You can select the type of emitter that you want to use when you create the object (in its Options window), or you can change the emitter type in the Attribute Editor.

To create an emitter:

1. From the Particles menu, select Create Emitter.

   By default, an Omni emitter is created, and its icon appears at the center of the grid. This is where the particles will be emitted (**Figure 18.8**).

2. Click Play ▶ in the playback controls.

   You will see particles emitting from the center of the emitter (**Figure 18.9**).

3. With the particles selected, open the Attribute Editor by pressing Ctrl/Control a.

4. In the Attribute Editor, select the particleShape1 tab.

5. Scroll down and open the Lifespan Attributes section.

6. From the pop-up menu, select Constant.

   You can now change the duration of the particles once they've been emitted. (Particle duration is the length of time that the particle is visible.) With a Constant value of 1, they will last for just one second and then disappear.

7. Click Play again to see the results.

   The emitter now emits particles from the center of the grid, and the particles' lifespan is one second.

Render Types

You determine the appearance of your particles by assigning to each a render type: Points, MultiPoint, Streak, MultiStreak, Sprites, Spheres, Tube [s/w], Blobby Surface [s/w], Cloud [s/w], or Numeric. Most of these types are rendered through the Hardware Render Buffer. The types whose names include [s/w] are rendered through software. (See Chapter 16, "Cameras and Rendering," for more information on hardware and software rendering.)

Figure 18.10 A selected particle object.

To change a particle's render type:

1. Select a particle object (**Figure 18.10**).

2. Open the Attribute Editor by pressing Ctrl /Control a .

3. On the particleShape1 tab, open the Render Attributes section and select the pop-up menu for Particle Render Type.

4. Select Cloud [s/w] from the list.

    The particles now look like circles in the Perspective view (**Figure 18.11**).

5. Click Add Attributes For Current Render Type (**Figure 18.12**).

6. Change Radius from 1 to 3 by adjusting the slider.

    This option allows you to interactively change the size of the cloud particle for the display as well as the render.

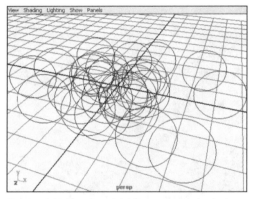

Figure 18.11 Cloud particles appear as circles in the Perspective view.

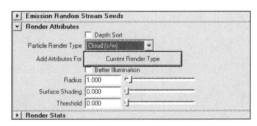

Figure 18.12 Each render type has a number of different attributes to adjust.

RENDER TYPES

Figure 18.13 The rendered particles appear in a cloud-like shape, making for a fuller looking set of particles.

Figure 18.14 Points render as dots.

7. To render the cloud particle, click the Render Current Frame button 🖼.

or

From the Window menu, select Rendering Editors > Render View.

Now the particles look like clouds (**Figure 18.13**).

Hardware render types

Maya offers the following hardware render types for particles:

◆ **Points**—Points render as dots on the screen (**Figure 18.14**). The radius is adjustable, but the particles will look like squares at larger sizes.

◆ **Multi Point**—MultiPoints render as clusters of dots on the screen (**Figure 18.15**). Additional attributes include Multi Radius, which controls the size of each cluster, and Multi Count, which controls the number of dots in each cluster.

◆ **Streak**—Streaks render as lines on the screen (**Figure 18.16**). Additional attributes include Size, Line Width, Tail Size, and Tail Fade.

continues on next page

Figure 18.15 Multi Points render as clusters of dots.

Figure 18.16 Streaks render as straight lines.

RENDER TYPES

◆ **Multi Streak**—Like Streaks, Multi Streaks render as lines on the screen (**Figure 18.17**). MultiStreaks have the same attributes as Streaks, plus Multi Count, and Multi Radius.

◆ **Sprites**—Sprites have an image file attached to them (**Figure 18.18**). From the Particles menu, select Sprite Wizard to choose the image file you want to use.

◆ **Spheres**—Spheres render as opaque spheres (**Figure 18.19**). You can assign any shader you want to a Sphere particle. Transparency is not supported.

◆ **Numeric**—Numeric particles have a number value associated with them (**Figure 18.20**). These number values can represent static, dynamic, or per-particle attributes. This allows the user to have single numeric values on particles that do not move, and multiple number values on fully moving particles.

Figure 18.17 Multi Streaks render as clusters of lines.

Figure 18.18 Sprites appear as images and support opacity and alpha channels.

Figure 18.19 Spheres render as polygonal spheres that can be textured.

Figure 18.20 Numeric particles appear with specified information pertaining to the particle. Numeric particles render as dots.

RENDER TYPES

Figure 18.21 Blobby Surfaces render as spheres but look as though they're melting or blending together.

Figure 18.22 Clouds render as foggy or cloudy surfaces that are partially transparent.

Figure 18.23 Tubes render as cylindrical surfaces and look a bit like Streak particles; the difference is that you can render them via the Software Render window.

Software render types

Maya offers the following software render types for particles:

◆ **Blobby Surface**—Blobby Surface particles render as spheres that can appear to melt into one surface (**Figure 18.21**). Attributes include Radius and Threshold:

   ▲ **Radius**—Determines the initial size of the particle.

   ▲ **Threshold**—Determines how much the particles blend together. As the Threshold attribute increases, the radius of the particle diminishes, and the particle begins to blend with other particles.

◆ **Cloud**—Clouds render as spheres that grow more transparent as you move farther from the center (**Figure 18.22**). Clouds behave like Blobby Surfaces but render with a Particle Cloud shader. You can adjust the shader's density, color, and other attributes in the Hypershade. (See Chapter 13 for more information on shaders).

◆ **Tube**—Tubes render as cylinders that grow as the animation progresses (**Figure 18.23**). You can specify where the cylinder begins and stops expanding with the Radius0 and Radius1 attributes. Tail Size determines the length of the tube.

Fields

Fields are used in conjunction with particle objects to give them a specific behavior. Maya has nine types of fields: Air, Drag, Gravity, Newton, Radial, Turbulence, Uniform, Vortex, and Volume Axis. You can use more than one field on any particle object to achieve the desired motion for your animation.

The following is a list of field types and their effect on particle objects.

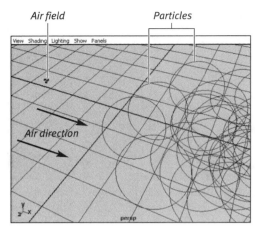

Figure 18.24 You can use an Air field to push particles in a specific direction.

- ◆ **Air**—The Air field produces the effect of a moving volume of air (**Figure 18.24**). The three default Air field types are Wind, Wake, and Fan:

  - ▲ **Wind**—This type of Air field blows particles in a specified direction until they catch up to the speed of the Air field.

  - ▲ **Wake**—As the Air field moves through a particle object, it disturbs the particles and drags them along, creating a wake effect.

  - ▲ **Fan**—This type of Air field pushes particles in a 45-degree spread, simulating a fan.

- ◆ **Drag**—The Drag field helps slow down, or add friction to, a moving particle.

- ◆ **Gravity**—The Gravity field simulates a real-world gravity effect on the selected particle; you can apply it in any direction you specify.

- ◆ **Newton**—A Newton field will attract particles.

- ◆ **Radial**—A Radial field will attract or repel particles in a spherical manner.

- ◆ **Turbulence**—A Turbulence field will disrupt the position of the particles. You can use this field type to randomize the movement slightly for your particle animation.

FIELDS

Figure 18.25 From the Fields menu, select Air.

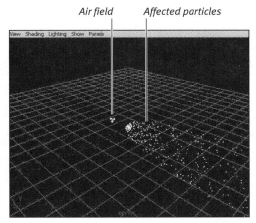

Air field   Affected particles

Figure 18.26 The Air field blows the particles in the X direction.

- ◆ **Uniform**—This field's effect is similar to that of the Air field: It pushes the particles in a specified direction.

- ◆ **Vortex**—A Vortex field exerts a spiraling force on the particles. You can use it to create a tornado effect.

- ◆ **Volume Axis**—A Volume Axis field is defined by a volume shape. This lets you affect particles with a shape, such as a sphere or cube.

Common attributes

The following attributes are common to all fields:

- ◆ **Magnitude**—Sets the amount of force exerted from the field.

- ◆ **Attenuation**—Sets the degree to which the force drops off as the affected object moves away from the field.

- ◆ **Direction**—Determines the direction of the force, usually as an X, Y, Z value.

- ◆ **Use Max Distance**—Allows you to set a maximum distance to define the area of effect.

- ◆ **Max Distance**—Sets the value, in units, that the field will affect.

To attach a field to a particle object:

1. Create an emitter.

2. Click Play ▷ once to emit the particles; click it again to halt playback.

3. Select the particles.

4. From the Fields menu, select Air (**Figure 18.25**). This will attach the field to the selected object.

5. Play back the animation (**Figure 18.26**).

continues on next page

FIELDS

6. Select the Air field.

If you have trouble selecting the Air Field, try selecting Window > Hypergraph and then clicking the Air field.

7. Open the Attribute Editor by pressing Ctrl / Control a.

8. On the Air Field Attributes tab, change Magnitude to 20 (**Figure 18.27**).

9. Play back the animation again to see the effect of the magnitude change.

The Air field pushes with more force as the magnitude increases.

✔ Tip

■ You can animate Air field attributes. Try setting keyframes on the Magnitude attribute to make its value change over time.

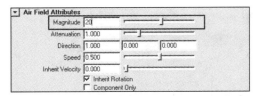

Figure 18.27 Increasing the Magnitude attribute of an Air field makes the particles blow away from it faster.

Selected CVs

Figure 18.28 Create a small hill for the particles to collide with.

Ground plane   *Particle object*

Figure 18.29 Select the ground plane and the particle object to make them collide.

Collisions

If we had added a Gravity field to our particle object, it would have simply fallen out of view because there was nothing in the scene to stop it. You can use the Make Collide command to tell Maya to make the particles collide with certain geometry.

For example, for a scene in which you want fog to roll along the ground, you could create a particle object, attach Air and Gravity fields, and have the particles collide with the ground. The particles then will fall to the ground and be pushed along by the Air field.

To create a particle collision:

1. Create a particle object and attach an Air field, following the steps in the previous task.

2. Select the particle and, from the Fields menu, select Gravity.

3. From the Create menu, select the box beside NURBS Primitive > Plane.

4. In the Options dialog box that opens, give the plane 10 patches in U and V.

5. Click Create.

6. Scale the plane so that it's large enough to represent the ground. Select a few CVs around the center of the plane and translate them in the positive Y direction to create a hill (**Figure 18.28**).

7. In object mode, translate the plane in the negative Y direction so that the plane is below the particles.

8. Select the particle object and the ground plane (**Figure 18.29**).

continues on next page

COLLISIONS

9. From the Particles menu, select Make Collide.

10. Rewind the animation by clicking the Rewind button ⏮ and then click Play ▶ to see the effect.

The particles now fall to the ground and are pushed along the surface by the Air field (**Figure 18.30**).

✔ Tip

■ So you can more easily see and select the particles, select the particle, open the Attribute Editor by pressing Ctrl / Control a, and change the render type to Cloud.

Figure 18.30 Particles collide with the ground geometry and flow over the hill.

Figure 18.31 A rendering from a rigid-body simulation. The ball collides with the pins, which in turn collide with the back wall, floor, and each other.

Rigid-Body Dynamics

For both rigid and soft bodies, you can connect dynamic properties to geometry. Define an object as a rigid body when you want it to collide with another object without yielding; if you want your object to behave with flexibility or elasticity, make it a soft body.

By using Maya's rigid-body dynamics, you can simulate what occurs when one or more objects collide.

Imagine trying to animate a bowling ball crashing into 10 pins at the end of the alley—it would take a lot of time and talent to make that action appear realistic. Maya solves this problem by letting you define objects that you want to interact with (or hit) each other; Maya can then simulate what happens when they make contact (**Figure 18.31**).

You can create active rigid bodies, which react to collisions and fields (Gravity, Air, and so on), or you can create passive rigid bodies, which are unaffected by collisions or fields. You use passive rigid bodies for things like floors and walls—basically, any unmovable object.

RIGID-BODY DYNAMICS

To create a rigid-body simulation:

1. Create a NURBS sphere.

2. Translate the sphere in the positive Y direction.

3. Create a NURBS plane and scale it up to create the floor (**Figure 18.32**).

4. Select the sphere.

5. From the Soft/Rigid Bodies menu, select Create Active Rigid Body (**Figure 18.33**).

6. Select the plane.

7. From the Soft/Rigid Bodies menu, select Create Passive Rigid Body.

8. Select the sphere.

9. From the Fields menu, select Gravity. This attaches a Gravity field to the sphere to make it fall to the ground.

10. Play back the animation to see the result (**Figure 18.34**).

Figure 18.32 A plane is used as a rigid surface for the ball to bounce off of.

Figure 18.33
From the Soft/Rigid Bodies menu, select Create Active Rigid Body.

Figure 18.34 A rigid sphere bouncing off a slightly rotated plane (to make the motion more visible).

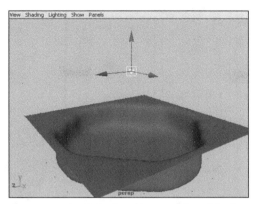

Figure 18.35 An Air field pushing part of a soft-body plane down in the negative *Y* direction.

Figure 18.36 Setting a keyframe at frame 40 in the timeline.

Soft-Body Dynamics

Unlike rigid bodies, Maya's soft bodies have elasticity. Each CV, or vertex, has an associated particle, which can be affected by other dynamics (such as fields) or by particle collisions, thereby deforming the object (**Figure 18.35**).

With particles affecting the surface, we can make flags wave in the wind, gelatin cubes wiggle when they hit the ground, or a belly jiggle as a character walks.

Soft bodies can also use non-soft objects as goal shapes. A goal shape represents a target shape for the soft body to settle into. The particles affecting the soft body are attracted to the CVs, or vertices, of the goal object—almost as if they were attached by springs. This means that you can animate the original geometry, and the soft body will lag behind it, overshooting the original geometry before finally settling into that shape. An overweight man with a double chin that jiggles and lags behind the chin bone's movement is one example of this.

To create a soft body:

1. Create a NURBS sphere.

   In the timeline at frame 1, set a keyframe on the sphere by pressing $\boxed{s}$.

2. Move to frame 40 in the timeline.

3. Translate the sphere 10 units in the negative Y direction (**Figure 18.36**). Set another keyframe by pressing $\boxed{s}$.

4. Move back to frame 1 and select the sphere.

5. From the Soft/Rigid Bodies menu, select the box next to Create Soft Body to open the options.

6. From the pop-up menu, select Duplicate, Make Copy Soft.

continues on next page

7. Check the boxes next to Hide Non-Soft Object and Make Non-Soft a Goal (**Figure 18.37**).

This will duplicate and hide the original geometry and make the duplicate a soft body. The goal then will be the original animated geometry that is hidden.

8. Click Create.

If you play back the animation now, the soft body will simply follow the original animation of the sphere. This is because the goal weights on the soft body are all set to 1.

Goal weights can be adjusted, even painted, on a soft body so that you can get just the right amount of movement from your object. In the next task, we'll make the top of the sphere lag behind and wiggle as the sphere stops.

To adjust goal weights for a soft body:

1. Select the soft-body sphere.

2. From the Soft/Rigid Bodies menu, select the box beside Paint Soft Body Weights Tool.

The Paint Attributes tool opens, and our soft body turns white (**Figure 18.38**).

3. In the Tool Settings window for the Paint Attributes tool (which looks like the Attribute Editor), click the Reset Tool button at the top right.

4. In the Paint Attributes section, change Value to *0.5*.

5. Paint the top of the sphere by clicking and dragging.

The color on the top should turn gray (**Figure 18.39**).

6. Play back the animation.

You should see the top jiggle as the sphere stops at frame 40 (**Figure 18.40**).

Figure 18.37 The options for creating a soft body.

Figure 18.38 You use the Paint Attributes tool to paint soft-body goal weights.

Figure 18.39 The Paint Attributes tool lets you interactively paint weight values on your objects.

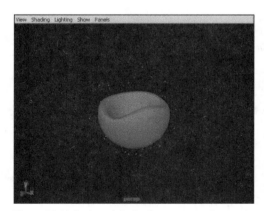

Figure 18.40 As the original sphere stops at frame 40, the soft body will jiggle on the top until it comes to rest in its original shape.

Figure 18.41 The Fire effect.

Figure 18.42 The Smoke effect.

Figure 18.43 The Fireworks effect.

Effects

Maya provides all sorts of premade particle effects to set objects on fire, emit smoke, produce lightning, even make a river flow through a valley. Typically these act as a starting point for something more complex, so you'll need to adjust them to get the desired effect.

By using a premade effect from the Effects menu, you can take advantage of a particle system with additional attributes that directly affect the way the particles react, or render. These attributes are made up of premade expressions and connections. When you make fire using the Create Fire effect, for example, Maya automatically connects Turbulence, Gravity, and Drag fields to the particles, as well as a premade shader and special expressions to give you added control.

Here is a brief description of each of the seven premade effects:

- **Create Fire**—Produces an emitter that has Gravity, Drag, and Turbulence fields attached to a Cloud particle. You can set Density, Radius, Direction, and Intensity using the Options menu. Fire can be emitted from a surface, curve, or directional point. A directional point will emit fire particles in a specified direction from any point in space (**Figure 18.41**).

- **Create Smoke**—Produces an emitter that uses Sprite images instead of Clouds or Points (**Figure 18.42**). To use a particular set of images, select Sprite Wizard from the Particles menu. A default set of images and directions are included with the program. You can set Lifespan, Opacity, Direction, Spread, and Speed in the Options menu.

- **Create Fireworks**—Produces a cluster of rockets and explosions according to the options you set (**Figure 18.43**).

continues on next page

- **Create Lightning**—Creates an animated electric bolt between two or more objects (**Figure 18.44**). You can adjust Thickness, Spread, Jagged Sections, and Glow and Light Intensity in the Options menu.

- **Create Shatter**—Lets you break apart an object into a specified number of pieces (**Figure 18.45**). There are three types of Shatter: Surface, Solid, and Crack.

- **Surface Flow**—Creates manipulators that will direct particles to flow along a NURBS surface (**Figure 18.46**).

- **Create Curve Flow**—Produces manipulators to control the flow of particles along a curve's path (**Figure 18.47**).

Figure 18.44 The Lightning effect.

Figure 18.45 The Shatter effect.

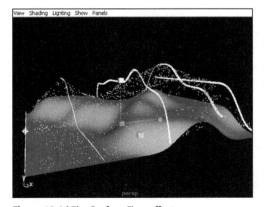

Figure 18.46 The Surface Flow effect.

Figure 18.47 The Curve Flow effect.

EFFECTS

Figure 18.48 A cylinder used to represent a log.

Figure 18.49 The fire effect during playback.

Figure 18.50 Extra attributes to affect the fire particles.

To make an object emit fire:

1. Create a polygon cylinder. Rotate and scale it to represent a log (**Figure 18.48**).

2. Select the cylinder and, from the Effects menu, select Create Fire.

3. Click Play ▶ to start the fire simulation (**Figure 18.49**).

4. Click Stop ■ at any point in the timeline and render the Perspective view to see the results.

5. Select the particles and open the Attribute Editor.

6. Under Extra Attributes, change Fire Density to *20*, Fire Lifespan to *0.2*, and Fire Speed to *10*; then play back the animation to see the effect (**Figure 18.50**). Try changing these and other attributes to get a different type of fire effect.

7. Make your changes. Rewind, play, stop, and render to see the results.

To create lightning:

1. Create two spheres and translate them so that they aren't overlapping (**Figure 18.51**).

2. Select both spheres.

3. From the Effects menu, select Create Lightning.

   A zigzag appears between the two spheres. Also created are two locators, a light, and a selection handle.

4. Select one of the locators and translate it away from the objects.

   The lightning will now have a curve in its trajectory (**Figure 18.52**).

5. Select the selection handle in the middle of the lightning object (**Figure 18.53**).

6. In the Channel Box, adjust the attributes for Thickness, Start and End, and Color to get the desired effect.

   You can also find these attributes in the Attribute Editor on the Lightning1 tab in the Extra Attributes section.

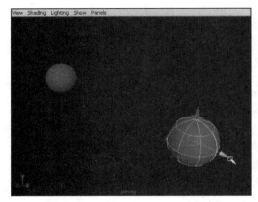

Figure 18.51 Two spheres used to create a lightning effect.

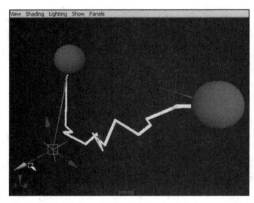

Figure 18.52 Select the locator and move it to put an arc in the lightning bolt.

Selection handle

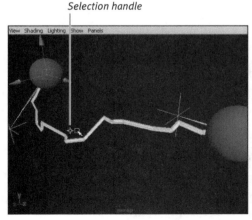

Figure 18.53 The selection handle for the lightning effect.

Figure 18.54 The Dynamic Relationships Editor.

Figure 18.55 Connecting a particle object to a gravity field in the Dynamic Relationships Editor.

The Dynamic Relationships Editor

Sometimes you'll want to attach a particle object or a rigid or soft body to an existing field or collision object. The Dynamic Relationships Editor lets you see a list of a scene's nodes as well as the existing fields, collisions, and emitters—all of which you can then connect.

To connect a field to a particle using the Dynamic Relationships Editor:

1. From the Particles menu, select Create Emitter.

2. From the Fields menu, select Gravity.

   If you play the animation at this point, the particles won't fall because the particle object wasn't selected when you created the Gravity field—which means the two aren't connected.

3. From the Window menu, select Relationship Editors > Dynamic Relationships.

   On the left side of the editor is a list of the scene's nodes. You should see emitter1, particle1, and gravityField1 in this column (**Figure 18.54**).

4. Select particle1 from the left column.

   Now, on the right side of the editor, gravityField1 should appear in the list. It's not highlighted at this point because the two nodes have not been connected.

5. Click gravityField1 on the right side of the editor (**Figure 18.55**).

   Particle1 is now connected to gravityField1.

6. Play back the animation to make sure the Gravity field has caused the particles to fall.

Fluid Effects

Fluid effects are used to create a realistic simulation of a particle's movement that depends on the surrounding environment; for example, if the temperature of the air is higher in a certain area, a particle will rise more quickly through that area. (The word *fluid* in this context refers to motion, rather than a simulation of actual fluid. You can use fluid effects to create such effects as explosions, smoke, flames, oceans, clouds, and thick liquids.

At the time of this writing, fluid effects are available only in Maya Unlimited.

About containers

At the heart of fluid effects is the container. All fluid effects take place inside a container; in fact, they can't exist outside a container. Containers are 2D or 3D rectangular objects.

◆ **2D containers** are useful for any effect where the camera is not moving around the effect. The container can be translated, rotated, and animated, but it has no thickness or depth (**Figure 18.56**).

◆ **3D containers** have depth, which you can set in the Options window when you create the container. These containers are useful for creating clouds, explosions, or any other effect that requires depth (**Figure 18.57**).

A container uses voxels (short for volume pixels) arranged in a grid to display the fluid effect. Each voxel has multiple associated attributes and values that determine the way the fluid effect behaves and appears (**Figure 18.58**).

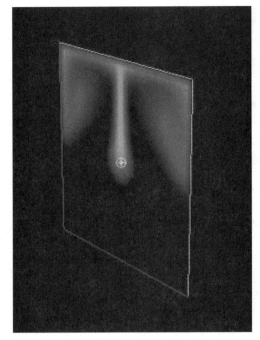

Figure 18.56 A 2D fluid container.

Figure 18.57 A 3D fluid container.

Figure 18.58 The Density grid values for a 3D container.

Grids are used for multiple attributes of fluid objects, and each attribute can use a different type of grid. The attributes for fluid effects are as follows:

- **Density**—The Density grid determines where the fluid will be visible as well as its opacity.

- **Velocity**—The Velocity grid determines the direction, or flow, of the fluid.

- **Temperature**—The Temperature grid determines the amount of heat emitted by a particular voxel. (Heat rises and dissipates as time passes—parameters that you can control.)

- **Fuel**—The Fuel grid determines where a reaction will take place within the grid. Temperature will ignite fuel to start the reaction. Thus, density is affected as the fuel burns off.

- **Color Method**—The Color Method grid determines whether the color will be a shaded color, dynamic grid, or static grid.

You can use three grid types for these attributes:

- **Static Grid**—This type of grid lets you define the values of each voxel in the grid. These values remain static throughout the simulation.

- **Dynamic Grid**—With this type of grid, you can assign a value to each voxel it includes. As the simulation plays, the value of each voxel dynamically changes depending on the forces acting on it.

- **Gradient**—A gradient assigns a linear value of 0 to 1 across the grid in any direction or out from the center. These values do not change over time.

There are a number of ways to get a fluid into a container: You can create an emitter, paint fluids, or use gradients. We're going to create a 2D container with an attached emitter.

To create a 2D Container:

1. From the Fluid Effects menu, select the box next to Create 2D Container with Emitter (**Figure 18.59**).

   In the options that appear, you can define the container's size (in units) and resolution (in number of voxels).

2. Rewind the animation and click Play ▶.

   As the simulation runs, you should see a white stream of particles being emitted from the center of the container (**Figure 18.60**).

Now that you've emitted a fluid, you can change the value of each attribute by using the Artisan Paint tool.

Figure 18.59 From the Fluid Effects menu, select the box beside Create 2D Container with Emitter.

Figure 18.60 The fluid is emitted upward from the center of the container.

Figure 18.61 From the Fluid Effects menu, select the box beside Add/Edit Contents > Paint Fluids Tool.

Figure 18.62 Setting the Density and Fuel grid to Dynamic.

Figure 18.63 A few strokes of Density and Fuel will change the behavior of the fluid effect.

To edit the contents of a container using paint fluids:

1. Select the fluid container.

2. Rewind the animation.

3. From the Fluid Effects menu, select Add/Edit Contents > Paint Fluids Tool > Options box (**Figure 18.61**).
   The Paint Attributes tool opens.

4. From the Paintable Attributes pop-up menu, select Density and Fuel.
   A dialog box appears informing you that you must set the attribute to Dynamic Grid; click Set to Dynamic (**Figure 18.62**).

5. Paint a few strokes into the container (**Figure 18.63**).

6. Click Play to see how Density and Fuel affect the results.

The same principles guide the creation of 3D containers. You get an extra manipulator to control where you're painting in the Z axis, or Depth. To create a 3D container, follow the steps you used to create the 2D container.

About fluid container attributes

Fluid containers have many unique attributes, which you can adjust in the Attribute Editor. The following describes each section of the Attribute Editor and its contents.

- **Container Properties**—Determines the resolution (number of voxels) and size of the grid.

- **Contents Method**—Determines the grid type for each fluid property.

- **Display**—Determines how the fluid appears in the View pane.

- **Dynamic Simulation**—Determines the gravity, viscosity (thickness), and friction of the fluid.

- **Contents Details**—Determines multiple parameters for each fluid property: Density, Velocity, Turbulence, Temperature, Fuel, and Color.

- **Grids Cache**—Determines the options for saving the simulation to a file.

- **Surface**—Defines how the surface renders. For various fluids, you can choose between Volume Render and Surface Render. Use a Volume Render for voluminous things like smoke or steam. Use a Surface Render for surfaces that need to look as though they have thickness, such as mud.

- **Shading**—Determines the fluid's color, incandescence, and opacity.

- **Shading Quality**—Displays options to control the way the fluid is depicted.

- **Textures**—Provides options for color, incandescence, and opacity texture types.

- **Lighting**—Lets you use Self Shadowing, which makes the effect cast shadows on itself. You can also use the lights in the scene by checking the Real Lights box, or you can set your own direction for lighting.

Figure 18.64 Importing a fluid example from the Visor.

Figure 18.65 The attributes for a fluid effect.

Sample fluid effects

Sometimes the best way to learn a new effects procedure is to look at systems that are already created. A great place to start is Maya's library of sample fluid effects. Import one of these sample effects into your scene, and then use the Attribute Editor to view the settings used to create it.

In addition, the Attribute Editor in Maya includes a new section at the bottom of the editor window called Notes. This area also includes an explanation of the procedure used to create certain effects. You can also use the Notes section to add your own comments about an effect. The comments are then saved with that specific node for later viewing.

To import a fluid example:

1. From the Fluid Effects menu, select Get Fluid Example.

   This opens the Visor, which contains the sample effects (**Figure 18.64**).

2. In the left column of the Visor, select the folder for the type of effect you want to import.

3. In the right column, right-click the effect you desire and select Import Maya File (your file.ma).

   The effect is imported into the scene at the center of the grid.

4. Experiment with the settings in the Attribute Editor by pressing Ctrl /
   Control a to change the way the fluid is displayed and evaluated (**Figure 18.65**).

FLUID EFFECTS

Maya Ocean and Ocean shader

Maya uses an advanced shading network along with fluid dynamics to create an Ocean object: With just one click, you can create a photorealistic ocean and control the calmness or storminess of the seas (**Figure 18.66**). By creating a locator and connecting it to the fluid simulation, you can even make objects appear to float in your ocean.

As with the other fluid effects, Maya provides ocean examples that you can import into your scenes.

Figure 18.66 A render of the Maya Ocean effect.

To create a default Maya Ocean:

1. From the Fluid Effects menu, select Ocean > Create Ocean (**Figure 18.67**).
   A NURBS plane is created on the grid in the scene.

2. Open the Attribute Editor and select the OceanShader tab.

3. Open the Ocean Attributes section and adjust Wave Height, Turbulence, Peaking, Speed, Frequency, Direction, and so on.
   Most of the adjustments for the Ocean effect are available in the Ocean shader, which uses the output to displace the NURBS surface.

Figure 18.67 From the Fluid Effects menu, select Ocean > Create Ocean.

Figure 18.68 Adding a preview plane to the ocean will help you interactively view the adjustments you make to the ocean.

✔ Tips

- Maya won't shade the ocean plane because it would slow playback too much. You can create a preview plane when you create the ocean by opening the Option dialog box and checking Create Preview Plane. You can add a preview plane to an existing ocean by selecting Ocean > Add Preview Plane from the Fluid Effects menu (**Figure 18.68**). The preview plane is a small patch with the Ocean shader attached to it so that you can see the results as you make adjustments.

- You may want to attach the ocean to the Perspective camera in the Create Ocean options. This will move and scale the ocean with the camera to give you an acceptable resolution wherever the camera is positioned.

Now that your scene includes an ocean, let's add an object that floats. We can use the Make Boat command to float objects or groups of objects and control their buoyancy and other attributes.

To make a boat:

1. Create an ocean by following the steps in the previous task.

2. From the Create menu, select Polygons > Cube.

3. Scale the cube to represent the size of a boat.

4. With the cube selected, choose Fluid Effects > Ocean > Make Boats (**Figure 18.69**).

   The cube is now parented under a locator, which is controlled by the ocean and in turn controls the movement of the cube (**Figure 18.70**).

5. Select the locator and open the Attribute Editor by pressing Ctrl/Control a.

6. In the Attribute Editor, open the Extra Attributes tab.

7. Click Play in the playback controls.

8. Interactively adjust Buoyancy, Water Damping, Air Damping, Roll, and Pitch to set the way the boat reacts.

   You will want at least 500 frames in the range slider to give you enough time to adjust and see the effect.

✔ Tip

■ Now that you've made a boat and familiarized yourself with the attributes, try creating a motor boat: Follow the steps in the preceding task, but in step 2 select Fluid Effects > Ocean > Make Motor Boat. The motor boat includes Throttle and Rudder controls so you can interactively drive the boat through your scene!

Figure 18.69 From the Fluid Effects menu, select Ocean > Make Boats.

Figure 18.70 A locator controls the way the ocean affects the boat.

FLUID EFFECTS

Figure 18.71 From the Fluid Effects menu, select Pond > Create Pond.

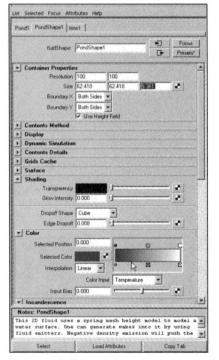

Figure 18.72 Changing the color in the Pond attributes.

Ponds

Ponds have similar controls to those for oceans and can have floating boats or other objects. Ponds are useful when you have a smaller body of water in your scene that may not look like a realistic ocean. To make small bodies of water, you'll use the Create Pond command.

To create a pond:

1. From the Fluid Effects menu, select Pond > Create Pond (**Figure 18.71**).

   A 2D fluid is created in the scene.

2. With the fluid selected, open the Attribute Editor by pressing Ctrl/Control a and select the pondShape1 tab (**Figure 18.72**).

   In the Shading section, you can adjust the color, opacity, and transparency, as well as other pond properties. We will keep the default properties for this example.

Now we'll create some motion for the surface of the pond. To do this, we will create a wake, which will ripple the surface of the pond.

To create a wake:

1. Select the pond you created in the preceding task.

2. From the Fluid Effects menu, select Pond > Create Wake (**Figure 18.73**).

   A spherical fluid emitter is created in the middle of the pond.

3. With the emitter selected, open the Attribute Editor by pressing Ctrl/Control a and select the PondWakeEmitter1 tab.

4. Open the Fluid Attributes section and set the Density/Voxel/Sec value to *1* (**Figure 18.74**).

   The Density/Voxel/Sec value defines how powerful the wake is; by default, the Density/Voxel/Sec value is set to 5. This setting creates a large wake, which may be too large for your scene.

5. To see the effect, click the Play button in the animation controls.

6. Adjust the Density/Voxel/Sec value until you get the desired ripple.

✔ Tips

- Wakes can be used with the Ocean object as well. Follow the same steps as in the preceding task, but in step 2 select Ocean > Create Wake.

- Wakes can also be attached to objects or boats. To do this, select the object and, from the Fluid Effects menu, select Pond > Create Wake. The emitter will now be parented to the object. If you animate the object, the emitter will follow and create a dynamic V-shaped wake behind it (**Figure 18.75**).

Figure 18.73 From the Fluid Effects menu, select Pond > Create Wake.

Figure 18.74 Adjust the size of the wake in the Attribute Editor.

Figure 18.75 An animated cube moves through the pond and leaves a wake in its path.

INDEX

INDEX

INDEX

INDEX